Mask and Performance in Greek Tragedy

Why did Greek actors in the age of Sophocles always wear masks? David Wiles provides the first book-length study of this question. He surveys the evidence of vases and other monuments, arguing that they portray masks as part of a process of transformation, and that masks were never seen in the fifth century as autonomous objects. Wiles goes on to examine experiments with the mask in twentieth-century theatre, tracing a tension between the use of masks for possession and for alienation, and he identifies a preference among modern classical scholars for alienation. Wiles declines to distinguish the political aims of Greek tragedy from its religious aims, and concludes that an understanding of the mask allows us to see how Greek acting was simultaneously text-centred and body-centred. This book challenges orthodox views about how theatre relates to ritual, and provides insight into the creative work of the actor.

DAVID WILES is Professor of Theatre at Royal Holloway, University of London. He has published widely on the topic of Greek theatre and his books include *A Short History of Western Performance Space* (2003), *Greek Theatre Performance: An Introduction* (2000), *Tragedy in Athens: Performance Space and Theatrical Meaning* (1997) and *The Masks of Menander: Sign and Meaning in Greek and Roman Performance* (1991), all published by Cambridge University Press.

# Mask and Performance in Greek Tragedy

## From Ancient Festival to Modern Experimentation

DAVID WILES

CAMBRIDGE UNIVERSITY PRESS

CAMBRIDGE UNIVERSITY PRESS
Cambridge, New York, Melbourne, Madrid, Cape Town,
Singapore, São Paulo, Delhi, Mexico City

Cambridge University Press
The Edinburgh Building, Cambridge CB2 8RU, UK

Published in the United States of America by Cambridge University Press, New York

www.cambridge.org
Information on this title: www.cambridge.org/9781107404793

© David Wiles 2007

This publication is in copyright. Subject to statutory exception
and to the provisions of relevant collective licensing agreements,
no reproduction of any part may take place without the written
permission of Cambridge University Press.

First published 2007
Reprinted 2009
First paperback edition 2011

*A catalogue record for this publication is available from the British Library*

ISBN 978-0-521-86522-7 Hardback
ISBN 978-1-107-40479-3 Paperback

Cambridge University Press has no responsibility for the persistence or
accuracy of URLs for external or third-party internet websites referred to in
this publication, and does not guarantee that any content on such websites is,
or will remain, accurate or appropriate.

# Contents

*Acknowledgements* [*page* vii]
*List of illustrations* [ix]

1 Introduction [1]

2 The evidence of vases [15]

3 The sculptural art of the mask-maker [44]

4 Mask and modernism [71]

5 Physical theatre and mask in the twentieth century [102]

6 Mask and text: the case of Hall's *Oresteia* [125]

7 The mask as musical instrument [153]

8 Masks and polytheism [180]

9 The mask of Dionysos [205]

10 Sacred viewing: 'theorizing' the ancient mask [237]

11 Mask and self [261]

   Epilogue: to the performer [286]

   *Bibliography* [291]
   *Index* [315]

# Acknowledgements

I have received help from many quarters. The necessary condition of research is time. Royal Holloway University of London granted me sabbatical leave, complemented by further leave from the Arts and Humanities Research Council. The Rockefeller Foundation provided me with a month of uninterrupted tranquillity at Bellagio. Victoria Cooper at Cambridge University Press has been, as always, unfailingly supportive. Those who have spared time to read chapters or shorter sections and give me their comments include Richard Seaford, Edith Hall, Stephen Halliwell, and my research students Stephe Harrop, Goze Saner, Angeliki Varakis, Chris Vervain. Practical work with Greek-style masks informs all that I have written. I have learned much from my collaboration with Michael Chase and Thanos Vovolis, and two short projects funded by the Arts and Humanities Research Board allowed me to experience the possibilities of the mask, so as to build bridges between the expertise of the modern practitioner and the historical concerns of the classicist. The participation of Danato Sartori at an associated symposium brought many issues and principles into focus. Teaching mask alongside Peter Bramley, and ongoing discussions with Chris Vervain (Lambert) about her forthcoming thesis 'Performing Greek tragedy in mask', have been an important part of my research environment. Observing Richard Williams' applied research into the New Comedy mask has been a stimulus and encouragement. I have lectured on the Greek mask in many contexts, including Paris VII, GITIS in Moscow, the IFTR scenography group in St Petersburg, the Getty Center, DESMI in Elefsina, an interdisciplinary community at Bellagio, the Athens festival, the Hellenic Society in London, the Cambridge Greek play symposium, the APGRD and a seminar series on mimesis in Oxford, and an inaugural lecture at Royal Holloway University of London. Feedback from these diverse audiences has on each occasion stimulated further thought.

Patricia Levasseur-Legangneux worked for a week on my behalf in the Bibliothèque Nationale, with great discernment. Dmitry Trubotchkin shared information about Stanislavski. Greg Hicks granted me an invaluable interview, and I have learned much from observing his work. Though I was privileged to meet two great mask-makers of the older generation, Jocelyn

Herbert and Abd'Elkader Farrah, alas both died before I was ready to interview them. Too many people have helped me with texts and references for me to note them all, but the list includes Florence Dupont, Richard Green, Barbara Kowalzig, Fiona Macintosh, Toph Marshall, Paola Piizzi, Richard Rutherford, Oliver Taplin, Michael Walton and Yana Zarifi. Pictures are an essential part of this book, and I am grateful to all who have assisted me: Ewen Bowie, Frank Brinkley, George Croft, Sandra Lousada, Paola Piizzi, Oliver Taplin, Dmitry Trubotchkin, Michael Vickers, Renato Villegas, Thanos Vovolis, Yana Zarifi. I have made every effort to contact copyright holders. The AHRC assisted with fees, and Victoria Cooper's assistants at Cambridge University Press helped with contacting museums. My greatest debt is of course to Gayna Wiles. Her delight in recreating the Greek line, and translating a 3-D artefact into a 2-D drawing, has led me to appreciate more fully the detail and artistry of ancient image-making, and left me in no doubt that the same sophistication must have shaped the work of Greek actors.

# Illustrations

**Drawings**

2.1 Men with horse heads + satyrs on the reverse. Athenian neck amphora. Berlin Staatlich Museen. 1697.   [*page* 17]

2.2 Mask. Detail of Plate 2.2.   [21]

2.3 Dancers on an Athenian calyx-krater. Vatican: Astarita 42.   [27]

2.4 Maenad mask. Detail of Plate 2.5.   [29]

2.5 Silenus on the 'Pronomos' vase. Detail of Plate 2.6.   [32]

2.6 Side view of the 'Pronomos' vase.   [34]

2.7 Fragment of an Athenian volute-krater. Martin Von Wagner Museum, Würzburg. H4781.   [35]

2.8 Fragment of an Athenian volute-krater, Archaeological Museum of Samothrace 65.1041.   [36]

2.9 Parody of *Antigone*. Apulian bell-krater. Museo Diocesano, Sant' Agata dei Goti.   [40]

3.1 Actors and Dionysos. Stone relief from Peiraeus. Athens National Archaeological Museum 1500.   [45]

3.2 Tympanum as mirror. Apulian bell-krater. Zurich. 3585.   [48]

3.3 Actor and mask. Stone grave relief from Salamis. Peiraeus Museum.   [49]

3.4 Oedipus and Antigone. Wall-painting from Delos.   [51]

3.5 Terracotta mask from Naples. Ashmolean Museum, Oxford.   [56]

3.6 Centaur. Temple of Zeus at Olympia: west pediment.   [63]

4.1 Antigone with Picasso's chorus of masks. Cocteau's *Antigone*, 1922. From a photo in *Le Théâtre-Comoedia*, January 1923.   [83]

9.1 Running hoplite on an eye-cup. Ella Riegel Museum, Bryn Mawr. P2155.   [208]

9.2 Satyr arming Dionysos. Athenian pelike from Vulci. Paris Bibliothèque Nationale, Cabinet des Médailles 391.   [209]

9.3 Satyr with eye-motif on his briefs. Dinos from Athens. Athens National Archaeological Museum 13027.   [211]

9.4 Men dancing round mask-idol of Dionysos. Lekythos from Athens. Brussels A262.   [215]

9.5   Libation for mask of Dionysos. Athenian stamnos, now destroyed. Berlin 1930.   [217]
9.6   Prometheus before a mask of Dionysos. Chous from Athens. Collection of the 3rd Ephorate.   [218]
9.7   Mask and krater. Etrurian bell-krater. Metropolitan Museum, New York. L.63.21.5.   [229]
9.8   Actor with Dionysos and masks. Athenian bell-krater from Spina. Museo Archeologico Ferrara. T161C.   [230]
10.1  Late sixth-century death-mask from Sindos, grave no. 115. Archaeological Museum of Thessaloniki.   [248]

**Plates**

2.1   (a) Choral dancers. Athenian column-krater. Antikenmuseum Basel. BS415. (b) Drinking scene on the reverse.   [19]
2.2   Boy with mask. From a fragment of an Athenian oenochoe. Athens Agora Museum P11810.   [20]
2.3   (a) Boy with mask and maenad. Athenian bell-krater from Spina. Museo Archeologico Ferrara. Valle Pega 173c. (b) Eos and Tithonos on the reverse.   [23]
2.4   Dancers with mask. Athenian pelike from Cervetri. Museum of Fine Arts Boston. 98.883.   [26]
2.5   Maenadic dancers. Fragment of an Athenian bell-krater from Olbia. Academy of Sciences Museum Kiev.   [28]
2.6   View of the 'Pronomos' vase. Athenian volute-krater from Ruvo. Museo Nazionale Naples 3240.   [30]
2.7   Actor and satyr, from the 'Pronomos' vase. Photo: François Lissarrague.   [31]
2.8   Parodic maenad dancers. Athenian bell-krater. Heidelberg Institute of Archaeology. B134.   [37]
2.9   Maenads and mask-idol. Athenian stamnos from Nuceria. Museo Nazionale Naples 2419.   [39]
3.1   Miniature terracotta mask from Lipari. Kelvingrove Art Gallery and Museum Glasgow. 1903.70.dt.1.   [53]
3.2   Helmet-maker. Cup. Ashmolean Museum Oxford. G267.   [58]
3.3   Orestes, Apollo and Fury. Athenian column-krater. British Museum, London. 1923.10.16.   [60]
3.4   Donato Sartori displaying the neutral mask made for Lecoq by his father Amleto. Photo: Renato Villegas.   [69]

*List of illustrations*  xi

4.1  Mask for Prometheus. From A. Gvozdev, A. Piotrovski, S. Mokulski et al., *Istoria sovetskogo teatra* (Leningrad, 1933).  [81]
4.2  Io. From *Prometheus Bound*, Delphi 1927. Photo by Nelly. Benaki Museum: Photographic Archive.  [91]
4.3  Prometheus. From *Prometheus Bound*, Delphi 1927. Photo by Nelly (detail). Benaki Museum: Photographic Archive.  [92]
4.4  The High Priest raises the dead. Sartre *Les Mouches* 1943. Photo: Studio Harcourt.  [96]
5.1  Jean-Louis Barrault holding the mask of Orestes, with Agamemnon mask in foreground. Photo sent to Amleto Sartori. Museo Internazionale della Maschera Amleto e Donato Sartori, Abano Terme.  [114]
5.2  Mask of Cassandra. Museo Internazionale della Maschera Amleto e Donato Sartori, Abano Terme.  [115]
6.1  Drawing of a Fury by Jocelyn Herbert. © Jocelyn Herbert Archive. Drawing no. 3320.  [136]
6.2  Mask of Orestes. Photo: Sandra Lousada. © Jocelyn Herbert Archive.  [137]
6.3  Drawing of Orestes by Jocelyn Herbert. © Jocelyn Herbert Archive. Drawing no. 3321.  [138]
6.4  Greg Hicks, demonstrating use of the body in mask-work. Mask by Tina Pople-Parali from the *Oedipus Plays*. Photo: Renato Villegas.  [142]
7.1  Masks for the *Oresteia* designed by Donato Sartori. Photo: Renato Villegas.  [155]
7.2  Michael Chase in his studio. Photo: George Croft.  [156]
7.3  Actress demonstrating a messenger speech in the Greek theatre at Bradfield: mask by Michael Chase. Photo: George Croft.  [159]
7.4  Rehearsal mask by Thanos Vovolis. Photo: Renato Villegas.  [166]
7.5  Rehearsal mask by Thanos Vovolis. Photo: Renato Villegas.  [167]
7.6  Mask of Messenger in *Oedipus the King*, by Thanos Vovolis. Photo: Thanos Vovolis.  [168]
7.7  Mask for *Oedipus at Colonus*, by Thanos Vovolis. Photo: Thanos Vovolis.  [178]
8.1  Nurse whispering to Hippolytus. From *Hippolytus* by Thiasos Theatre Company, 2004, with commissioned Balinese masks. Photo: M. J. Coldiron.  [191]

8.2 Actor and mask. From a fragment of a bell-krater from Taras. Martin Von Wagner Museum, Würzburg. H4600. [194]

8.3 Actor with masks. Apulian bell-krater. Museo Provinciale, Brindisi. Faldetta collection. [196]

9.1 Women worshipping an idol of Dionysos. Stamnos from Etruria. Museum of Fine Arts Boston. 90.155. [216]

9.2 Mask of Dionysos in a *liknon*. Chous from Athens. National Archaeological Museum Athens: Vlasto collection 318. [217]

# 1 | Introduction

I have no choice but to employ the word 'mask' in the title of this book, yet that word already carries embedded within it an unsatisfactory interpretation of my subject. In English, to 'mask' something is to hide the reality. Yet when fifth-century Greeks spoke of masks, they had only the word *prosōpon*, the regular term for 'face'. This in turn is derived from the preposition *pros* ('before') joined to *ōps*, a noun related to words for seeing and the eye. 'Before the gaze...' yet the gaze in question might equally belong to me the seer or you the seen. Slippage from seer to seen was easy in a classical world where *I am* coincides with *who I am seen to be*.[1] Later Greeks coined the word *prosōpeion* to separate false faces from real ones, but no such distinction was made in the age of Sophocles, when donning a face was no negative act of concealment but a positive act of becoming.[2] Roman terminology is a step less remote from ours. The Latin term for a theatre mask, *persona*, was not the same as *vultus*, 'face', and it gave birth to handy modern terms like 'personality', the front that we present to the world.[3] This brief journey through semantics reveals something of how other people once saw the world. If my overt topic, 'mask and performance in Greek tragedy', were redefined as 'fore-gaze and mimesis in goat-song at the Dionysia', we would enter a less secure cognitive domain, but might have more chance of intuiting what it is to inhabit another culture.

Greek theatre masks were made of light perishable materials, and have not survived. Yet even if, by good fortune, a set of masks were available to us, housed in a glass case in the British Museum, we should still be a long way from understanding how different those masks looked on the body of a mobile actor, trained in an unfamiliar tradition. We would still be at a loss to know why ancient Greeks chose to place such apparently constraining objects over their heads. When tragedies are staged today at Epidaurus, there is no call to wear masks under the powerful stage lights. Masks would seem

---

[1] Cf. Frontisi-Ducroux (1995: 10–34).
[2] Frontisi-Ducroux (1995: 14–16). Stephen Halliwell points out to me that the first appearance of the term *prosōpeion* is unusually problematic, being found in inferior manuscripts at Demosthenes 19.287, and a corrupted passage in Theophrastus *Characters* 6.3.
[3] Cf. Frontisi-Ducroux (1995: 39); Dupont (2000: 155–7).

an aesthetic intrusion, either archaeological pedantry, or the pretension of an avant-garde director. Why then did the Greeks find it necessary to wear 'masks'? The best way of answering will be to turn the question around: why is it necessary for us *not* to wear masks in *our* theatre?

This book stands at the nexus of four major debates. The first concerns the disputed ownership of 'Greek tragedy', a piece of academic turf which classical philologists (often reinvigorated by 'Critical Theory') and theatre historians (often set in their ways) jostle to claim for their own. Though it is self-evident that each contingent benefits from the other's help, there is a point of principle at stake: is a Greek tragedy essentially a text that happens to have been performed, or are the words a mere component in a historical, participatory, acoustico-visual event, such that a reading of the text which marginalises performance distorts its historicity? My own allegiance will be obvious. I have attempted in this book to recover some sense of the lost festive event, so the text can be more readily imagined in its performative context.

The second debate concerns the actor within Greek tragedy. The recurrent question of whether actors are in constant conscious control of their craft, or whether they are, in the best cases, somehow possessed by their part, seems particularly pressing in respect of Greek tragedy with its potent mix of formalism and emotionality, of political speech-making and divine intervention. The conclusions which I once reached about New Comedy are not the same as those to which I come in respect of fifth-century tragedy.[4] I am in broad agreement with Ismene Lada-Richards when she places fifth-century tragedy in the cultural sphere of Dionysos and argues that 'to retain one's cognitive hold over reality, is in the eyes of the god a grave insult, entailing the human being's disaster and delusion ... More precisely, within the Dionysiac dramatic area, it is the mask, an inherently Dionysiac property, which guarantees for the performer the possibility of becoming "other", of acquiring a different identity.'[5] For the modern actor approaching Greek tragedy, enigmatic asides about acting culled from Aristophanes or treatises on oratory are of little practical assistance, but the simple fact of the mask is overwhelming. To wear a mask changes everything: one's voice, one's movement, one's awareness of self and other. For the practitioner, to understand the mask is to have an entry point into the historical practice of Greek acting.

---

[4] Wiles 1991.

[5] Lada-Richards (1997: 96). Lada-Richards (1999: 168–9) reverts to an orthodox view of the theatre/ritual distinction. Duncan 2006 gives only passing attention to the mask. On Greek acting, see Lada-Richards 2002 and Hall (2006).

The third issue concerns the relationship of theatre to ritual. This is a matter of heated debate within Classics, whilst Theatre Studies has found its own definitions challenged by an American discipline called Performance Studies, which extends the notion of 'theatre' to multiple areas of social interaction. Anthropologists have so often associated the mask with secret societies, power enforcement, encounters with gods, and engagement with death, that we might sensibly expect it to belong to the domain of ritual. In Greek vase painting, the mask is clearly an attribute of Dionysos, like fawnskins and fennel rods, and if tragedy is indeed *something* to do with Dionysos, then the mask must be at the centre of that something.[6] If, however, one takes the festival of Dionysos to be merely the residual frame for a new aesthetic activity generated by the new democratic system, then masking has to be explained in purely artistic and practical terms. So far as we can tell, the mask was invented to serve tragedy and was not the product of evolution from a primitive ritual source.[7] Attention to this creative leap, however, offers no answer to my inversionary question: why should the mask in theatre today seem such an alien object? The modern dichotomy between theatre (or art) and ritual requires further attention to semantics, for there are no classical Greek terms equivalent to *ritual*, *art*, or our institution of *theatre*. The Greeks conceptualised the world on the basis of different categories, which we must struggle to make sense of.

The fourth area of debate concerns the way faces are bound up with personal identity. For Cicero, the orator's performance 'is wholly a matter of the soul, and the face is an image of the soul, while the eyes reflect it'.[8] It is but a small step from here to the formulation of the American psychologist Paul Ekman: 'Emotions are shown primarily in the face, not in the body. The body instead shows how people are *coping* with emotion.'[9] One finds a different ideology at work in Lévi-Strauss, for whom 'the face of man is in opposition to the body of man: as the state of society is in opposition to the state of nature'.[10] The mask in this structuralist view provides escape from the socially constructed domain of facial expression, not a barrier to viewing authentic feelings. There are thus competing ways today of understanding face and self. When we turn to the sculpture of classical Greece, eyes are always powerful, enhanced in bronzes by the insertion of precious stones,

---

[6] Winkler and Zeitlin 1990 put the catch phrase 'Nothing to do with Dionysos?' at the centre of current debate, but their volume has little to say about masks.
[7] See Halliwell (1993: 199).
[8] *De Oratore* iii.221, translated in May and Wisse (2001: 294). Dupont (2001: 130–1) prefers to translate *imago* as mirror, though the term alludes to a death-mask cast from the face.
[9] Ekman and Friesen (1975: 7). [10] Lévi-Strauss (1961: 11 – my translation).

but there is no evidence for a strong binary opposition between face and body. The Parthenon frieze, lowered to eye-height in the British Museum to provide the sort of intimate encounter we like, often leaves viewers troubled by the emotional coldness of these figures, despite their bodily perfection. When we scan these Athenian faces, it is hard to escape our own cultural hunger for a world composed of individuals. These males who exist only as part of a collective, who inhabit an uncertain limbo between human and divine worlds, and who have no existence over and beyond their harmonious bodies, collide with our modern need to place individuals in front of our eyes.

I have focused this book on tragedy, for comedy would require a separate volume.[11] Fifth-century Athens was a place of cultural ferment where tragedians were responsible for some unique performance events that have left their trace in the form of canonical scripts. Though this book may be seen as a sequel to my *Masks of Menander*, my methodology will be entirely different. There, my analysis of New Comedy masks relied on huge numbers of artefacts, and contemporary physiognomic treatises, material which lent itself to a semiotic and cognitive approach. In the fifth century, philosophical writings are more fragmentary, and philosophical thought had not percolated into the common-sense of ordinary Athenians, though all were aware of its presence. The iconographic evidence, mainly in the form of vase painting rather than terracotta replicas, is more enigmatic, but implies that masks, far from making distinctions which a semiotician can interpret, served to obliterate distinctions. Masks are never found as isolated objects, but only as functions of relationships. Whilst materialist philosophy provided a secure basis for explicating Greek New Comedy, in Greek tragedy the gods are a defining presence, and cannot be set aside. A more phenomenological approach is required. We have to ask how people felt when they watched or wore such masks? We need to explore the relationship between masking and a sense of the divine.

My intellectual stance in this book is broadly anthropological. In a recent survey of the discipline, Wendy James takes her title *The Ceremonial Animal* from Wittgenstein. Her thesis is that: 'Ritual, symbol, and ceremony are not simply present or absent in the things we do; they are built in to human action . . . because all human action relates in some way to arenas of culturally specified significance . . .'[12] If we start from the premise that the human being is essentially a 'ceremonial animal', then distinctions between different

---

[11] An essay, 'The poetics of the mask in Old Comedy' is forthcoming in 2008.
[12] James (2003: 7).

sorts of ceremony become more nuanced. In Theatre Studies, the logic of such a position was established by Richard Schechner, under the influence of Victor Turner. Even though Schechner's ritualised and participatory *Dionysus since 69* remained firmly within the domain of artistic expression,[13] his 'theatre anthropology' has established the intellectual grounds for loosening the distinction between 'theatre' and 'performance'. In an essay of 1966, for example, dismissing the notion that Greek theatre descended from a primal ritual, he argued that ritual, theatre, play, games, sports, dance and music are parallel performance activities that should not be placed on any developmental ladder.[14] Two other anthropological studies have helped to inform my approach. In *The Anthropology of Art*, Robert Layton examines Eskimo shaman masks and demonstrates how ongoing creative innovation and aesthetic pleasure are central to the practice of controlling spirits.[15] This helps us understand how Greek theatre may meaningfully have functioned as an offering to Dionysos, with a convergence of ritual and aesthetic concerns. In *Art and Agency*, Alfred Gell argued provocatively that the anthropologist should not think in terms of discrete art objects and ways of seeing them. The aim should be to investigate a network of relationships within which artefacts themselves acquire agency. The mask lends itself to analysis in Gell's terms, not a thing sitting on the face to be viewed, but endowed with agency, an 'index' pointing always at a reality elsewhere.[16]

There are two major strands to my methodology. In the first instance, I shall take a fresh approach to the main primary source, vase painting. I shall not view representations of masks as more or less imperfect renderings of a 'real' artefact, but will concentrate on the function of the vase as a whole, asking why painters chose to portray masking. I shall argue that the vase image communicates not a fixed state or a moment in time but a process of transition, and I shall look at the mask not as an *object* manipulated by humans but as an *agent* engaged in a set of transactions. French research on the Greek gaze, drawing inspiration from the intellectual tradition of Lacan and Sartre, provides an important stimulus for this re-examination. Vase imagery tells us much about Greek ways of seeing, for masks are visible as appurtenances in the sanctuary of Dionysos, but vanish from tragic scenes where we may imagine them to have been worn. Since we never glimpse tragic actors concealed by masks, we may draw appropriate inferences about how Greeks viewed enactments in their festivals. Masks,

---

[13] See Zeitlin 2004.   [14] 'Approaches' in Schechner (1988: 1–34).   [15] Layton (1991: 193–8).
[16] Gell 1998. Edinborough 2003 called my attention to the relevance of Gell; cf. James (2003: 97–9).

furthermore, are conspicuous in Dionysian iconography but absent from discourse. The silence of our written sources relates to the lack of a distinguishing name for the mask-object, this thing that can never be dissociated from the effect of its gaze, and from its condition of being subject as well as object. Images and words had different emphases in the classical world: the spoken and written *logos*, when separated from music, related to logic, and logical ways of organising the polis, whilst vision lent itself to more visionary or metaphysical areas of human experience.

My second methodological ploy is to draw on the evidence of twentieth-century practice. The history of reception is a burgeoning area in Classical Studies, on account of a professional crisis concerning the relevance of Antiquity to the modern world, and of an epistemological crisis concerning the difficulty of writing any positivist, fact-based history of the ancient world. The Archive of Performances of Greek and Roman Theatre in Oxford, and The Reception of Classical Texts and Images Project at the Open University have given a particular impetus in the UK to research into modern performances of Greek drama.[17] Studies of how the ancient world has been received can be conservative, tracing an unbroken line to the present in order to justify the timeless value of the past, or they can be radical, stressing the otherness of the past, and the socially constructed nature of all interpretations. It is the cultural otherness of the Greek world that I shall stress in this book, whilst not undervaluing the remarkable properties of texts and artefacts capable of engendering such diverse perceptions. I shall look at realisations of the Greek mask in modern theatre with equal attention to the functions of actor, writer and spectator, and the variety of work that I document will serve to relativise my own twenty-first-century viewpoint. Whilst I cannot finally escape from a historically and geographically conditioned way of seeing the world, I can at least open up a menu of choices.

It is axiomatic in Theatre Studies that theory and practice should converge, and a further strand in my methodology has been practice-based research.[18] I have worked on masks with students over many years,[19] and have also undertaken two focused projects sponsored by the Arts and Humanities Research Board, which I shall discuss in Chapter 7. The value of such research

---

[17] I should also signal the importance of three Greek-based organisations in stimulating academic activity: DESMI, the European Cultural Centre of Delphi, and the European Network of Research and Documentation of Ancient Greek Drama Performances – together with the individual contributions of figures like Erika Fischer-Lichte in Berlin, Helene Foley in New York and Marianne McDonald in San Diego.

[18] The place of practice in historical research has been marginal to debates within PARIP at the University of Bristol. Methodological issues are discussed in Bratton and Bush-Bailey 2002.

[19] Wiles 2004a offers an example of my practice.

does not lie in clinching what *must* have been done in antiquity, for it would be absurd to claim that that masks two and a half millennia ago meant the same and had the same effect as masks today. The point is rather to demonstrate what potentially *can* be done with a mask, and what masks *can* do to us. Moreover, even the most determined cultural relativist must accede to certain biological universals. For purposes of studying the mask, scientific experimentation could embrace the effects of sensory deprivation upon those who wear masks, the physics of producing sound within a shell formed like a second skull, and the brain-structure which 'wires' us to respond in special ways to faces.

This book builds on much earlier scholarship. Archaeologists have provided the bedrock by locating, classifying, dating and photographing artefacts. The tireless work of T. B. L. Webster and Richard Green in collating mask images, in association with the Institute of Classical Studies in London, has been of particular assistance, as has Arthur Pickard-Cambridge's handbook on the festivals of Dionysos, rewritten by John Gould and David Lewis.[20] If Webster's catalogue of *Monuments Illustrating Tragedy and Satyr Play* remains unrevised since 1967, this may in part be due to the inherent difficulties of the early material.[21] While most comic images present overt signs of their theatricality, the relationship between theatricality and images of heroes or satyrs is more elusive. Many data have been gathered, and the major need in the twenty-first century is for a higher level of theorisation. By 'theory' I refer not to a specific body of postmodern thought, but merely to sustained reflection about why mask research matters, and what the implications are of categorising masks in one way rather than another way.[22] Françoise Frontisi-Ducroux has done valuable work on Dionysian masks in a theoretically self-conscious manner, as has David Napier but their focus has been on ritual as distinct from theatre.[23]

Within Theatre Studies an overarching theoretical study of the mask remains to be written. Publications fall into three main categories: generalist books where the text is a support to photographs, manuals setting out the method of a particular practitioner, and specialised historical studies. I recommend to students Efrat Tseëlon's brief 'Reflections on mask and carnival' as the most useful overview of the subject I have encountered because it

---

[20] Pickard-Cambridge 1968. An appendix was added in 1988.
[21] Webster 1967. Eric Handley tells me that he has gathered materials for a future revision. I await eagerly Oliver Taplin's forthcoming study of theatre-related vase images, to be published by the Getty Foundation in 2007.
[22] Green 1991 sets out his methodology and rationale clearly and helpfully.
[23] Napier 1986; Frontisi-Ducroux 1991, 1995.

draws alike on Theatre Studies and on the social sciences, unconfined by the parameters of what we now classify as 'theatre'.[24] Standard introductions to Greek theatre contain many sensible observations about masking in Greek tragedy. Oliver Taplin in *Greek Tragedy in Action* related masks to a theatre of outward action,[25] and Rush Rehm has explained well the importance of the audience's imagination in projecting expression onto the mask.[26] While Taplin tends to privilege the dramaturgical function and Rehm the directorial, Michael Walton does more to place acting at the centre of the ancient theatrical experience, seeing the masked face as a positive asset in the creation of a physical acting style.[27] Writing in the 1970s before Peter Hall had demonstrated the potential of masked tragedy, Taplin suggested that the emotional singing of the chorus 'compensates' for the 'immobility' of the mask when Theseus absorbs Phaedra's suicide note, but as a practitioner, Walton was already clear that: 'Far from being a hindrance to the presentation of emotion, the mask concentrates feeling and focuses the attention of the audience'.[28] In *The Cambridge Companion to Greek Tragedy* Pat Easterling confronts the paradox that on the one hand masks, 'fixed and unchangeable, are a visible reminder to the audience of the fictive nature of the dramatic events', while on the other hand 'the mask in performance may create the illusion of facial movement and fluidity of expression', and she relates this complexity of the mask phenomenon to the cult of Dionysos.[29] In the recent *Cambridge Companion to Greek and Roman Theatre*, however, Greg McCart leaves any such cultic context aside, and draws on his own practice to redefine the gestural nature of Greek acting.[30]

The gap between ancient and modern understandings of the mask is best treated in two studies not available in English. Siegfried Melchinger in 1974 concluded that the classical mask effected useful distinctions of age, gender and class, while at the same time it essentialised the face in the manner of sculptors like Phidias or Polygnotos, whereas in the modern era masks usually result in monotonous clowning. When reality belongs to the actor's face, he argued, Brechtian alienation becomes the only viable aesthetic option.[31] Patricia Vasseur-Legangneux in 2004 examined the utopian impulses behind revivals of Greek tragedy. Most modern masked productions, she maintains,

---

[24] Tseëlon 2001. Grimes 1992 offers a useful perspective on ritual. Aslan and Bablet 1985, Mack 1994 and Malik 2001 provide valuable collections of individual essays.
[25] Taplin (1978: 14).
[26] Rehm (1992: 41). His description of the mouth and eyes of the mask betray the influence of Tony Harrison.
[27] Walton (1984: 54–9); Walton (1991: 161–7).
[28] Taplin (1978: 95); Walton (1991: 167). Walton's book first appeared in 1980.
[29] Easterling (1997: 51). [30] McCart 2007. [31] Melchinger (1974: 201–16).

either constitute a celebration of the ancient world, thereby aestheticising the mask, or use the mask to establish a radical break with conventional readings, resulting in obscurity. Successful use of the mask today, as in the work of Ariane Mnouchkine or Benno Besson, involves deliberate play with theatricality. This, she suggests, is not so far removed from the practice of the ancient world, which created a gap between the audience and the mythic world of the play through creating masked bodies devoid of any interiority.[32]

Within mainstream Classics, the theatre mask sits in a curious limbo, welcomed neither in literary criticism nor in the analysis of Greek religion. Once the Cambridge ritualists had been sent packing in intellectual disgrace because no one accepted any longer their romantic but reductive vision of a Frazerian Ur-ritual from which all drama stemmed, the main post-war source of intellectual nourishment became Marxism, with its claim that art should be understood as a function of society.[33] The great question to ask of tragedy now concerned its relation to the *polis*. But if drama was just a continuation of politics by another means, then the place of masks was unclear. The mask had impinged much more obviously on other big questions asked of tragedy by earlier generations – about the sources of its emotional power, for instance, the construction of psychological archetypes, or the power of the gods. Historians of religion in the meanwhile, once the umbilical link with Frazer's Ur-ritual had been cut, left theatre aside as a no-go area, artistic rather than religious terrain. Texts could be quarried for information about religion, but tragic performance belonged now to practical people like Arthur Pickard-Cambridge, who could explain how things were done in nuts-and-bolts terms.

There is a bigger picture here, of course, for in the wake of the Renaissance and Kant the divide between ritual and 'art' has entered the common-sense of the modern world, shaping such institutions as the Arts Council, or Faculties of Arts in universities. This apparently natural division underpinned, for example, Vernant's contention in 1968 that the role of the tragic mask 'is not a ritual but an aesthetic one'.[34] In an extreme statement of the anti-Dionysiac case, Scott Scullion attacks 'those moderns for whom the mask serves to put a cultic face on dramatic representation', and is content with 'the obvious and sufficient reason for wearing masks in drama, namely that they help performers look less like themselves and more like the characters they are representing'.[35] Other critics more eager to retain some relationship between theatre and ritual nevertheless use the mask to help define the

---

[32] Vasseur-Legangneux (2004: 163–74).  [33] Goldhill 1997 offers a useful overview.
[34] Vernant and Vidal-Naquet (1990: 24).  [35] Scullion (2002: 116).

demarcation line. Rainer Friedrich, for example, argues that connections between Dionysos and theatre should be traced on the plane of narrative; exaggerated claims by ritualists that Dionysos is god of the mask, he remarks, simply add glamour to the god's modern *c.v.*[36] In an extensive account of the relation between tragedy and religion, Christiane Sourvinou-Inwood confines the function of masks to 'mimesis': her mimetic mask effects a shift of perspective, distancing what is shown from the ritual enactment in order to privilege the otherness of the past.[37] This is the Brechtian Verfremdungseffekt by another name.

All these accounts are premised on a distinction between theatrical mimesis and authentic ritual. Pat Easterling opened the door a crack in 1988, when she concluded a survey of ritual *in* tragedy with a paragraph on the passage of *Eumenides* where the chorus blesses the city of Athens, making the critical admission: 'despite what I have said about the metaphorical status of the ritual elements in tragedy, I do not think we can rule out the possibility that some sequences of words, music and actions could be felt to have exceptional power, something that went beyond the fictional world of the drama and was able to affect the world of the audience for good or ill'.[38] An important recent development has been recognition that tragedy often provides the aetiology for a cult. Robert Parker, for example has described tragedy as part of 'the soil in which Greek hero-cult grows'. He adds that it provided 'the directest "theology" to which Athenians were ever exposed', and 'the Dionysus of, say, *Bacchae* or *Frogs* was part of an Athenian's experience of Dionysus no less than was the Dionysus of the Anthesteria'.[39] Despite these insights, he proves unwilling to relinquish the orthodox view that 'the use of masks in Dionysiac cult is quite unlike the theatrical, and it is not clear that Dionysiac delusion and theatrical illusion are compatible'.[40] It seems to me that 'theatrical illusion' is a concept we have foisted onto Greek goat-song, aided and abetted by Plato, in order to make it comprehensible in our own terms.

The most influential post-war account of the tragic mask has been that of John Jones, who related the neutrality of the classical mask to Aristotle's privileging of plot over character.[41] Another authority on Aristotle's *Poetics*, Stephen Halliwell, investigated the mask in 1993 in the context of a broad interest in mimesis, and likewise emphasised the aesthetic value of neutrality. He assumed that 'tragic masks were regarded as entirely theatrical, not

---

[36] Friedrich (1996: 268).   [37] Sourvinou-Inwood (2003: 163).   [38] Easterling (1988: 109).
[39] Parker (2005: 141, 146, 152). On aetiology, cf. Seaford (1994: 123–39).
[40] Parker (2005: 139, n. 14).   [41] Jones 1962.

religious, in classical Athens', and part of his aim was 'to demystify the power of the mask, and to suggest that its function in the classical Greek theatre will not bear the gaze of scrutiny which a modern imagination may too easily incline to give to it'; he criticised in passing my own 'incautious claims about the Dionysiac nature of Greek theatre masks'.[42] My purpose in this book is to make some more considered claims. While mystification is bad academic practice, the experience and representation of mystery cannot be dissevered from the phenomenon of religion.

Aristotle's *Poetics* has for centuries provided a basis for western theatre aesthetics. University departments of Drama came into being to deal with dramas written by named individuals, and to examine how those written works were staged. Much progressive theatre work in recent decades starts from an alternative basis, such as collective improvisation, the performer's body, the animation of spaces, or audience interaction. In modern Theatre Studies or Performance Studies, the authored play has increasingly been dislodged from its pivotal position. It is helpful in this context to turn from Aristotle to Plato, who envisages tragedy as a distinctively Athenian category of choral dancing. In his *Laws*, where the divine gift of festivals is seen as necessary to human life, he accepts some forms of choral mimesis like armed dances performed in honour of Athena and in imitation of her,[43] but opposes the Athenian practice of bringing a medley of choruses to the scene of a sacrifice, where their words, rhythms and music reduce the audience to tears. He refers to tragedy again when he urges that a lament should be performed in costumes that are dark not glittering.[44] Tragedy should properly represent the noble life, he declared, and the problem with Athenian tragic performance was the way it jumbled traditional forms.[45] He nevertheless leaves space in his ideal city for irrationality, permitting Dionysiac dancing that imitates satyrs and nymphs, for this belongs outside the political sphere, and he relates theatre to the wine-god when he prescribes choral dancing for older men under the rejuvenating influence of wine.[46] Plato's understanding of tragedy not as a text that needed to be staged but as a local variant on competitive choral dancing gives twenty-first-century Theatre Studies, with its orientation towards physicality, a point of purchase. The authored text was nevertheless a crucial component within the performance, as it was equally in dithyrambs, dances celebrating sporting victories, paeans, wedding hymns, and other forms generally categorised as ritual.

---

[42] Halliwell (1993: 202, 209, 197, n. 4).   [43] *Laws* 796.
[44] *Laws* 800.   [45] *Laws* 668, 817, 700.
[46] *Laws* 815, 665. On Plato's choral perspective see Kowalzig (2007).

Religion has failed to wither away, but remains a potent factor in geo-politics, whether we think of Belfast, Cyprus, Palestine, Kashmir or the American Bible belt. The drive to 'demystify' Greek tragedy stems from a liberal, secular value-system that declines to engage with religion as a driver of human conduct. Postmodernism's account of the transcendental signifier does little to explain the power of religious experience. I shall take issue with a 'postmodern' criticism at several points in this book, and recognise my own stance better in terms of two related coinages: post-secular, and post-dramatic. I take my first from a recent lecture by Jürgen Habermas, who engages with the predicament of liberal democracy in a 'post-secular' age. To expect religious citizens to articulate themselves in rationalistic ways is not necessarily democratic, he argues, calling for a 'post-metaphysical' category of thought which, while remaining agnostic, avoids narrow scientism and does not exclude religious doctrines from 'the genealogy of reason'.[47] My second term is drawn from Hans-Thies Lehmann, who sums up his distinction between dramatic and 'post-dramatic' theatre by citing Paul Claudel's reaction to an encounter with Japanese masked theatre: 'Le Drame, c'est quelque chose qui arrive, le Nō, c'est quelqu'un qui arrive'.[48] For Lehmann, this encapsulates the idea that post-dramatic theatre eschews Aristotelian plot or action in favour of apparition, and representation in favour of 'performance'. Claudel's aphorism sums up my own argument about the classical mask: the mask made someone happen. It brought about a transformation, and the epiphanic appearance of a being who was not present before. The Aristotelian argument is not in itself wrong, and I am in full agreement that masking helped to generalise character and clarify plot. My contention is that masking added another dimension to the experience of performance, which we need a post-metaphysical language in order to describe. This further dimension relates to the liveness of performance, something that theatre practitioners have increasingly learned to value in an age when technology makes a far better job of representation and reproduction.

The organisation of this book may appear counter-intuitive. One of my referees for the Press advised that I should write this book in the obvious order: antiquity first, and then see what later generations made of the mask. I have rejected linear historiography because we understand the past only through the present, and the present through the past in a continuing dialectic. I devote an initial pair of chapters to the archaeological data, the primary

---

[47] Habermas 2005. Lecture first given in Lodz, April 2004.
[48] 'A drama is something that arrives/happens; Noh is someone who arrives/happens.' Lehmann (2006: 58).

source material, and raise questions about the art of the mask-maker. From there I pass in Chapter 4 via German idealism to early twentieth-century modernism, where European artists were preoccupied by the idea of the mask.[49] This chapter is centred on the creative work of the writer, exploring the influence of Nietzsche's mystic idealisation of the mask, and runs chronologically parallel with my next, which explores the work of the actor and traces the influence of Copeau. I describe a tension between Copeau's transformative, quasi-religious conception of the mask, and a politicised Brechtian conception of the mask as a visible and material sign. My next two chapters also form a pair. Chapter 6 is focused on the proposition of Peter Hall and Tony Harrison that the function of the mask was to foreground text, while 7 considers how the voice is an intermediary between body and text, testing the proposition that the mask was an instrument to enhance sound. In these four chapters on modern western theatre I examine specific performance problems that relate to our interpretation of antiquity, and am not attempting a comprehensive survey of modern performances in Greek masks.[50] In Chapter 8 I pass to the issues involved in interpreting non-western mask performance. Masking in Asian and African tradition is perfectly normal, not avant-garde and exotic, and I argue that this difference is linked to polytheistic beliefs, tied conceptually and experientially to a more plural conception of self. In my final three chapters, in the light of all that masks can potentially achieve, I return to fifth-century Athens. Chapter 9 relates the mask cult of Dionysos to masked tragedy at the Dionysia, and I go on in 10 to analyse the religious inflection involved in viewing a masked tragedy. In my final chapter I show how masking assumed and fostered a less inward, less monolithic conception of self than the one we have adopted today.

I had the good fortune to write the final two chapters of this book at the Villa Serbelloni on Lake Como, thanks to the generosity of the Rockefeller Foundation. Since I was writing about images, I naturally took a special interest in all the images that I found about the grounds, and two became particular friends. The first was Pliny the Younger, who sat in his sunny *aediculum* with a hand pointing to his heart, and the inscription HIC TRAGEDIA on his pediment. The legend 'Here is Tragedy' had three levels of reference. Firstly, Pliny is supposed to have built a villa called Tragedy on this spot, perched on the crag like a Roman tragic actor on high buskins; second, the words refer to the personal tragedy of Duke Serbelloni, who erected

---

[49] See Sorell 1973.
[50] Wiles 2004b gives some attention to Koun and Guthrie, notable omissions from this book.

the statue in the year of his death, 1826; and third is a reference to tragedy as text, since a codex and papyrus rolls sit at Pliny's side, a reminder that he wrote a tragedy in his youth. This statue encapsulates the romantic notion of tragedy, an affair of the human heart, best expressed through the solitary act of writing, and available to the leisured elite with time for introspection. My second cherished image was Bernadette of Lourdes, who inhabited a lonely grotto on the north side of the headland, the creation of gardeners in the early twentieth century. She knelt on a small stage of rough limestone blocks, looking up at an alabaster Virgin armed with a disciplinary rosary and skull. As a common mortal the luckless Bernadette was only made of plaster, she had lost an arm, and her face was little more than a white blob since drips from the roof had washed off the protective paint and eroded the plaster. In the gloom, the illusion of a transfigured face was stronger than any detailed sculpting and painting could have created. Her face was much more expressive than that of the alabaster Virgin, or the sun-bleached Roman sage, and this expressivity stemmed in part from the passage of time written into her features, which tied the past to the here-and-now of present performance.

The comparison of these two images was a source for meditation. Was Bernadette a work of art? Or should we deny her that label of cultural approval and dismiss her as a work of rustic superstition, modified by happenstance. Like Pliny, she is expressive of an ideology, but a more populist ideology. Between the religiosity of the gardener and the educated secularism of the aristocrat there lay a gulf of understanding which finds its echoes in the twenty-first century. The sculptor of Pliny laid claim to the great classical tradition, while Bernadette has a medieval ancestry. Yet Bernadette for the sake of realism was painted as Greek statues were and Pliny was not. She is associated with an apprehension of the divine, as fifth-century sculptures normally were, and Pliny is not. With Pliny, emotional truth is rooted in a psychological interior whereas Bernadette has no inner world, truth lying out there in what she sees and how she is seen. These questions take us back to Greek tragedy which was written and performed for a mass audience, predominantly male and free, but nevertheless more gardener than duke. How did this audience apprehend tragedy at the Dionysia? Not as 'art', certainly. Nor 'theatre'. Nor did they look upon 'masks'.

# 2 | The evidence of vases

When he states that in comedy no one knows who introduced the *prosōpa*, but changes in tragedy are well known, Aristotle implies that the tragic mask was introduced at a specific historical moment.[1] Horace declares that the first actors used the dregs of wine-making to smear their faces, but this sounds like an inference to underline the wine-god's connection with theatre, and most late texts speak of faces covered in white lead or white plaster.[2] Our sources agree that the masks used in Athens at the Dionysia were made of linen, but whether the stiffening agent was plaster or animal glue cannot be told. Though one source refers to glue, there was doubtless much experimentation.[3] The first linen masks are said to have been plain, until Aeschylus introduced colour.[4] The origin of the mask in crude white make-up suggests that the first purposes of masking were transformational rather than mimetic. Fortunately, we are not reliant on these paltry antiquarian references because fifth-century vase painting offers a rich source of data on tragic and satyric masking.[5]

The uniting of 'mask' and 'face' in the one word *prosōpon* helps explain the vase painter's convention that tragic and satyric masks become faces the moment a dramatic scene is presented. The technical term used by archaeologists is 'melting': the mask melts into the face so no distinction of body and mask can be seen. We have nothing, therefore, that can in modern terms be regarded as a documentary record of a classical tragedy in performance. We never see actors acting. The closest we come is in three vases of the 440s which appear to depict Euaion, the son of Aeschylus, playing the tragic roles of Perseus, Argiope and Actaeon. The name of the actor appears on the vase, but there is no other sign of theatrical performance, and Actaeon's face is in the process of metamorphosing to acquire the features of a stag.[6] The lack of any representation of performance is striking, whether we explain it as a tribute to the power of the theatrical imagination, as a religious taboo, or

---

[1] *Poetics* v.3.  [2] Sources in Pickard-Cambridge (1962: 71–9).
[3] Plato, the fifth-century playwright, refers to linen: Pollux x.167; the scholiast on *Frogs* 406 refers to glued rags.
[4] Suidas, cited in Pickard-Cambridge (1968: 190).
[5] *LIMC* 'Dionysos' 6; Csapo and Slater (1995: 125–6).  [6] See Krumeich 2002.

as an example of how cultures differ in their 'ways of seeing'. In order to make sense of the iconography today, we need to start with the function of classical vases, which was in most cases to contain wine, the gift of Dionysos. Wine-vessels were often placed in tombs because of the association between Dionysos and the afterlife. Gell's proposition is fundamental, that 'aesthetic properties' must not be abstracted from 'social processes'.[7] When we look at the corpus of vase images representing masks, we see that masks are always a function of relationships, both internal and external to the vase, and not autonomous objects of painterly representation. All of them compel us, when we possess more than fragments, to make a connection between theatrical artefacts and the sphere of the divine. Halliwell's proposition that 'tragic masks were regarded as entirely theatrical, not religious, in classical Athens' is in flat contradiction with the message of vases.[8]

We may begin with a well-known amphora in Berlin from the age of Thespis, the supposed originator of tragedy in the 530s. It depicts three men bent in horse-like fashion to display their fine buttocks, wearing horse-masks that do not actually conceal their faces (Drawing 2.1). They carry on their shoulders three riders who sport animalistic crests on their helmets, and face an *aulos*-player. Theatre historians like Margarete Bieber have seen this image as a record of the work of some predecessor of Aristophanes, and an indication of how Aristophanes staged his chorus of mounted knights.[9] If we turn to the other side of the vase, which theatre historians have seen no reason to reproduce, we find that the *aulos* is now being held by a satyr with equine legs who dangles the *aulos*-case from his erect phallus. Standing before him, ready to dance, are five figures in line: three naked satyrs with human legs, horsy ears and tails and huge erections, and two androgynous figures, who may be awaiting sexual penetration from behind. On each side of the vase we thus have three couples and an equine theme. One side shows us masks and riders, the other a Dionysiac world where human bodies are available for mounting; on the one side we see humans performing mimetically as animals, on the other the animal instinct in males is embodied by satyrs, who are part horse, part human. Within the ambit of the wine-god, dramatic enactment yields to the world of the divine, which we might also term the world of the imagination. In more psychoanalytic language, we could say that desire is sublimated into choral dance. All the 'theatrical' images of masks that we investigate on vases need to be interpreted in the same way,

---

[7] Gell (1998: 5).   [8] Halliwell (1993: 202).
[9] Bieber (1961: 37). For the vase, see Hedreen (1992: 136–8). The words render some inarticulate cry.

**Drawing 2.1** Berlin horse-dancers.

in regard to their Dionysiac function. They are teasing fantasies concerned with the metamorphosis of mental states and physical beings. We may infer that some sixth-century Athenian dancers did indeed wear horse-heads in the manner shown, but these figures might also be a fantasy of the artist to suggest a transition between the states of human and satyr.

A vase of *c*.490–480 in Basel is often held to represent a half-chorus of tragedy performing in masks, at a time when the theatrical mask was still a relatively new phenomenon (Plate 2.1). This krater or bowl for mixing wine depicts six members of a chorus singing in front of a tomb from which a bearded figure appears to rise, like Darius in Aeschylus' *Persians* (472 BC). The vase is a prime exhibit for Erika Simon, who writes in *The Ancient Theatre*: 'When one considers this picture, the few remains of the Archaic layout which W. Dörpfeld found in the theatre of Dionysus are filled with life'. The play which inspired this image, she continues, 'strongly impressed the vase painter, who must have been seated in the audience'.[10] Richard Green confirms that the words coming from open mouths, the profile and the pronounced line around the jaw hint at the features of a mask.[11] Is this truly, however, actually a tragedy in performance? A water jar of the same period in St Petersburg depicts what seem to be chorus-men with similar costume, profile and text, but these aged men are being led reluctantly to the god Dionysos, and here there is no question of a performance being pictured.[12] The common theme turns out to be reluctance.

If we rotate the krater, we see on the reverse side a krater that is clearly a self-referential image. A young satyr proffers wine to a mature satyr, who, despite his extreme erectile condition, declines the advances of the youth as he moves out of the frame. Turning back to the 'masked' side, we find clues to the connection. Firstly, decorating the shoulder of the front dancer, a tiny satyr is running away from the tomb towards his colleagues on the reverse. And second, on both the tomb and the self-referential krater is the inscription KALOS, the standard generic dedication to a beautiful youth.[13] The homoerotic theme is obvious in the Dionysiac world of the satyrs, less so in the world of human performance until we notice the buttocks protruding through the skimpy tresses of the skirt, and the fabric hitched up in the area of the crotch. The twin inscriptions point up a symmetry between two containers: the tomb from which the hero (possibly Dionysos himself)

---

[10] Simon (1982: 9).
[11] Green (1994a: 18 and fig. 2.1); 'certainly' masks according to Simon (1982: 10); 'at least something between masks and faces' in Csapo and Slater (1995: 57); 'reminiscent' in Green (1991: 35). Full documentation in Slehoferova (1988: 21–3).
[12] See Green 1995.   [13] For the convention see Lissarrague 1999.

*The evidence of vases* 19

Plate 2.1 (a) Dance at tomb. Basel. (b) Reverse: drinking scene.

is conjured, and the krater from which wine is taken. The first is decorated with funereal myrtle, the second with Dionysiac ivy. The word 'phe' uttered by the bearded man, garlanded in myrtle, suggests 'pheu' ('alas!'), and the way he pulls his cloak about him likewise signifies reluctance. He is unwilling to return to life when summoned up by young men, just as the older satyr on the reverse is unwilling to be seduced by youth. This much-reproduced vase painting is not an image of tragedy in performance but a

Plate 2.2 Boy with mask. Athens.

riddle about wine and the attractions of youth for party-goers to decode. As in the Berlin amphora, there is subtle interplay between a pure Dionysiac world and a world of human mimesis. Though nothing precludes the inference that the vase painter has been inspired by a motif from tragedy, and is evoking the theatrical mask, we must insist on the difference. Tragic costume was designed precisely in order to eliminate the carnal viewing proper to a drinking-party. The young choral dancer concealed his body, at least until the satyr play, and normally played a woman or an old man opposite to himself, not a handsome youth like himself.

The earliest image of a mask separate from its wearer is in Athens, on a fragmentary wine-jug of 470–460 BC (Plate 2.2). The viewer is confronted by female figures and a small boy holding a mask, which Webster identified as a maenad on account of the purple band round the hair.[14] The hair is cropped, however, which suggests mourning, and thus tragedy. An unshod

---

[14] Description in Talcott 1939; cf. Webster (1967: AV9). Gould and Lewis refuse to confirm that this is a maenad: Pickard-Cambridge (1968: 181 and fig. 32).

**Drawing 2.2** Mask. Detail of Plate 2.2.

woman is walking away from the mask, but on another fragment a woman similarly dressed wears pointed theatrical boots, and on another there is a laced boot, so the context seems choral, but at the same time a world in flux. The mask is held by multiple cords secured to the headband, and cords also hang below the base of the mask, indicating how the mask was tied to the head (Drawing 2.2). The mouth is open but not gaping, with an indeterminate expression closer to a smile than grief. The line of the nose connects with that of the brow in the manner of contemporary sculptures. The eyes were originally painted in, complete with their irises, so the mask stared out at the viewer. Close study of the paint reveals that the artist began by painting the eyes and mouth, an archaeological detail which reveals something about the psychology of viewing faces.

Though most photographic reproductions of the mask create the impression of blank eyes, leaving the modern viewer in the secure position of gazing objectively at an inert object,[15] the normal convention in fifth-century vase painting was to make the eyes of the mask alive. This mask, picked out by its white pigment, was designed to arrest the gaze of the user, and the exposed ear hints that it may be listening to the viewer as well as watching. It is also not obvious in photographs that the artist has been at pains to represent the mask in motion, swinging left and back as one can tell from the free-hanging strings. The perspective on the nose, the height of the ear, and the disproportionate width of the face in relation to height combine to create a sense of foreshortening as the chin moves away. Also, one does not at first notice that the eyes are on a different axis to the nose, which again creates the illusion of movement. As this artist understood, the essence of theatrical masks is that they come to life in movement, and have no meaning as static objects. It was in the motion of tipping that wine-jugs likewise had their *raison d'être*.

In the museum of Ferrara, from perhaps ten years later, a largely intact krater depicts a dancing maenad wearing a fawnskin and theatrical footwear. The vacant eyes, defined jaw and open mouth show the maenad is wearing a mask (Plate 2.3).[16] The mask has a fine Grecian profile, but no indications of mood or character. A bound hair-piece extends over the back of the head, and tiny strands of hair falling below the cloth onto the neck distinguish the dancer's own hair from the false hair on the mask, while less clearly the dancer's own ear seems to be exposed. However, there are no eyes behind the empty eye-sockets, so the actor has in this sense vanished. On the left, an adolescent boy hangs from his hand, in a focal position facing the viewer, a mask of indeterminate sex with long auburn hair, and he has turned his head towards the maenad in a look of astonishment. On the reverse side of the vase, in a more conventional image, the winged goddess Dawn advances rapaciously upon Tithonos, a young Trojan prince who carries a lyre and is destined to be her consort. She extends her arms towards him, while he backs away.[17] There is a strict symmetry between the two sides. On both, a mature and threatening woman advances upon an immature and beautiful youth who will undergo transformation. On one side we are in the world of myth, on the other we seem to be in the world of performance. On the one side, by virtue of the lyre, we are in the domain of Apollo, while on the other, by virtue of the mask and fawnskin, we are in the domain of Dionysos.

---

[15] For example Bieber (1961: fig. 74); Pickard-Cambridge (1968: fig. 32).
[16] Riccioni 1959. Reproduced as Pickard-Cambridge (1968: fig. 33).
[17] *LIMC* 'Eos' 166, with commentary in Woodford (2003: 57–60).

*The evidence of vases* 23

Plate 2.3 (a) Boy with mask. Ferrara. (b) Reverse: Eos and Tithonos.

Again we must resist the instinct to read the first image in quasi-photographic terms as a dressing-room scene. If we look more closely at the boy, we see that he wears a long Ionian chiton, which could be a regular female garment or a ceremonial male garment. Pointed theatrical boots have been rendered in a strange frontal perspective, ungainly in their immobility, and his *himation* (cloak) has been pinned up at the shoulder and belted in an unusual way as if to allow freedom to dance like the maenad. Passing to the mask, we notice the excessive length of its chin, and the ears which sit too high and too forward, a bit like the equine ears of a satyr.[18] The hair is shorter on our right, while the right pupil is larger, the right eyebrow higher, the mouth tending rightwards, and the nose-line incomplete on the left. It is as though the mask's features are being pulled towards the dancer. The asymmetry of eyes, mouth, brows and hair induced Gould and Lewis to apologise for the artist's 'not very accomplished drawing',[19] but this is absurd for the boy's face is drawn with great delicacy and no lapse of professional standards. The sketchy, irregular drawing of the mask is an artistic ploy, designed to suggest the crude and transitional nature of the mask-object. As we shall see in later chapters, mask-makers often use asymmetry to make a mask seem like a living face. Though the mask is irregular, the composition of the image as a whole is carefully balanced, with the toes and thumb of the dancer defining an axis line. The mask is part of a process, swinging towards the central axis while also holding the gaze of the viewer.

Tithonos was doomed to shrivel away, granted immortality at the cost of losing his ephemeral beauty. If we think of the Dionysiac youth as a fellow victim, one choice is to regard this mask as a disembodied head, staring forward like the decapitated head of a Medusa. The blank eyes of the maenad mask could evoke the unseeing eyes of Agave in Euripides' *Bacchae*, possessed by Dionysos and unable to recognise her son, while the long auburn hair of the mask would help to legitimate Agave's perception that she enters carrying not Pentheus' head but that of a lion.[20] However, the boy's youth suggests that the mask belongs rather to Dryas, whose father Lycurgus hacked off his head in a fit of Dionysiac madness, mistaking his son for a vine. In an Attic vase of the late fifth century depicting this scene, a maenad wields Dryas' head, characterised by similar long hair.[21] There is an

---

[18] On the signifying force of ears, cf. Bérard and Bron (1989: 140).
[19] Pickard-Cambridge (1968: 182). I am grateful to Dr Fede Berti for allowing me to inspect this vase.
[20] *Bacchae* 1196.
[21] *LIMC* 'Lykourgos' 12, also reproduced as 'Pentheus' 65. Lycurgus was the subject of a celebrated trilogy by Aeschylus.

obvious correspondence between the execution of Dryas, the obliteration of the young performer's beauty by the mask, and the destruction of Tithonos' beauty by time. The blind eyes of the dancer's mask echo the delusion of the Dawn-goddess who thought she could conquer time.

The Ferrara image is richly suggestive. It is not a rehearsal scene but a meditation on Dionysiac madness and the transformative effect of wine. Whether the performer of the maenad's part is *actually* male or female is not an appropriate question to ask, for the image is not framed in such realist terms. The mask in the centre of the image, like the mask on the Athens jug, looks out at the viewer, so that objective viewing becomes impossible. On another vase of the same period in Berlin, much reproduced by theatre historians, a bare-breasted maenad brandishes a limb torn from a fawn, and dances in front of an *aulos*-player. One face of the vase shows the maenad in profile, the other is identical save that her face is turned towards the viewer,[22] and play upon sexuality is suggested by the KALOS inscription.[23] As in the Ferrara vase, the male viewer is invited to think that he might be the next victim, punished for his desires. In both vases, the mask/face is placed at the centre of a puzzle designed to provoke debate at a symposium.

Moving ahead to the time of Sophocles and Euripides, *c*.440–435, we come to a jar now in Boston. On the left, a maenad dances, holding a cloak, and on the right a young man pulls on theatrical boots, while a mask sits on the ground (Plate 2.4).[24] The mask is identical to the head of the dancing maenad, though there is no sign of the latter being a mask. The dancer wears theatrical boots, but bare arms suggest that this is not a straightforward theatrical costume. The placing of mask and cloak on the central axis of the image affirm that the main concern of the vase is the process of metamorphosis. The youth donning his boots lacks the cloak worn by the dancer, so the garment must be intended for him, and this juxtaposition of cloak and mask on the central axis of the jug demonstrates that masking and costuming were not fundamentally different modes of transformation.[25] On the reverse of the vase, a bearded man leaning on his staff creates a voyeuristic context, suggesting that the feminisation of the young man is related to his desirability.[26] Whether the fully realised face of the mask in this image is

---

[22] Korshak (1987: 29) notes only two other front-facing maenads.
[23] Green (1991: 33–4 and plates 5a–b); on gender permutations in satyr/maenad vases cf. Caruso 1987.
[24] Pickard-Cambridge (1968: 182 and fig. 34), with a date of *c*.430 BC. Webster (1967: AV 20) gives a date of 450 BC. I follow Oakley 1990. The costumes are identified as maenadic in Caskey and Beazley (1931: i.56).
[25] On the Agora wine-jug, fabric hanging next to the mask may have had a similar import.
[26] Caskey and Beazley (1931: i. fig. 40).

**Plate 2.4** Dancers with mask. Boston.

closer to the historical mask-object than the crude face of the Ferrara vase is a conundrum to which we have no answer. What matters is the power of the mask to turn a young Athenian into a maenad.

The same painter is also responsible for a remarkable krater in the Vatican (Drawing 2.3).[27] The lower register contains some conventional maenads and satyrs, but on the upper register women are engaged in a dance. Nine women use cloaks as masks, concealing a greater or smaller proportion of the face, but one dancer in lieu of a cloak wears a mask, defined by a clear and non-organic line across the jaw. She is shown in profile and occupies the centre position on one side of the base, balancing the *aulos*-player on the other side. Again the painter is playing with levels of reality, the masked maenadic figure providing a link between the human performers on the upper register and the supernatural figures beneath. The vase painter's theme

[27] Oakley (1990: 38 and plates 52–4). He dates the vase 445–440 BC.

Drawing 2.3 Masked dancer with two muffled dancers. Vatican.

may by now seem familiar: a Dionysiac world of the imagination merges with the observed world of mimesis and Athenian cult. One of the muffled dancers looks directly out at the viewer, creating a live encounter with the drinker of the wine. Boundaries of subject and object are broken by the gaze, assisting the viewer's journey into the realm of Dionysos.

Plate 2.5 Maenads. Kiev.

From around 430, a fragment of a krater in Kiev shows us two crowned maenads dancing and wearing masks, which are clearly defined as such by the crude white pigmentation which separates mask from neck and emphasises the deep false chin. High ears form part of the mask, and it looks as if they are designed somehow to hook over the ears of the dancer (Plate 2.5 and Drawing 2.4).[28] An *aulos*-player stands in the middle, whilst a garlanded boy is clapping or presenting something to the left-hand dancer, confirming the context is ceremonial rather than an unprecedented glimpse of a play in action.[29] The women wear decorative chitons, but lack the theatrical sleeves of the *aulos*-player, which suggests that they are not in any straightforward way positioned as Athenian performers. The crudeness of the masks may take these maenads back towards the age of Thespis rather than refer to contemporary practice. Alas, without the remainder of the vase, further decoding of the image becomes impossible.

The most famous of all images of Athenian theatre is the Pronomos vase in Naples, a large krater dated to the end of the fifth century.[30] It appears to depict the personnel of a satyr play gathered in the sanctuary after the

---

[28] First published in Froning 2002. I am grateful to Oliver Taplin for calling it to my attention, and to Ewen Bowie and Frank Brinkley for helping me to secure a photo.
[29] Note, however, the presence of unmasked boys in some representations of New Comedy, like the two mosaics by Dioskourides in Naples.
[30] See a drawing of the complete image in Bieber (1961: figs. 32–3). I have not yet been able to view the VRML reconstruction by Theatron Ltd.

Drawing 2.4 Maenad mask. Detail of Plate 2.5.

performance, while Dionysos and Ariadne sit on a banqueting couch in their midst (Plate 2.6). Beneath them at the centre of the main face sits Pronomos the famous Theban composer playing his *aulos*. The three bearded actors are unnamed, but nine satyr chorus-men bear the names of citizens. Eight of the eleven chorus-men hold masks, while the one closest to the music has been prompted to dance, his mask 'melted' to become a satyr face. The three actors hold masks, whilst a woman holds a female mask next to the head of the Heracles actor, suggesting that he doubled the two roles. The eroded features of this mask are invisible in photographs, but its cap implies an oriental setting.[31] The woman holding the mask wears a costume which echoes that of the actor on the left of Dionysos but her coiffure and profile echo Ariadne, and she thus conflates the heroine, whom 'Heracles' will become when he dons the female mask, with Ariadne the beloved of Dionysos. The dancers, horses and personification of Victory on her costume

---

[31] Most critics opt for Heracles' seduction of Hesione, princess of Troy: see Pickard-Cambridge (1968: 187); Simon (1982: 19) argues plausibly for Omphale.

Plate 2.6 'Pronomos' vase. Naples.

conduct us into a further world of procession and celebration. The masks of both Heracles and heroine are rendered in white paint while the human faces are in the natural terracotta of red-figure vases, so these masks are literally an imposed surface. The white attracts the gaze of the viewer, and evokes the power of masks in the theatre. Since Ariadne's flesh is distinguished from that of Dionysos by whiteness, we may also think of the mask as a feminisation of the face. Though the female mask is even whiter than the male masks worn by actors, there is no firm evidence here that gender on fifth-century masks was systematically coded by colour.[32] Gender in tragic texts is too fluid to sit comfortably with such a restrictive convention.

Any inference about performance must start from an assessment of the vase's multiple layers of reality. Pronomos himself, for example, was not a young man at the end of the fifth century so his youthful features are an idealisation, like the youthful features of Athenians on tombstones.[33] By

---

[32] For the Hellenistic performance convention see Wiles (1991: 152). White for female skin was also the normal convention in sixth-century 'black-figure' vases.
[33] Cf. Webster (1967: 48).

**Plate 2.7** Actor.

the same token, the masks held by the actors are the product of fantasy. The mask of the king is far more animated in its brows and eyes than the impassive face of the actor, and with its living gaze it seems to be an object that has come to life (Plate 2.7). The Heracles mask peers anxiously upwards with pupils upturned, and the mask of Silenus likewise squints quizzically at the actor who holds the mask, its mouth enhanced by the addition of a few teeth (Drawing 2.5). The masks held by the chorus-men are also more expressive than their own faces, and each mask's direction of vision is clearly defined. The gaze of one (below right in Plate 2.7) engages the viewer while another (above left) engages the wearer. The power of the mask's gaze is one of the most important facets of the mask that we must relate to the realities

**Drawing 2.5** Silenus.

of tragic performance. The satyrs dangle or handle their masks casually and without apparent reverence, and it is the effect of the mask, not its material substance, which defines it as a sacred object.

Theatre historians commonly reproduce only two-thirds of the painted image, creating the *trompe l'œil* effect that this is some kind of cast party.[34] The ancient viewer, passing his eyes around the circuit of the vase, in fact encountered no dividing line at the point where the mimetic world yields to the divine world depicted on the reverse of the vase.[35] Here, in an idealised wilderness, Dionysos dances with Ariadne, accompanied by two maenads who resemble Ariadne, and four satyrs, who are no longer in theatrical shorts, but naked with horse-tails. The winged figure of Desire, who on the front of the vase implores the heroine mask to love Heracles, now celebrates with castanets the realised desire of Ariadne, whilst two of the satyrs seem intent on satisfying their desire for maenads. The panther whose skin was worn by Silenus has now come to life. The transition between the front and

---

[34] For example Pickard-Cambridge (1968: fig. 49); Csapo and Slater (1995: plate 8); Wiles (2000: plate 11).

[35] As noted in Bérard and Bron (1989: 143); Green (1982: 239).

the back of the vase is a fluid one. On the lower register a satyr mask gazes at the anus and horse-tail of an equine or 'real' satyr; on the upper register, an equine satyr extends a wine cup, to pour wine over the head of the actor-satyr who stands on the lower register (Drawing 2.6). The satyr beneath the spilled wine and the cloaked satyr next to him are not labelled with names, suggesting that they are on their way towards losing civic identity and entering the oblivious world of the gods.

Images in two-dimensional photographs create a static frame that seems to offer the viewer objective knowledge. The Greek user of the vase, however, moved around it or rotated it, seeing only one aspect of reality at a time. To view the vase was a process of engagement, and a process is also what the vase represents: a movement between the visible world of the performer and the invisible world of the god, mediated by music and the mask. As part of that process of transformation, the masks become more alive than the faces of the wearers. The circularity of the vase invites an analogy with the theatre itself, which placed spectators around the performance space, much as banqueters were placed around the krater. The Greek audience did not occupy the modern position of detached observers, who look through a proscenium frame at a mimesis of reality, but were caught up in an interplay of gazes and in collective emotion.

Fragments of a krater in Würzburg, of similar date and scale, help us place the Pronomos vase within a genre.[36] Again the painter portrayed an enthroned Dionysos and the tokens of a theatrical victory: a tripod, cauldron and bowl. The upper level seems to include a couple of actors as well as a maenad and an enthroned bare-breasted woman who may be Aphrodite because of the Eros next to her. On the lower register, three or four women who appear to be members of a chorus hold pallid female masks with wild hair, open mouths and animated eyes, yet their bare arms and feet suggest that this is not full theatrical costume. There is no hint that these are men playing the role of women (Drawing 2.7). We discern a spectrum in this vase running from the sleeved actor through feminised choric figures to the god and his maenads, and the point of the image lies in its multiple realities. The *aulos*-player is not yet making music, but the masks themselves look possessed, pointing to a transition that will take place both in the theatre and in the drinker of the wine. As in the Pronomos vase, the mask has come to life, for it is via the mask that Dionysos touches the performer. In a further parallel with the Pronomos vase, sexual desire is an aspect of the divine power which takes possession of human beings.

---

[36] Hölscher (1981: 59–61 and plate 41). Cf. Pickard-Cambridge (1968: fig. 50 a–c).

Drawing 2.6 Side view of the 'Pronomos' vase.

**Drawing 2.7** Maenad mask. Würzburg.

Another set of fragments in Samothrace helps place the Pronomos vase within a genre.³⁷ On one of them, shown in the drawing, a pair of masks, apparently male and female, hangs next to temple columns, and Richard Green suggests that this evokes a theatrical rite of dedication (Drawing 2.8). We also see the heads of Dionysos and Ariadne, who lie on a couch. On other fragments we find an Eros, and Dionysos again, drunkenly cavorting in the wilderness with his lyre. On the neck of the vase, a maenad swings the body of a child, evoking the violence of extreme Dionysiac madness. The two hanging masks are of most interest, again picked out by white pigment. A man and a woman, or perhaps two women, look at them, and we notice

³⁷ Green (1982: 238–42).

**Drawing 2.8** Masks, with Dionysos and Ariadne. Samothrace.

not only their darker complexion but also the contrast between their neat coiffure and the long flowing hair of the masks. Similar skin colour and hair characterised the Pronomos and Würzburg kraters. The coiffure of the mask marks a release from the constraints of civilisation, and we must recall that the heroic world of tragedy did not share the social norms of democratic Athens, there being less restriction, for example, on the public behaviour of women. Next to the roaming Dionysos, a woman in translucent dress holds up a female mask with its back to the viewer, and only tumbling hair is to be seen. This woman is in a mid-way state, neither clothed nor naked, and the mask is likewise in an intermediate condition.

I shall postpone until Chapter 10 discussion of one other important late fifth-century krater from Ferrara. When we reach the early fourth century, images of masks proliferate though many of the vases were produced in southern Italy. I shall confine my discussion to one unusual Athenian krater in Heidelberg which offers a variant on the theme of mask and

**Plate 2.8** Parodic dancers. Heidelberg.

metamorphosis (Plate 2.8).[38] The figure on the left, to judge from the unattractive face and from the left arm which beneath the cloak mimics an erect phallus, can be taken as a man in drag, which is to say a man performing a woman but letting his gender remain recognisable. The youth on the right wears a pelt with a design that echoes the cloak, and he is in the process of removing a mask which, with its snub nose and hanging lip, echoes and mocks the features of the 'drag-artist'. The pelt, torch and dance suggest the functions of a maenad, but the physique and beautiful face tell us this is a young male. The closed eyes of the mask are an unusual feature, which lend it the air of a dead face. A Greek mask is normally painted to look alive, both when it is viewed as a disembodied head and when it has melted to become an integral head, but in this half-on, half-off position it is necessarily dead and unseeing. The vase painter is playing with old ingredients, concerned to capture in a fresh way the process of mental and physical transition involved in masking. In this fourth-century treatment, one senses

[38] Kraiker (1978: no. 239); cf. Webster (1978: AV 16).

a new point of view. The mask itself has become inert, and we identify the male beneath the female disguise. The representative of the Dionysiac world is no longer a true maenad but a man acting a maenad. In this new and more rationalised way of seeing, the spiritual journey from young man to feminised companion of Dionysos can only be a partial one.

I shall not linger on a group of fourteen vases from Apulia which depict female masks being handled by Dionysos or placed in his sanctuary.[39] I could have gone on to trace a progression in our iconography from the maenad pursued by satyrs to the courtesan of New Comedy pursued by young citizens. The important point is that these masks are female. Within the corpus of fifth-century images to which I have confined myself, subsequent to the homoerotic vases in Berlin and Basel, the relation between mask and maenad seems critical. I shall examine in Chapter 9 a group of mid-fifth-century vases which represent women in a ritual context worshipping a masked idol of Dionysos, but it may be useful now to glance at one late example from about 420 BC which offers us the names of the nymphs or maenads who have passed into a state of ecstasy. Dione is a name associated with Zeus that fits the leader dispensing wine, and her companions include the Muse Thaleia ('blooming'), Choreia ('dance') and Mainas ('maenad', 'mad') (Plate 2.9). These labels provide an allegorical rationalisation of maenadic figures in a way that would not have been necessary earlier in the century, and certify that we are not watching Athenian ladies having a wild night out on the mountainside. There may of course be an allusion to ritual practices as there is also an allusion to those mythological nymphs who reared Dionysos on Mount Nysa and were his first companions.[40]

To explain the ubiquity of maenads on 'theatrical' vases on the basis that the choruses of Aeschylus' *Bacchae* and *Bassarids* had a unique hold on the imagination is the product of literalistic viewing.[41] Maenads and masks alike belonged to the metamorphic world of Dionysos, and we notice that the idol here wears something akin to tragic costume. Whilst the distinction between satyr and citizen is absolute and obvious, maenads are liminal figures because no horsy ears or tails separate them physiologically from human women. Women's innate emotionality was thought to make them instantly susceptible to the god's influence, with no physical transformation required.[42] The maenad embodied a natural female capacity for being possessed, whilst men needed the intervention of the mask, along with wine

---

[39] Webster (1967: TV 27–40).
[40] On maenads see Henrichs 1978, and Peirce (1998: 64–5); on the names, Carpenter (1997: 80–2).
[41] For example Simon (1982: 9–10).   [42] Cf. Frontisi-Ducroux 1986; Caruso 1987.

**Plate 2.9** Maenads and mask-idol. Naples.

and music of the pipes. There is much force in Froma Zeitlin's argument that in a culture preoccupied with masculinity the feminine figure is 'the mistress of mimesis, the heart and soul of the theater'.[43]

Maenads are associated with satyrs, and satyr plays were closely tied to tragedy, being danced by the same chorus-men in a rite of closure. In comedy, the practices and conventions of tragedy were reversed. Writers of Old Comedy delighted in referring to the circumstances of performance, and vase painters accordingly depicted the costumes, props and stage doorways of the theatre, so comic images can provide useful information about tragedy. When an old man in comedy impersonates Sophocles' Antigone, he is depicted carrying the actor's tragic mask. We see the comic phallus beneath the dress, and tights worn over the legs of the guards to signify their nakedness. The image is 'metatheatrical' in the sense that it represents the conventions of performance, but not in the sense of calling attention to the body of the performer beneath (Drawing 2.9). In representations of comedy we never see actors in the process of donning comic masks. Children may handle such masks but never adults,[44] for within this obscene and slanderous

---

[43] Zeitlin (1990a: 86).    [44] See Pickard-Cambridge (1968: 211–12).

**Drawing 2.9** Parody of *Antigone*. Sant' Agata.

genre the anonymity of the actor had to be conserved. When a vase representation of comedy includes the tragic figure of Aegisthus *in propria persona*, as distinct from a comic figure acting the part of Aegisthus, then the mask 'melts'. There is no hint of a mask on the face, and we discern the lineaments of a heroic body beneath the tragic costume.[45] Tragic costume in lieu of heroic nudity was a sufficient sign of performance.

The evidence of comedy assures us that the material presence of a mask with its open mouth and amplified scale was visible to the audience of tragedy if they chose to see it. The refusal of vase painters to portray tragedy in performance can be explained in several ways. (1) Psychologically: the transformative power of the text was such that the audience simply forgot, or chose to forget, that a mask was being worn. (2) A religious prohibition: a formal or informal taboo may have prevented representation of what was a sacred activity – a milder version of the prohibition on revealing what was seen in the Eleusinian Mysteries. (3) An aesthetico-philosophical explanation:

---

[45] Taplin (1993: nos. 21.22 and 9.1).

the vase painter declined to fall into a Platonist trap and construct an illusion of an illusion. (4) Function: vases were like masks, designed for a specific ceremony, and that ceremony was concerned not to represent but to transform the perception of the user. These four modes of explanation involve no contradiction.

Vase images have proved a treacherous guide to the artefacts themselves. Nevertheless, if the vase painter is a creative *bricoleur*, working with recognisable components, then we can risk a few cautious inferences.[46] The mask covered the front and crown, without greatly amplifying the scale of the head, and the mouth was open but not gaping. The wig was made of hair that was often long and could animate the face through its movement. The performer's ears may have been covered by hair alone, which would have assisted in balance. The bold painting of the eye is consistent with later sculpted masks in suggesting that the actor must have looked through circular holes bored in the position of the iris, with restricted vision in consequence. The lightness of the material is confirmed by the way the mask is dangled on cords. There is no evidence to confirm the supposition that female masks were distinguished by their whiteness in the fifth century,[47] but it is consistent with the written record to infer that early masks were paler and more luminous than normal flesh colour and relied on moving shadow to create expression. Masks provide no indication of character, but hair-pieces carry important social signals. Beyond this, the evidence is contradictory. Masks can be portrayed as crude makeshift objects, but can also be seen as delicate sculptural creations. A mask can be handled casually, but one can equally be transfixed by its features. This ambivalence of the tragic *prosōpon*, as it resists reduction to objecthood and a single essence, is what makes it so interesting. The failure of fifth-century vase iconography to supply us with scientific data about the lost artefact is not something to be lamented, for what the vase evidence offers us instead is a rich source of information about what masks *meant*. My concern throughout this book will not be with masks *in themselves* but with comparative cultural practices and ways of seeing.

Classical masks were conceived not as artefacts but as agents of transformation. Just as Athenians used a krater to mix the wine of Dionysos with some three parts of water, so images on the krater mixed a Dionysiac world, too strong for human consumption, with inert elements from the human world of performance. The classical mask is indeed like a wine-vessel since

---

[46] On 'bricolage' see Green (1991: 39), citing Metzger.
[47] *Pace* Marshall (1999: 190). Marshall cites MacDowell and Sommerstein.

its purpose is defined not just by how it looks but more importantly by what it contains. Athenians used the mask not to conceal but to effect a transformation of the substance within. It was a sacred object in large part because of the intoxicating effect it had on those who wore it, turning men into maenads.

Yet the mask can also intoxicate the onlooker. Our vase imagery testifies to the peculiar intensity of the mask when its eyes are fixed upon the viewer, who becomes the object of a gaze that is at once animate and inanimate, and cannot be controlled by normal social interaction. In an important essay on the mask, Claude Calame comments on the way disembodied masks on vases often face the viewer, whilst masks in use merge with the face, and are seen at an angle. On the basis of this observation he seeks to differentiate vase representations of the tragic mask from actual masks in the theatre. In the theatre, he argues, given the 'essentially veiling and nonfigurative nature' of the mask, a degree of distance is set up between the actor and the spectator. The theatrical mask breaks down the assimilation of the enunciator ('I, Oedipus') with the actor. The function of the actor 'materializes in the look... appearing from behind the two holes made in the mask'.[48] I shall argue in the course of this book that such a view of the fifth-century mask is mistaken, and derives from the experience of masks in modern theatre. We should take the evidence of vases more seriously, and recognise that the tragic mask was a tool for achieving presence, not distance. Bérard and Bron are closer to the mark when they infer from the Pronomos vase that 'the actor would become, in the heat of the moment, a real satyr'.[49] I shall examine in the course of this book the recurrent experience of actors that they are somehow changed by the masks they wear.

Calame's conception may be applied far more plausibly to the Roman mask. Cicero, in a celebrated passage, argues that the orator needs to experience emotion in order to represent it, and he draws a comparison with theatre. 'I have often seen myself how the eyes of an actor seemed to blaze forth from his mask, when he was speaking these lines at another's prompting...' – i.e. prompted by the verse of the tragedian Pacuvius.[50] Cicero's sense of the emotional actor behind the eyes of the mask derives from a Roman aesthetic that was very different to the Greek,[51] and we should remember also that Cicero was a senator who sat in the orchestra, physically close to the actor. Fifth-century Athenian images give us no such sense of the feeling or personhood of the actor behind the mask. Calame discards the

---

[48] Calame (1986: 135–6).   [49] Bérard and Bron (1989: 143).
[50] Cicero (2001: ii.193). The last phrase is textually problematic.   [51] Cf. Dupont (2000: 155–6).

evidence of iconography in order to recycle a familiar modern distinction between ritual and art, imposing a detached modern way of seeing upon the ancient material. As revealed to us on vases, the milieu of Dionysos was a homogeneous one, admitting no clear-cut boundaries between theatre and Dionysiac cult. The boundary that mattered lay between mundane experience and an encounter with the god, and the crossing of that boundary is the rich theme of our iconography.

Masks must have changed to some degree in the period between early Aeschylus and late Euripides, but these changes were probably of the same order as developments within red-figure vase painting, perceptible to the connoisseur, but never touching the fundamentals of the form. A particularly striking change in Athenian conventions of representation during this period lies in the way a bearded and virile Dionysos gave way to a young androgynous Dionysos.[52] In late fifth-century vases like the ambitious Pronomos, Würzburg and Samothrace kraters, we see the beardless Dionysos presiding over his sanctuary. Why the image of Dionysos changed so radically and so quickly remains a mystery. If young men dancing in tragic choruses became the pre-eminent servants of Dionysos, it was reasonable, perhaps, that the god should come to reflect their looks.[53] In the first part of the century, it was the simple power of the mask to come alive that caused wonder in the Athenians, and we see this mystery played out in the ceremony of the masked and bearded idol. By the end of the century it was the ability of the mask to turn male into female that seemed its most conspicuous feature, and the androgynous conception of Dionysos meshed with that power.

---

[52] Cf. Carpenter (1997: 98–9). Much turns on the identification of a lanky beardless figure on the Parthenon pediment.
[53] Cf. Kowalzig (2004: 50); Kowalzig (2007).

# 3 | The sculptural art of the mask-maker

Vase painting is crucial to any investigation of the Greek mask for two reasons. First is the survival capacity of baked clay: pottery cannot be melted down like bronze, or worn away like stone, so the evidence is available. And second is the identity of the god of wine with the god of theatre. Stone had its own very different connotations, associated not with the transient moment of banqueting (though banqueting did indeed extend symbolically into the underworld) but with creating lasting memorials for the dead.[1] In the age of tragedy a prestigious new technology invented to represent and honour the gods involved building a hollow frame clad in sheet gold and ivory, regularly oiled to preserve the sheen, but this particular sculptural form, which like the mask put appearance before substance, has failed to withstand the ravages of time. There was no generic term for a 'sculpture' in the classical Greek world, and it was only when Roman generals carried off sacred images as loot to decorate their gardens that the concept of an art object began to emerge. The normal Greek term for a statue was an *agalma*, a gift or honour to the gods.[2] Masks were *agalmata* for Dionysos.

Our earliest piece of direct sculptural evidence for the tragic mask is a plaque from Peiraeus, which presents fascinating riddles to the modern visitor who looks at it in the National Archaeological Museum in Athens (Drawing 3.1).[3] As on vases, Dionysos remains the god of wine, reclining on a couch and holding a bowl in one hand, a drinking horn in the other. On the couch in front of him is a maenad, identifiable by her fawnskin, functioning as an intermediary between the human, male world of the Athenian performer and the divine sphere of the wine-god. On the left side of the plaque, approaching Dionysos, are three slightly smaller figures, whom we must take to be the three actors of a tragedy. They are not bearded like the actors in the Pronomos vase, but have youthful features, idealised in the

---

[1] On the phenomenology of stone see Vernant (1990b: 29).
[2] See Burkert (1985: 91); Spivey (1996: 45); Gordon 1979.
[3] Bieber (1961: 32); Webster (1967: 32); Pickard-Cambridge (1968: 188); Slater 1985; *LIMC* 'Paidia' 13.

**Drawing 3.1** Peiraeus relief.

same way as the Pronomos playwright and musicians in the lower register. They wear soft theatrical shoes designed for dancing, and long ceremonial chitons belted above the waist, reminding us for example of the charioteer of Delphi. The central figure has a curious tunic over his chiton of unknown ceremonial significance,[4] perhaps identifying him as *protagonistēs* or leader. The actors wear theatrical sleeves, and the stone must have been painted to create ornately decorated costumes.

The relief belongs to a genre that emerged in the late fifth century, which depicts worshippers approaching a banqueting hero who enjoys a privileged life in the world of the dead. Rather than a conventional bearded hero, this is the beardless god known for his androgynous features. Dionysos like Heracles could be worshipped as a 'hero' because he occupied a liminal position between god and human, having once died and been reborn, and this liminality relates to the mediating function of tragedy, and of the mask in particular.[5] A hero relief in Cagliari shows a similar female attendant

---

[4] Dentzer (1982: 507 n. 633) notes such a garment in the worship of Apollo – cf. a fourth-century sculpture of Apollo Patroos in the Athenian Agora. Cf. also the krater from Altamura in the British Museum where the leader of tragic dancers wears a distinctive overgarment: Pickard-Cambridge (1968: 185 and fig. 42).

[5] For the mortality of Dionysos, see Henrichs (1993: 18).

sitting on Dionysos' couch and gazing at a tragic mask, while three more tragic masks hang on the wall, represented as isolated artefacts separable from their wearers now we have reached the mid-fourth century.[6] A hero relief in Athens inscribed as a choregic dedication supports the inference that the Peiraeus plaque commemorated a theatrical victory.[7] Dionysos' gaze is fixed on what appears to be a griffin at the base of a conventional drinking horn, and the symbolism supports an association with the dead.[8] The right-hand worshipper holds up one hand, now missing, in a gesture of devotion to Dionysos, while his other grips a mask by the mouth. Though the stone is eroded, one can discern the remnants of a moustache and beard,[9] together with a ceremonial headband, and a tress on one temple that looks female or oriental, suiting the Dionysiac encounter. The actor in the centre holds by the hair the mask of an old man which gives added emphasis to his own youth. The mask, shown in profile, has a gaping mouth, and ample wig, strongly defined lips and an intense gaze, with a strong Grecian nose that makes it clear this is no Silenus from a satyr play. As on the Cagliari relief, these are tragic rather than satyric or maenadic masks, for this is a monument in stone, not a container for wine.

The plaque cannot actually commemorate the victory of Euripides' *Bacchae*, with Cadmus, Teiresias and Pentheus dressed in maenadic attire, but it relates nevertheless to a transitional area of Bacchic experience.[10] The left-hand actor holds a tympanum beside his missing head, and his pose looks feminine, with hand on hip and some swelling about the bosom. Since he holds no mask, vase analogues lead me to surmise that he wears a mask which has 'melted' to become a head, transforming the male actor into a feminised inhabitant of the Dionysiac world. The two tympana held by the two actors on the left symbolise that world, being standard attributes of maenads attending Dionysos. Bent into a hoop, the tympanum could only be circular, and their oval shape on this relief tells us that *trompe l'œil*

---

[6] Dentzer (1982: 505–6 = R449); Froning (2002: plate 94). Cf. also a relief in Eleusis, where a figure holding a slave mask approaches Dionysos: Dentzer (1982: 507 = R236).

[7] See Dentzer (1982: 512–13; also 506 for a bibliography of interpretations). Slater 1985 offers insufficient evidence to support his argument for a hero.

[8] My observation concurs with Slater (1985: 335); on the associations of the griffin see Flagge 1975. Dentzer (1982: 341) perceives a winged horse. Visitors to the British Museum can see a similar griffin on a drinking horn sported by the Lycian king on the Nereid Monument, a tomb the king designed to elevate himself to 'heroic' status.

[9] Having inspected the monument I concur with Dentzer, Webster and Pickard-Cambridge rather than with Slater: a strong line around the upper lip and an ampleness of jaw imply a beard.

[10] Slater 1985 demonstrates that the doubling is impossible – *pace* for example Simon (1982: 11).

painting must have been used to create the illusion that, as on most vases, the tympanum is held up at an angle to the viewer.

To complicate matters, the monument seems to have been recycled in antiquity. An inscription was added identifying Dionysos and giving an allegorical name to the maenad. Thereafter, her name was smoothed away, leaving just the last two letters, allowing a fresh name to be applied in paint. The missing head is an unlikely break and the neat hollow has been chiselled out, with the dowel hole in the centre being used to peg a substitute head into place.[11] This suggests that the original head was found unsatisfactory when the monument was reused to commemorate some subsequent Hellenistic victory. In a more rationalistic age I surmise that it became necessary to substitute the 'melted' female head with a male head or an overtly theatrical mask, adding at the same time an allegorical explanation for the supernatural maenad. Next to the missing head is the blank face of a tympanum held up in the manner of a mirror. A krater in Zurich provides an analogue suggesting there was once a face painted on this tympanum (Drawing 3.2). In the vase a male figure, reaching for a Dionysiac thyrsus, looks at a tympanum as if into a mirror, and sees in it a face that melds his own features with those of an advancing maenad.[12] The shield of Perseus protected the male hero from a dangerous female gaze, and the tympanum on this vase may also confer protection. The organisation of the relief suggests that similar play with identity was its theme. While the actor on our right looks in the direction of the god, I surmise that the actor on our left looks into a tympanum/mirror where he sees a face that melds his own maenadic features with those of the young actor beyond in some sort of Dionysiac compound. Possibly this new face looks out at the viewer of the plaque. This dynamic interaction of 'melted' mask and mirror is balanced below by the inert relationship of a hand-held mask and a reversed tympanum. The original mystic meaning of the relief would have seemed irrelevant when the image was recycled to commemorate a victory by Hellenistic actors, and a meditation upon mutability became a more humanistic celebration of victory.

The other important early monument that probably belongs to the fifth century is the upper portion of a tombstone found in Salamis (Drawing 3.3).[13] The head of an idealised young man gazes impassively

---

[11] Cf. Dentzer (1982: 508); Slater 1985.
[12] For the painted face of a maenad's tympanum, cf. a krater of the same period depicting Dionysos' sanctuary: *LIMC* 'Dionysos' 863. On tympana images and mirror effects, see further Seaford (2001: 223). Amy C. Smith in the on-line 'Perseus' sculpture catalogue wrongly classifies the tympana as mirrors. The Zurich vase is examined in Seaford 1998.
[13] Tsirivakos 1974; Slater 1985.

**Drawing 3.2** Tympanum as mirror. Zurich.

at a mask which he must be holding by a strap. The mouth is open but filled, to avoid creating a gaping cavity, and there are signs of a hollow at the back where the actor's head should enter. It was common for tombstones to portray attributes of the dead man's profession or passion, so this must have commemorated an actor and/or playwright. The archaeologist who first published this tombstone assumed that the mask was female, comparable to Pollux's young talking woman, but in his photograph, upon which the present drawing is based, there are traces of a beard, and the features seem unambiguously male and heroic.[14] He was probably misled by the luxuriance of the hair, inappropriate on the tombstone of a normal Athenian, but characteristic of the tragic mask as we can see in the Pronomos vase, serving to conceal the neck-line. While the transition from male to female is an

[14] Tsirivakos gives scant attention to the mask. He published sketches which clearly depict male bearded features, along with a photographic plate that reconstructs long falling female hair. Slater (1985: 341) notes that the photographic reconstruction is incorrect and the locks did not descend further, but he does not question the female attribution. The museum has been closed for refurbishment so I could not inspect for myself. Slater accepts Tsirivakos' dating of c.410 BC.

**Drawing 3.3** Grave relief from Salamis.

appropriate theme for a wine jar, the encounter between youth and maturity is more apposite for a grave. The most interesting feature of this monument is the gaze. The young man's face expresses deep concentration, but his eyes are set upon the hand that manipulates the mask rather than the facial features of the mask. One is reminded of the concentration of young men on the Parthenon frieze controlling their horses. We find the same depiction of the gaze on later sculptures, such as the Lyme Park relief of *c.*380 BC, where one comic mask engages the viewer and another the actor/playwright, while the latter seems lost in his own world, or the Lateran relief which depicts Menander holding a comic mask which gazes back at him, while his own gaze is fixed upon his Muse beyond.[15]

In respect of comedy, the sculptural record is more copious. Late fifth-century figurines, found in an Athenian grave and mostly now in the

---

[15] Bieber (1961: figs. 201, 317a–b). Cf. also her figs. 300b, 308.

Metropolitan Museum in New York, yield precise information about the wide mouths and bulging eyes of the mask, and show how the mask integrates with bulging stomach and buttocks to create a single corporeal composition. Tights covering the arms and legs ensure that the spectator has no sense of the corporeal person of any particular actor.[16] Only by inference can we proceed from these images to tragedy. If sculptors in the fifth century never produced figurines of masked tragedians caught in the act of performance, but preferred to concentrate on direct images of gods and heroes, the reason must be that tragic mask-makers aimed somehow to make people *see* those very gods and heroes.

For an unambiguous depiction of tragedy in performance, we must turn to another medium with other conventions, namely wall-painting. A painting in Delos, dated to the second century BC but probably based on a fourth- or early third-century original, seems to depict Antigone and Oedipus, standing on a stage, and the pair are perhaps arriving in Colonus (Drawing 3.4).[17] He is blind, and she is leaning towards her father to guide his hand. The pale mask which signifies Antigone's gender is rendered almost grotesque by the open mouth, which the medium of painting cannot commute into movement. The mask of Oedipus is more textured thanks partly to damage and partly to the rendering of shadow cast by the *onkos*, the elevated hairline that was introduced to tragic masks in the later fourth century.[18] The pair are dressed in long chitons and cloaks of plain but rich fabric, which give bulk to the body in order to compensate for the extra size of the mask, but do not encourage vigorous movement. It is the subtle inclination of the two bodies towards each other, complemented by the angle of mask in relation to body, that creates the emotional dynamic. Whilst the curvature of a vase lends itself to the idea of transformation, the flat surface of the wall-painting creates an illusionistic world that mirrors the spectator's world. The mixing of colour tones creates mystery and shadow in a way that cannot be achieved with the sharp lines of a vase image. In this Hellenistic medium the crude materiality of the heroine's mask stands out precisely because wall-painting aspires to illusionism.

Using a flat surface, the medium of wall-painting was better equipped to represent the frontal performance of actors on a shallow Hellenistic stage than the three-dimensional interaction of actors and chorus in the

---

[16] Bieber (1961: figs. 185–98); dating in Green (1994a: 34).

[17] Bezerra de Meneses (1970: 168ff. and plates 21–2); Webster (1967: DP1); *LIMC* 'Antigone' 2. The inspiration could be Euripides' *Phoenician Women*, but see Easterling (2006: 6–11) on the popularity of Sophocles' *Oedipus at Colonus*.

[18] Pickard-Cambridge (1968: 196).

*The sculptural art of the mask-maker* 51

**Drawing 3.4** Oedipus and Antigone. Delos.

fifth-century orchestra. The actors in the Delos image are relatively static, as though reliant upon text rather than movement, and the monochrome costume throws emphasis upon the features of the mask. We know classical sculpture to have been polychrome, and Vinzenz Brinkmann has shown how elaborate geometric ornamentation on painted stone served to emphasise the plasticity of the moving figure.[19] The vase tradition suggests that ceremonial rather than everyday costume was the norm in fifth-century tragedy, and when Aristophanes mocks Euripides for dressing characters in rags, we should not take him literally.[20] The costumes of fifth-century tragedy were securely belted to allow free movement, they evoked a world of myth rather than everyday reality, and they arrested the vision in a sunlit orchestra, relating the head to the body rather than isolating the head. The monochrome costumes of the Delian painting, reflecting the wardrobe of itinerant actors rather than the conspicuous expenditure of a choregos, evoked a less exotic world and called more attention to the semiotic detail of the face, giving impact also to the actor's silhouette against the wall of the *skene*.[21]

Our last major archaeological source is a collection of some thirty-three miniature terracotta masks of tragedy found in fourth-century tombs on the island of Lipari. The masks appear to derive from a single workshop, and other finds in the tombs have been used to support the hazardous claim that some are dateable to the first quarter of the century. Open mouths, which define the theatrical nature of these miniatures, and the lack of an *onkos* associate them with the classical rather than Hellenistic tradition. The workshop is thought to have been a local one, since no comparable masks have been found elsewhere. A research project based in Glasgow has created wearable, computer-generated replicas of comic masks from Lipari, their theatrical viability demonstrated by a Venetian *commedia dell'arte* company.[22] This work has revealed the theatrical energy of the masks, and their capacity to change expression when viewed from different angles.[23] There is no reason to doubt that the smaller and perhaps earlier corpus of tragic masks would yield similar results. I illustrate with the example of a youngish man in an oriental headdress. Richard Williams has published a computer-generated image which reveals how frown-lines above the eyes gain emphasis once the mask is lowered.[24]

Luigi Bernabò Brea, the archaeologist responsible for most of the excavation, has attempted to cast the groups of masks found in different tombs to fit different plays.[25] The mask which I illustrate, for example, is said to be Polymestor (Plate 3.1). Though Brea's publication is of superb visual

---

[19] Brinkmann and Wünsche (2004: esp. 95–7).
[20] Pickard-Cambridge (1968: 199–202) surveys the evidence. See also Battezzato 1999/2000.
[21] See pp. 55–6.
[22] For the Glasgow project, see most recently Williams 2004, and video extracts on www.iah.arts.gla.ac.uk/masks.
[23] Cf. Wiles (1991: 80–3).   [24] Williams (2004: 149, fig. 2).
[25] Bernabò Brea 1981, Bernabò Brea 2001. For difficulties, see Battezzato 2003.

**Plate 3.1** Terracotta mask. Glasgow.

quality, his classificatory system rests on speculation.²⁶ In his quixotic mission to find specific roles for all the masks, Brea was able to point to two things. First there is great variety in the coiffure, which is of course a social sign and may point to eastern, royal or (in the case of horns) divine status. And second there are signs of mood or temperament, communicated most obviously by the brows, but also by eyes, mouth and overall shape. Brea gave the earliest dating to a pair which he identified as Philoctetes and Paris, from a lost play by Sophocles.²⁷ He alighted on Paris because of the oriental tiara,

---

²⁶ Regrettably, for reasons that may be inferred, I have been denied permission to reproduce masks from the Aeolian Museum in this book.
²⁷ Bernabò Brea (2001: figs. 5–6).

similar to headgear on the Pronomos vase, combined with soft, feminine but not youthful features, while signs of physical pain – striations around the nose and cheekbone as well as on the brow – led him to Philoctetes. After consulting the first of Brea's volumes many years ago, I was misled by a printer's error, which transposed two captions, and in lectures to students I erroneously placed these two figures as Oedipus and Jocasta. I was suitably impressed by the features of a monarch psychologically tormented by his quest, and saw no cause to doubt that the companion mask was female. The power of suggestion to determine how we read masks is precisely what gives masks their efficacy.

Though Brea was the victim of self-persuasion, his enterprise calls attention to nuances of expression, and serves to stimulate the imagination more effectively than the scientific taxonomies of Green and Webster. His publications remind us that masks in the theatre acquired meaning in relation to a dramatic narrative, and never existed as works in isolation. The clay models buried in the tombs of Lipari carry signs of their theatricality. One does not at first notice that the eyes and mouth of both 'Philoctetes' and 'Paris' are asymmetrical, and this asymmetry creates the illusion that the faces are mobile rather than frozen in time. The mouths seem to be caught in the act of speaking, rather than gaping as in the Delian wall-painting, and the overall expression changes when viewed from different angles. The hair creates a slight overhang as it meets the forehead, which creates an unexpected change of perspective when the head is bowed, anticipating the later function of the *onkos* that gave heroic stature to Hellenistic tragic figures.[28]

Pollux's catalogue of masks belongs to the later era, and is of very little use in helping us understand fifth-century practice. His rigid distinctions of slave and free, male and female cannot be transposed back to the fifth century. It is nevertheless worth noting that Pollux never thinks of a fixed 'Orestes' or 'Oedipus' mask because the character of ancient heroes would shift from play to play; only when Achilles cuts his hair in mourning can a particular hero be identified by a distinctive mask.[29] C. W. Marshall has argued that fifth-century tragic masks fell into the categories of old, mature and young, male and female, making up six basic types.[30] Though they are of course from the fourth century, the Lipari masks prove incompatible with that theory. 'Paris' with his feminine features is neither mature nor youthful, and 'Philoctetes' seems prematurely aged by his troubles, beyond his prime

---

[28] Bernabò Brea (2001: 275); Wiles (1991: 68, 109).
[29] Calame (1986: 130); catalogue in Csapo and Slater (1995: 398–400).
[30] Marshall (1999: 191).

but not yet an old man. The tortured expression of 'Philoctetes' is not typical of the Lipari collection, and most of the masks are more impassive. Though a few figures in our tragic texts are confined to a single mood, like Madness in Euripides' *Heracles* to take an extreme example, the major characters run through a gamut of feelings, and would lend themselves better to a polyvalent mask like Brea's 'Oedipus'. We may see in 'Philoctetes' a face where suffering has engendered a temperament, reflecting a growing fourth-century interest in physiognomy.[31]

One mould was apparently used to produce a set of casts that were subsequently modified for headdress and expression, so the same mould for example could generate a divine 'Acheloos', an aged 'Priam', an impassive dignified 'Oedipus' and a figure with hair more like a Centaur.[32] As Brea observes, this may point to principles that guided the making of real theatrical masks. The Glasgow project has demonstrated the theatrical efficacy of the comic mask, though some of the detail seems to me too crude, and the quality of the painting cannot be recovered from surviving flecks of paint. The purpose of the miniatures was to evoke a memory of the theatrical mask, imperishable mementoes providing cheer in the world of the dead, and their level of reference should be understood in those terms. Just how far these masks reflect a fourth-century practice distinct from that of the fifth century is not easy to say, but it seems to me safe to apply at least some of the aesthetic principles back to the earlier period: that masks should not individualise; that they should look alive, by virtue of subtle asymmetry; that they should respect the proportions of the human form; that a finite number of moulds can serve a range of theatrical needs; that simple taxonomies of role-types are of little help to analysis.

I argued in *Masks of Menander* that the physiognomic detail of Greek New Comedy masks was related to a transformation of the space. In the south-facing Theatre of Dionysos, with the sun behind the actors, performance in the orchestra meant that the actors' faces were mostly in shadow. Meaning was principally created through the conformation of the body to the mask, and through the spatial relationship of actor and chorus. Masks supported a brilliantly costumed body. The move to a high stage entailed not only a different acoustical principle, with sound reflected off the orchestra floor, but also a different visual principle, with a more frontal presentation of the mask. When all the actors stood in the shadow of a high *skene*, the spectator's eye could accustom itself and perceive visual detail. Consistent shadow was better for this purpose than frontal sunlight would have been

---

[31] Wiles (1991: 85–90).   [32] Bernabò Brea (1981: 34–6). The last is now lost.

**Drawing 3.5** Mask of New Comedy. Oxford.

in a theatre with a different orientation, for direct sun would have created harsh contrasts and flattened out the masks.³³

It is always salutary to pass from photographs, whose publication already enshrines a point of view, to the actual artefacts. Visiting my local museum, the Ashmolean in Oxford in 2004, I found a fine life-size terracotta mask of a young man from Naples labelled as a mask of tragedy (Drawing 3.5).³⁴ The mouth seemed to close when viewed from above, and the cylindrical holes bored into the iris changed the shape of the eye when the angle of vision changed. In the same room I could turn my eyes to a Roman copy of a bronze head by the fifth-century sculptor Polycleitus. The serene, meditative expression of the bronze face appeared constant, while the theatrical mask kept changing its expression, and transcendence of time stood in contrast to the art of mutability. The features of the mask are flattened to create the illusion of movement, so when the mask changes its angle, my eye is deceived because my brain assumes I am looking at a normally proportioned face. A lumpiness in the brow catches the light in different ways, there is a

---

[33] Wiles (1991: 36–40); cf. Wiles (1997: 77).
[34] Fortnum bequest. Webster (1995: 5XT4). The attribution to tragedy stems from Vafopoulou-Richardson (1981: 30). The gallery in question has now been refurbished.

marked asymmetry in the mouth, and the eyes are angled in slightly different directions to create the illusion of movement. A curious anecdote records that the actor Roscius first donned a mask to hide his squint.[35] Behind this story may lie Roman amazement that a heroic mask in the theatre could be designed to squint. An idealised Polycleitan head would never squint, but Japanese Noh masks provide a living example of why the divided gaze was so important, creating the illusion of moving eyes when the mask is in motion.

We know almost nothing about the men who made Greek masks, the *skeuopoioi*.[36] The term 'makers of equipment' implies that mask-makers also had responsibility for costume and other design aspects. Lucian's dream of becoming a sculptor conceals, beneath its satire, a long-standing prejudice in the Greek world against manual labour:

You will be nothing more than a workman, doing hard physical labor and putting the entire hope of your life into it; you'll be an obscure person, earning a small ignoble wage, a man of low esteem, classified as worthless by public opinion – neither courted by friends, feared by enemies, nor envied by your fellow citizens – but just a common workman ... Even if you should become a Pheidias or a Polykleitos and produce many marvellous works, all will praise your art, but not one of those who see your art, if he were in his right mind, would pray to be like you.[37]

Makers of masks were for this reason of lower status than writers of plays. To create the body beautiful was a messy business – a paradox which all visual artists had to endure.

Since we have no image of a mask-maker at work, I shall turn by default to a restored cup of *c.*480 in Oxford which depicts a helmet-maker in his studio equipped with lathe and furnace (Plate 3.2).[38] A boy is putting the finishing touches to a traditional Corinthian helmet. Since the vase is inscribed with the familiar legend that 'the boy is beautiful', we must as always be on our guard, for this pretty lad is no common artisan. His gaze modestly drops below the eye-line of the helmet/mask that he holds in his hand, as if the empty helmet represents the absent older lover, the role-model for adulthood. The competing planes defined by the floor and by the handles of the cup give the helmet a feeling of lift or movement. To be a citizen of consequence in fifth-century Greece was to serve as a hoplite, and the armour of a hoplite included a heavy bronze helmet, designed not only to protect but also to intimidate the enemy with the power of its depersonalised gaze. The traditional Corinthian helmet was refined in the sixth century, so that

---

[35] Diomedes, cited in Beare (1955: 293).   [36] First used in Aristophanes *Knights* 232.
[37] Lucian *Dream* 9, cited in Pollitt (1990: 228); cf. Plutarch *Pericles* 2.1.
[38] Restored cup from Orvieto: Beazley (1927: 6).

Plate 3.2 Helmet-maker. Oxford.

a precisely measured gap separated the single sheet of beaten bronze from the skull, allowing the metal to be lighter yet absorb blows.[39] To wear such a helmet in the summer heat, deprived of normal hearing and peripheral vision, was a feat of endurance, and for this reason hoplite races became part of the Olympic games. In the period when the theatrical mask emerged, the Athenians began to make military helmets lighter, freeing the ears and revealing somewhat more of the face. Mask-maker and helmet-maker were confronted by similar technical problems.

The traditional accomplishment that made it possible to serve as a hoplite imparted the skills needed to serve in a tragic chorus. Though John Winkler overstated his case when he argued that tragic choreography was like military drill, neglecting the importance of gender inversion and the simulation of cult,[40] it is clear that dancing in a tragedy would have helped young men function in a phalanx. Masks would have helped them adjust to sensory

[39] Snodgrass (1967: 51ff.); Feugère (1994: 18). Cf. also Bollini 1988.
[40] Winkler 1990; cf. Wiles (1997: 89–90, 93).

deprivation in extreme conditions and find intuitive or kinaesthetic means of sensing the collective rhythm of a group. Actors and warriors alike benefit from the removal of self-consciousness that characteristically follows concealment of the face. Young Athenian males had a strong motivation to go through the pain barrier involved in wearing a mask in a way that modern student actors do not.

The Greek mask-maker had certain technical constraints. Holes must be pierced for the eyes, the mouth had not to muffle the voice, the actor needed to hear in order to compensate for restricted vision, and had to breathe. Just as the base of the Parthenon was curved in order to make it look flat, so the proportions of the mask had to be corrected to make it appear animate and mobile. Leaving these generic requirements of the theatre mask to one side, I shall turn now to the broader question of an underlying aesthetic. Masks were simply 'faces', and there is no reason to suppose that the aesthetic effect sought by mask-makers differed profoundly from that sought by other representational artists. Idealisation and the absence of facial emotion are characteristic fifth-century traits. If we look at vases representing mythical scenes closely related to the action of tragedies, for example, where faces are always bare and male bodies normally nude, it is a guiding principle that these bare faces are not used to signify emotion. We might take, for instance, a vase of c.480 BC which depicts maenads tearing Pentheus limb from limb in front of a bearded Dionysos. The lower half of the body has been torn off, but the upper half is heroic and beautiful, with no pain in its features; nor is there any hint of ecstasy in the faces of the women.[41] Another example in Oxford actually shows blood streaming from a serene head of Pentheus.[42]

Representations of the Furies assailing Orestes as he clings to the *omphalos* in Delphi offer another revealing example. A fifth-century Athenian vase in the British Museum depicts three faces in profile: Orestes, Apollo and a Fury (Plate 3.3).[43] Sun hat, wreath and horns are the primary signs that secure recognition, while on closer inspection Orestes' hair is seen to have been cropped, Apollo has some locks gathered in ringlets and the Fury's hair is gathered at the back. Once we eliminate the coiffure, however, there is no basic facial distinction between human, god and demon, or between male and female, and no expression. Orestes' legs are extended to the maximum, and he has twisted his body round; Apollo steps towards Orestes and echoes his pose, but his upper half is turned to confront the Fury, who in turn seems to be part walking, part flying, part dancing. It is the bodies

[41] *LIMC* 'Pentheus' 43.   [42] Attributed to the Berlin painter – see Beazley (1963: 208.144).
[43] *LIMC* 'Erinys' 43.

Plate 3.3 Orestes, Apollo and Fury. London.

that communicate narrative, relationships, and thereby emotion. We could perform the same analysis on a more elaborate fourth-century rendering of the same scene, also in the British Museum.[44] Here females wear decorative costumes that echoes theatrical attire, Athena is identified by her helmet, and a chorus of Furies by snakes in the hair, but in the ungendered faces of the Furies there is no hint of fury. Once you remove the headgear, you are again left with what we may best describe as a neutral mask.

In the light of vases such as these, Stephen Halliwell's argument is a cogent one:

> For it is predominantly and strikingly true of the figurative arts altogether in the classical period – it is, in fact, a defining quality of the 'classical style' – that they eschew delineation of pronounced facial expression. The relevance of this stylistic trait to tragic masks increases when we register in particular the absence of facial expression in visual portrayal of acute suffering, violence and grief. If the exclusion of facial suffering represented a *limitation* in the case of masking, how could the same tendency have been positively embraced in the painting and sculpture of the period?[45]

To understand tragic masking, we must come to terms with this 'classical style', which had an important ethical and political dimension, associated

[44] *LIMC* 'Erinys' 52.   [45] Halliwell (1993: 203–4).

with terms like *sophrosyne* (level-mindedness) and *kalokagathia* (gentle-manliness – literally the 'fine-and-good'). Pericles, or so Plutarch tells us, trained himself never to despair, and never to weep at funerals, a resolve that finally crumbled when he laid the wreath for his last legitimate son.[46] The ethic of self-mastery appeared not only in the funeral but also in the gymnasium, a place where mature men learned to control themselves in relation to beautiful naked bodies.[47] In the competitive environment of the Greek *polis*, where beautiful bodies were the product of intense physical training, the body rather than the face was the key to a man's moral nature. Just as emotions had to be mastered, so genetic features that helped make faces distinguishable had to be ignored in the solidary public art of the *polis*. In portraits on tombstones and in honorific sculptures, people were immortalised on the basis of idealised and uniform traits.[48] There may indeed be a connection between theatrical masking and the art of making idealised memorials to the dead. When the latter activity was abruptly halted in Athens at the end of the sixth century, because immortalising the aristocracy was incompatible with new democratic ideals,[49] there emerged with equal rapidity the industry of making heroic faces for the theatre, faces of historical or mythic heroes who were the property of all.

The aesthetic idealism of the Periclean age is well summed up by Cicero, in a discussion of Pheidias the great sculptor of the Parthenon. A copy, Cicero claims, can never be as beautiful as the original 'as is the case with a mask copied from the face', but Cicero here uses the term *imago*, which refers not to theatre masks but to lifelike wax images of Roman ancestors. When Pheidias created his famous versions of Zeus and Athena, Cicero concludes, he relied upon 'some extraordinary vision of beauty' that 'resided in his own mind'.[50] Nigel Spivey has described the classical sculptor as a vicarious agent, through whom the divine could be glimpsed.[51] Sacred statues needed to seem alive in the sense of possessing sensory powers, but not in the sense of possessing a unique identity, and the quest for perfection in Greek art was bound up with a quest to solve the mystery of aliveness. Contrary to modern norms, faces did not have to be particularised in order to seem animate. Aliveness was a function of beauty, and beauty was a link to the divine.

The emergent sculptural mode in the early fifth century was bronze, and the 'lost wax' method of casting allowed fine detail to be etched in wax,

---

[46] Plutarch *Pericles* 36.   [47] See for example Von Reden and Goldhill 1999.
[48] Cf. Zanker 1995.   [49] See Parker (1996: 133–5).
[50] Cicero *Orator* 8–9, cited in Pollitt (1990: 223–4). On the *imago* see Flower 1999.
[51] Spivey (1996: 48–52).

with more delicacy than could be achieved with a simple clay mould.[52] It is evident that theatrical masks were likewise a product of casting, with linen soaked in a stiffening agent pressed into a negative mould.[53] The expertise and creative excitement fostered by the development of bronze sculptures at the start of the fifth century must have assisted in the development of theatrical 'faces' that seemed more alive than any wearer. However, whilst bronze sculptors filled the eye cavities with glass and precious stones and metals, mask-makers had to rely on the actor's skill to animate the iris. The famously impassive and meditative face of the Delphic charioteer has, in the end, more to tell us about the actor than his mask.[54] The charioteer's absolute concentration on the contest and the management of his horses can be related to the athletic demands of the theatrical contest, which required the actor likewise to be in a state of complete readiness and control. The analogy with other plastic arts breaks down when we consider the technical need of a mask to come alive in movement.

Stone reliefs are more obviously theatrical than standing bronzes because they tend to represent a narrative. Most evocative of all are the pediments and metopes of Olympia, completed around the time of the *Oresteia*. The east pediment portrays Pelops, founder of the house of Atreus, about to engage in a fateful chariot race, and the famous spectating seer creates a sense of performance tension, but the west side is more dynamic, portraying the battle of Centaurs against Lapiths. The theme echoes, in a more violent idiom, the Dionysiac motif of equine satyrs pursuing maenads. John Boardman, in a standard work on classical sculpture, does not hesitate to refer to 'centaur masks', and Nigel Spivey writes of how the furrowed brows and square open mouths of the Centaurs 'look indebted to the nascent tradition of theatrical masks'.[55] J. J. Pollitt likens the east pediment, with its dramatic timing and moral perplexity, to 'a scene out of Aeschylean drama', and continues: 'In looking at the Lapith women and Centaurs on the west pediment at Olympia, one has the feeling that we are looking at the sort of faces which poets and *choregoi* would have demanded to express *ethos* and *pathos* on the stage'.[56] None of these authorities, however, comments directly on one of the most remarkable images, where a Lapith woman strives to tear a mask from the Centaur's face.[57] The contours of the mask are unmistakable in

---

[52] Boardman (1993: 99).
[53] See Chapter 7 on the work of modern mask-makers like Sartori, Chase and Vovolis. A mask built up around a positive mould would be too heavy.
[54] Cf. Fo (1991: 27).   [55] Boardman (1985: 39); Spivey (1996: 35); cf. Simon (1988: 10).
[56] Pollitt (1985: 108–9).
[57] Figure 'N'; for good photos see Ashmole and Yalouris (1967: plates 98, 99, 105).

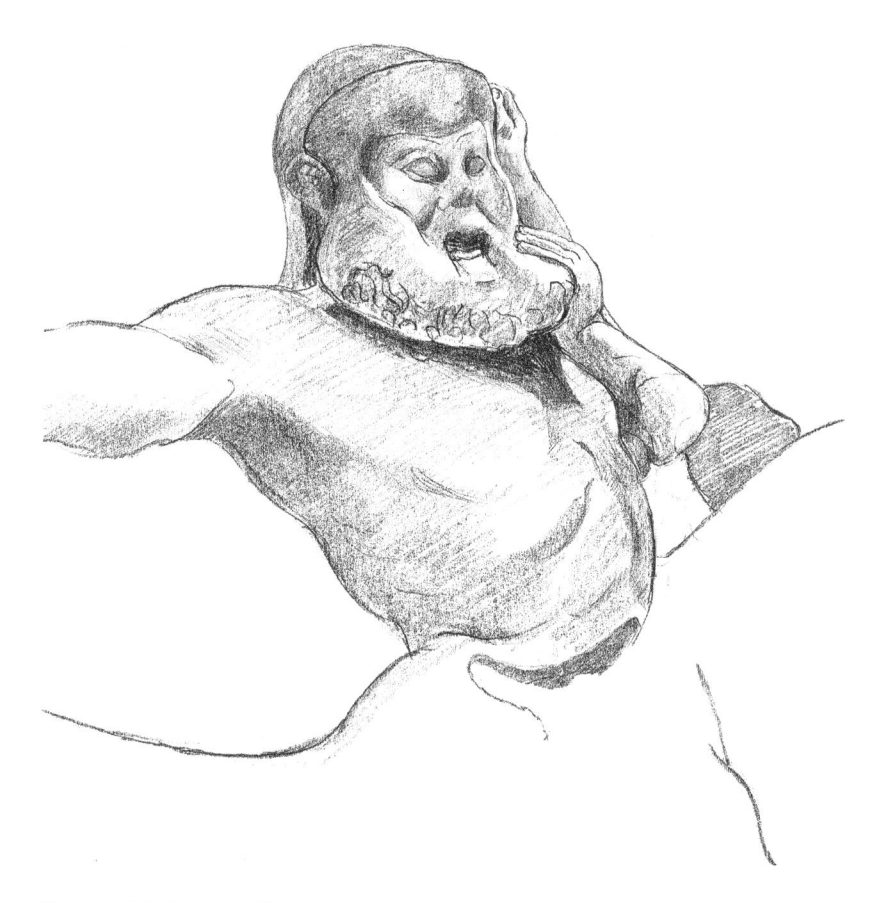

**Drawing 3.6** Centaur. Olympia.

the modern museum, but would have been invisible when the pediments stood high above the viewer (Drawing 3.6). This mysterious Centaur offers an intriguing reflection of how the sculptor related his evolving art to the new genre of masked tragedy.

Like the maker of a theatrical mask, the sculptors of Olympia had to think how faces would look when viewed from afar and from an extreme angle. On some of the metopes, features are adjusted for the sake of frontal viewing. Whilst a bronze figure was complete and perfect in its own three-dimensional space, these stone reliefs inhabited a kind of stage set, where the gaze had to be manipulated. And yet one is struck also by the care taken over detail. Toes and fingernails are perfectly rendered, even though any viewer would be some twenty metres distant.[58] This is an important principle for us

---

[58] Cf. Barron (1981: 81).

to bear in mind when we think about the execution of tragic masks. Masks had to work optically at a distance for an elevated audience, but we may guess that they too were perfect in their finish. Masks may have been inspected in the temple after the festival was over, or used in tiny deme theatres, but more to the point is the presence of the statue of Dionysos in the front row as a privileged spectator.[59] Theatrical masks like the carvings of Olympia were attached to a cult and must in some sense have been experienced as sacred objects.

On the west pediment, it is the Centaurs who show emotion, whilst the Greek Lapiths are generally impassive, though the Centaur's vicious bite does manage to elicit a couple of wrinkles.[60] Emotion belongs to the symbolic barbarian, the human in his animal state, while self-control marks the civilised Greek. This impassivity does nothing to mitigate the violence of the fight, or the urgency in the gaze of the woman who watches from the sidelines. As in vase painting, emption is communicated by posture and juxtaposition. If the Lapiths were human actors in a modern play, we should say that they had avoided internalising, but had transferred all their energy into the execution of objectives. They triumph precisely because they know how to hold back surplus energy that might be wasted on the face, and focus completely on what needs to be done. There was no movement in this period towards psychologism. On the Parthenon, a decade or more later, the same theme is treated again, and the Lapiths appear even more uniform in their expression, distinguished again from the more emotional features of the Centaurs.[61] In respect of theatre, we are left with a teasing question. Did tragedy only depict noble Lapiths, or was it concerned equally with their antithesis? To what extent was the bestial Centaur dimension in humankind relegated to comedy and the satyr play? Aristotle provides some sort of answer with his theory of mimesis, whereby tragedy represents men as better than people of today, comedy as worse. He goes on to specify that laughter is associated with ugly (*aischron*) behaviour, and the comic mask accordingly is ugly and distorted.[62] It follows that the normative tragic mask was an idealisation 'better' than a normative human face.

The ideal, impassive Greek face of the later fifth century was replaced in fourth-century sculpture by more expressive features. In Pollitt's terms, there was a shift back from ideal forms to transient phenomena, and from *ethos* or 'moral character' to a celebration of *pathos*, 'feeling'.[63] When Skopas

---

[59] Pickard-Cambridge (1968: 60).   [60] Barron (1981: 80).
[61] Osborne (1998: 179). The remains are in much poorer condition.   [62] *Poetics* ii.4; v.1.
[63] Pollitt 1985.

in the mid-fourth century created a maenad's face out of stone, a Platonist explained how 'all the soul displays when stung by madness, all the signs of passion, shone out through the sculptor's skill blended with secret reason'.[64] This is a far cry from the blank maenad masks we saw in the Athens, Ferrara and Boston vases. We glimpse the new era in the miniatures of Lipari, where signs of emotional disposition may be written onto the features, though the process is much more marked in comedy than in tragedy. The evolution of fifth-century sculpture does not encourage us to think that masks changed profoundly between the ages of Aeschylus and Euripides.

There was a change of mind-set in the fourth century, and two apocryphal anecdotes sum up the great cultural shift. According to the first, when Pheidias had created the gigantic face of Zeus in Olympia, surfaced with strips of ivory, he hid behind the doors of the temple to hear what people said, and later made fine adjustments in the light of all the comments overheard.[65] The principles that determined the classical face were thus consensual, and the artist was a craftsman who realised a collective ideal. In the second, Seneca, father of the Stoic playwright, tells of a fourth-century painter who tortured an enslaved Greek to death so he could depict the contortions of pain on the dying man's face, and place in the Parthenon a satisfactory likeness of Prometheus.[66] Artists now copied from real-life models, and were fascinated by facial emotion. Seneca's tale brings out the latent voyeurism implicit in an art form focused on personal feeling.

Polycleitus, a contemporary of Pheidias in the Periclean age, is famed for tying theory to practice with his sculpture called the Canon. His accompanying treatise defined a 'canonical' set of proportions for all the components of the human body.[67] These proportions held until Lysippus, in the age of Alexander, made the head smaller to create the illusion of a taller, more heroic body.[68] It may be no coincidence that in the age of Lysippus masks were made taller through the extension of the *onkos* to create a similar illusion. Scale was the major technical difficulty that faced mask-makers who wanted to replicate in the theatre the aesthetic ideals of sculptors, since Greek 'helmet' masks perforce made the head disproportionately large in relation to the body of the wearer. The *skeuopoios* necessarily had responsibility for costumes as well as masks since a voluminous and vibrant costume was the key to deceiving the spectator into imagining that a perfect classical body stood before him. Long and ample hair served the same purpose. The

---

[64] Kallistratos *Descriptions* 2, cited in Osborne (1998: 215).   [65] Barron (1981: 93).
[66] Seneca *Controversies* 10.5.   [67] Galen cited in Pollitt (1990: 76–7).
[68] Pliny *Natural History* 34, cited in Pollitt (1990: 98–9).

audience on the hillside viewed from above, so their eyes had to correct some foreshortening of the human figure and could easily correct further.

The technical difficulties of mask-making, most notably the size of the head and the open mouth, are compensated for by the practical gain of a clarified face whose features can be caught at a distance, and can seem more expressive than those of the natural face thanks to the play of shadow. The technical pros and cons of masking should not divert us from recognising the principle that masking was concomitant with the idealising conventions of fifth-century art at large. To find masks self-evidently more appropriate than faces seems counter-intuitive in our individualistic era, with its preference for the particular. Universality, Aristotle famously claimed, is what distinguishes the 'poetic' from the historical and merely contingent.[69] The universal was also and necessarily the beautiful, because beauty was bound up with normative proportions based on agreed mathematical formulae. The 'impersonality' which today makes classical statues seem emotionless or impenetrable was a defining feature of the classical mask.[70] Siegfried Melchinger debates whether the primary purpose of masking was to distinguish in order to create a recognisable image, or to simplify in order to essentialise.[71] I have argued that facial recognition was largely irrelevant to the needs of an ancient spectator. Text, costume and hair-piece were enough to make the narrative clear. The power of the tragic mask lay rather in the transition that it effected, from the world of Athens to the world of myth. As I demonstrated in Chapter 2, all our fifth-century representations of masks are bound up with the mystery of transformation.

The Furies or 'Erinyes' provide a test case if we are to understand the principles of tragic masking. Echoing the vision of Orestes at the end of *Libation Bearers*, the Priestess in *Eumenides* describes the Erinyes (who are not yet visible to the audience) as black, with ooze dripping from their eyes, reminding her of Gorgons or Harpies. Alan Sommerstein infers that the masks are black and the ooze is blood.[72] Yet in the half-century which followed the *Oresteia*, the iconographic tradition is consistent in giving the Erinyes standard female faces, ideal faces with no sign of age, and snakes attached to the hair usually fix their identity.[73] Commenting on a vase of *c*.450 which portrays the Erinyes pursuing Orestes, Susan Woodford remarks: 'The Furies themselves are disappointingly tame-looking, quite lacking in the impact they were supposed to have had in the theatre (and the terror they

---

[69] *Poetics* ix.1–4.  [70] For this reaction, cf. Boardman (1993: 90).  [71] Melchinger (1974: 215).
[72] Sommerstein (1989: notes to *Eumenides* 52, 53–4). Cf. also Frontisi-Ducroux (1991: 48).
[73] Prag (1985: 48); cf. Knoepfler (1993: 70).

struck into Orestes, according to the play)'.[74] Seduced by a fanciful tale in Aeschylus' biography, she betrays unrealistic expectations about the relation of text and image,[75] but she is in good company, for Pausanias experienced the same surprise. When he visited the Areopagus in Athens, he remarked on the contrast between the Aeschylean description and the entirely unfearsome statues, probably of the fourth century, which he saw in the shrine of the Erinyes.[76] Yet facial neutrality is in fact what makes it possible for the Erinyes at the end of Aeschylus' trilogy to metamorphose into the *eumenides*, the 'kindly ones'. The universalising features of the mask allow and encourage figures to change, in a way that would necessarily be restricted by the unique features of one particular actor's face. The transformative power of masking helps us see how, historically, the remarkable literary power of Greek tragedy derived from the mask. Characters are not delineated and contained by the mask, but are allowed to become. Greek tragedy both portrayed and embodied a metamorphic world. The potential for transformation was a property of Greek political systems, and also of the Greek polytheistic system with its fluid boundary between human and divine worlds.

C. H. Hallett uses the term the 'neutral' in order to characterise the classical face, a face which had to reconcile the 'lifelike' with the 'symbolic' and 'otherworldly'. He argues that fifth-century artists saw no need to develop those glimmerings of expression discernible on the Olympia pediments because the classical face was so flexible:

> the neutral Classical expression appears to take on a subtly different emotional tenor in different situations – largely through the postures and gestures of the figures. In a violent struggle it can seem resolute and intent; in a stately procession serene and composed; in a grave stele melancholy yet resigned; in a victor statue modest and reflective; and in cult image inscrutable – passionless and perfect. Its apparent vacancy is in fact its greatest strength; for it renders the expression potentially ambiguous, or – more correctly – multivalent; and the beholder will tend to supply feelings appropriate to the context.[77]

This account of the classical face will have many resonances for theatre practitioners who have worked with 'neutral' rehearsal masks. Jacques Lecoq (1921–99) placed the 'neutral' mask at the centre of his pedagogy, and his methods have been influential. Although Lecoq insisted that his neutral mask was a vehicle for rehearsal not public performance, it remains the basis of intense performances within the rarefied and arguably ritualised atmosphere

---

[74] Woodford (2003: 108).   [75] Anecdote in Nagler (1952: 5).
[76] Pausanias i.28.6; cf. Prag (1985: 48).   [77] Hallett (1986: 80).

of his school.[78] It is in some degree a tragic mask, for one definitive exercise asks the actor to wave farewell from a quayside to someone they will never see again.

A classical aesthetic lies behind Lecoq's account of the neutral mask, emphasising economy, balance and beauty. The chemistry that underlies all mask work ensures that the qualities of the mask communicate themselves to the wearer:

> The neutral mask is an object with its own special characteristics. It is a face which we call neutral, a perfectly balanced mask which produces a physical sensation of calm. This object, when placed on the face, should enable one to experience the state of neutrality prior to action, a state of receptiveness to everything around us, with no inner conflict... With an actor wearing the mask, you look at the whole body... Every movement is revealed as powerfully expressive. When the actor takes off the mask, if he has worn it well, his face is relaxed... The mask will have drawn something from him, divesting him from artifice. His face will be beautiful, free.[79]

We may cast our minds back to the Delphic charioteer, whose beautiful and tranquil features signify his readiness for action: his 'neutrality' is recognisable in Lecoq's description. The word 'neutral', however, has troubled many of Lecoq's pupils, in part because the word has a deader ring in English than in French. A current teacher in the UK opts for the term 'potent mask' to suggest both potency and potential.[80] An American pedagogue in the 1970s cited Walter Pater on how the Greek sculptors sought to display 'the breadth of humanity', and substituted the term 'universal' mask.[81] Some two decades later, in a 'politically correct' cultural climate, another American pedagogue found the racial and gender implications of the 'neutral' mask intolerable, and worked with a mere sheet of paper.[82] The concept of 'neutrality' remains a contested one. Modern psychological experimentation using morphed photographs has demonstrated how the perception of beauty is bound up with symmetry and normalisation of features in ways that may cut across ethnic distinctions.[83] Such research invites a fresh engagement with the universalising ideals of Greek antiquity.

Lecoq places his emphasis upon action, in a way that Aristotle would have approved. We have to understand, therefore, why this mask familiar to so many theatre practitioners cannot play the classical repertory. The problem is not simply one of emotion, for feeling can be conveyed through narrative and gesture. We know what the figure on the quayside feels because

---

[78] I owe this point to Chris Vervain.   [79] Lecoq (2000: 36–8).
[80] Jos Houben, cited in Edinborough (2003: 17).   [81] Rolfe 1977.
[82] Eldredge 1996.   [83] Bruce and Young (1998: 134–40).

Plate 3.4 Donato Sartori with neutral mask.

we know what he or she is seeing. The lack of inner conflict, the lack of memory, and the inability to relate which characterise the Lecoq mask offer more serious difficulties. To understand the difference between ancient and modern neutrality, we must turn to the actual artefact, the leather mask made for Lecoq by the great Italian mask-maker Amleto Sartori (1915–62) (Plate 3.4). The mask is in many respects a 1950s interpretation of a classical face, owing something to Matisse and Picasso.[84] Flat planes which reflect the light evince a cubist influence. The sculptor's chisel marks leave their trace on the moulded leather, so this is a provisional creation waiting to be completed by the work of the actor. The smooth brow is not covered by a headpiece, and the mask therefore lacks any social identity. The continuous curve joining nose to brow creates a Grecian profile, and the half-open mouth is classical in concept, though the full lips echo the Gallic features of Lecoq himself. The fundamental difference lies in the large teardrop eye cavities extending back round the side of the head which create a blankness of gaze that denies all possibility of recognition. The lack of eyes, eyelids, bags beneath the eyes and brows capable of contraction eliminates the capacity for memory and

---

[84] Cf. Edinborough (2003: 28–9). Sartori regularly worked as a sculptor in the classical idiom: see for example his Hercules and Antaeus of 1948 in Sartori and Piizzi (1996: plate 4).

thought. This is a mask with a gaze but no eyes, and with the eye vanishes personhood.

Lecoq and Sartori took what they needed from the classical tradition: a mask that taught the actor simplicity, balance, grace and a heightened awareness of body, while discouraging manifestations of ego. Yet their mask remains a modernist abstraction. They could not or would not take the next step and stage a modern-day version of Apollo or Athena, at once universal and lifelike. Fascist celebration of the Greek body as an Aryan body was too close a memory. Actors in Lecoq's school use the neutral mask as a step towards creating their own 'clown', a stage persona that draws on their own personality and body-type, so they can walk on stage as individuals without egocentricity, effectively shedding their own psychological masks. Lecoq's method has been so successful because it serves the needs of a culture preoccupied with the individual. In Greek tragedy, the mask permitted a total relinquishment of self: the actor could let go of his gender, age and body-type and play any role. In modern professional theatre the body of the actor has become a marketable commodity, confining him or her to a particular type of role, and the naked face is a vital part of this commodification.

I have examined the Greek mask in this chapter in terms of the technique that governed its manufacture, and in terms of the aesthetic ideal to which it aspired. The purpose of the technique was to make a face seem alive, with the emphasis not on obliterating the actor, but on bringing a mythic figure to life. Rather than call attention to its own material properties, the tragic mask had to become an integral part of a heroic body. It belonged historically to the great idealist project of the mid- and later fifth century. Idealism was bound up with a political ethic, which held that individual difference should be subordinate to collective values, and with a religious system, which used art as a means of drawing together the human and divine spheres. It is hard for us to respond to this idealism in a more secular and individualistic age. We can only see Greek art through eyes that have been trained to see in a certain way, and in order to understand antiquity better we have to understand ourselves better. To grasp the Greek ideal of neutrality, for example, we have to differentiate it from the modern ideal of neutrality. I therefore pass on in the next section of this book to an account of how the twentieth century saw Greek masks, for our own twenty-first-century perceptions are rooted in the work of the generations that have preceded us.

# 4 | Mask and modernism

The archaeological evidence leaves many questions unanswered. Whilst images on containers of wine offer us a mask that is to be understood as a tool for Dionysiac possession, the sculptural evidence yields a more Apolline theatrical face which, when taken in isolation, is remarkable for its serene impassivity. The 'real' tragic mask of the fifth century continues to slide from our grasp. Our surmises about Greek acting are inevitably shaped by our sensory and emotional experience of theatre in our own lives. Archaeologists and literary scholars with no applied experience of theatre are unlikely to be our best guides when we seek to understand how the mask functioned in practice, and amateur enthusiasts reach simplistic conclusions after donning masks for some brief experiment. In the ensuing chapters I shall seek what can be learned from the varied work of twentieth-century professional performers who have pushed the possibilities of their medium to the limits. I shall open up a range of possibilities, ideals and debates that will provide, at the minimum, a sensible platform from which to interrogate the evidence of antiquity. Through most of the twentieth century Athenian tragedy has furnished artists with a utopian vision of the possible, spurring them to new forms of creative expression. Greek theatre needs to be studied and imagined afresh in the twenty-first century if it is to sustain that utopian impulse.

The post-classical world has construed the Greek mask in many different ways, and it is salutary to trace that endeavour back to the Renaissance. Juan Luis Vives, the Spanish humanist and tutor of Mary Tudor, fancifully imagined the earth as a stage, with the gods seated above in an ancient amphitheatre watching tragedies and comedies. On this stage Man appears from behind the curtain as a Graeco-Roman pantomime. Under Jupiter's direction he dons a series of masks, impersonating plants, different species of animal, and then a well-socialised human being. As he peers through the mask, Man is tempted to reveal the god-like body he hides beneath, until finally Jupiter allows him to depict the gods, with a decorous impersonation of Jupiter himself the climax of his performance. The gods applaud frenetically, delighted to see a figure on stage who looks like themselves, and invite him to unmask and join them on the seats of the spectators. When they examine his mask, they admire the sculpting of the eyes, measure of the soul, and the ears, so well protected against dust and insects. Having banqueted with the gods, Man puts on the mask again, but now his mask is endowed with the power of perception. The mask, in other words, becomes the face.

Inspired by the conventions of the court masque, Vives finds in the Greek mask a positive metaphor for the human condition. It is an outer shell which conceals the soul within, but at the same time it is an object of beauty which replicates the form of the divine. Despite the carping of rival performers, Man's masked performance offers spectators no disjuncture between the actor and the role he plays. No comment is made, incidentally, on the mouth of the mask, for dancers in renaissance court masques like those in ancient pantomimes did not speak. Lucian in the second century AD contrasts the beauty of the pantomime mask with the gaping masks of tragedy that looks as if they could swallow up the spectators.[1] In this renaissance context the utopian force of the mask is clear, legitimating a celebration of the perfect human body that Christianity could not tolerate. In his neo-Platonist celebration of the classical past, Vives privileges the mask over the spoken text because it is the eyes that lead human beings to a vision of the divine.[2]

The Counter-Reformation took a much less kindly view of the ancient mask. While the reference point for Vives at the start of the sixteenth century was the aristocratic banquet, the relevant experience for Claude Noirot a century later was public masking which broke the peace at carnival time. In a treatise on the origins of masks, this otherwise unknown provincial French lawyer traces a transition from smeared paint or foliage to the hideous mask of tragedy worn by Aeschylus, called the father of tragedy because he unified the chorus and made the rites of Bacchus somewhat more orderly. Noirot cites axioms from the Fathers to support his argument – for example Tertullian: 'The lover of truth hates what is false: all that is false is adultery towards Him'. The Greek word for acting is *hypokrisis*, and acting thus becomes by definition hypocrisy, a concealment of what God has created, with the representation of women by men being a particular offence against the order of God's creation. Noirot typifies a long-standing Christian assumption that the mask is a means of concealing shame. He provides a useful corrective to twentieth-century perspectives on the ancient mask

---

[1] *On the dance* 27–9. Lucian adds that in former times these pantomime masks of Hecuba, Andromache or Heracles were also used for singing.
[2] Vives 1948; cf. Lucian *On the Dance* 27–30.

through his premise that masking is part of a seasonal ritual, and an integral part of a pagan religion. Theatre, regarded from Noirot's historical angle of vision, is a part of carnival and not in any sense an autonomous art form.[3]

For a representative Enlightenment view of the tragic mask, we need simply turn up the entry on *masque* in Diderot's great *Encyclopaedia*.[4] The conception of theatre here seems a much more familiar one, and all talk of ritual is gone. The convention of the Greek mask, however, is distinctly puzzling for the eighteenth-century practitioner since: 'These masks caused the spectators to lose the pleasure of seeing the passions, and of recognising their different symptoms on the faces of the actors'. It is assumed that signs of passion in the face will affect the spectator more than voice or gesture. The core emotions identified by Descartes were moulded into shape by the actor on the basis of a mechanical conception of the body.[5] To explain the Greek mask, the *Encyclopaedia* falls back on a set of practical explanations related to outdoor performance. Like the use of an all-male cast, the hollowness and bronze mouthpiece of the mask increased the acoustical power of the play. For spectators seated some twenty-two to twenty-five metres away in a Greek theatre, subtle changes in the human face become impossible to discern, and sunlight, it is assumed, can only create unhelpful shadows. Quintilian (11.3.73) is the source for a belief that the classical masks showed fixed expressions: Niobe fixed in grief, Medea ghastly and Ajax beside himself. Ancient drama was compatible with such immobile masks, for actors in the oratorical tradition were trained to control their emotions and show no change in the face. The ancient mask necessarily increased the scale of the human body, which in eighteenth-century terms was an offence against verisimilitude. The *Encyclopaedia* concedes, however, that in view of widespread belief that heroes and demi-gods actually were larger than life, the convention of the mask would not in fact have offended.

For Diderot and his associates, French neoclassical theatre represented an advance on the primitive practices of the Greeks and Romans. Diderot himself moved towards ever greater realism as a dramatist. But at the end of the eighteenth century such bourgeois realism was anathema to German idealists, who saw in the Greek mask something worthy of their aspirations. Kant had put paid to the Enlightenment view that the universe out there is unproblematically knowable, and championed a new category of 'aesthetic' perception. If human life is driven by more than psycho-physical passions,

---

[3] Noirot (1838: esp. 19, 89); cf. Carpenter and Twycross 2002.
[4] *Encyclopédie* (1765: 172–6).    [5] See Wiles (1991: 114–21).

then the human face can no longer be a sufficient guide to the human condition, and the mask offered new possibilities for the educated spectator. August Schlegel in his celebrated lectures of 1808 despatched the French neoclassical emphasis on verisimilitude, offering a new justification for the masks of the Greeks:

Fidelity of representation was less their object than beauty; with us it is exactly the reverse. On this principle, the use of masks, which appears astonishing to us, was not only justifiable but absolutely essential; far from considering them as a makeshift, the Greeks would certainly, and with justice too, have looked upon it as a makeshift to be obliged to allow a player with vulgar, ignoble, or strongly marked features, to represent an Apollo or a Hercules; nay rather they would have deemed it downright profanation.[6]

Goethe, in a sketch written for the opening of the Lauchstädt theatre in 1802, brought on a boy carrying ancient masks, and representing Art. The mask, proclaimed 'Art' in solemn iambics,

permits us to discern a grave and universal reflection of the High and the Beautiful. Banish the personality of the famous actor, and there enters a host of other figures, at the bidding of the playwright alone, a very multitude to delight your gaze.[7]

For Schlegel and Goethe, Greek theatre required the trained actor to become an instrument in the hands of the poet, with all hint of his own personality obliterated. Movement was in service of the text. The poetry of Greek tragedy, wrote Schlegel, 'required a certain degree of repose in the action, and the keeping together of certain masses, so as to exhibit a succession of *statuesque* situations', in an art of display that he related to the bas-relief.[8]

Goethe visited Italy to see carnival masks absorbed as part of a living theatrical tradition, and commented that masks 'which in our country have as little life and meaning for us as mummies, here seem sympathetic and characteristic expressions of the country'.[9] Yet the main influence on Goethe and Schlegel was Greek statuary, which epitomised the sublime. Understanding that heroic nudity could not be reproduced on stage, Schlegel saw that the enhanced scale of the mask had to be counterbalanced by padded clothing and the raised cothurnus, to re-create perfect proportion. His experience of wax masks in the Roman carnival convinced him that, at a distance, a perfect illusion could be achieved.[10] Yet there remained problems in moving from sublime statues of Apollo to any viable stage equivalent, and the Lucianic

---

[6] Schlegel (1846: 59).
[7] *Was wir bringen*, scene xix, cited in Trevelyan (1941: 254 – my translation).
[8] Schlegel (1846: 62–3).  [9] Goethe (1962: 87).  [10] Schlegel (1846: 62–3).

problem of the gaping mouth was never confronted. Goethe staged in 1801 a successful production of Terence's *Brothers*, with masks and costumes inspired by the recent excavations at Herculaneum.[11] Since the comedy of Terence was clearly analogous to the *commedia dell'arte*, comic effects were not hard to achieve with masks. However, when Goethe directed Schlegel's adaptation of Euripides' *Ion* in 1802, he felt able to use masks only for the two negative characters of Phorbas the slave and Xuthus the stepfather, and not for the two positive characters of Ion, the son and human likeness of Apollo, and of his mother. The perfect face of Ion could not be reproduced in plastic form on stage, and recourse to a human face was the only way. No performer with an enlarged head could have reproduced the perfect contraposto pose of an Apollo Belvedere which Goethe's theatre demanded, so the role was given to a petite actress noted for her blue eyes and golden curls.[12] There were to be no masks either for Goethe's revival of his own *Iphigenia* in the same year, a play which he considered 'rich in internal vitality, but poor in external life'.[13] As in French neoclassicism, so in Goethe the face remained by default the privileged pointer to an internal psychological life; to find a very multitude of masks capable of reflecting the High and the Beautiful would remain a utopian dream. In principle theatre was the perfect medium for creating a vision of the ideal, but in practice its mundane exigencies were insuperable.[14] Kleist's celebrated essay of 1810 'On the Marionette theatre' showed the only way forward for idealist theatre. Actors are necessarily flawed because they have eaten of the tree of knowledge, and a dancer trying to represent Daphne or Paris is tied to the material realm by the forces of gravity, so puppetry alone allows the theatre to present symmetry, mobility and lightness.[15]

'Modernism' is a convenient historical and generic label to attach to the conspectus of artistic movements, focused in the early twentieth century, which rejected the notion that art should replicate either exterior reality or a neo-Platonic ideal.[16] To express irrational inner experience now seemed the most important role for the artist. Modernism had many prophets – Darwin with his breakdown of the distinction between human and animal, Marx with his assertion that we live in false consciousness and are subject to transpersonal economic forces, and Freud with his distinction between a struggling ego and the inchoate but energising id. However, it was above all Nietzsche who served as a guru for modernist artists, with his assault on

---

[11] Carlson (1978: 161–2). [12] Carlson (1978: 166, 95). [13] Carlson (1978: 176).
[14] Cf. Boyle (2000: 724). [15] Kleist 1972.
[16] Helpful accounts include Bell 1999 and Butler 1994.

the fundamentals of western epistemology. The mask is a recurrent motif in Nietzsche's thinking, serving as a metaphor for the human condition, and his scandalous philosophy offered up a fresh rationale for the mask in the theatre. The mask was no longer a barrier between the psycho-somatic human organism and the scientific gaze of the spectator, nor did it offer a glimpse of a transcendent ideal, but as an intermediary between inner and outer was part of how it felt to be alive.

Nietzsche's *The Birth of Tragedy out of the Spirit of Music* (1871) set the sculptural ideal of the Apolline, Goethe's concept of the Greek mask, against an underlying demonic, dithyrambic conception more reminiscent of Noirot. In the theatre Nietzsche contends that

> until Euripides, Dionysus never ceased to be the tragic hero, and that all the celebrated characters of the Greek stage – Prometheus, Oedipus and so on – are merely masks of that original hero, Dionysus. The fact that a divinity lurks behind all these masks is the major reason for the typical 'ideality' of those celebrated characters that has so often aroused astonishment. Someone, I do not know who, claims that all individuals, as individuals, are comic and consequently untragic: from which we can deduce that the Greeks were actually *unable* to bear individuals on the tragic stage.[17]

As an interpreter of classical drama, Nietzsche reasserted the primacy of the chorus, an aspect that the neoclassical tradition neglected. Following the archaeology of the day which taught him that the chorus danced in the orchestra, while the actors performed on a high shallow stage, he compared the shape of the primitive Greek auditorium to 'a lonely mountain valley' filled with maenads who had swarmed down from the mountains. The stage building, like 'a luminous cloud formation', provided a 'wonderful frame in the middle of which the image of Dionysus is revealed to them'.[18] He conceived the composition on stage not as Schlegel's bas-relief, but as a two-dimensional vision conjured up by the votaries of the god, 'a light-image cast on a dark screen'.[19] When tragedy becomes a formalised genre, he argued, the dance and music of the chorus stir the audience 'in such a Dionysiac way that when the tragic hero appears on the stage they do not see, for example, an awkwardly masked man, but rather a visionary form'.[20]

Inspired by a visit to Pompeii, he reflected in *The Gay Science* (1882) on the nature of ancient life: 'What can one understand about it when one does not understand the delight in the mask, the good conscience in everything mask-like! Here is the bath and the recreation of the ancient spirit . . .' While he found the comic mask restorative, and a release from the

---

[17] Nietzsche (1993: 51).  [18] Nietzsche (1993: 42).
[19] Nietzsche (1993: 46).  [20] Nietzsche (1993: 45).

northern culture of shame, he turned firmly against the Aristotelian theory of catharsis, developing a theory of critical distance. The Greek spectator discovered 'the art of regarding oneself as a hero, from a distance and as it were simplified and transfigured – the art of "putting oneself on stage" before oneself'.[21] Frustrated now by the way Wagnerian opera drowned the text in symphonic music, he celebrated the power of the mask to foreground poetic language:

> It delights us now when the tragic actor still finds words, reasons, eloquent gestures, and altogether a radiant spirit where life approaches the abyss and a real human being would usually lose his head and certainly his fine language . . . The Greeks go far, far on this road, terrifyingly far! . . . just as they make facial expressions and easy movement impossible for the actor and transform him into a solemn, stiff masked puppet, so they also have deprived passion itself of any deep background and dedicated to it a law of beautiful speech; yes, on the whole they have done everything to counteract the elemental effect of images that arouse fear and compassion . . .[22]

When he argued that the greatest offence of the actor was surrender to emotion, he anticipated Brecht and the 'alienating' theory of the mask.

In *The Birth of Tragedy* the key to Nietzsche's Dionysos was not wine but the myth of dismemberment, for Dionysos is the god who can revert from being individual to being multiple, individuation being the major source of human suffering. In *Beyond Good and Evil* (1886), Nietzsche wrote in a more autobiographical vein, presenting himself as a disciple of Dionysos, the smiling god who declares that he wants to make human beings '"stronger, more evil, and more profound; and more beautiful"'.[23] He himself is compelled to wear masks that are the opposite of himself, just like Dionysos: 'Everything profound loves masks; the most profound things go so far as to hate images and likenesses. Wouldn't just the *opposite* be a proper disguise for the shame of a god?' Masks in Nietzsche are never simulations of reality but always opposites. Nietzsche portrays himself as a man who 'wants and encourages a mask of himself to wander around, in his place, through the hearts and heads of his friends. And even if this is not what he wants, he will eventually realize that a mask of himself has been there all the same'.[24] It is easy to explicate this pessimism in terms of Nietzsche's anxiety about his homosexuality, and relate his mask obsession to the monstrous moustache which he wore to conceal his effeminate features.[25] But Nietzsche's sentiments chimed also with a broad consensus in the artistic community about the falseness

---

[21] Nietzsche (2001: 78).    [22] Nietzsche (2001: 80).
[23] Nietzsche (2001: 177).    [24] Nietzsche (2001: 38).    [25] See Köhler 2002.

of bourgeois values, and a feeling that all inner lives are fragmented. Nietzsche went on to develop a theory that anticipates Artaud, claiming that 'almost everything we call "higher culture" is based on the spiritualization and deepening of *cruelty*'. Negative examples of cruelty, which act on the spectator like a narcotic, include the Roman arena and Wagnerian opera, but Greek tragedy had a nobler function, involving cruelty inflicted not just on the other but knowingly on oneself. Nietzsche maps a tension between that part of his spirit which keeps manufacturing masks, and another which keeps cruelly searching for truth. Though speaking of 'honesty' involves the empty language of old metaphysics, to confront *homo natura* remained a necessary task.[26] The logic of Nietzsche's argument is that Greek tragedy, as a masked form, had the highest possible function, that of allowing a painful engagement with one's own human nature.

Building on Goethe, Nietzsche demonstrated that the mask was not merely an accessory to the text but an integral part of the *Gesamtkunstwerk*, the total work of art. His complex theory of the mask lent support to many kinds of modernist performance – those spurred by primitivism and a search for origins, or by symbolism interpreting life as a dream, hieratic productions interpreting theatre as a pagan ceremony, or anarchistic ones tearing the veneer from bourgeois society. Nietzsche could be embraced equally by those seeking a romantic ecstasy in the moment of performance, a detached poetic theatre, or an expressionistic theatre of cruelty. What he ruled out of court was any idea of social realism, or any scientific aspiration to replicate an essentialised classical past.[27]

The extraordinary force of the mask in the modernist era is vividly illustrated by Hugo Ball's account of how masks were introduced to the Dadaists as they sheltered in Zurich from the insanity of the First World War:

Janco has made a number of masks for the new soiree, and they are more than just clever. They are reminiscent of the Japanese or ancient Greek theatre, yet they are wholly modern . . . We were all there when Janco arrived with his masks, and everyone immediately put one on. Then something strange happened. Not only did the mask immediately call for a costume; it also demanded a quite definite, passionate gesture, bordering on madness. Although we could not have imagined it five minutes earlier, we were walking around with the most bizarre movements, festooned and draped with impossible objects, each one of us trying to outdo the other in inventiveness . . . All at once we realized the significance of such a mask for the theatre. The masks simply demanded that their wearers start to move in a tragic-absurd dance . . . What fascinates us all about the masks is that they represent

---

[26] Nietzsche (2001: 120–4).   [27] Cf. Foucault 2001.

not human characters and passions, but characters and passions that are larger than life. The horror of our time, the paralyzing background of events, is made visible.[28]

Ball's diary evokes the mood of a Nietzschean chorus, freed from individuation to become possessed by the mask. This was no escape from reality because realist art could not do justice to a world of such horror, more adequately expressed by the excesses of a cardboard mask. A few weeks earlier, Ball had been thinking about Kandinsky: 'The image of the human form is gradually disappearing from the painting of these times and all objects appear only in fragments. This is one more proof of how ugly and worn the human countenance has become...'[29] Masks offered a solution to the problem of representing the human face in the age of cubist and abstract art, and Picasso's African masks became emblematic of a new ideal.

W. B. Yeats was one of the many in this generation inspired by Nietzsche to develop a theory of the mask,[30] and his discovery of masked Noh drama pointed him to a true poetic theatre where:

A mask never seems but a dirty face, and no matter how close you go is yet a work of art; nor shall we lose by staying the movement of the features, for deep feeling is expressed by a movement of the whole body. In poetical painting & in sculpture the face seems nobler for lacking curiosity, alert attention, all that we sum up under the famous word of the realists 'vitality'.[31]

In practice, this poetic theatre only suited the few. The mask served Yeats well enough in his coterie dance plays, but when it came to staging 'a plain man's *Oedipus*' at the Abbey in 1926, both mask and verse had to be discarded in the interests of accessibility. Yeats could sense in rehearsal 'the actual presence in a terrible sacrament of the god', but public performance was a more secular affair.[32] At the time of *Oedipus* he was also drafting *Resurrection* for his coterie audience, specifying a mask for the face of a fused Christ/Dionysos figure. In an island of entrenched religious views, this Nietzschean view of the world, with its concomitant language of the mask, would not have been acceptable. Tyrone Guthrie revealed the possibilities of Yeats' *Oedipus* for actors in masks, but in 1955 his hieratic production lacked the subversive energy that Nietzschean thinking provided in the 1920s.[33]

Not even Stanislavski, father of naturalist actor training, could escape engaging with the mask. He wrote eloquently about the principle of the mask in the opening chapters of *Building a Character*, where his protagonist Kostya smears make-up over his face, and unexpectedly discovers the character of

---

[28] Ball (1974: 64–5).  [29] Ball (1974: 55).  [30] See Bohlmann (1982: 130–9).
[31] Pound (1916: vii).  [32] Jeffares and Knowland (1975: 178–9).  [33] See Wiles (2004b: 251).

the Critic. In the manner of a Dadaist, Kostya recounts how 'almost as though I were in some delirium, I trembled, my heart pounded, I did away with my eyebrows, powdered myself at random, smeared the back of my hands with a greenish colour and the palms with light pink'. He is taken over by a voice and manner of moving that function as an autonomous alter ego. 'I divided myself, as it were, into two personalities. One continued as an actor, the other was an observer.' Kostya learns that only behind a mask can one actually reveal one's self, for 'a characterization is the mask which hides the actor-individual. Protected by it he can lay bare his soul down to the last intimate detail.'[34] There are distinct echoes here of Nietzsche's idea that sensitive souls need masks.

Stanislavski's critical encounter with the Greek mask came in 1925–7, when Nemirovich-Danchenko sponsored at the Moscow Art Theatre an ambitious Prometheus Trilogy, incorporating a masked version of Aeschylus' tragedy.[35] As an allegory of revolution, this was set to be a crucial production in rebranding the MAT as a Soviet enterprise. Stanislavski was not the director, but when he came in on rehearsals he did not like what he saw, and started coaching V. Kachalov who played the part of Prometheus. Stanislavski was unhappy with the interpretation of Prometheus as some kind of god, and worked for a more human Prometheus 'who walks on Earth, but his soul flies up to the sky'. This desire for naturalism could not be reconciled with a dramaturgical conception that was more symbolist and poetic, and the resulting tension was one reason, though perhaps not the only one, why this politically significant project collapsed after nearly two years of rehearsal. A drawing of the Prometheus mask survives (Plate 4.1). It is in the antique style, inspired by late classical statuary, with a 1920s coiffure. The solid Soviet neoclassical jowls, chin and nose are in tension with sloping eyes, brows and mouth that hint of art nouveau, and the face as a whole is locked in an expression of pain. It is hard to imagine how an actor in this mask, immobilised against a rock, could have found the earthly, human qualities which Stanislavski sought. Kostya's 'soul' remains available to him to observe his 'masked' performance, but for Kachalov beneath his mask it would have been hard to retain that vital contact between self and role.

[34] Stanislavski (1950: 16, 21, 30).
[35] The failed production is noted briefly in Flashar (1991: 142) and Trubotchkin (2005: 268). Context in Benedetti (1999: 273–4). I am grateful to Dmitry Trubotchkin for sharing with me his archival research, upon which this paragraph is based, and for locating the photo. Rehearsals began in March 1925, Stanislavski became involved in November, and rehearsals were abandoned early in 1927. The guest director was V. Smyshliáev, who also at this time directed an unmasked *Oresteia* for MAT II. On this see Trubotchkin (2005: 262–8).

Plate 4.1 Mask for MAT Prometheus.

I shall focus this chapter on three productions of the 1920s where a conception of the classical mask was realised with a significant degree of success. Cocteau's *Antigone* of 1922/3 influenced Ezra Pound amongst many others,[36] and its triumph stemmed from the collaboration of so many talented modernist artists. Picasso designed the set, and Chanel the costumes, while Honegger composed the music; Charles Dullin played Creon and Antonin Artaud the prophet Teiresias. The authority figure of the play, Dullin, also managed the Atelier theatre in Montmartre where the play was staged. The production combined a streak of Dadaist anarchy with a reverence for Sophocles. Cocteau prided himself that he had managed to trouble the critics with a classical play, removing the play's 'patina' which was normally all that people respected.[37] His script stripped the play down to half length, and masking faces was another means of stripping out redundant detail.

[36] Pound (1956: 67); Steegmuller (1970: 299).    [37] Cocteau (2003: 328).

The production was received enthusiastically by the artistic elite, who included François Mauriac, novelist and future Minster of Culture:

We could never have imagined a more moving Antigone than Mlle Génica Anastasiou. Against a deep blue backdrop like the Attic sky and the gaudy colours of the Parthenon, she slid forward her immobile plaster face, evoking the face of the Greek actor, avoiding that particular plastic, sculptural conception which we can never separate from the 'antique'. Thanks to Cocteau, the drama of Sophocles, exhumed from all that had covered it through the ages, emerged in its youth and original purity.[38]

Another observer commented that the Greek actress 'wore a white mask, and the immobility of this plaster face made one feel that Sophocles' rebellious royal daughter, majestic, cruel, but just, had left the tomb where she had lain for millennia, to utter amidst the maelstrom of Paris the luminous words of her Greek truth that a French poet had restored to life'.[39] Asked why he 'made those inestimable performers Mlle Anastasiou play *cold* and Charles Dullin play *dry*', Cocteau replied: 'So the emotion is engendered solely by what they express'.[40] The mask threw the attention onto story, and created also a sense of the ancient, but an ancient rediscovered for the present. The art nouveau eyes, straight brow-line and pursed mouth imposed on Antigone's white face were of their era. Her close cropped hair and the concealment of her figure beneath a voluminous woollen cloak helped turn her into an iconic figure for the male gay community, and she spoke to a rebellion that was more sexual than political.[41] Cocteau announced in the programme that his play was a sketch done in a museum,[42] and he borrowed from sixth-century vases the convention of painting all male limbs in tones of red or ochre, all female limbs in white. The alternation of frontal with profile delivery and immobility of the performers reinforced the idea that these stage images were lifted off a classical amphora. The bright unchanging light ruled out any romantic manipulation of mood, so the classical story could evolve with stark clarity. Cocteau lamented at the end of a month of performance that the actors were 'rebecoming themselves',[43] but the convention of the make-up mask clearly had provided them, like Stanislavski's Kostya, with a viable technique for integrating head, limbs, costume and voice in an image that appeared definitively other. Antigone's strong Greek accent obliterated any idea of traditional declamatory acting, turning the voice into another sort of mask.[44]

---

[38] *La Revue hebdomadaire*, 6 February 1923. Cocteau (2003: 1656).
[39] Maurice Sachs cited in Steegmuller (1970: 298).   [40] Cocteau (2003: 328).
[41] Cf. Steegmuller (1970: 298).   [42] Cocteau (2003: 1652).
[43] Steegmuller (1970: 300).   [44] Steegmuller (1970: 298).

Drawing 4.1 Cocteau's *Antigone*, 1922.

Above a classical pediment at the centre of the ultramarine backdrop, Picasso placed a tableau of some thirty painted waxwork masks (Drawing 4.1). The faces of these women, boys and old men were diverse and intensely alive, more alive thanks to the genius of Picasso than the impassive faces of the performers. From a dark hole in the rucked curtain, in the midst of the chorus, Cocteau declaimed the choral text in the rapid impersonal tones of a person reading the news, wanting, he said, to capture the distinctive timbre of the Athenian megaphone mask.[45] One critic reported that the chorus initially suggested to him a scene of massacre, but as he gradually made out the distinctive expression and unique soul behind each choral mask, he became caught up in the illusion.[46] Seeming to emerge through the roof of a Doric temple, the chorus was at once part of a Sophoclean monument, frozen in time, and fully animated, reaching out to engage with the living Creon and Antigone. The juxtaposition of made-up faces and faces in relief placed the idea of the mask at the centre of this production. Susan Harris

[45] Cocteau (2003: 307, 327).   [46] Dorhoy 1924.

Smith in her study of masks in modern theatre argues that Cocteau used the mask convention in order to emphasise that man is subject to fate, helpless in the hands of the gods.[47] Clearly Cocteau did intend his 1922 *Antigone* to unwind like an accelerating machine, yet the spirit of rebellion made the mood anything but fatalist. The aliveness of the masked body was always in tension with the imprisonment of form. In a dynamic manner the mask mediated between death and life.

In a 1927 revival, Cocteau changed the mask convention, dressing the actors in black body-suits, and covering their heads with large plaster masks. The face was covered by a mesh on which ethereal features were embroidered, allowing the features of the actor to be glimpsed behind. The aesthetic elegance of his 1922 production yielded to a 'sordid but regal carnival' in which the performers were like a 'family of insects'. The change may reflect the loss of the beautiful man he loved, or a drug-inspired fascination with double vision, but is also symptomatic of ongoing modernist rebellion, since too many conservatives had praised his production for being true to the spirit of the classical past. Cocteau's work with Greek masks culminated in his 1952 production of Stravinski's *Oedipus Rex*. Responding to a critique of his earlier head-masks by Picasso, he sought to avoid creating dwarves with large heads, wanting the audience to be in no doubt that these were actors sporting strange false heads.[48] The fusion of actor and mask had given way to a clear disjunction.

In the USA, Eugene O'Neill wrote *The Great God Brown* as a kind of Nietzschean parable, and was seen attending rehearsals with a copy of *The Birth of Tragedy* stuffed into his pocket.[49] The play was first performed in January 1926 in Greenwich Village, mounted by Experimental Theatre Inc., a company managed by the 'triumvirate' of O'Neill, Kenneth MacGowan, and the expressionist director Robert Edmond Jones. Through use of the mask, the triumvirate sought to align themselves with the European modernist movement, and fight the dominant American mode of psychological realism.

In an 'author's foreword' which he never published, O'Neill stated: 'This play is not merely naturalistic or realistic. It is also an attempt to express the vast inarticulate before which these isms are, of necessity, dumb.' The theatre, he continued, should 'give us what the church no longer gives us – a meaning. In brief, it should return to the spirit of its Greek grandeur. And if we have no gods, or heroes to portray we have the subconscious the

---

[47] Smith (1984: 72–3).   [48] Cocteau (1956: 177).   [49] Alexander (1992: 242).

mother of all Gods and heroes. But for this realism is insufficient.'[50] He was unmoved when critics found the play confusing, having replied to one sceptical friend before the opening that

> there's enough in it to get over to unsophisticated audiences. In one sense *Brown* is a mystery play, only instead of dealing with crooks and police it's about the mystery of personality and life. I shouldn't be surprised if it interested people who won't bother too much over every shade of meaning, but follow it as they follow any story. They needn't understand with their minds, they can just watch and feel.[51]

Subsequent critics have repeated the accusation that the play is flawed because the use of masks is so confusing. Susan Harris Smith echoes the consensus when she writes that 'O'Neill mistakenly forsook language in favour of a device incapable of assuming complexity of expression', and accepts G. W. Gabriel's verdict that the play 'is ball-and-chained to this embarrassing trickery of masks'.[52] The irony here is that the play was intended to confuse and disorientate, in pursuit of its aspiration to be a Nietzschean mystery play. Reaching for the inarticulate, the play refuses a definitive decoding, and the discomfiture of intellectualising critics on the first night was a necessary part of the endeavour. Most subsequent critics have been mesmerised by biography, and emphasise how the two central characters echo O'Neill's relationship with a brilliant alcoholic brother, while overlooking the significance of a masked dramatic form harnessed to the pursuit of a philosophical ideal.

The play develops the relationship of Billy Brown, a self-made entrepreneur and demi-god of American materialism, with the artist Dion Anthony, who symbolises the conflicting principles of pagan Dionysos and a guilt-ridden Christian hermit: Dion[ysos] is yoked to Saint Anthony. Brown initially wears no mask because he is 'inwardly empty and resourceless', whilst Dion's 'spiritual, poetic, passionately supersensitive' face is forced into its opposite by a moulded classical mask, that of a mocking Pan.[53] Dion is a Nietzschean hero, forced into masking by his shame, which is to say the sensitivity and vulnerability of a self liable to disintegration. On one level of masking, which Erving Goffmann would analyse thirty years later in *The Presentation of Self in Everyday Life*, the mask simply represents a social front, and this was indeed how O'Neill first developed his mask concept.[54] However, O'Neill lamented that in performance this was the only aspect that

---

[50] O'Neill (1968: 29).   [51] Clark (1933: 146).   [52] Smith (1984: 134).
[53] O'Neill's 'explanation' in Clark (1933: 142–5); O'Neill (1995: 67).
[54] Goffmann 1956; Ffloyd (1981: 47).

he communicated, the 'defensive double-personality of people in their personal relationships – a thing I never would have needed masks to convey'.[55] On a more significant level, the mask moulds the face beneath and starts to possess the wearer. The mask changes the wearer, but in a process of dialectical interaction changes in its turn. In the course of writing the play, O'Neill developed a further level of meaning. When Dion dies, he bequeaths his identity to Brown through the vehicle of the mask. As MacGowan explained in a programme note, 'The skull or the mask of a dead man grips his soul, and whoever puts it on must be ready to have the soul enter his body'.[56] Like theatrical masks in *The Birth of Tragedy*, which are all covers for a single god, so O'Neill used masks in his play to suggest the breakdown of individuation as one character collapses into another. He originally wanted the great tragic actor John Barrymore to play Dion, and then take over Brown's role after Dion's death.[57] For this finale, O'Neill had wanted the mask to transmute into an object of stone, an apotheosis of the modern materialist god who opposes the creative principle embodied by Dionysos.[58] It was an ambitious project.

O'Neill's conception of the mask owed much to his collaborator Kenneth MacGowan, who in partnership with a Dutch stage designer published a documentary account of the mask in 1924. O'Neill had followed the course of their research.[59] The book addresses itself to a man looking at a mask drawn by Edward Gordon Craig and offers him photos of the 'ancestors' of that mask, implicitly providing a Nietzschean critique of Craig's aestheticism. MacGowan places the early tragic mask in the midst of an array of primitive masks, tracing them to an animist 'democracy' of men and spirits. MacGowan explains how a mask offers man 'a kind of release from his inhibited and bashful and circumscribed soul' and offers the example of how a contemporary 'black-face' American comedian becomes, by virtue of his crude make-up, a 'demoniac creature, privileged in his humor, insensate in his vitality'.[60] He emphasises the primitivism of the Greek mask, for if a man 'has the sensitive mind of a Greek, he will know that a human face is absurdly inappropriate to a god', and Dionysiac masks must have been made out of 'wood and leather, cloth and cork and paint'. MacGowan traces an evolutionary line from Iroquois, Brazilian, and Zuñi masks through the Greek world to the Noh where 'hard on the heels of the Greek tragedy, the mask finds itself at the highest point of perfection'. Though Greeks and Japanese

---

[55] Alexander (1992: 78).   [56] Bogard (1988: 267n).   [57] Alexander (1992: 241).
[58] Alexander (1992: 68, 75–6).   [59] Alexander (1992: 237).
[60] MacGowan and Rosse (1924: xii).

managed to turn ritual into drama, nowadays, MacGowan concludes, 'the mask must come upon the stage shorn of the religious spirit' for 'mystical religion has gone out of our life taking its symbols with it. The task of the artist of the theatre may be to seek out new symbols' which one may experience 'in one of the greatest of symbols, the ancient and mysterious mask'.[61] The book was a manifesto, and O'Neill rose to the challenge.

Though he had confidence in his script, the production process caused O'Neill much frustration. The masks, he lamented, 'were never right, and we had neither the time nor the money to experiment and get them right before we opened — the old story that prevents anything really fine from ever being done in the American theatre!'[62] The mask-maker had similar ideals to the rest of the team, writing in a 1924 programme that: 'The mask alone is consistently true, the sublimation of the attributes of the god — a face that human eyes can bear', but in reality he had other commitments, and the actors were cast too late. The actual masks were made of rubber and covered the whole face, flexible enough to allow movement of the lips.[63] The technology of rubber was in one sense necessary to the conception, allowing the mask to be fluid almost like flesh, and to borrow facial features from the performers. Yet it was at the same time a material designed for illusion, not of a substance in which the actors might expect to find the spirit of Dionysos embedded. The ceremony of taking the mask on and off, to which MacGowan's book had called attention, became awkward, and the mask-object could not function happily in scenes where it became a venerated icon. O'Neill was pleased with the way the actors' bodies came to life in a mask, contrasting this with his normal experience of bodies on stage which 'remain bored spectators that have been dragged off to the theatre when they would have much preferred a quiet evening in the upholstered chair at home'.[64] It is not clear, however, that this amounted to the 'totally new kind of acting' that O'Neill envisaged in experienced masked performers.[65]

When he adapted the *Oresteia* to create *Mourning Becomes Electra* (1931), O'Neill wrote the second draft for half-masks, hoping to catch 'the unrealistic truth wearing the mask of lying reality', but he rapidly abandoned the convention, which introduced a 'duality-of-character symbolism' — the simplistic dualism that he had worked so hard to complicate in *The Great God Brown*. Along with period costume, he decided that make-up would be sufficient to create the necessary mask-like effect — that of a death-mask

---

[61] MacGowan and Rosse (1924: 123, 125, 161).   [62] Alexander (1992: 78).
[63] Wainscott (1988: 190, 193).   [64] O'Neill (1961: 70).   [65] O'Neill (1961: 71).

'suddenly being torn open by passion'.[66] He also rejected physical masks because 'the Classical connotation was too insistent', and incompatible with his modern speech idiom.[67] Yet, in an article written a year after the production he expressed regret at this decision:

> I should like to see *Mourning Becomes Electra* done entirely with masks, now that I can view it solely as a psychological play, quite removed from the confusing preoccupations the Classical derivation of its plot once caused me. Masks would emphasize the drama of life and death impulses that drive characters on to their fates and put more in its proper secondary place, as a frame, the story of the New England family.[68]

Freud and Nietzsche had shown him that quasi-divine forces lurked in the subconscious, and there was a world beyond appearances. Jones, who designed *Mourning Becomes Electra*, had shown him a possible way forward with his puppet-based production of the Stravinski/Cocteau *Oedipus Rex* in the same year. Yet the social realism of *Mourning Becomes Electra*, set as it is before a neoclassical mansion evoking a Greek *skēnē*, was probably incompatible with any archetypal mask convention stripped of classicism.[69] In *The Great God Brown* O'Neill made deliberate play with the Greekness of the mask, which supported the doubling of actors and was bound up with Dionysiac cult. To find a new visual language capable of symbolising the universal unconscious lay beyond O'Neill's scope as a writer, and he began a slow retreat from the modernist ideal of a total theatre.

The label 'modernist' is not the most obvious one to apply to the 1927 *Prometheus*, performed in the context of a Delphic festival.[70] The production was financed and directed by the American heiress Eva Palmer-Sikelianos, in association with her husband, the Greek poet and visionary Anghelos Sikelianos. Along with industrialisation, the modern movement in art had largely passed Greece by, and the Sikelianos couple set store by the traditionalism of Greece, which gave access to 'the sources' of life. They wanted their festival to tie people to the earth, of which Delphi was the symbolic centre, and to break down national divisions in pursuit of cosmic wholeness. The strand of modernism which linked people to machines, exemplified by the Bauhaus Theatre Group's *Triadic Ballet* where the body was subsumed by

---

[66] Bogard 1988.   [67] O'Neill (1961: 69).
[68] O'Neill (1961: 69) – originally published as 'Second Thoughts' in *The American Spectator*, December 1932.
[69] O'Neill envisaged the set itself as a classical mask disguising ugliness: Ffloyd (1981: 265).
[70] See Wiles (2000: 183–9).

geometric shapes,⁷¹ ran counter to their organic principles. Yet this was a modernist event in the sense that it looked to the future. Crucially, this was an event inspired by Nietzsche's *Birth of Tragedy*, which placed the chorus at the centre of tragedy.⁷² The breakdown of individuation was an ideal that the Sikelianos couple embraced with enthusiasm.

The choice of text relates to the privileged position of *Prometheus* in *The Birth of Tragedy*. Nietzsche contrasts Prometheus as the active masculine rebel of Aryan myth with Eve in the guilt-ridden Semitic account of the Fall of Man. Prometheus became in the 1920s the archetypal modernist hero, standing for creativity, the use of new technology, and the rejection of established religion. Nietzsche described Prometheus as 'a Dionysiac mask' because on the one hand he embodies Apolline intellect and a rational search for justice, but on the other commits an act of sacrilege on behalf of the human race, and assimilates himself with a Dionysiac force, as a wave is part of a tide.⁷³ The use of masks was inevitable in a production that sought to realise cosmic wholeness. Though masks were not used for the chorus of some thirty young women, who danced in the orchestra as worshippers of the god, ignoring the audience in order to concentrate on devotional dance, they were worn by the actors, who performed on a stage at the foot of an artificial mountain. The unmasked chorus represented and embodied not only initiates, but also the feminine side of the universal self that lies beneath every male life-mask.⁷⁴

In her autobiography written after her return to the USA, Eva set out her conception of classical theatre:

it was as if the Greeks had consciously raised barriers against all the usual theatrical tricks which are devised to turn personality to account . . . In the ancient theatre an actor could not smirk and look pretty, because, even without a mask, he never could be sure that anyone was looking at him. His only sure spectator was his own inner conscience, and what ever god he believed in. And it is significant that the acclamations of the audience, in the end, were for the play, and not for the actors.⁷⁵

In a Greek theatre it is impossible for actors to make eye contact with the full auditorium, which means that true unity between actors and audience can only be achieved through shared concentration on 'the Word'. Eva added that 'this psychological phenomenon of unity realized outside of themselves

---

⁷¹ See Arndt Wesemann's account in Fiedler and Feierabend (2000: 532ff.).
⁷² For Eva's reading of Nietzsche, see Palmer-Sikelianos (1993: 171–4). For Anghelos, see Sherrard 1956.
⁷³ Nietzsche (1993: 51).   ⁷⁴ Cf. Sherrard (1956: 162).   ⁷⁵ Palmer-Sikelianos (1993: 223).

was accentuated also by the use of the mask'.[76] She rejected technical explanations of the mask as a megaphone since 'the Greek-theatre is itself a loud-speaker'.[77] For Eva, the mask helped save Greek tragedy from the perils of modern American acting, focusing attention on the drama. Her husband, in an article published in 1926, went further, claiming that Aeschylus, as a native of Eleusis, took the convention of the mask from the Eleusinian Mysteries. The mask was 'still warm from the breath of the great Mystagogical Orgy' when Aeschylus, 'removed it one day from the narrow enclosure of the initiates into the midst of an entire people'. Anghelos explains that the Eleusinian ritual 'found an aid worthy of its purpose in the form of the mask, impassive and wholly saturated in the idea of Grandeur and Eternity'. The *prosōpopoiēsis* (masking or face-making) 'of the Gods or Heroes is plainly unachievable except through rigorous unifying and simplifying of the most representative and general expressions of an ephemeral individual – like the stamp of an ideogram, limitless in range and forceful in purpose'.[78] It was Eva's task to realise Anghelos' idealistic conceptions.

Though Eva studied Greek vases for her choreography, the masks used for the Sikelianos *Prometheus* were not heavily classicised, bearing no relation for example to the MAT *Prometheus* locked in eternal anguish. The music owed much to a Byzantine tradition which supported 'the Word' rather than overwhelming it like Wagnerian orchestral music, and the iconographic conception in the same vein assimilated *Prometheus* to a Christian Passion play, with Prometheus nailed to the mountain in cruciform position, and the mountain itself evoking Golgotha. Prometheus looked like a Christ figure, or a bearded orthodox priest, though in the conception of the play he also evoked Aeschylus himself, 'crucified' by ungrateful Athenians seduced by Socratic rationalism.[79] Hephaestus sported a red beard recalling Judas, and the trio of Hephaestus, Strength and Violence echo the three soldiers who nailed Christ to the cross in Christian tradition. There was a more overt classicism in the figure of Hermes, with a single curved Greek line joining nose to eyebrow; Hermes speaks on behalf of the Olympian gods, so an Apolline image was appropriate. Io, on the other hand, wore a horned mask obviously inspired by the Japanese Hannya mask, the tormented woman transformed to a demon (Plate 4.2). Since Io is destined to travel into Asia, where the roots of ancient Greek spirituality were understood to lie,[80] the cultural associations were appropriate. The flowing white hair of Oceanus evoked an Old Testament prophet, forewarning of doom.

[76] Palmer-Sikelianos (1993: 222–3).   [77] Palmer-Sikelianos (1993: 224).
[78] Sikelianos 1998. I am grateful to Yana Zarifi for a translation.   [79] Sherrard (1978: 90).
[80] Cf. Sherrard (1956: 132–3); Sherrard (1978: 84).

**Plate 4.2** Io. Delphi 1927.

The masks survive as beautifully crafted objects,[81] simplified and generalised in the way Anghelos sought, encouraging each actor to devise a distinctive code of movement. The mouths are relatively small, the eyes finely painted, with narrow slits beneath ensuring that the actor was locked in a world of self-communion. All the masks are asymmetrical in the cheekbones and mouth, creating a sense of facial mobility. The squared jaw and flattened nose of Io ensured that the mask created shadow and a sense of movement in this the most energetic and poignant of the characters, while bovine features legitimated the disproportionate scale of the masked head, without detracting from the beauty of the actress's animalesque movement.

---

[81] The masks are in the Theatre Museum, Athens. Photos in Sikelianos 1998. A film record was published by the Cinematic Service of the Greek Armed Forces in 1971.

**Plate 4.3** Prometheus. Delphi 1927.

For the classicised Hermes, the impression of a large head was corrected by the wearing of a helmet. Hephaestus was a grotesque, and made maximum use of his body in the crucifixion scene, while Strength and Violence wore raised clogs to restore proportion. One has to scrutinise the mask of Prometheus very carefully in order to be sure that it is a mask, testimony to the skill of the mask-maker. The masks testify to the power of illusion that is possible when masks are used in Greek theatre spaces under natural light (Plate 4.3).[82]

---

[82] Less than three weeks before the performance, *Le Journal des Hellènes* reproduced as the mask of Prometheus a mask later worn by Strength: *Eos* (1998) 137, 87; and the mask is missing from Sikelianos 1998. I am grateful to Pantelis Michelakis for scrutinising the film and extracting stills which confirm that a mask was finally used.

Set against the artificial mountain, the masks gave the performers an imposing presence they would otherwise have lacked. The costume designer Antonis Fokas, half a century later, recalled the performance and in particular:

> the entrance of Hephaestus and the two other allegorical figures of State and Violence. All three were wearing masks, but these were not masks that one would notice immediately. The way that these three personae of the tragedy entered the stage, their decisive and somehow unreal step, their intense colors in broad daylight made the surrounding silence even more imposing. It is difficult to analyse an impression that has deeply moved one. And I had to think about it after the performance in order to realize what an important role the masks had played in the ecstasy that we felt during the passage of these three poetical figures ... The masks had achieved their aim. They had kept reality at a distance.[83]

The success of the masks lay precisely in the fact that people did not notice them – only their effect. In the studio theatres of Montmartre or Greenwich village, the mask is perforce a self-conscious aesthetic device, a directorial statement. In an outdoor Greek theatre, in a daylight performance, the mask has a very different potential. The convention seems a more natural one in an environment where perceptible reality cannot be mirrored.

In the course of the 1930s the vogue for masks in artistic circles started to wane. Fascism and Stalinism were inimical to experimentation, and cast their shadow over the era. In order to suggest the tensions involved in the decline of modernism, I will focus on Jean-Paul Sartre's adaptation of the Electra story, *Les Mouches* ('the Flies'), staged by Charles Dullin in 1943 at the former Théâtre Sarah Bernhardt. Whilst Dullin was a committed modernist whose work was rooted in the aesthetic of the 1920s, Sartre spoke for the new age, more interested in moral commitment than formal innovation. His title was inspired by Chapter 12 of Nietzsche's *Thus Spake Zarathustra* with its central image of flies buzzing in the market-place, evoking a Nietzschean world where God is dead and the state a false idol.[84] The text alludes to Nietzsche in order to counter him.

Charles Dullin proclaimed in 1922 that 'a return to the mask is today the norm. It is forced upon us by the Ballets Russes, and by cinema. People had lost the way of it, and long imagined that the mask was not alive. But the mask *is* life, intense and concentrated life.' This life of the mask, he continued, stems not from itself but from the way it makes actors work the body. His trainees gained courage and confidence from the mask so

---

[83] Fotopoulos (1980: 158). Kratos is here translated as State not the familiar Strength.
[84] Sartre (2005: 1262–3); Louette (1996: 56–8).

that 'by hiding their face, they can reveal their personality more freely'.⁸⁵ I shall examine in the next chapter the training of Copeau which Dullin replicated. A mask, Dullin later observed, 'has a life of its own, not always that which the sculptor wanted to give it. There is often something that escapes the maker.' The student actor must therefore develop a relationship with the mysterious mask, making it his companion and confidant, not pounce on it like a carnival mask; that would be sacrilege 'for the mask has indeed a sacred character; it demands an audience of initiates'.⁸⁶ Dullin rejected antiquarianism and had a utopian vision of the mask's place in performance. 'People wanted to go back, to revive lost forms. Mistake. The use of the mask in modern theatre is not something to rediscover, but to be created in every play. It fosters a dramaturgy that has yet to find its poet.'⁸⁷ In broad terms his aim in theatre was to shake off the yoke of naturalism, to position the poet as the source of inspiration, and to restore the place of instinct.⁸⁸ He staged Cocteau's 1927 version of *Antigone*, but found few other occasions where the dramaturgy seemed to demand masks. *Les Mouches* was a notable exception. Masks became part of a modernist design concept that responded to the energy of Sartre's text, while compensating for its verbosity.

In his school for actors, Dullin employed Sartre alongside Jean-Louis Barrault to co-teach a course in performance – a remarkable collaboration of theorist and practitioner that owes much to the principles of Copeau. Together Sartre and Barrault explored, for example, the portrayal of fear, and the inadequacy of purely psychological methods for rendering emotion.⁸⁹ Barrault was to have staged *Les Mouches*, but they fell out over the leading actress. Sartre wrote the play for De Beauvoir's protégée, Olga Kosakiewics, pretty, but inexperienced, and Barrault refused, accusing Sartre of seeking the role for his mistress.⁹⁰ Whatever the truth of the accusation, Sartre wanted for Electra an ingénue who would resonate authenticity and naturalness, without any declamation or actorishness in her voice, and not a traditional actress 'in corsets'.⁹¹ This quality of truthfulness was central to his philosophical project. Dullin accepted that Olga had potential, and took the risk of staging the play in a large theatre that demanded spectacle, with a cast mainly drawn from his students.

---

⁸⁵ Brindejont-Offenbach 1922.   ⁸⁶ Dullin (1946: 122).
⁸⁷ Dullin (1946: 123).   ⁸⁸ Dullin (1946: 41).
⁸⁹ Document from the Dullin Archive exhibited at the exhibition on 'Sartre'. Bibliothèque Nationale, March–August 2005.
⁹⁰ Galster (1986: 51); Sartre (2005: 75); De Beauvoir (1981: 238).
⁹¹ Sartre (2005: 76); for an analysis of the voice, see Galster (1986: 140–1).

Sartre described his play not as a tragedy of fate but as a 'tragédie de la liberté'.[92] Orestes' decision to kill Aegisthus and then his mother is the archetypal act of free existential choice, an act unsupported by any code of social or religious values, so the chooser must take absolute responsibility. There was an analogy in Sartre's mind, largely imperceptible to contemporary spectators, with the act of the resistance hero who kills Germans at the cost of condemning French hostages to execution in reprisal.[93] Orestes resolutely makes his choice, while Electra succumbs to guilt, absorbing herself back into an Argive community which replicated the moral paralysis of the French majority under the Pétain regime. Dullin's philosophy of the mask, identifying the mask as a quasi-sacred tool used for revealing personality, was incompatible with Sartre's insistence that persons have no essence. Dullin's idea that the actor could be possessed by a character was alien to Sartre's conception of moral autonomy.

Sartre knew that Dullin had long wanted to mount a modern tragedy, and would later explain the director's conception in Nietzschean terms:

He had a complex understanding of Greek tragedy: savage and unrestrained violence was to be rendered with thorough classical rigour. He managed to bend *Les Mouches* to this double necessity. He wanted to harness Dionysiac forces and organize them, expressing them through a free and packed deployment of Apolline imagery.[94]

The set was cubistic, and dominated for much of the play by a statue of Zeus that might have been sculpted by Picasso. The eponymous flies were the Erinyes, feminine figures with black wings and piercing eyes – a visual echo of the old women who greet Orestes in the first scene. The High Priest, pictured in the photo raising the dead, had a Chinese aspect (Plate 4.4). The ordinary soldiers and citizens of Argos wore bold masks inspired by abstract art, fixing them as reified beings incapable of authentic action living in the existential state of '*en soi*'. A hostile right-wing critic would condemn this 'implausible cubist and Dadaist bric-a-brac, an avant-garde long since become rear-guard'.[95] Dullin, in the role of Jupiter, wore heavy make-up (as he had in the role of Cocteau's Creon), but the make-up was cleared around the eyes and lips to create for this trickster god the impression of a mask. Clytaemnestra wore heavy make-up to suggest, in more social realist

---

[92] Preface to the 1943 edition.
[93] As Sartre maintained at the Liberation in 1944: Sartre (1992: 269). Cf. Sartre (2005: 1269).
[94] In a 1966 tribute to Dullin: Sartre (1992: 271).
[95] Alain Laubreaux in *Le Petit Parisien*, 5 June 1943. Cf. Galster (1986: 135). The masks are conserved in the Bibliothèque Nationale, and I inspected four in the 'Sartre' exhibition of 2005. Photos in Surel-Tupin 1974.

Plate 4.4 *Les Mouches* 1943. Raising of the dead.

terms, a woman hiding from guilt with no inner animation. Electra and Orestes sported bare faces on which nuances of expression could be read. Faces in this production belonged to characters who exist *pour soi*, capable of choosing *for themselves*.

In Sartre's neo-Cartesian conception of the human being, the self defined by its moral choices is separable from the biological human being. In the final act of the play, set in the temple of Apollo, Jupiter uncovers an image of the cosmos, and bids Orestes 'return to nature, unnatured son!' – but

Orestes holds firm: 'Freedom melted onto me and transformed me, nature leapt back... Beyond nature, anti nature, no excuses, no other recourse but myself.'[96] This conception of an autonomous self that transcends biology and environment is at odds with the holistic thinking of practitioners like Jacques Copeau or Eva Sikelianos. Sartre's text insists again and again on the semiotic force of the eyes, which provide a unique key to the *moi*, the self hidden within. Electra has eyes full of fire but acquires the dead eyes of her mother when she repents. She imagines Orestes will have red eyes of anger, but his eyes are in fact shining. The Argives have read in Aegisthus' eyes that he lacked the courage of his convictions. This privileging of eyes and face belongs not to modernism but to the neoclassical tradition of Racine, or of Giraudoux whose *Electre* was revived two months before *Les Mouches*. By masking the minor characters, Dullin in fact highlighted the special function of the face as an index of self-realisation. The blank eyes of Jupiter's statue and the prominent eyes of the masks helped emphasise verbal references to the protagonists' eyes. The gaze is a preoccupation of Sartre's philosophy, which asserts that people can become fixed in an immovable identity by the gaze of the other. Electra in the play tries to keep herself safe in the gaze of Orestes, then becomes transfixed by the gaze of Aegsthus' corpse. Dullin's masks in this respect served Sartre's purpose well, emphasising the controlling power of the eyes in human relationships.

Critics at the time wondered if the philosophy had not been submerged by the production.[97] Sartre's attitude to Dullin's production was ambivalent. On the one hand there was respect, for Dullin had taken a risk in supporting him, and had taught him much about theatre, summed up in the maxim 'never play the words, play the situation'.[98] And yet, as he looked back on *Les Mouches* thirty years later, he remarked: 'The work of the director was so crucial that I never truly felt myself to be there on stage. It was something that started from what I had written, but it was not what I had written. I never had that feeling afterwards, with other plays...'[99] In his subsequent and most successful plays, like *Huis clos* or *Les Mains sales*, he tended to use intimate domestic settings, where people could talk about their moral dilemmas, and express them through the face. Modern theatre, he declared in 1946, 'must be contemporary. I would not write again a play like *Les Mouches*.'[100]

In 1943 the budding novelist explained his decision to use the mode of Greek tragedy not in terms of censorship but of genre. 'The condensed

---

[96] Sartre (2005: 64–5). [97] Galster (1986: 142).
[98] Tribute to Dullin in 1966: Sartre (1992: 272).
[99] De Beauvoir (1981: 238–9). [100] Sartre (2005: 1263).

nature of theatre required a dramatic situation of peculiar intensity. Had I invented my hero, he would have aroused horror, condemning him to a cruel misunderstanding – hence my recourse to a character who, in theatrical terms, was already situated.'[101] Existentialism meant the prioritisation of *situation* and *existence* over any *essence* of character or a priori definition of *human nature*. Though this equates with Aristotle's position in the *Poetics*, what Sartre failed to do was dramatise the actual turning point of the plot, the *proairesis* when Orestes *chooses* to kill his mother and determines who he is. Sartre offered no equivalent to the Aeschylean scene where Pylades breaks silence and doubt is actively overcome. Dullin responded to this dramaturgical weakness by conjuring up an expressionist nightmare, into which Electra finds herself sucked. Sartre had created a feminised Orestes with pale skin and a girlish face, the opposite of his father, and Dullin pointed up the androgyny, giving his hero long hair, decorative buskins, and bare knees beneath a short tunic. When Orestes led the chorus of Erinyes away at the end of the play, he thus became a version of Dionysos leading out his wild chorus of maenads after a ritual purging of the city. For Nietzsche, Dionysos was of course the universal face behind the mask. Through the person of Orestes, the figure strong enough to wear no mask, Dullin represented on stage the liberating force of an impassive, amoral god. An enthusiastic German review of the production in the *Pariser Zeitung* concluded that Orestes acted not for democracy but for the glory of the Übermensch, and saw the play as 'Nietzsche dramatised'.[102] Sartre's philosophical thought was finally turned upon its head by the production.

In theatrical terms, Dullin's instincts were sound: raw young actors left to vocalise philosophy in a 1,250-seat theatre would have stood no chance of success. In political terms, the question is an open one. Dullin challenged the idealist picture of an ordered Aryan classical world beloved by fascism, his primitivist masks paid tribute to African art, and he reasserted aesthetic values dismissed as decadent and effeminate by right-wing critics. These modernist traits added up to an oppositional statement, as forceful in its own way as the new Sartrian philosophy of personal liberation.[103] Yet the philosophical and theatrical tide was turning in Sartre's direction. While the First World War left an aftermath of moral confusion, the Second World War left a clear-cut sense of good and evil, against which a theatre of moral commitment could define itself. In the light of Goebbels' success in harnessing mass emotion, surrender to the forces of Dionysos was no longer admissible as an aesthetic goal. Rather, as Sartre urged, people now had to accept the

---

[101] Sartre (1992: 269).   [102] Sartre (2005: 1287).   [103] See Galster (1986: 135ff.).

loneliness of their selfhoods, and take responsibility for his own destinies. Domestic settings were the natural means to render such isolated selfhoods. Mask theatre, with its transgression of the boundaries that normally define individuation, had no obvious place in this new world.

Ezra Pound was a renegade with his feet in the old world when he published his *Women of Trachis* in 1956, which we may see as a final fling of the modernist impulse. He likened the play to a 'God-dance', hoping that his version of Sophocles might be performed by the same Japanese dancer who had animated Yeats' plays.[104] Pound's protagonist, Herakles Zeuson, is a Nietzschean Übermensch who, like the *shite* in a Noh play, changes his mask at the climax of the action. The hero strips off the 'mask of agony' that has been fixed on his face for most of the play to reveal a made-up face signifying solar serenity, an image which recalls how Nietzsche's Dionysos was hidden beneath the mask of tragedy. Revealed as the principle of 'solar vitality' Herakles urges his son to:

put some cement in your face,
Reinforced concrete, make a cheerful finish
Even if you don't want to.[105]

Through the modernist image of concrete Pound communicates his distaste for the facial representation of suffering. Pound's dramaturgy proved as unpalatable in the 1950s as his fascist politics, and his masked drama was performed only through the medium of radio. The obsession of pre-war artists with the mask was no longer compatible with a post-war mentality that preferred a theatre of moral seriousness and formal orthodoxy.

The 1960s yielded a culture inimical to the mask, with the emphasis placed on self-revelation and the aspiration to 'let it all hang out'. There was a celebration of nudity in the theatre, the antithesis of the mask principle, exemplified most obviously by Schechner's *Dionysus in 69*.[106] The decision of Living Theatre to play *Antigone* in the jeans and sweat-shirts of everyday living represents the same ideal: the actor needed to display his or her authentic self to the audience, if genuine communication in an alienated bourgeois world was to take place.[107] Grotowski, another emblematic figure of the 1960s, trained his actors to create organic masks using the musculature of their faces, but he left their bodies exposed, interpreting the classic text as 'a sort of scalpel enabling us to open ourselves'.[108] By the 1990s,

---

[104] On Pound's collaboration with Yeats see Harrop and Wiles (forthcoming).
[105] Pound (1956: 23, 24, 59, 67, 70).   [106] See Zeitlin 2004.
[107] See Jacquot (1970: 217–43).   [108] Grotowski (1969: 69, 57).

however, the idea that authentic self-revelation was possible had vanished. The new politics of gender and multi-culturalism sapped the confidence of radicalised white males that they knew deep inside who they actually were. Bodies were back on the agenda. In this climate there was space for the Greek mask to reappear.

In *Les Atrides* (1990–3) Ariane Mnouchkine staged the *Oresteia*, prefaced by the *Iphigeneia in Aulis*, with the help of eastern-style make-up masks and costumes. For her company, the Théâtre du Soleil, the mask was the '*discipline de base*', the basis of actor training.[109] The production was rooted in rhythm, its tempo controlled throughout by Jean-Jacques Lemêtre on multiple instruments, and the dancing chorus had a dominant role. Mnouchkine's perception that Greek tragedy was rooted less in text than in the spirit of music drew her back inevitably to Nietzsche, who lent support to the idea that the actor's own body has to be invested in the cruelty which Greek tragedy represents:

> If one stages [Greek tragedy] while censoring oneself, entirely repressing one's own drives, then I think the essence of the tragic is lost. The person who articulated this best was Nietzsche ... In terms of the central question, 'What is it to perform a Greek tragedy?', what is essential lies in the relationship between Apollo and Dionysos, and this philosopher sitting at his desk, without any physical relationship to the theatre, went straight for it. It is all there. Greek tragedy attained its apogee in the balance between Apollo and Dionysos, where Dionysos weighs with greater weight than Apollo, yet without abolishing him.[110]

In her production, the mask as Apolline form gave necessary artistic shape to a violent Dionysian content.

Mnouchkine's actors made themselves up with red lips and bold black lines around the eyes alluding to Kathakali, over a white pancake base which alluded to Kabuki and the European white-face clown tradition. The eyes and mouth amplified basic emotions, while the white base generated chorality. An advantage of make-up was that, while creating uniformity and eliminating psychology, it left individual actors recognisable as they doubled from one role to the next in strategic ways. When the player of Agamemnon became Orestes, the face became more obviously human, and the pancake was largely wiped off in the *Eumenides* as the four-part play emerged into a fictional present. Mnouchkine could be accused of manipulating the mask convention when she allowed Clytaemnestra's eyes to be less heavily lined, so the audience would immediately find the character more

---

[109] Williams (1999: 193).    [110] Williams (1999: 194) from an interview in 1990.

sympathetic.[111] The white pancake base did not cover the whole face as in kabuki, but was a defined imposition on the front of the face in the manner of a Noh mask, setting up a tension between the performer and the role, an Apolline cover for the biological energies of the actor. Upon arrival the audience glimpsed the actors making themselves up, becoming witnesses to a ritual of metamorphosis. A further dimension was provided by subterranean sculptures in the forecourt, monumental replicas of the performers evoking an archaeological past which the actors were charged to reanimate.[112]

Like Nietzsche, Mnouchkine in her understanding of the mask combines a notion of critical distance with a notion of inner transformation. As she wrote in 1982: 'I believe theatre is a to-and-fro between what exists in our depths, our most unknown, and its projection, its maximum exteriorization to the audience. The mask demands exactly this interiorization and maximum exteriorization.'[113] Mnouchkine is postmodern in her stylistic eclecticism, and her recognition that the past is a lost world which can only be cited, not recovered, but is at the same time drawn by feminism to insist that rational thought cannot be separated from emotion. Cultural trends are hard to identify when one is too close to them. I believe, however, that Mnouchkine's reaffirmation of Nietzsche marks a swing in the cultural pendulum. Following Sartre's emphasis on acts of individual free will, and postmodernism's separation of language from body, Mnouchkine's work is symptomatic of the desire to restore a mind-body connection. For this purpose, the mask was a necessary tool.

[111] See Salter (1993: 71) – a discussion with the actors; photos by Michèle Laurent in Théâtre du Soleil 1992; Williams (1999: 199); Bryant-Bertail (1994: 14).
[112] Lallias and Arnault (1992: 22). The statues were not brought over for the UK performance.
[113] Aslan and Bablet (1985: 233).

# 5 | Physical theatre and mask in the twentieth century

Paris through the twentieth century has been the crucible of experimentation in modern mask work, and Mnouchkine, whilst acknowledging the philosophical tradition, belongs squarely within a French tradition of performance practice. The importance of Paris for the development of masked acting stems largely from the influence of one man, Jacques Copeau. Peter Hall's enthusiasm for the Greek mask stems from workshops conducted in Stratford by Copeau's nephew, Michel Saint-Denis;[1] Jacques Lecoq drew his main inspiration from Jean Dasté, Copeau's son-in-law;[2] Etienne Decroux was another famous pupil, and Dullin an associate. It is through programmes of training and not through books or exposure to performances that modes of practice are transmitted. Indeed I should not be writing this book now if I had not been exposed to French-trained mask teachers in my early twenties.

My focus in Chapter 4 was upon writers who found in the ancient mask a means of articulating their modernist view of humanity. In this chapter my concern will be with the twentieth-century actor, who has kept returning to the mask as a means of engaging mind with body, driven less by politics or philosophy than by the simple aim of achieving a quality of presence in the here-and-now of performance. I shall frame this chapter around two significant encounters: Copeau's meeting in 1915 with Edward Gordon Craig, which helped him forge his own understanding of the mask as a tool for actor training, and not an artistic vehicle for the scenographer; and then, forty years later, Roland Barthes' scathing review of Jean-Louis Barrault's *Oresteia*. Barrault was France's most celebrated body-based actor, and the mystical language through which he articulated his engagement with the body made no sense to a mind trained at the Sorbonne. Barthes argued for a politically engaged theatre free of mystification, and the argument between Barrault and Barthes remains of the greatest relevance today, when critics argue whether Greek tragedy was essentially a political form, or a religious and ritual form.

In September 1915, following the first season of his experimental Théâtre du Vieux Colombier, Copeau went to Florence, the seat of High Art, in

---

[1] See for example *The Times*, 2 November 1981; Hall (1993: 310).  [2] Lecoq (2000: 5).

search of a guru. He was intrigued by Edward Gordon Craig's controversial theory that the ideal actor was the Über-marionnette, the super-puppet, a term inspired by Nietzsche's *Übermensch*. Though charmed by Craig's character, Copeau found himself dismayed by his aestheticism and emotional detachment from the war devastating France. Copeau viewed cabinets filled with masks, mementoes of Irving, and puppets. He listened to Craig over supper explaining how the actor cannot be an artist, and how in particular 'you can do nothing artistic with the human face'.[3] In a later meeting Copeau describes him clasping his hands and sweeping them through his hair as he said: 'I don't believe in the actor – that's no doubt one of my weaknesses. *I see. You believe in the actor*.'[4] In fact Craig had no shortage of admiration for old-style actors like Irving, or the *commedia*-based Ermete Novelli, and sent Copeau to see the aged Italian in a poor play designed as his vehicle. The supporting actors seemed to Copeau faceless, because Novelli could manipulate his own face so well. To create each expression, Copeau recalled, Novelli 'models a new face, hardening his features, digging in this bit, projecting that bit, like a sculptor, consciously deploying every muscle. What one sees is a sequence of masks.'[5] While appreciating the technique, Copeau was unimpressed by a star system that fostered mere virtuosity. He was looking for a deeper level of communication in art, and wondered how he might contemplate a Fra Angelico not with a merely aesthetic eye but with a 'fervour so tenacious that it consumes its object'.[6] On the final day of the visit, having given a demonstration with his Javanese shadow puppets, Craig also produced a magnificent wooden puppet, and delighted in getting Copeau to operate its male organ.[7] An Egyptian Dionysos described by Herodotus was of just this kind, and Craig may have been pointing Copeau to the origins of theatre.[8]

Craig's theory of the super-puppet owed much to German idealism and Kleist's famous essay on the marionette theatre, and nothing to Russian constructivists with their celebration of the machine.[9] In an essay of 1910 he explained the link between his aesthetic theory and the primitive mask:

And then the mask, that paramount means of dramatic expression, without which acting was bound to degenerate. Used by savages when making war at a time when war was looked upon as an art; used by the ancients in their ceremonies when faces were held to be too weak, too slight, an element; used by those artists of the theatre,

---

[3] Copeau (1991: 716–19).
[4] Copeau (1991: 734). Copeau quotes the last two sentences in English.
[5] Copeau (1991: 748–9).   [6] Copeau (1991: 741).   [7] Copeau (1991: 750).
[8] Herodotus ii.48.   [9] Taxidou (1998: 166–72).

Aeschylus, Sophocles and Euripides . . . Human expression is for the most part worthless, and the study of my art tells me that it is better, provided it is not dull, that instead of six hundred expressions, but six expressions shall appear upon the faces of the performer.[10]

As a modernist concerned with the future, he had no truck with a revivalist desire that 'masks, sham-Greek in idea and modern in their quality, should be brought into the theatre, appealing only to the curious by creating a subject for small talk. No! The mask must only return to the stage to restore expression – the visible expression of the mind – and must be a creation, not a copy.'[11] The problem in practice was that Craig had no means of moving from puppets, sketches and masks in glass cabinets to actual masked performances. Copeau urged Craig to reactivate his school, the Arena Goldoni, which had been stripped of students by the war, but when Craig showed little interest in pedagogy, Copeau only gained a stronger sense of his own vocation – to create a theatre of the future through the training of actors.[12] Craig's understanding of the actor as puppet sat comfortably with Nietzsche's view of the tragic actor, but left Nietzsche's dithyrambic chorus out of account. Copeau was committed to the choral and collective aspect of theatre, and to the ideal of communion between actor and character, actor and spectator, something he held more important than Craig's abstract quest for beauty. He sought a theatre that was both religious and popular. As he sat in Florence leafing through copies of Craig's mouthpiece *The Mask*, however, he noted down one text with approval: 'I ask you: can all this be possible when you are not acquainted with the principles of Greek theatre? . . . If we could only be content to begin at the beginning.'[13]

After a sojourn in America, Copeau reopened the Théâtre du Vieux Colombier in Paris at the start of 1920, and with it an embryonic school. Alongside his stage stripped of ornament, he wanted actors stripped of affectation. In November 1921 he launched his training programme in earnest and decided that Greek theatre should be the focus of the work. Like Craig, he was not interested in revival, but in first principles. He saw Greek theatre as a model because it was a 'religious and popular theatre summoned to link men together and make them communicate'. In a nihilistic age devoid of principles, he saw Greek theatre as 'the most potent remedy against the ills we suffer from'. Art in France 'faltered the day it lost sight of its Graeco-Roman origins'. Copeau admired Attic art as the height of civilisation on account of its hatred of false ornament, its dislike of exaggeration, its natural

---

[10] Craig (1983: 20).   [11] Craig (1983: 23).
[12] Copeau (1991: 738).   [13] Copeau (2000: 55).

purity.[14] Though his belief in 'le pur naturel' seems a far cry from Nietzsche, he was entirely at one with Nietzsche in the premise that Greek tragedy was rooted in the spirit of music. In 1923 he cited with approval Nietzsche's idea that one can live and act through bodies other than one's own.[15]

In January 1922 Copeau began his course of lectures with one on the Dionysia and a second on the Eleusinian Mysteries, establishing the religious basis of Greek drama, and moving on to a technical analysis of choral lyric, which he interpreted as a popular celebration of gods and heroes. At this point he began to theorise the process of inhabiting other bodies and other souls. He identified a mystical 'transport' or emotional transformation in the actor who sought to become a god or a hero, while the common crowd reached out towards the actor who was their representative. By late February he had arrived at the mask, which he related to the actor's 'feeling of unworthiness vis-à-vis the hero or god who was represented'. Since the actor had to be instantly recognisable as a new character when he changed role, the hair and features were largely symbolic. After two weeks on the mimetic basis of Greek dance, Copeau returned again to the theme that Greek theatre was instantly comprehensible to the masses, with the author's text simply an extra, a finishing off. The mask demanded more discussion:

The first to wear the mask were the priests of Dionysos, to celebrate religious ceremonies. The mask is born from a feeling of shame, a need to hide. The first masks were made of canvas and not painted – they were white . . . The characters wore the mask of their role-type [*emploi*]. Variety in the appearance of tragic characters was restricted. The sobriety of means, the austerity, the few facilities they allowed themselves contribute much to the greatness of their art.[16]

What Copeau envisaged in the fifth century was essentially a neutral mask, with a few distinguishing elements, religious in function but not hieratic in its visual form. A later essay evokes the colossal scale of the Greek actor, standing on the minimal bare stage that Copeau loved so much, while the chorus dancing in the orchestra expresses the collective feelings of the people.[17]

In the following year Copeau passed on to broader theoretical principles, and we have only some notes taken by his daughter Marie-Hélène, known as 'Maïène'. To understand the living tradition we are part of, comments Maïène, one must possess the timeless laws of theatre rooted in the ancients. The training of contemporary French actors has for centuries been centred on language, whereas drama should be a 'spectacle of the soul', which is

---

[14] Copeau (2000: 286–8); Copeau (1990: 40).   [15] Copeau (1955: 37).
[16] Copeau (2000: 289–94).   [17] *Le Théâtre populaire* (1941) in Copeau (1990: 178).

why, in antiquity, so much emphasis was placed upon song and dance. In Copeau's course of training it was assumed that 'music' should be the basis, but the term music should embrace, as in Greece, both 'la culture musicale et la culture physique'.[18] Although this sounds like a manifesto for 'physical theatre', Copeau did not ignore text, but employed a teacher who would read the Greek to his students and translate before them so they could sense the poetic force of the text.[19] Ancient hymns from Delphi were committed to heart.[20] Copeau himself gave a public reading of *Antigone* in the 1922/3 season, which he followed next year with a repertory of seven Greek plays.[21] One of these was the *Persians*, which he would perform again in Brussels in January 1940, linking the suffering of the Belgian people to the chorus, and the excesses of the doomed protagonists to Hitler.[22] Copeau was famed for the power of these readings, where he sat at table, or in an armchair with his back to the light, using only voice and face. One listener compared the interplay of his different voices to a string quartet.[23] Copeau's musical sensitivity to text and his commitment to corporeality were, unfortunately, never to be reconciled in the full-scale performance of a Greek tragedy.

While Copeau's historical and theoretical course of lectures on Greek drama was unfolding, practical experimentation was taking place alongside. A visitor in 1922 commented on the close relationship between historical and practical study in the School, even though direct work on a text was taboo.[24] To get back to the origins of theatre was for Copeau like getting back to the naturalness of childhood before the posturing of adolescence.[25] Through the first half of 1922, Louis Jouvet oversaw a mask and improvisation workshop with six teenage students, and it was here that a new method of actor training evolved, based on mask and improvisation. The same quality of sincerity uncontaminated by theatrical tradition, which Stanislavski sought through 'emotion memory', Copeau sought through the mask. Where Stanislavski's reference point tended to be Chekhov, Copeau's was Molière, and experiments in the *commedia* style had shown him how alive the masked face could be.[26] Copeau shielded his teenage students from professional theatre, and regarded them as a *tabula rasa* for the creation of a better future. It was a logical principle to start by making a *tabula rasa* of the face. Jean Dasté explains Copeau's aim as being to 'help us rediscover spontaneity, the ability to invent and transform ourselves, to be children.

---

[18] Copeau (2000: 295–7).   [19] Copeau (2000: 412).   [20] Copeau (2000: 334).
[21] Copeau (1993: 495).   [22] Copeau (1993: 505).
[23] Joseph Samson cited in Leabhart (1995: 86–7); Mignon (1993: 74–6); cf. Copeau (2000: 346–7).
[24] Bidou in Copeau (2000: 325).   [25] Copeau (2000: 366).
[26] Doisy (1954: 118); Leigh (1979: 12, 22).

When your face is masked and hidden, you feel less shy, you feel more free, you risk more, and lack of sincerity is instantly detected.'[27]

The evolution of the work is summarised by another pupil, Jean Dorcy:

This instrument, the mask, had to be discovered. To begin with, we felt our way. First we covered the face with a handkerchief. Then, linen was followed by cardboard, raffia, etc.; in short, any malleable material. Finally, aided by our sculpture teacher Albert Marque, we found a solid material together with modifications that gave form to this new instrument. Without Albert Marque we should have carried on making 'small and pretty'. A good mask must be neutral: its expression is dependent on your movements.[28]

Maiène details seven different techniques of mask-making used in the initial workshops, and explains that the early masks made the forehead too small, the eyes too close, and placed the mask next to the skin, which made them sweaty and encumbered the voice; only in 1924 were the main technical problems overcome.[29] It was an important principle in Copeau's holistic vision that students should make their own masks. As Dasté explains, 'by making the mask oneself, one has time to try out, to modify, to remake the mask, until it becomes incorporated in us'.[30] The presentations in July 1922 were dominated by demonic masks of different kinds, including 'keres', Greek spirits of the dead hovering about a corpse like Erinyes, inspired by Copeau's lecture on the Anthesteria, and nightmare figures with raffia hair preyed upon 'Goldoni', a Venetian puppet inspired by the visit to Craig. There must have been a certain mismatch between graceful adolescent bodies in leotards and these grotesque masks.[31] However, an idealist conception of the mask also surfaced in an improvised playlet about Psyche, the product of charades in which the spectator had to guess the Greek myth.[32] Marque, who guided the students towards a workable neutrality, was the man famously dubbed in 1905 a 'Donatello among the *fauves*', because of his neoclassical contribution to an aggressively modernist exhibition.[33] The wild, fauvist strand in modernism was not for Copeau. Maiène describes the group learning that the mask needed, despite the inferiority of the available materials, not a complicated grimace but a 'large, beautiful and simple expression'.[34] During the third year of the academic course, tragedy gave way to Aristophanes and Plautus, but practical work on Greek music and

---

[27] Dasté (1977: 89).   [28] Dorcy (1958: 31); cf. Leigh (1979: 30–1).
[29] Copeau (2000: 274–5, 396).   [30] Dasté (1987: 169); cf. Leabhart (1995: 95).
[31] Copeau (2000: 328).   [32] Copeau (2000: 315–16).
[33] Louis Vauxcelles, cited in the programme for 'A la belle époque des Fauves': Musée Fournaise, Chatou, 2005.
[34] Copeau (2000: 300).

chorality continued. The climax came in February 1924, when the students performed a masked chorus of maenads in accompaniment to Copeau's public reading of the *Bacchae*.[35] The projected summation of the course, however, lay not in Greek tragedy, for which there were no available models, but in the full performance of a Noh play, a more accessible vehicle to unite poetry, chorality and the neutral mask.

Maiène's notebooks give us a detailed account of a learning process that would be shared by countless students in the future. She discovers how the mask lends strength and scale to every movement, and a strong sense of pacing. Any particular mask demands movements that need to be selected, simplified, and 'purified' to echo its *style*. The group learned how a mask displayed at different angles will present a whole variety of expressions. Maiène describes the core discipline of learning to see or hear in a mask: face the wall, put on the mask, and after a moment of stillness the eye or ear must lead, the head follows, then the body, and last the feet. The principle is to isolate the separate components of the action in order to simplify and clarify. More elaborate individual improvisations followed, which would be discussed by the group: fear generated by an imagined noise, crossing a river in spate, or sitting on an ants' nest. There is a natural affinity in this workshop process between masking and improvisation, for the mask imposes a set of rules and generates form, giving the sense of an impetus coming from outside the individual. Maiène also describes a minimalist but effective choral exercise. The six students sit cross-legged in a semi-circle with heads lowered until a sound makes all heads rise, drawing the body to follow, and then the heads drop back. The power of the exercise lies in its shifts of tempo, first two-time, then three-time. As she remarks, 'a group exercise with masks, well coordinated and controlled, whatever it may be, is always beautiful'.[36] Such exercises prepared the students to improvise a tragic masked chorus representing bereaved fisher-folk, or women on a battlefield.[37] The ideal of chorality underlay Copeau's whole programme.[38]

For participants in these workshops, the experience of wearing the mask was powerful and diverse. Maiène writes quite analytically in her private notes about how the mask creates 'a kind of self-awareness and self-command', and the technical need to make emotions more 'legible'.[39] Doisy cites ancient tragedy as proof that the mask has its own style and sublime language.[40] Dorcy offers more sense of the psychological experience. The

---

[35] Copeau (2000: 345, 400).   [36] Copeau (2000: 305).   [37] Leigh (1979: 45).
[38] Copeau (2000: 415); cf. Doisy (1954: 114).   [39] Copeau (2000: 300).
[40] Doisy (1954: 118).

actor who puts on a mask 'isolates himself from the external world. The darkness to which he subjects himself will first let him throw off all that encumbers him. Then, by an effort of concentration, to attain emptiness. From that moment on, he will be able to live again and act, but this time dramatically.' This acting must take place 'according to the law of the mask, namely *grosso modo*: to create and submit oneself to the rhythm imposed by the theme, sharpen the angles, rarefy and amplify movements'. He describes in great detail the ritual of putting on the mask: controlling the breathing, closing the eyes, and clearing the mind of thought. If the process works, the actor can then be 'possessed by characters, objects, thoughts; he is able to act dramatically'.[41] Dasté takes mysticism further, describing how he used to close or half-close his eyes when putting on a mask in order to let himself be 'inhabited by something that was not my usual self; as if a double was living in my place: I needed different gestures, different poses to express what I felt. I wasn't trying to perform, but to be.' The mask, he continues, 'made me discover a world that we have inside us, an unknown world, forces that let us communicate with the universe'. He also emphasises the ethical dimension in Copeau's mask work, teaching sincerity since in a mask one cannot deceive. When the actor was not genuinely carried away by an inner force, when he 'wasn't there', this was always clear to the group.[42] He summed up in his old age what had drawn him to Copeau's School: a 'return to the joy of childhood and the sense of the sacred'.[43]

Copeau's best attempt to theorise his practice can be found in his 1928 preface to Diderot's *Paradoxe sur le comédien*. Diderot had been much impressed by Garrick's party-piece, a private demonstration of how he could project his head through a curtain and create a series of facial masks with absolute control, and he developed on this basis a rationalistic view of the actor compatible with the thinking of the Enlightenment. For Diderot the actor should be in absolute control of his or her art, while surrender to real emotion only breeds mediocrity on the stage. Copeau responded that Garrick was demonstrating a technical mask exercise of the kind he used with his pupils; in full performance the good actor must make play with his immortal soul.[44] Unhappy recollections of Novelli must still have been in his mind. Copeau arrives at his own paradox, that the actor's body is his material, so he must at once *act* and *be* what he acts, at once natural man and marionette. Copeau rejects Craig's Cartesian dualism when he attacks those who 'resolve the problem by separating the spirit from the machine and,

---

[41] Dorcy (1958: 30–1, 145–6).   [42] Dasté (1987: 88–9).
[43] Copeau (2000: 405).   [44] Copeau (1955: 24, 18).

rejecting the actor, prefer the marionette'.⁴⁵ The actor does not get under the skin of the character (*personnage*); the character comes to him. It is not enough to see, understand and possess the character; you must be possessed by it. And the relationship of actor to character is symbolised by the mask:

From this cardboard object he takes the reality of his character. He is commanded by it, and obeys it irresistibly. Barely has he donned the mask, than he feels flowing into him an existence that he was empty of, that he never even suspected. It is not just his face that is changed, it is his whole person, the very nature of his reflexes, with ready-formed feelings that he could neither experience nor falsify with an uncovered face. If he is a dancer, the whole style of his dance, if he is an actor, his actual vocal intonation will be dictated to him by his mask – in Latin *persona* – which is to say a *personnage*, lifeless until he weds with it, a newcomer from outside which takes hold of him and replaces him.⁴⁶

Though Copeau turned to the Greeks in order to get beneath the superficiality of Parisian theatre and rediscover the sources of his art, his engagement with Greece remained on the level of pedagogy. With his *Oresteia* of 1955, Jean-Louis Barrault took over where Copeau left off. As a student of Dullin and close collaborator with Maïène, he worked in the same body-based tradition. He was not a minimalist like Copeau, however, and inspired by the Artaudian ideal of 'total theatre', he took the risk of staging the great Aeschylean trilogy. An essay by Jean Gillibert, published in Barrault's journal in 1955, explains how Copeau engaged with Greek theatre only as a man of letters, and thought, mistakenly, that he could separate the form of Greek tragedy from its content. Copeau's background lay in a French neoclassical tradition which preferred to adapt Greek tragedy rather than translate it.⁴⁷ Mounet-Sully's landmark *Oedipus* at the start of the twentieth century was an inimitable *tour de force*, and there had been no French equivalent to Gilbert Murray, who popularised the texts of Euripides on the English stage. Barrault's production was thus a landmark attempt to reclaim the Greek original for the modern professional stage. His production was greeted with rapture when it opened in Bordeaux, but in Paris there were reservations, and then Barthes' devastating review; the 1962 revival at the Odéon proved something of a flop.⁴⁸ From the perspective of the twenty-first century it is hard to make qualitative judgements. My concern will be to unpick Barrault's thinking, which can be seen as a throwback to Nietzschean modernism, but in other ways anticipates the interculturalism, stylistic eclecticism and holistic philosophies of the twenty-first century.

---

⁴⁵ Copeau (1955: 19).    ⁴⁶ Copeau (1955: 26).
⁴⁷ Gillibert (1955: 90–1).    ⁴⁸ Lallias and Arnault (1992: 15).

Barrault's production of the *Rape of Lucrece* in 1932, with Maïène as Lucrece, showed him how Copeau's method with mask and chorus could generate a modern form of classical tragedy.[49] He established his reputation in modernist circles in 1935 with *Autour d'une mère* at Dullin's studio theatre, doubling mother and son in a story taken from Faulkner. Barrault played the doomed mother in a mask made of cheesecloth with steel buttons for eyes and a huge mop of hair above, prompting Artaud to describe this as a perfect instance of 'holy theatre', with gestures so beautiful that they acquired symbolic meaning, so the actor became a shaman expelling evil.[50] Jean Dasté acted in the production, and Félix Labisse the designer went on to design the set for the *Oresteia*. In 1941 Barrault tackled Aeschylus' *Suppliants*, putting on the play in an athletics stadium. Maïène headed the chorus of fifty maidens, Parisian firemen in masks played the Egyptians, and young athletes played the heroic Argives. Unfortunately there was a loss of focus in the summer heat, since night-time performance was forbidden, the masks melted and musicians fainted. Given the Nazi cult of the heroic sporting body, Barrault's theatrical metaphor had a certain political ambivalence.[51] Playing the *Oresteia* in a proscenium theatre converted to a thrust stage, he had more control over events, but lost the sense of total theatre. His *Oresteia* was also influenced by the 'unforgettable' 1936 production of *Persians*, performed by students in the courtyard of the Sorbonne with mask, costume and choreography after the ancient manner.[52] This *Persians* was limited by its amateur performers, and by an audience that could not be construed as pilgrims to the Dionysia, but it showed Barrault that a formalist production could communicate a Greek play with its basis in chorus to a diverse modern audience. Gillibert praised the students because they had not been afraid to put Greek tragedy back on its pedestal.[53]

The key to the *Oresteia* was found in a visit to Brazil in 1950, when, accompanied by Labisse and Maïène, Barrault made the connection between the Greek chorus and dancing in trance. The three pivotal points of the trilogy would be Cassandra's possession by Apollo, inspired by 'white magic' at Rio, the *kommos* over Agamemnon's tomb inspired by *candomblé* at Bahia, and Clytaemnestra's 'black mass' celebrated with the Erinyes, inspired by diabolic *macumba* in the rain-forest. These experiences in Brazil seemed like a fissure in the ground that gave him access not to classical Athens, but to the primitive Athens of Aeschylus' youth that vanished with the Persian

---

[49] Mignon (1999: 26).   [50] Christout (1996: 189–90); Mignon (1999: 50).
[51] Barrault (1962: 93); Christout (1996: 192); Mignon (1999: 105–7).
[52] Barrault (1962: 94).   [53] Gillibert (1955: 92–3).

wars.⁵⁴ In the tradition of Copeau, Barrault's concern when developing the production lay not with argument and character but with choral form. He was at pains to beat out every sung line in its original metre, and then with the translator to find a French equivalence. The shape of the production was worked out in ternary rhythmic patterns. He and Maiène studied vase images in the Louvre, finding hints of wild trance-based dancing frozen into pictorial form.⁵⁵

As for content, long conversations with Sartre when they taught together in Dullin's studio had made it clear to Barrault that the subject of the trilogy was 'justice', but he interpreted justice in apolitical terms as the biological justice of life, a rebalancing of the equilibrium which located humans between animal and god. This was what mattered to the modern world. 'As for the civilising theme developed by the *Oresteia* – the transition from the order of the family, then the order of the clan, then order in the city, we leave to expert commentators the trouble of developing it.'⁵⁶ His rationale for tragedy was cathartic. Anguish is part of the human condition, a toxin excreted by the spirit, and the painful task of tragedy is to release it. This conception owed much to Artaud, who saw theatre as a lancing of the abscess in a plague-ridden world, and interpreted Greek tragedy in terms of the Eleusinian mysteries where a vision of terrifying evil was revealed.⁵⁷ And prior to Artaud there was of course Nietzsche, whom Barrault first read at the age of eighteen, and whose lifelong influence he would celebrate with his 1974 adaptation of *Thus Spake Zarathustra*, where Zarathustra became an alter ego of Dionysos.⁵⁸ The absorption of self into the Dionysian collective was the ideal that drove Barrault's *Oresteia*. Where Sartre famously proclaimed that Hell was other people, Barrault countered that other people are salvation.⁵⁹ His devotion to the mask was that of an unreconstructed modernist fighting individuation.

Following Strehler's successful revival of the *commedia dell'arte* in Italy, Barrault commissioned at great expense seventy-five leather masks from Amleto Sartori, and his design team painted the leather to match the authentic African fabrics used for Maiène's costumes (Plate 5.1). Embodiment in the here-and-now required authentic organic materials. The design resisted any influence of Greek statuary, for statues, Barrault commented, have an 'empty' gaze to preserve the spatial integrity of the figure, whilst masks require a 'visionary' gaze. Leading with the gaze was a foundational

---

⁵⁴ Barrault (1962: 94–101); Barrault (1974: 206).  ⁵⁵ Barrault (1962: 109–11).
⁵⁶ Barrault (1962: 94, 122–3); Barrault (1974: 123).
⁵⁷ Barrault (1962: 124–6); cf. Artaud (1970: 20–2); Barrault (1961: 8).
⁵⁸ Barrault (1975: 240, 234, 249).  ⁵⁹ Barrault (1975: 44).

exercise in Copeau's workshops, and we have observed this principle in fifth-century vases. Though Barrault comments that donning a mask affects an actor much more than the application of make-up,[60] the masks must have been comfortable enough to wear with their large eye apertures and unobstructed mouths. One reviewer in Bordeaux wrote that the masks created the faces of golden idols, another described Clytaemnestra as a Hindu goddess, a third applauded the way the 'hieratic' half-masks harmonised with the uncluttered line of the costumes.[61] In design terms at least, the masks reinforced Barrault's religious conception of the trilogy.

In his published account of the production Barrault develops the paradox that the mask is at once an inert object, and alive. 'Simultaneously the mask expresses a maximum of life and a maximum of death. The mask opens both on the visible and the invisible, on appearances and on the absolute. The mask brings one's deeper being to the surface, and by bringing to the surface deeper being, it allows instinct to be rediscovered.'[62] Opening up the taps was Barrault's metaphor for this unblocking of natural instinct. Like Copeau, he believed that the mask should transform the actor:

Beneath the mask one is no longer oneself, one is the character. Timidity vanishes, and one gains a completeness of expression. The toes regain their personality, the abdominals regain their *raison d'être*, the body recovers its full theatrical function, and just as Greek theatre is total theatre par excellence, so the mask helps us regain totality of expression in the human being.[63]

In his unpublished notebooks, Barrault extends his mystical conception of the mask. The face is interpreted as a six-part microcosm of the body, which in turn has a magnetic connection to the universe. Thus on the manifest level the intellectual brain is located in the bulge of the forehead, the two eyes radiate into three-dimensional space, the tip of the nose like a radar is in charge of external relations, and the play of the lips round the cavernous mouth is linked to sexual pleasure and visceral needs; but on the macro corporeal level, the brain corresponds to the whole head, the eyes to the breasts, the nose to the solar plexus, the junctions of the lips to the viscera and sexual organs. These add up to the six heads of the integral body, while the legs are rooted in the forces of life.[64] Whatever one's view of the occult principles, which can be traced back to the cabbalistic teaching of Artaud,[65]

---

[60] Barrault (1962: 114).
[61] R. Kemp in *Le Monde*, 29–30 May 1955; M. Lebesque in *Carrefour*, 1 June 1955; R. Saurel in *Information*, 1 June 1955: press cuttings in the BN.
[62] Barrault (1962: 113).   [63] Barrault (1957: 277).
[64] Barrault n.d.; cf. Barrault (1974: 58).   [65] Cf. Barrault (1974: 83).

114  *Mask and performance in Greek tragedy*

JEAN-LOUIS BARRAULT

*Pour Sartori, qui, par ses masques,
est aussi sur cette photo.
Avec mon amitié et mes vœux pour l'avenir
    JLBarrault   MAI. 58*

**Plate 5.1** Barrault with mask of Orestes.

**Plate 5.2** Cassandra in Barrault's *Oresteia*.

one can see how, taken as metaphor, Barrault's conception of the face as a map of being would have helped the actor to shift energies normally located in the face down to the body as a whole. In one notebook Barrault sums up as follows:

By virtue of the mask you pass to the expanded format of the body which, through its continuous exchanges with universal life unites with *the great body of the universe*. Such is *my religion of the human body*.
The universe reproduces itself in my Being, in my body where I discover in the position of my face all the symbolic signs.

*When I wear the mask*
I think with the vertebrae of my neck
I look and see with my breasts
I smell with my diaphragm
*From the mirror of my face*
*to the magnetic machine* of my body
I put myself in contact with *the presence of the universe*

Barrault developed this symbolic system on the basis of Polynesian masking, but he also found relevant spiritual values in African masking: love through marrying the skin of another, enrichment through rediscovering the kingdom of Instinct, piety through the practice of Ancestor cult, and protection through appropriating the power of the enemy.[66] His anthropological source defined an important difference: the Polynesian mask is detached from the wearer, whereas when the African mask is placed on the face 'instinctive energies run like molten metal into a mould whose form and power they take on'.[67] When Barrault adopted an Afro-Brazilian idiom for his *Oresteia*, and particularly for the masks of the Erinyes, he must have hoped for a metamorphosis of this kind in his actors.

Roland Barthes, as a Marxist semiotician, saw the world in diametrically opposite terms, and an interpretation of the classical mask was no less central to his aesthetic agenda. Barthes had helped to set up *Théâtre Populaire* in 1953 as a journal that would foster a theatre at once populist and politically radical. In 1954 came a moment of enlightenment, when the Berliner Ensemble production of *Mother Courage* revealed to him the Marxist aesthetic he had been seeking.[68] Here was a production imbued with political thought, artistically triumphant because the actors had time to develop their art unconstrained by the laws of capitalism, and based upon the laying bare of signs. In 1955 he was in the midst of the brilliant series of essays that would be published as *Mythologies*. In these he considered, for example, why the face of Garbo had once plunged cinema audiences into ecstasy. Her face seemed to him sculpted like a classical mask made of plaster. Unlike a *commedia* half-mask which implies the secret and the hidden, the Garbo mask has a Platonist force, evoking an archetypal or essential human creature, yet somewhere in the relation of the nostrils to the curve of the eyebrows, the psychological, individualised 'Hepburn' face is beginning to emerge. A touch of nostalgia emerges when Barthes looks back to

---

[66] Barrault n.d.  [67] Buraud (1948: 157).
[68] 'J'ai toujours beaucoup aimé le théâtre...': Barthes (2002: 20–1).

an age when the mask as Idea could engender ecstasy in the early cinema audience.[69]

This was the context in which Barthes condemned Barrault's *Oresteia* as an icon of the bourgeois theatre he had come to detest. He blamed the production in the first instance for its timidity, failing to push the Artaudian notion of total theatre to a point where the experience would embrace the audience.[70] He identified a conflict between the choral ideal, evident in Barrault's own rendering of the chorus leader, and the old-fashioned rhetorical acting of the leads. As Clytaemnestra, Marie Bell demonstrated 'a dramatic art of the intention, of the gesture and the glance heavy with meaning, of the signified secret, an art suitable for any scene of conjugal discord and bourgeois adultery...' Barrault was delighted by the psychological complexity he uncovered in Clytaemnestra during rehearsal,[71] but Barthes associated such a psychological approach with an essentialist ideology that tells of timeless, universal passions. Heavy beards made the three-quarter masks of men look like full masks, but the female masks were more like ball-masks leaving a sense of the expressive face hidden beneath (Plate 5.2). When a press cutting announced that 'Marie Bell will be Clytaemnestra beneath the mask at the Bordeaux Festival' the phrasing is eloquent: the actress is tantalisingly concealed along with her character.[72]

Barthes castigated the production for its irresponsible mixing of aims: to create archaeological authenticity, to aestheticise, to exoticise through the evocation of voodoo, and to essentialise through representing the moral debate of the play as timeless. Half a century later, some of Barthes' charges seem puritanical. The idea of mixing archaic costumes for the older generation and classical costumes for the younger is entirely in accordance with twenty-first-century norms. Barthes' conclusion that, since cultural knowledge of Greek dance is lost, it would be better to follow Claudel and have the chorus seated like a choir in church, seems defeatist in the wake of Mnouchkine. Yet Barthes' central charge of dehistoricisation continues to resonate. Most classical scholars now take it for granted that 'the *Oresteia* is a profoundly politicised work. . . . the work of a specific period, of a definite social condition, and of a contingent moral argument'. Given this premise, Barthes insists that any modern director must address two questions: 'what was the *Oresteia* for Aeschylus' contemporaries? What have we in the twentieth century to do with the ancient meaning of the work?' Having answered these questions, the director must choose between transposing the play to the

---

[69] Barthes (1983: 82–4).   [70] Barthes 1972.   [71] Barrault (1962: 112).
[72] *Encore*, 24 May 1955: press cutting in the BN.

present, and creating historical distance. Though this is a familiar dilemma in modern translation studies, Barthes' idea that the play can be reduced to a definable message seems reductive, as though the transition from patriarchy to matriarchy was a full and sufficient explanation of what the play 'meant' to its audience.

Barthes had a profound interest in Greek tragedy, for as a student in 1936 he was co-founder of the Groupe de Théâtre Antique which restored to *Persians* its original performance conventions, albeit in a modern translation that made the text accessible. This experience convinced him that distancing Greek tragedy was a means to theatricality. In 1953, soon after his well-known *Mythologies* essay on wrestling, which demonstrated that the purpose of a fight was not to win but to communicate ideological meanings, he published in *Théâtre Populaire* a major essay on Greek tragedy, and argued that the physical storm of tears generated by a tragedy could only be likened in the twentieth century to the emotions of a sporting contest:

> Alongside the suffering face of the pinned and vanquished wrestler, presenting his head to the encircling audience as an allegory of ravaged humiliation, set the ancient mask, fixed for ever in an emotional type [*emploi*], charged with signifying to the popular audience that the man whom the mask exhausts and signals is the seat of a true 'concrete essence' of Suffering. Identity is not in dispute. In both cases, over and above the proffered story-line, the audience finds release from the world's ambiguity, and clear signs to consume, with psychology abolished since the art of both wrestler and tragedian lies in making all such flow to the surface, gathering it for a direct reading by the people, letting no crease or cavity survive as a refuge-place for some indefinable part of self. The Athenian sun and 'Mutualité' lanterns have the same surgical function, which consists in bringing out from the signifying creases of the face an interiority that, if concealed, would have no dramatic function, for theatre can only offer what is visible for consumption ... The tragic mask, fixed in advance to a basic motivation ... left the dialectic of competing passions full freedom to develop.[73]

With his customary eloquence Barthes sets out his case for regarding the mask as pre-eminently a sign. Cognition is a pre-condition of emotion. Music like the mask comprises a system of discrete signs, despite the metaphysical claims of Nietzsche and Copeau. Greek theatre is not a religious ritual but essentially 'political history in the making, with men in complete control of it'. In the conclusion he makes it clear why this was a manifesto article for *Théâtre Populaire*: the Parisian Boulevard audience is alas not a

---

[73] 'Pouvoirs de la tragédie antique': Barthes (2002: 40–1); cf. 'The world of wrestling' in Barthes (1972: 18–30).

collectivity but a collection of voyeurs in a theatre devoid of civic function, and the democratic chorus has been sealed up in a tomb.[74]

In a 1965 essay written for a performance encyclopaedia Barthes refined his archaeology but not his underlying semiological principles. He now distinguishes Hellenistic masks which develop a 'metaphysics of psychological essences' from the mask of the Aeschylean period which had no fixed expression but was simply 'a neutral surface'. Drawing on his memories of 1936, he is less uncompromisingly secular in his interpretation of the early mask:

> It disorientates: first by censoring movement in the face, nuances, smiles, and tears, without replacing them by signs of however general a nature; then by altering the voice, made deep, cavernous and strange, as though coming from another world. A mix of inhumanity and emphasized humanity, it is now fundamentally a function of the tragic illusion, and its task is to allow communication between gods and men to be read.[75]

In the neutral fifth-century mask a complex dialectic is involved. Barthes explores a to-and-fro between the symbolic and the real in the convention of the mask, where much depends on the prior expectation of the audience. The famous terror supposedly caused by the first entry of Aeschylus' Erinyes can be explained as the disruption of a code, since previously the chorus had always entered as a coordinated group.[76]

Barthes found his theatrical utopia in Brecht, where overt sign-systems were deployed with Marxist intent. As a Brechtian purist, Barthes in 1958 sat on the tribunal which attempted to deny Jean Dasté the right to transfer his production of *Caucasian Chalk Circle* to Paris.[77] Dasté replicated the external forms of the Berliner Ensemble production, with its proliferation of half-masks for the epic tale, but in the spirit of Copeau, and a review of his production in the provinces commented revealingly: 'What did Berlin offer us? A wonderful succession of Persian miniatures, a Morality Play in distanced images. What does Saint-Etienne offer us? The very principle of timeless theatre: marionettes made of flesh, possessed of a heart.'[78] Before Brecht died, he gave Dasté his personal approval for this undertaking which Barthes sought to censor. In this context we must ask what Brecht meant when he said that classical theatre 'alienated its characters' by making them wear masks,[79] and whether any pure Brechtian theory of the mask exists. In 1929 Brecht cited as an exemplary piece of epic theatre Weigel's deadpan

---

[74] Barthes (2002: 42–5).   [75] 'Le théâtre grec': Barthes (2002: 325).
[76] Barthes (2002: 327).   [77] Dasté (1987: 33); Calvert (1994: 115).
[78] Morvan Lebesque in *Carrefour*, 5 February 1958: press cutting in the BN.
[79] 'A short organum for the theatre' (1948): Brecht (1978: 192).

rendering of the messenger in a version of *Oedipus the King*. 'She did not abandon her voice to horror, but perhaps her face, for she used white make-up to show the impact which death makes on all who are present at it'. Alas, he continued, empathy with Oedipus prevented most of the audience appreciating how Weigel was highlighting Jocasta's moral decision to kill herself.[80] As so often the audience resisted the attempt to create an epic theatre of pure signs. It was this very resistance that made his theatre feel alive.

What we see repeatedly in Brecht's practice is a mask of psycho-social alienation juxtaposed against the unmasked face of a natural human being. Piscator pointed the way with his 1928 production of *Schweik*, using masks and marionettes to surround the 'good soldier' who represents venial humanity. Brecht's Young Comrade in *The Measures Taken* (1930) dons a physical mask to become a faceless agent of the all-seeing party, but pulls it off and tears it up when instinctual human sympathies overcome his reason; Shen-Te, heroine of *The Good Person of Setzuan* (1943), dons a mask in order to prevent her tobacco business from being destroyed by her own good nature; and in the 1954 production of *Caucasian Chalk Circle* there is a mask for the Governor's wife, the biological mother, but not for the penniless adoptive mother Grusche, who gives the child her love.[81] An eastern setting legitimates the formal mask convention in these three plays. The Marx behind this masking conception is less the scientific economist than the romantic Marx of the 'Paris Manuscripts', with his vision of humans in an unalienated state before the division of labour.

In *Antigone* (1948) the classical setting also legitimated experiment with masks. Brecht and Neher his designer created Dionysiac masks on staves – flat, square, crudely painted faces, signs but also material carnivalesque objects – which echoed barbaric horse-skulls set around the stage. The four chorus elders used their masks for a Bacchic dance to celebrate peace, and also considered their actions in relation to the alter ego of the mask. In the finale they reversed their masks to lay blood-red faces over the body of Haemon while Creon's grinning mask stood implanted as a juxtaposition to his heavily made-up face now fixed in grief.[82] This was a strategy Barthes would surely have approved: antiquity set at a distance, with complete physical separation between the wearer and the mask of the god he worshipped. The mask was a sign making legible the dialectic of opposed emotions. Yet for all the brilliance of this solution to the historicity of the Greek mask, the dynamic of Weigel's Antigone replicates that of Shen-Te and Grusche: Weigel is the

---

[80] 'Dialogue about acting': Brecht (1978: 28).
[81] Berliner Ensemble 1961 documents the *CCC* production, and also the use of the make-up mask in *Puntila*. Cf. Smith (1984: 31–4); Tenschert 1961; Brecht 1977.
[82] Brecht and Neher (1949).

unmasked emblem of natural human emotion, whose instinctual goodness emerges despite all the socio-political pressures that demand she put on a false face. Brechtian theatre is scarcely less gendered than Greek theatre in its equation of the female with the instinctive.

Barthes' purist vision of Brecht was a dream of the impossible, and he gradually cut his links with a consumerist theatre that he could not redeem.[83] His last major theatrical essay, 'Lesson in Writing' (1968), is a celebration of Bunraku – and returns us full circle to Craig's ideal of the marionette. In Japanese puppetry the western dichotomy of inner/outer with its mystery of the soul is definitively abolished. The spectator is offered three autonomous sign-systems via the speaker, the puppeteer and the puppet, adding up to a 'total spectacle, but divided'. Barthes claims that the Brechtian ideal is here perfectly realised as 'emotion becomes matter for reading'.[84]

At the same time, however, Barthes' faith in the objectivity of the semiologist was crumbling, and a post-structuralist Barthes set about reinstating his own subjectivity. In his autobiographical *Roland Barthes par Roland Barthes* (1975) he included as one fragment of his past a photograph of himself in the role of Darius in 1936, arms akimbo, declaiming from the classical portico in the Sorbonne to the crouched chorus beneath. Above he set the caption:

Darius, whom I always played with utter nerves, had two long speeches where I was continually in danger of getting entangled. I was fascinated by the temptation to *think of something else*. Through the small holes in the mask I could see nothing, except the far distance, high up. While I churned out the prophecies of the dead king, my gaze fell on still, singular objects, a window, a corbel, a corner of sky. They at least had no fear. I resented the way I had let myself get caught in this uncomfortable trap – and meanwhile my voice continued its steady flow, resisting the expression I should have given it.[85]

There are many ironies in this recollection of a theatrical moment that inspired many in the audience. Gustave Cohen, academic mentor of the group, recalled how Darius 'as a white ghost, appeared between the brazen doors of the Chapel of Richelieu . . . which slowly opened, a long frisson ran through, and you could have heard, despite some thousand spectators, the fluttering of a bird's wing on the columns of the temple'.[86] The mismatch between the experience of the spectator and that of the disengaged performer must have helped Barthes see how meaning is created by context. Indeed, in the context of a 1945 revival the production spoke about liberation from Germany without any alteration to the external form.[87] The towering

[83] Barthes (2002: 20–1). [84] Barthes (1983: 305–13). [85] Barthes (1975: 37).
[86] Le Groupe de théâtre antique (1962: 25). [87] André Müller in GTA (1961: 23).

half-mask worn by Barthes was made for him by Maiène, and Jean Dasté taught him the technique, while the director was trained by a student of Copeau.[88] Barthes signally failed to maintain the qualities of presence or possession that his mentors sought. His later politicised commitment to the mask as sign was bound up with a personal psychological resistance to embodiment. Barthes described his post-structural autobiography as 'the book of my resistances to my own ideas', and a product of the 'imagination controlled by a series of masks (*personae*), layered according to the depth of the stage (and yet *personne* behind)' – which is to say, 'nobody' behind.[89] The empty mask became a metaphor for his own selfhood. Barthes describes a recurrent gap between his emotion and his ability to signify that emotion, resulting in an aura of 'serenity', which is simply 'the constraint of an actor scared to go on stage for fear of acting badly'.[90] The authoritative 'I' once capable of decoding bourgeois sign systems dissolved into the subject position of a student actor unable fully to inhabit the mask allocated to him.

Barthes' onslaught upon Barrault in 1955 was a significant moment. Copeau and Barrault celebrate the mask because of the way it forces the actor to connect mind and body, seeing the actor's body as the unifying centre of meaning in theatre. Barthes on the other hand values the mask because it suppresses psychological empathy, and turns the face into a legible sign. For both parties, the masked theatre of Greece was a utopia, and its historical nature needed to be properly understood if moral and aesthetic value was to be restored to the theatre of the present. For Barrault and Copeau, Greek theatre was fundamentally a religious experience, and the mask was a powerful tool in transformation of the spirit, while for Barthes Greek theatre was essentially political, creating collective emotion through the vehicle of thought. For Barrault and Copeau, great art was timeless, whereas for Barthes every work of art was a function of its historical context. Barthes' conception accorded with the Zeitgeist, and Barrault's apoliticism, as he realised when students sacked the Odéon during the Events of 1968, left him out of touch with the times. The students, he lamented, 'found themselves before a void',[91] but for Barthes the sense of void behind the mask was a quality to celebrate. In the twenty-first century, with the collapse of the Marxist world-view, it is possible to have more sympathy with Barrault in his attempt to engage with the cultural other, his sense of the human being as a citizen of the planet, and most importantly his sense of the human animal as a psycho-somatic unity; though it is impossible at the same time to forget

---

[88] Le Groupe de théâtre antique (1962: photo caption, 32, 25).
[89] Barthes (1975: 123).   [90] Barthes (1975: 180).
[91] Barrault (1975: 119); cf. Barrault (1974: 311–25).

his political naivety, and his failure to see that by 1955 he had enmeshed himself in a glamorous mainstream theatre incompatible with the Artaudian ideal of 'total theatre'. Committed to a philosophy of immersion, Barrault attempted to play chorus leader in a theatrical culture that demanded the rigorous external eye of a director.

The key concept which divides the two schools of thought is 'possession', a term much invoked by Copeau and his followers, for whom the experience of being taken over by the mask was fundamental. Barthes in an essay of 1958 was withering about 'the myth of the possessed actor'. Society, he argued, paid actors so poorly that it had to reward them with the notion that they exercised a priesthood.[92] The possessive theory in the Anglophone world received sustenance from Keith Johnstone's account of the mask in his 1979 manual on improvisation.[93] Johnstone learned his mask technique at the Royal Court from George Devine, who like Peter Hall was taught by Copeau's nephew Michel Saint-Denis. Johnstone valued the idea of possession because it led him to a form of theatre where the actor could improvise in front of the audience, to the consternation of the Lord Chamberlain. Johnstone vividly recalls Devine's workshop with a 'tragic mask', a neutral mask covering the full face, and the minimalistic method recalls early Copeau workshops: the actor sits in a chair, puts on a mask with head lowered, then raises the head to look into the distance. 'When the mask is still, or when it moves smoothly or decisively, or in slow motion, then the room seems to fill with power. Invisible ice forms on the walls.'[94] Johnstone cites the mask of Garbo as a memorable tragic mask, but where Barthes was content to analyse the face alone, Johnstone argues that we should rather celebrate Garbo's spine which controls the mask/body relationship.[95] For Johnstone the actor's technique, as in Bali, involves generating a 'serious trance state'. In the tragic mask, a 'different kind of spirit is involved from that which inhabits the half Mask'.[96]

By no means all modern mask practitioners subscribe to this language of possession.[97] Though Lecoq discovered the power of theatre through watching Barrault's *Autour d'une mère*,[98] and subsequently taught with Barrault, he was reticent about the idea of possession, and his popularity in the late twentieth century owes much to his secularisation of the mask, within a pedagogy that fostered the existential freedom of the individual, liberated from masks imposed by society. Whilst Copeau and Barrault were Nietzschean

---

[92] 'Le mythe de l'acteur possédé': Barthes (2002: 234–7).   [93] Johnstone (1981: 143–205).
[94] Johnstone (1981: 186).   [95] Johnstone (1981: 184–5).   [96] Johnstone (1981: 190).
[97] For example, Britain's Trestle Theatre Company, who in the Craigian tradition treat masks as sculptural creations.
[98] Lecoq (2000: 4).

modernists who sought a dissolution of self, Lecoq aimed to foster a more honest and secure sense of self. This helps us see why Lecoq was never a proponent of public masked performance.

The historian of classical theatre has much to learn from twentieth-century arguments about masked acting, and from examining the phenomenology of wearing a mask. When masks change bodies, they also change minds. Philippe Hottier, an associate of Mnouchkine, explains the process like this. The actor first looks at the mask to see how its form can be echoed in the body. When put on, the mask unlike make-up actually hurts, and creates pressure points which act on the body. This helps the actor create a physical posture that echoes the physical form of the mask and, through the way it constrains the lungs or throat, generates the voice of the mask. A prolonged period in this physical position shapes the way the actor thinks, and mind becomes a function of body. In the climax of this process, the actor like a shaman becomes capable of physical and mental feats that are impossible for them in an everyday context.[99] Technique is a necessary condition of effective mask work, but good technique needs to be absorbed to the point of becoming unconscious, and consciousness of self in the present, as in the painful experience of Barthes as Darius, is usually counter-productive. It has therefore proved important to generations of actors that they surrender conscious control and receive impulses perceived to come from the mask.

The association between the god Dionysos and the classical mask relates to this experience of transcendence on the part of the actor or dancer. The strict dichotomy between objective political analysis and the subjective world of myth and religion, though taken for granted by the Marxian Barthes, makes little sense in relation to Copeau, Barrault and Mnouchkine. The distinction between art and ritual, which might have held meaning for Craig or Lecoq, seems far less applicable to Copeau or to Barrault, at least Barrault in his Artaudian youth. An understanding of how the mask acts upon the performer will help us see how the religious and political concerns of Greek theatre were in fact inseparable. Copeau and his successors were determined to tie mind and body together, despite cultural pressures to foreground the verbal or psychological dimension of theatre. The masked dance theatre of Athens also deployed the whole human organism, and it is a challenge for the modern historian to recover the lost corporeal dimension. An appreciation of the power of the mask is a first step.

---

[99] 'La structure du masque agit sur le corps et le mental du comédien': Aslan and Bablet (1985: 235–9).

# 6 | Mask and text: the case of Hall's *Oresteia*

We saw in Chapter 5 how the mask in twentieth-century European theatre was bound up with an ideal of 'physical theatre'. The mask proved an efficacious means to reanimate the body within an increasingly sedentary society. The experience of enhanced living provides an explanation for the spiritual language so often used to describe what it feels like to wear a mask.[1] The physical theatre tradition, however, in centring on the body, has decentred the dramatic text. It insists on the way masks foster improvisation, actors generating their own spontaneous text as if possessed by the spirit of the mask. The related ideal of 'total theatre' likewise excluded any received text from its notion of totality. Artaud, in his essay 'No more masterpieces', admired *Oedipus Rex* for its themes of incest, plague and the amorality of nature, but lamented the text, for 'all this is clothed in language which has lost any contact with today's crude epileptic rhythm. Sophocles may speak nobly, but in a manner that no longer suits the times.'[2]

Jean-Louis Barrault's roots as a performer lay within this physical and Artaudian tradition. The voice was by no means something he ignored, for he writes of how words are creations of the body, and he celebrates the animalistic sensuality of language. Speech is understood as a physical act in which the breath touches different vital organs, and language as the encoding of an idea is subordinate or supplementary to the act of shaping sound.[3] Accounts of his *Oresteia* suggest that his holistic approach to the body led him to develop exciting choral sequences where dance, movement and sound could coalesce, but that in some other respects the textuality of Aeschylus defeated him, even though the language was stripped down and its rhythmic structures foregrounded. He was unwilling to engage with the political argument of the trilogy, displayed little interest in the narrative art of the storyteller and does not seem to have reined in the orthodox declamatory acting of his star, Marie Bell. There seems to have been a gap between his ideal of the embodied actor and the given of the classic text, between language as sound and text as meaning.

---

[1] Cf. Damasio (2004: 284).   [2] Artaud (1970: 56).   [3] Barrault (1975: 50–3).

Many besides Barrault have attempted to explore the language of Greek plays as emanations of the body. In Iran in 1971 Peter Brook worked on the Greek text of Aeschylus' *Persians*, and explained to his actors how traumatic the sack of Athens had been:

We seldom go through experiences of this force. Our own interpretation of it is likely to be weaker than the experience lying inside the play itself. If we feel our way into the text, knowing in general what it's about but not in detail, and take a word, several words, a dialogue, with imaginations open to the words, it will literally put words into our mouth. The more we experience the sensual flavour of the words, the more we experience the person who went through it. Suddenly and mysteriously they become our words: words so strong, alive, vibrant, affecting our imagination through their sound and movement, that suddenly we find all our feelings flowing with the words.[4]

The project culminated in *Orghast*, which attempted to uncouple words from precise semantic meanings and create a language of pure sound. The event included part of the Greek text of *Persians* performed at the tomb of Xerxes, the actors having been provided with Greek sounds but no meanings. There was constant tension through the rehearsal process as actors attempted to pin meanings to words, and thus lost the pure imaginative qualities Brook was seeking. For Ted Hughes, who created the language and mythology of Orghast, the translation of sound into movement was never a concern. As translator of Seneca's *Oedipus*, he had been impressed by a rehearsal when Brook's actors declaimed the text at double speed with no movement but total concentration. 'The field of electrical power became nearly unbearable', he recalled. 'Maybe this was how the rigid, stilted, masked actors of the Greek amphitheatre performed their megaphone tragedies and sent members of their audience raving in iambics for days afterwards. Those Greek plays were close to liturgy. The gods and the underworld were still listening, and it was intended they should hear.'[5] In Hughes' mind the mask belonged to a Graeco-Roman theatre which suppressed movement in order that energy might be concentrated on the transcendent power of sound.

Andrei Serban, who worked with Brook on *Orghast*, carried Brook's line of investigation forward, arguing that

The ancient Greek language is perhaps the most generous material for actors that has ever been written ... It is a matter of discovering the paradox that the head, the heart and the voice are not separate but connected with each other ... Movement

---

[4] Smith (1972: 122).   [5] 'Inner Music' (1988) in Hughes (1994: 245–6).

and voice rediscover one another in a common effort... What is it then that touches us in *Electra*? What is its message transcending time? What does Electra say during her long lament? It is difficult to determine. Let us take a word that she often repeats: 'eee.' It is simply what one hears: a prolonged 'e.' What does this continual repetition of a vowel mean? Nothing that can be translated; 'e' means nothing other than 'e.' The meaning is in the sound itself. The fundamental character of the tragedy can be rediscovered in this unique sound – impossible to translate.[6]

Though few would disagree with Serban that the sound of poetry is indisseverable from its meaning, many would reject the rider that the play has a timeless emotional essence, made available to all through its sound. Though Serban has proved an inspired director, and his *Fragments of a Trilogy*, which included the Sophoclean *Electra*, was a successful reworking of Greek material incorporating fragments of many languages,[7] his method of working from sound did not in fact encourage him to tackle Greek texts as they have come down to us. Discussing a production of *Persians* inspired by Brook, which translated the ritual sounds of the Greek into movement, Jacqueline Martin sums up the fundamental dilemma: 'By placing the emphasis on the "medium" rather than the "message", vocal delivery seems to run the risk of losing its ability to activate an audience to think and thereby hold its attention'.[8]

The tension between thinking which is by definition retrospective and visceral experience in the here-and-now is explored in Derrida's critique of Artaud. Artaud, wrote Derrida, 'knew that all speech fallen from the body, offering itself to understanding or reception, offering itself as a spectacle, immediately becomes stolen speech'. In order to reclaim speech, to make it feel other than stolen from a bygone author, Artaud sought to abandon the fundamentals of classical art. Yet, Derrida maintains, this is an impossibility and leads to a situation of infinite regress. 'In soliloquy as in dialogue, to speak is to hear oneself. As soon as I am heard, as soon as I hear myself, the I who hears *itself* who hears *me*, becomes the I who speaks and takes speech from the I who thinks that he speaks and is heard in his own name; and becomes the I who takes speech *without ever cutting off* the I who thinks that he speaks.' Total physical embodiment is no less impossible since one is always aware of one's limbs as being 'other'. Artaud, Derrida argues, wrote in an anguish of dispossession. Seeking to do away with the figure of the God-Author, whose speech becomes the stolen property of actors and directors, his only recourse was to create a new and more rigid textuality with a system

---

[6] Serban (1976: 26).   [7] Aronson (2000: 102–7).
[8] Martin (1991: 183) citing a 1988 production by Mirka Yemendzakis.

of shouts and sounds instead of words, and masks instead of faces. Only by this means could Artaud be sure that he was truly hearing himself, and come to terms with his double.[9] Collapsing the metaphysics of presence, Derrida insists like Barthes on the otherness of the theatrical sign, and the inevitability of personal dissociation. Given the postmodern account of a fragmented self, the idea that the text can be fully inhabited is philosophically untenable. It follows that the text must remain out there, a stolen thing which the actor can cite but never finally own. In Derrida's world of difference and infinite deferral, the classic text becomes less of an embarrassment than it was for Artaud, and its textuality is rather something to be celebrated. A positive role for the mask may be envisaged if one assumes that its purpose is to separate the once-written text from the vocal apparatus of an ever-absent actor.

The potential usefulness of the mask becomes obvious when we turn from the perspective of the speaking actor to that of the spectator in receipt of a dramatic poem. Two eminent authorities on Greek theatre, Oliver Taplin and Helene Foley, when presented with an unfamiliar 'Greek tragedy', a lengthy pastiche by John Barton played in masks, both commented on how the masks helped them listen more attentively. The masks, wrote Taplin, 'drew attention to the words in a way that would have been harder to achieve if such a long production were to have had all the expressiveness of the human face'. Foley remarks that 'in a production of this length I don't think I could have continued to listen without them'.[10] Greg Hicks, a performer in the production, confirms their view, saying that when a good cast wears masks 'it's like light being switched on. It's a mutual dance between the intensity of concentration of the actors and intensity of concentration of the audience. Masks encourage an audience to look and listen with more intensity. That's why I love doing it.'[11] Peter Hall, co-director of the production, confirms that 'The bonus of the mask is that it forces the audience to concentrate on the text'.[12] This phenomenon of intensified listening may be explained in the first instance in terms of information overload. The psychologically expressive face demands superfluous mental activity in order to decode countless tiny cues.

As always, caution is needed before we jump from the experience of Taplin and Foley to conclusions about ancient theatre. In a modern, thousand-seater theatre with strong lights that pick out the face, the mask is inevitably

---

[9] Derrida (1978: esp. 220, 223, 233).
[10] Taplin 2002; Foley 2001a. First performed in Denver in 1991, *Tantalus* was directed by Peter and Edward Hall, with masks by Dionysis Fotopoulos.
[11] Hicks 2002b.   [12] *The Times*, 2 November 1981.

seen in negative terms, as a means to eliminate the customary facial detail. In a large open-air sun-lit theatre, I have argued that the effect was rather to make the face visible. Though he is right to distinguish simple and subtle fifth-century Greek masks from gargantuan Roman masks, Peter Hall confuses scale with clarity when he adduces that: 'The mask is not a device to enhance visibility in the large Greek amphitheatres; a mask of human scale is perfectly visible in Epidaurus before ten thousand people'.[13] Since twenty metres is the approximate threshold needed for an actor to make eye-contact with an audience,[14] painted and moulded eyes would have made a face seem more immediate to a spectator seated further away in a Greek theatre, while shadow on the heightened geometry of the face increased the degree of expressivity. The broad point remains, as I argued in relation to the terracotta masks of Lipari, that polyvalent tragic masks required prior knowledge and imaginative interaction in the audience in order to create their theatrical effect. They did not burden the audience with excess information.

In his poem *Balaustion's Adventure* (1871), Robert Browning framed the text of *Alcestis* as a narrative told by his heroine to the people of Syracuse. The Syracusans rescue Balaustion and her companions from pirates because they have been so transfixed by Euripides' dramatic poem. Sitting on temple steps, Balaustion recounts the dramatic action as she saw it in an island theatre many years after the first performance in Athens, so *Alcestis* was already for her and the Syracusans a classic text. Her account of what she saw and heard prompts a pedantic protest:

> Why mark!
> Even when I told the play and got the praise,
> There spoke up a brisk little somebody,
> Critic and whippersnapper, in a rage
> To set things right: 'The girl departs from truth!
> Pretends she saw what was not to be seen,
> Making a mask of actor move, forsooth!
> "Then a fear flitted o'er the wife's white face," –
> "Then frowned the father," – "then the husband shook," –
> "Then from the festal forehead slipt each spray,
> And the heroic mouth's gay grace was gone"; –
> As she had seen each naked fleshly face,
> And not the merely painted mask it wore!'

---

[13] Hall (2000: 29).   [14] See Watt (1992: 116–22); Andrew Todd in Todd and Lecat (2003: 243).

Belaustion responds:

Well, is the explanation difficult?
What's poetry except a power that makes?
And speaking to one sense, inspires the rest,
Pressing them all into its service . . .

She goes on to describe three senses related to the separate art forms of poetry, painting and music:

and what if but one sense of three
Front you at once? The sidelong pair conceive
Thro' faintest touch of finest finger-tips, –
Hear, see and feel, in faith's simplicity,
Alike, what one was sole recipient of:
Who hears the poem, therefore, sees the play.[15]

The Syracusans themselves have no difficulty using their imaginations when listening only to the woman's voice. The theatre audience on Balaustion's island, however, projected onto the blank masks the emotions of fear, anger, shock and grief which the language told them they needed to see. Just as one *hears* the words spoken in a narrative painting or *participates* in the physical emotions of the composer, so in the mask one *sees* the face move. Poetry is celebrated as *poiēsis*, an activity of *making*, less an art of imitation than of stimulating the senses.

We can translate Browning's romantic formulation into the language of modern neurology. What happens when the visual image is transferred from the retina to the visual cortex is not a simple process of pictorial mimesis. The same parts of the brain are stimulated when one sees a face and imagines a face, for our neurons engage in an act of remaking. We do not simply see what is there, because out there is far more information than any brain can process, certainly quickly enough for survival; rather, we see for the most part what our brains have learned *ought* to be there. In Richard Gregory's formulation, 'perceptions are like the predictive hypotheses of science'.[16] We form the hypothesis that a certain configuration of lines and shadows is a face, and on that basis read expressions into it. Ernst Gombrich quotes the best formulation of this principle in antiquity, voiced by Apollonius: 'Even if we drew one of these Indians with white chalk . . . he would seem black, for there would be his flat nose and stiff curly locks and prominent

---

[15] Browning (1928: 13–14).   [16] Gregory (1998: 10).

jaw... to make the picture black for all who can use their eyes.'[17] An Asiatic face rendered in white chalk is seen as dark rather than pale because the Greek brain has learnt to predict, on the basis of experience and in the context of a visit to a foreign country, what skin pigmentation will accompany certain facial features. Another aspect of prediction in face recognition is the way people infer form from shadow,[18] and Greek masks were clearly designed to exploit this aspect of the seeing process. When Belaustion's theatre audience read emotions into painted three-dimensional faces, such principles of prediction explain the psychological process at work.

The journey from retina to cortex is complicated by the way the brain is hard-wired to respond to faces. Thanks to evolution, special parts of the brain are dedicated to the perception of faces. Babies have been shown to track schematic faces composed of three blobs at the age of forty-three minutes, while in two days they start to recognise their mother's face and in two to three weeks can imitate facial movements.[19] It follows that the simplified features of a theatre mask will make it hold the attention of the spectator with unexpected force. Recognising faces upside-down is generally harder than recognising other objects upside-down, but, in a celebrated illusion, a face with inverted mouth and eyes will disturb us greatly, whilst the same face viewed upside-down will scarcely disturb at all.[20] This illusion helps explain why eyes and mouth are so critical to mask manufacture. Because of the semi-autonomous systems used in viewing faces, we find it easier to accept the relationship of mask and body when the two are of different substances. Hearing has been shown to be bi-modal, involving the reading of the jaw and lips as part of an integrated physiological process,[21] and this too may have implications for the viewing of a speaking mask. When distance interferes with the synchronicity of sight and sound, it may be easier for the brain to predict and project movement onto a mask than to be confronted with a real moving jaw.

An even more important area of research concerns the brain's sensitivity to the perception of gaze direction, which is a basic requisite of social interaction and inferring intentionality.[22] The eyes of the Heracles mask in the Pronomos vase track the actor holding it in a way that no real mask could

---

[17] Philostratus *Life of Apollonius* in Gombrich (1977: 155).
[18] See Gregory (1998: 189–90); Bruce and Young (1998: 78–84).
[19] Bruce and Young (1998: 250–3); cf. Trevarthen (1995: 163–4).
[20] Gregory (1998: 73–4); cf. Bruce and Young (1998: 237).
[21] Bruce and Young (1998: 208); Massaro (1998: 3ff.).
[22] Edinborough 2003 calls attention to the fundamental work of Simon Baron-Cohen on 'mindblindness'.

actually do. While shallow or two-dimensional images like those of Medusa in Greek art may create the illusion that the eyes follow the viewer,[23] three-dimensional theatre masks normally require that the angle of gaze should correlate with the angle of the head. In Chapter 3, I contrasted the blank gaze of Lecoq's neutral mask with the more dynamic gaze we find in classical bronzes and vase images. Establishing the nature of the gaze is crucial if we are to understand the technique of Greek tragic acting. Part of the normal seeing process is ambient, and keyed to movements of the whole of the viewer's body, while part is foveal, the focus flickering from one tiny point to the next.[24] Masks may set up the illusion that they only possess ambient vision, ruling out psychological interaction in the way that Lecoq's mask does, or they may create the illusion of foveal activity.

A neurological account of the interactive brain does much to support Browning's picture of the senses conceiving from each other so that 'who hears the poem' indeed 'sees the play'. To perceive the mask is not a matter of responding passively to sensory data or analytically decoding signs, but a more active process of building a relationship with the mask in order to make meaning. The Derridean model of self-awareness does not tally with modern understandings of the brain, where so much activity is now understood to take place beneath the threshold of phenomenal consciousness. Dramatic speech need not appear 'stolen' when the brain receives speech through both eyes and ears, or when feelings are triggered by an autonomic nervous system prior to any rational thought process.[25] Far from serving as an alienation device, I believe, the classical Greek mask generated in the spectator a more integrated and powerful emotional response to the words of the play. The mask served rather to repsychologise than depsychologise the face – using the word *psyche* in its Greek sense to imply the presence of a living spirit.

The proposition that masks enhance the reception of text was put to the test in the 1981 *Oresteia* performed in the Greek-style auditorium of Britain's National Theatre. The director, Peter Hall, has done more than anyone to bring the importance of the Greek mask to public attention, and as a director, he is famed for giving first priority to the text. Hall works from the clear theoretical proposition that art requires form in order to contain emotion, and in Greek tragedy he sees the dominant containing form as the mask. In his Cambridge lectures of January 2000 published as *Exposed by the Mask* he uses the mask as a metaphor to speak of how

---

[23] Bruce and Young (1998: 211–14); Perrett *et al.* in Gregory, Harris, Heard and Rose (1995: 117–19).
[24] Trevarthen (1995: 172–6).   [25] Bruce and Young (1998: 237–43); Damasio (2004: 59–61).

music in Mozart's opera or verbal rhythms in Shakespeare and Beckett likewise formalise performance, lifting it above mere impersonation. The 1981 *Oresteia* is of particular interest because the translator Tony Harrison aspired to write what he would publish as 'a rhythmic libretto for masks, music and an all-male company'.[26] Harrison's attempt to work out what language properties are required by masked performance will be of help when we return to the original Greek texts and seek to define in what sense they too were written as texts for masks.

Hall's working method, developed in the *Oresteia* and sustained in *The Oedipus Plays* (1996) and *Bacchai* (2002), is curiously schizophrenic. For half the day Hall, as a sometime student of Saint-Denis, will often pursue the methods of Copeau. He explained to his Cambridge audience: 'When the actor first puts on the mask, he finds it almost impossible to speak. If he works honestly, he goes through a period – and it can sometimes take two to three weeks – where all he can do is make guttural sounds. He ignores everyone.' Eventually social interaction, sounds and even words become possible. 'This somewhat alarming process of growing up, of becoming part of a group and learning how to live in it has happened every single time I have conducted a mask workshop.'[27] Hall draws from the tradition of Copeau three principles: the mask takes you back to a pre-civilised state so you must grow up afresh, the mask inculcates the ethical principle of honesty, and the mask has a spiritual dimension evident in the way it acts on you. He elaborated in a 1996 interview: 'We contain in ourselves all that we have been and might be and the mask can take you anywhere – to the feminine side of yourself, the brutal side, the old side. It's a terribly liberating device. That sounds terribly Pseud's Corner but it's true, don't ask me why, it's one of those mysteries.'[28] While Hall the hierophant spends part of the day running mask workshops, it is a more secular Hall, sometime founder of the Royal Shakespeare Company, who runs text rehearsals, eyes on the script rather than the actor's body, paying minute attention to verbal rhythms. There is an inevitable tension between these two modes. Hall discovered in the course of rehearsing the *Oresteia* that it was impossible to give notes to actors in masks because naming them individually 'was to break the spell'. From the point of view of Greg Hicks the actor, this was like swapping telephone numbers in the middle of a High Catholic Mass.[29]

At a certain point the actors know the form and rhythm of the text and are in a position to work in masks, but Hall is much less clear about the

---

[26] Harrison 1982a.    [27] Hall (2000: 35–6).
[28] *The Independent* (section 2), 14 August 1996. Pseud's Corner is a column in the satirical magazine *Private Eye*.
[29] Hall (1993: 313–14); *The Sunday Times*, 29 November 1981; Hicks 2002b.

psychological processes now involved. In a 1982 interview he is quoted as saying that when an actor puts on a mask: 'You become it. The actor is possessed by it, and must go with it.' Yet later in the same interview he qualified: 'These actors do not feel. They tell. If they emote in the mask they begin to shake. Yet they have to experience it to tell it.'[30] The mask somehow contains emotion which in early rehearsals was once 'primal'. Hicks proves more illuminating when he explains how the mask gives the performer a frame, and allows him to hold onto huge feelings without indulgence or sentimentality. The mask allows the energies of the text 'to play through you as an instrument, as a controlled, spiritually disciplined, emotionally disciplined, physically disciplined performer. And actually that doesn't happen very much in acting, it's a messier palate without the mask.'[31] Within the cast Hicks was unique in achieving an effective movement vocabulary in the production, working with his feet and articulating mask against body.[32] A drawback in Hall's method is that the voice and movement which the actors have discovered in workshop is not necessarily related to the particular mask they have to wear. As Hall once wistfully remarked: 'It's always a problem with masks, you can't design them until you know what you're doing, and you can't know what you're doing until you've got the masks. It's a vicious circle.'[33] For the *Oresteia* the masks were available earlier than in subsequent productions, and the process was better integrated. One wonders how the Greeks managed the rehearsal process. Plutarch tells the story of how Euripides was teaching his chorus a rather elaborate song when one of the performers burst into giggles, which seems to imply a level of unmasked rehearsal at the point of absorbing text.[34] Given the 'neutral' and familiar nature of the Greek mask, one may assume that performance masks were available from the start.

A major gain of Hall's Copeau-inspired mask work was choreographic. Using senses other than vision alone, the *Oresteia* chorus instinctively formed organic and aesthetically pleasing groupings. As a movement passed through the group the actors functioned in Hall's metaphor like a shoal of fish or a flock of starlings, while without masks their instinct was to create dull straight lines.[35] What Hall could not or would not do, having locked each

---

[30] *The Observer*, 4 April 1982.   [31] Hicks 2002a.
[32] Timothy Davies commented on the failure of the rest in a National Theatre platform discussion of 10 May 2001: 'National Theatre: Twenty Five Years on the South Bank', chaired by Al Senter.
[33] Croall (2002: 36); cf. Reynolds (1996: 19–20).
[34] *De audiendo* 46b, cited in Marshall (2004: 27).
[35] Cf. Fay (1995: 286); Timothy Davies in a National Theatre platform discussion of 10 November 2001.

actor into a sense of personal isolation, was to transfer that visual chorality to the domain of language. He insisted that synchronised verbal delivery would become mechanical, creating 'verbal Tiller girls', and that a single voice suffices for choral text because no movement of the mouth serves to identify the speaker. He also rejected the notion that a text so complex as a Greek chorus can be sung or danced.[36] For Michael Walton this represents 'a fundamental misunderstanding of the nature of masked acting' because it denies the physical discipline of listening which should always tell us which mask is speaking.[37] Hall's desire to avoid the mechanical mode of the musical has led him paradoxically into a style that often seems rather analytic. Techniques that work well for dense Shakespearean text do not necessarily work well for choral text – equally dense but of a different substance.

Jocelyn Herbert, who designed the masks for the *Oresteia*, had also experienced the Saint-Denis method, and was formerly the partner of George Devine. She had much more experience of masks than Hall, who did not know Saint-Denis' work on the quasi-tragic full-face mask, but only the training in comic masks, which included the development of primitive speech.[38] Herbert reflected wryly upon Hall's initial statement that the cast would take six months before they could speak. 'Before I was involved, they had been given a mixture of masks that had nothing to do with *The Oresteia* so, naturally, they couldn't speak.' The inwardness of the improvisatory work that Hall describes related to the fact that the outward image of their masks led them nowhere. Herbert released the actors from gazing introspectively at mirrors, asking them just to contemplate the mask so the text could motivate their moves and gestures.[39] Herbert's years at the Royal Court had given her a strong commitment to the primacy of text. As a devotee of Edward Gordon Craig, she was less interested in the improvisatory force of the mask than she was in the aesthetic image and its close relation to the word. For Tony Harrison, she proved far more congenial than Hall as a collaborator.

Herbert understood that masks needed to be monochrome, so that shadows cast by the moulding would have the main job of creating animation, and she was committed to simplicity in the mask image so spectators could concentrate on the text. One of the difficulties of mask research is that normally the researcher has to work from static photos or video. Hall chose to film the play in close-up, with the masks rather brightly lit so one could see

---

[36] Hall (2000: 30–3).   [37] Walton 2002.
[38] *The Times*, 2 November 1981. For the Saint-Denis method see Saint-Denis (1960: 103–5).
[39] Herbert (1993: 120).

Plate 6.1 Fury drawn by Jocelyn Herbert.

the actors' mouths, eyes and throats, placing his camera level with or below the masks to create heroic stature in the small-screen image. Almost all photos are from the London production, though the performance at Epidaurus was better lit. I found it helpful, therefore, to see some of her masks of Erinyes exhibited in 2003 alongside chorus masks from the 1996 *Oedipus Plays* made by others. The *Oedipus* masks were more rounded, duller in colour, more blank in expression, with mouths conceived in two dimensions, seeming round-eyed in horror but passive in response to fate. Herbert's masks had a stronger geometry, angular cheekbones to catch shadow, and more energy in the arch of the brows. She caught faces in action, actively looking and apparently always on the point of speaking (Plate 6.1).[40] Hall rightly praised

[40] 'A stage for Dionysos', curated by Spyros Mercouris. Dublin Castle, March 2003.

Plate 6.2 Mask of Orestes.

her ability to create the ambiguous mask of Greek tragedy which 'must laugh when the sound of laughter is heard and . . . cry when the sound of sobbing is heard'. For Harrison, her masks 'had a beautiful neutrality until, that is, they were worn by the actor and became animated by the emotions expressed by means of the text'.[41]

Greg Hicks testifies to the way Herbert studied him in the rehearsal room, then rendered something of his physical presence into the form of his Orestes mask (Plate 6.2). This mask seemed to him to combine angularity with softness, weakness, vulnerability and tenderness. He explains how he got a charge from looking at it, so that 'every time I put it on it was an event, in my personal psyche, my acting psyche'.[42] Most of the actors had been cast for their authentic northern voices, and Herbert's special response to

[41] Herbert (1993: 224, 230).   [42] Hicks 2002b.

Plate 6.3 Orestes drawn by Jocelyn Herbert.

Hicks related to his exceptional physical skills. Herbert's published workbook includes a preliminary sketch of Orestes with his head expressively in profile, but all subsequent photographs are frontal (Plate 6.3). Hall was emphatic that 'The mask goes dead in profile. It is always the full face that expresses what the heart is feeling.'[43] Hicks developed the same conviction that Greek masks need to be frontal, and speaks of tracking the house with his gaze like a spotlight beam, or dragging the audience around with him as though they were shards of metal drawn by a magnet, building up an unbreakable symbiosis. Even in Epidaurus his task was to attract the audience to the front of the mask. Brief moments in profile might be admissible but no more.[44]

---

[43] Hall (2000: 33).   [44] Hicks 2002b.

Herbert explained that the 'effect of the mask lies in the opposition of the stillness or stylization of the face with the expressive movements of the body'.[45] Though her masks seem alive, there is an element of modernist abstraction in them, allowing no spectator to forget that this is a masked performance, a recreation of an ancient ritual. As a practising designer, her main contact with masks had been through Brecht, and this encouraged her to make masks that were less for *becoming* than for *seeing* and *telling*. The strong plain coloration of the masks creates a surface that separates the body of the actor from the horrors of which he tells. Her masks undoubtedly reflect the influence of Tony Harrison, who experimented in rehearsal with the words masks could utter. She quotes one of his many postcards sent to her:

A Greek theatrical mask is part of the existential survival gear. It gives the bearing of survival to the actor wearing it. It represents a commitment to seeing everything through the eyes that never close. It represents a commitment to going on speaking when the always open eyes have witnessed something unspeakable. The masks must witness the unendurable. That is why they are created with their eyes open. The mouth must continue to speak in situations where the human being would be speechless or screaming or unable to articulate its agony.[46]

In the *Oresteia* programme he likened the masks of the production to the protective masks used by welders. Hall's own formulation in the programme placed less emphasis on seeing, more on how the mask is seen: 'The screaming, naked face repels; the screaming face of the mask does not ... In tragedy it makes possible the expression of hysterical emotions which would be disturbing and unacceptable with the naked face.' While Hall responded to the serenity and classical form of Herbert's masks, Harrison was drawn to the energy of the mouth and above all the empty yet staring eyes of these masks, a feature emphasised by the lighting from above. Cassandra and Aegisthus had large startled holes in place of the iris, while most of the other masks had the full eye cut out as in a Sartori neutral mask.

In an unsympathetic review of the production, Michael Billington dismissed Harrison's theory of the mask as 'absolute poppycock', maintaining that the unmasked *Oresteia* of Peter Stein in Berlin in 1980 was much more successful in keeping the audience's eyes open. The mask in his view restricted emotional variety.[47] In a poem on the excavation of a smiling Gorgon, Harrison nevertheless developed his conception without apology:

---

[45] Herbert (1991: 283).   [46] Herbert (1991: 282–3).   [47] *The Guardian*, 30 November 1981.

> The tragic mask of ancient days
> looked with eyes that never close
> straight into the Gorgon's gaze
> and sang Man's history through its throes.[48]

The mask witnesses horror, and thereby inherits the power of a Gorgon's stare. He prefaced the poem with a quote from Nietzsche to the effect that 'Art forces us to gaze into the horror of existence, yet without being turned to stone by the vision'.[49] In Barrault's production the leather sat close to the face and the actor's eyes remained visible, a stylistic option which helped the actor feel in full control of his body, and also allowed them to perpetuate a received style of acting. In the Sikelianos production, by contrast, the iris was painted in because the characters were enclosed in a mythic environment glimpsed from afar by the audience. Having developed an expressive language of the body, the actors were free to turn their backs when climbing the mountain to look at Prometheus. Herbert's empty eye-sockets were an artistic choice designed to mesmerise the audience and they answered perfectly to Harrison's specification. Her masks recall sculptural images of the first century BC and later, a period when actors stood and sang, describing horror in a manner we can best imagine through Seneca's surviving tragedies.[50] Fifth-century vase paintings and early sculptural replicas are absolutely consistent in their indication that the eyes were vividly painted in and active rather than passive in the quality of their seeing.

The playwright John Arden was inspired to write for masks by George Devine's workshops, and discovered that 'an actor with a mask does not need elaborate language – the mask is so powerful in itself that it needs a more naked expression of emotion'.[51] Masks change what is required of language. In the *Oresteia* programme Harrison wrote that

> I had never examined, or imagined, all the implications of a 'masked text'. The entire meaning of lines spoken by masked actors is strangely different from the way those lines work if delivered unmasked. I found myself, in fact, in an area of poetry quite unlike anything we are familiar with. The differences largely determined the style I adopted for the translation.

Yet it is not easy to glean from Harrison's discussion of his own work what makes a 'masked text' so distinctive. On one level, the notion of 'masked

---

[48] Harrison (1992: 73).   [49] Harrison (1992: 59).
[50] Cf. Levasseur-Legangneux (2004: 168–9). Compare for example the eyes of Herbert's Cassandra with Webster (1967: plate VIIb). Halliwell (1993: 207) also rebuts Harrison's theory.
[51] Arden (1967: 42).

text' is pure metaphor, and relates to the formalised nature of any poetic language. In relation to style Harrison explains that 'when we take into account at an early stage the masked nature of these plays... which makes speeches one block of solid colour rather than the lurches and subtextual twists we associate with Stanislavskian readings of more modern texts, or intimate screen acting, the sense of necessary weight and momentum is linked to a world of primary emotional colours which complicate their palate by accretion and cumulative effects rather than by a prismatic surface.'[52] Herbert's masks and costumes provided simplified slabs of red, white and dull gold that had their verbal equivalent in Harrison's text. It is not mere pedantry for the theatre historian to note that fifth-century Athenian actors wore patterned and variegated robes that helped the mask to vanish into the body and picked out the limbs,[53] while blocks of solid colour, to judge from wall-paintings, helped the more expressive Hellenistic mask to stand out. Fifth-century dramatic verse was likewise more variegated and prismatic.

Harrison cites Aristotle in support of the view that vowels are of the spirit, consonants of the body. His own preference was for the material body, and his alliterative northern verse shortened southern vowels while emphasising initial consonants. This tendency assisted speaking in masks because when 'vowels were lengthened it caused a vibration in the mask that fogged the language and seriously disturbed the actors' concentration'. Harrison associates lengthened vowels with 'worn out traditions of English acting and English culture', and a 'rather self-regarding style of acting'.[54] Greg Hicks is a great admirer of the Harrison text which he likens to a 'mouthful of armoury', a text that makes him shiver when he picks it up, 'wonderful stuff recommended for anyone beginning mask work'.[55] He qualifies nevertheless that Harrison's text is hard to do 'from a technical point of view, because the aperture of the actual mouth must be quite unnaturally large to get plosive consonants out'.[56] Herbert's masks did little to help articulation, and when Harrison Birtwistle, who composed the *Oresteia* score, went on to stage his *Masks of Orpheus*, she had no hesitation in cutting away the mouths of masks worn by singers. In his subsequent Greek productions, when southern vowels were let loose on the iambic pentameter, Hall introduced an electronic 'bass enhancer' into the masks, in order to deal with the issue of vibration and eliminate a certain 'boxy' sound, while providing an

---

[52] Harrison (2002: 21–2).
[53] On evidence for costume see Pickard-Cambridge (1968: 198–202).
[54] Harrison (2002: 9, 22); Herbert (1993: 230).  [55] Hicks 2002b.  [56] Hicks 2002a.

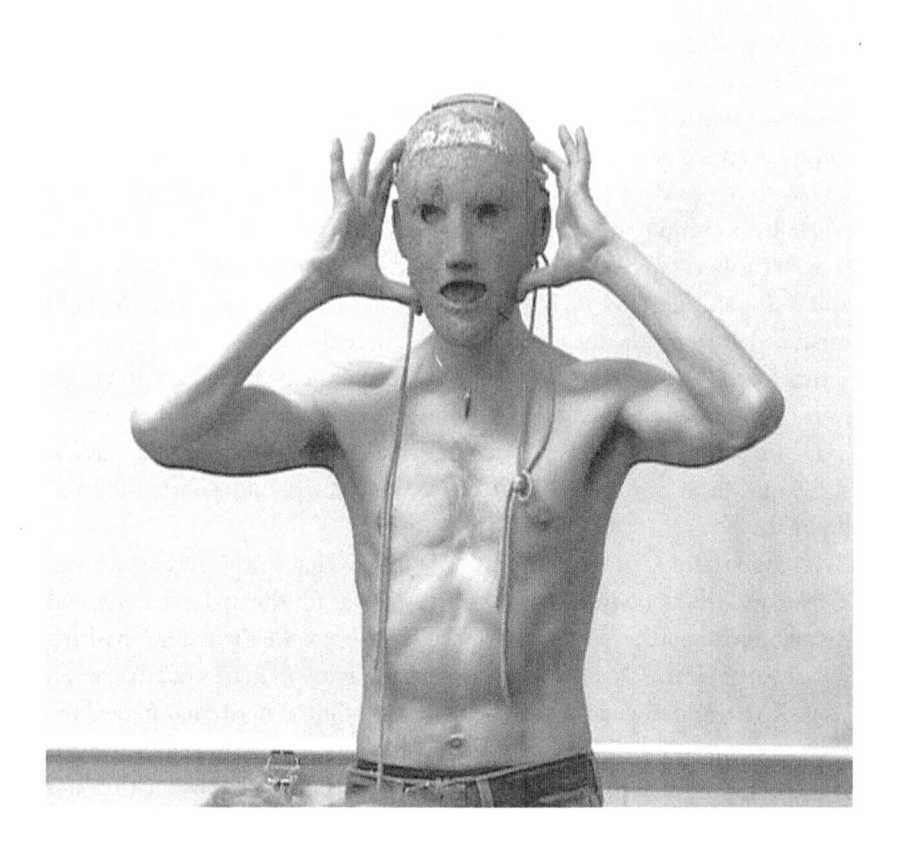

Plate 6.4 Greg Hicks in a mask demonstration.

amplification of some 20 per cent.⁵⁷ Though Hicks denies that the 'microphone' changed his performance, actors in *Bacchai* were discouraged from shouting. The psychophysical union of body with sound was not on Peter Hall's agenda.

Hall's brief to Harrison was to find the right sound to come out of a mask. The result was a heavy line with four pulses, a northern alliterative verse form with links back to Anglo-Saxon. In order to achieve momentum, the lines were timed in order to be spoken at ninety-two crochets to the minute. Hall saw that this language was ideal for his purpose, but without masks would seem hopelessly mannered.⁵⁸ Harrison was using essentially the same verse form that he had used for his adaptation of the York mystery

---

⁵⁷ Croall (2002: 35, 63). Reynolds (1996: 19).    ⁵⁸ *The Sunday Times*, 29 November 1981.

plays, where the actors had to present themselves as everyday tradesmen, and there could be no question of masks. This opens up the historical question of whether there was something in the language of fifth-century tragedy that belongs to the mask, or whether we can only account for the mask in terms of the horrific content of tragedy, and matters of cultural and spatial context. Oliver Taplin, for whom the classical mask 'was fundamentally the sign of the act of impersonation', finds scant logic in the thesis of Hall's Cambridge lectures that the Greek mask was equivalent to the Shakespearean iambic pentameter. 'Put like that, I find the idea pretty strange, because there is no doubt that the Greek equivalent of the iambic pentameter is the iambic hexameter, what we now normally call the iambic trimeter (metrically speaking there are remarkable similarities between the Shakespearean spoken line and the Greek)'.[59] An unsympathetic reviewer of Hall's *Bacchai*, though conceding that the Agave mask seemed to have its expression altered by the words, insisted: 'it would be far more moving to see the face of a real actor registering this terrible shift in perception. "The screaming, naked, human face would repel," Hall insists in his book, *Exposed by the Mask*, to which I can only reply nonsense. Does Lear repel when he comes howling on to the stage with the body of the dead Cordelia in his arms? Of course not. Would Hall dream of staging this scene in masks? He would be mad if he did.'[60] In the remainder of this chapter I shall seek to address the issue: in what sense is the Greek trimeter, with its basis in six iambs, a language for masks where the Shakespearean line of five iambs is a language for faces?

Hall came closest to providing an answer in a platform discussion of *The Oedipus Plays*, where he made two historical premises clear. First, he assumes that Greek tragedy grew out of storytelling, not choral lyric; and second, he relates his mantra that masks must never look at each other to a spatial assumption that the chorus belonged to the orchestra, the protagonists to a stage from which they addressed the chorus and the gods. He envisages a theatre of the word where members of the chorus, forbidden to look at each other, were forced to rely on listening. Hall's concept of the physical action is restrictive, for 'The only action in any Greek play is someone coming on or someone going off. It's not like modern American movies, you don't blind yourself on stage. You hear how Oedipus has been blinded, which is even more horrifying, then he comes out blinded. The whole thing is based on the worship of form.' Hall went on to discuss the

---

[59] Taplin 2002. [60] Charles Spencer. *The Daily Telegraph*, 21 May 2002, citing Hall (2000: 24).

blinding of Gloucester in *King Lear*, and argued that 'Shakespeare knew his Greeks' so must have deliberately introduced 'a piece of meretricious violence, in my opinion, which wasn't quite the full tragic dimension, otherwise he would have kept it off the stage or described it, or put it in some form other than naturalism.' For Hall, Greek tragedy is much purer in its formalism, shaped by three language modes: the 'great arias for the solo protagonists', complex choruses which are 'about the subconscious', and then stichomythic dialogue where people confront each other and argue. Turning to Shakespeare Hall reiterated that Shakespeare's verse was his mask. 'You can't do Shakespeare in a mask and it's quite interesting why. Because it's like putting a mask on a mask. The text is too complex and metaphorical to exist behind a mask.'[61] The key point is clear: not only is Shakespeare less formal and static, but something in his metaphorical density resists the mask. A rider to the argument emerges in the Cambridge lectures, where Hall describes the Elizabethan theatre as 'an unrepresentational space, which, like a mask, became what the actor said it was – a palace, or a prison'.[62] The actor projected a reality onto the walls of the Rose or the Globe in a way that cannot happen in a Greek space. Shakespearean language had a different job to do.

Greg Hicks, as an experienced Shakespearean actor, is in full agreement with Hall that a masked *Hamlet* could not work: the language 'does not sit in a mask'. While rehearsing the role of Coriolanus in 2002, he read David Mamet's controversial *True and False*, and found himself in sympathy with the argument that there is no such thing as character, only text. He undertook no method-type research for the role: 'I just talked, found my way in by opening my mouth. That is why Peter is such a rock about language – look at the iambics etcetera, then you'll find out. I've had a positive response about what I'm doing, suggesting I've captured the essence of the character.' In Greek drama, despite the soaring and ecstatic language, the characters seem to him sharper than those of Shakespeare. 'Teiresias comes on and confronts Oedipus, then Jocasta says don't pay any attention to that old man. The storytelling aspect is so sharply defined.'[63] For Hicks, character is a function of narrative in Greek tragedy, but of language in Shakespeare. When he observes that 'the essence of a character's motive is absolutely spotlighted when you are in a mask', we recall the Aristotelian principle that character in Greek tragedy should be a function of plot. Hicks discovered the importance of Greek space at Epidaurus where he experimented

---

[61] Hall 1996.  [62] Hall (2000: 63).  [63] Hicks 2002b.

with performing bits of Shakespeare and Harrison's *Oresteia* without a mask and felt himself a smaller, humbler human being, so the text became more difficult to play 'whereas somehow in mask I felt okay I'm part of the archetype here, I'm part of the archetypal structure, psychically, at this place, in this mask'.[64] Though this experiment takes us back from language to spatial context, Hicks' terminology calls attention to the archetypal quality of Greek dramatic characters.

With these indications in mind, let us attempt some close reading of text. To establish a parallel context in Greek myth, I shall take my Shakespearean samples from *Troilus and Cressida*. We shall begin with six lines where the manipulative Odysseus attempts to manoeuvre his companion into supporting the Argive cause. In Shakespeare Odysseus (Ulysses) works on Achilles, and in Sophocles he works on Achilles' son. Odysseus' motives and aims are never in doubt and the dramatic interest lies in how his victim will respond. Shakespeare's handsome sulking hero is now being spurned by the Greeks, who have conspired to treat him as misers do beggars, and this prompts Ulysses to launch into what will be a thirty-line simile:

Time hath (my Lord) a wallet at his backe,
Wherein he puts almes for obliuion:
A great siz'd monster of ingratitudes:
Those scraps are good deedes past,
Which are deuour'd as fast as they are made,
Forgot as soone as done: perseuerance, deere my Lord,
Keepes honor bright . . .[65]

Ulysses paints an elaborate verbal picture of a beggar, but literalistic miming of a wallet or becoming the monstrous Time would only confuse. The physical person of the beggar is neither impersonated by Ulysses, nor projected onto Achilles, but left to be conjured up as a vision on the empty stage. An audience reared on masques, morality plays and sermons would have found this language of allegory easy enough to grasp, and would have formed an appropriate mental picture when 'Perseverance' is in turn personified.

In my contrasted lines of Sophocles, Odysseus tries to spur Neoptolemus into undertaking an immoral act. In order to clarify the metre I have emboldened short syllables and indicated the three feet of the trimeter:

---

[64] Hicks 2002a.
[65] *Troilus and Cressida* III.iii.145–50. Spelling and punctuation from the first Folio.

all'autò toû-/**to** deî **so**phis-/thênai, **klop**eùs
**hó**pos **gen**é-/sei tôn **an**ik-/éton **hóp**lon.
éxoida, paî,/**phús**ei **se** mè/**pe**phuk**óta**
toiaûta pho-/neîn me**dè** tech-/nâsthai **kaká**.
all' he**dù** gár/ti ktêma tês/**ní**kes **lab**eîn,
tólma **dík**ai-/**oi** d'aûth**is** ek-/**phan**oúmetha.[66]

Odysseus sets out his measured arguments in three pairs of lines. In the first pair Neoptolemus is told that this act of sophistry is necessary: he will be a thief (*klopeus*) of the unconquered bow. In the second pair Odysseus tells Neoptolemus that he knows his nature (*physis*) and breeding is to speak and engineer no evil (*kaka*). In the final pair he declares that sweet is the taking hold of victory; be bold! (*tolma*) – 'as righteous men later can we appear!'

The Shakespeare text is pure metaphor, and the word-image sits at a remove from the two bodies engaged in an agon, while the repeated 'my lord' maintains the tension of the face-to-face relationship. The Sophoclean text is much more direct, more abstract than pictorial, using verbs where Shakespeare prefers nouns. 'Like a thief' is too literal to be called a metaphor, and the hint that acquiring the bow would be like a military victory suggests exactly how the deed will be regarded. Just as in Shakespeare, the direct address to 'pai' – 'boy!' and the imperative 'tolma' maintain the tension of the relationship, and we may or may not be satisfied with the insistence of Hall and Hicks that such tension has to be maintained through sideways motions of the body. In Sophocles there is no gap between language and body, so everything that is said advances the argument and thus the situation: 'But you must . . . I know that . . . but . . . be brave . . . and afterwards . . .' The concern in Sophocles is with Neoptolemus' 'nature' which may or may not be like that of his father, and this true nature will be revealed as the play unfolds. Nothing in the looks of the mask or the actor's body language should afford a clue. There is no pre-existent hidden nature concealed by the mask, for this is a boy whose nature has yet to be formed by experience and acts of choice. Rather than regard the mask in Barthesian terms as a theatrical sign, or in Harrison's terms as an existential survival kit, it seems preferable to follow Copeau who saw the mask as a device to simplify the narrative, unify the body and eliminate any separate ego of the actor. When we turn to Shakespeare, we find that Achilles has been preoccupied with an existence constructed by the gaze of others: 'nor doth the eye itself, / That most pure spirit of sense, behold itself, / Not going from itself.'[67] The

---

[66] *Philoctetes* 77–82.   [67] *Troilus and Cressida* III.iii.105–7.

audience have become surrogate Greeks, their eyes from the diverse viewing angles of the Elizabethan playhouse helping define the beauty and honour of Achilles. When the focus is upon the physical person of Achilles rather than on the narrative, and when that person is preoccupied by the nature of his selfhood, the mask becomes an incompatible convention.

Turning to the verse form, we see that Shakespeare is making a sophisticated use of the iambic pentameter. Against the pulse of the five-beat line he counterpoints a different rhythm to mark the rhetorical argument. He reverses the iambic foot to emphasise the two key words in the first two lines: 'Tíme hath' (not Time háth) and 'álms for' (not alms fór). Then things become more difficult. The natural phrasing to preserve the pulse runs counter to the formal line endings in the printed text:

Those scraps are good deeds past, which are devoured [5 beats]
As fast as they are made, forgot as soon as done. [6 (accelerated) beats]
Perseverance, dear my lord . . . [3 (slow) beats]

The pulse demands that the actor swallow the words 'as soon as', to emphasise the rapidity with which Achilles' good deeds will be forgotten, while three missing syllables in the third apparent line evoke the slow drawn-out nature of 'per-séverance' when polishing armour. Though English metre is based on stress, Shakespeare makes significant use of length. 'Time' and 'almes' which break the regular iambic beat are also the solitary long syllables within their lines. The following line, 'A great-sized monster of ingratitudes', has a regular iambic metre, but when three long syllables 'great sized monst-' are followed by a run of shorts, the sound image contrasts the monstrous nature of the beggar Time with the rapid way gifts vanish. The long 'almes' is likewise followed by a run of shorts in 'for oblivion' as the line fades away into nothingness. Ulysses' visual images are thus complemented by sound images which exist outside and beyond his own physical presence. Since Shakespeare's metrical technique consists in counterpointing one rhythm against another, there is no way the actor's body can commit itself either to the one or to the other. If both latent rhythms and the formal structure of the pentameter are to be kept in play, the body must partially disengage itself. To dance the language is impossible.

The Sophoclean text keeps a more even rhythm, maintaining the rules of the iambic. Built-in flexibility is provided by the freedom of the first syllable of each foot to be short or long, and likewise the final syllable of the line is often short to accommodate a micro-pause marking the line ending. Odysseus uses a lighter, quicker rhythm for his knowledge of Neoptolemus' nature and rearing in the third line, and a slower or heavier rhythm for the dreadful things he has to do in the next line. He likewise speeds the verse for his throwaway conclusion that it's okay to be good later. The metrical structure based on length is modified by pitch accents.[68] An acute accent suggests that the voice must rise on many words which have morally upbeat loading, such as *hóplon* (weapons), *phúsei* (nature), *pephukóta* (reared), *tólma* (courage!), *díkaioi* (righteous). A grave accent cautiously halts a natural rise on *klopèus* (thief) and *hedù* (sweet). A circumflex denotes a rise and immediate fall on the trickiest and most ambivalent words that Odysseus uses: *sophisthênai* (deal subtly), *paî* (boy), *technâsthai* (to engineer), *ktêma* (possession), *aûthis* (later). The lilt of the voice thus creates a highly nuanced delivery, while the rhythm of the action correlates with the impulses of the body. The stress-based verse of Shakespeare is essentially percussive, so we can think of the actor using the wooden walls of the Globe as his drum; the length-based verse of Sophocles is more akin to the *aulos*, with the flow of sound from two pipes controlled by a single breath.[69] Harrison writes to the English drum, not the Greek *aulos*. The Sophoclean verse-form allowed the actor to move with the words rather than stand beating his rhythm, attuning his body to the rising and falling, speeding and slowing of the verse. While Shakespearean verse is based upon the background beating of the heart at the core of the body, Sophoclean metre asks to be measured out in footsteps, generating a physical dance of ideas. The mask belongs to Sophoclean rather than Shakespearean verse because it is a means to bring life to the limbs.

Since Aeschylean language differs greatly from that of Sophocles, and is plainly rich in metaphor, a second exercise in close reading needs to be undertaken. Here are some lines where a character flatters Agamemnon by endowing him with a sequence of positive characteristics. First Ulysses/Odysseus addresses the assembly:

*Agamemnon*:
Thou great Commander, Nerue, and Bone of Greece,
Heart of our Numbers, soule, and onely spirit,
In whom the tempers, and the mindes of all
Should be shut vp: Heare what *Vlysses* speakes[70]

When Ulysses describes Agamemnon, independent epithets converge to form a single intellectual conceit: qua monarch, Agamemnon is the physical

---

[68] Stanford (1983: 72–3) is an accessible discussion.
[69] Allen (1987: 132) notes, however, that length must not be entirely set apart from stress; cf. Stanford (1983: 65–6).
[70] *Troilus and Cressida* I.iii.53–6.

embodiment of the nation. As in my previous example, the metaphor sets off on a journey of its own. In a well-known passage of Aeschylus, however, a string of metaphors makes a direct sensory impact, with no overarching conceit or theoretical frame. I have again emboldened short syllables. Clytaemnestra addresses her husband, in the presence of the assembly:

nun tau**ta** panta tlas', **ap**enthetoi **phreni**
**leg**oim' **an** andra ton**de** ton stathmon **kuna**,
sote**ra** naos **protonon**, hupseles **steg**es
stulon **pod**ere, **monogen**es teknon **patri**,
kai gen **phan**eisan nau**til**ois par' el**pida**,
kallis**ton** ema**r** eis**id**ein ek cheim**atos**,
**hod**oi**por**oi dipson**ti** pegaion **rheos**.

Harrison renders as follows:

All that I suffered but no longer feel fettered,
I'm free to say welcome, my lord, to your house,
welcome as the watchdog is in the sheepfold,
mainmast of our vessel, chief central rooftree.
Like an only child to its father you're welcome,
welcome as land is to those on the ocean,
welcome as dawn is after long nightsqualls,
as a spring is to travellers thirsting for water.[71]

Reference to the Greek reveals that Harrison has made life easier for himself, in terms of flow and forward movement, by repeating the word 'welcome' five times. He also gives the actor a chance to pause for breath after 'rooftree' by creating a sentence break. Aeschylus secures additional rhythmic variety by wrapping one image around the line endings, and the final long syllable of 'steges' permits the necessary enjambment. Harrison's pseudo Anglo-Saxon compounds – rooftree, nightsqualls – lend weight and character to the verse,[72] hinting at Aeschylus' use of a diction and syntax that are far from everyday Athenian usage. Harrison's main concern is to preserve mass and momentum with his marked line endings and heavy caesura, while the Greek is lighter and more nuanced. My point in making this comparison is not to criticise Harrison, whose translation I admire, but to point up the different resources of the Greek language.

---

[71] *Agamemnon* 895–901; Harrison (1982a: 27).
[72] Taplin (2006: 241–2) plays down the Anglo-Saxon dimension in favour of a more general 'foreignising' in Harrison's text.

In order to examine Clytaemnestra's string of images, it will be helpful to enumerate each one separately:

| | |
|---|---|
| 1  ton stathmon **kuna** | *of the building dog* |
| 2  sote**r**a naos **protonon** | *keeper of ship tensile* |
| 3  hupseles **ste**ge**s**/stulon **pod**ere | *of lofty roof pillar footed* |
| 4  **monogen**es teknon **patri**/ | *only-born child to father* |
| 5  kai gen **phan**eisan nau**ti**lois par' el**pida**/ | *and land appearing to sailors against hope* |
| 6  kallis**ton** ema**r** eisi**d**ein ek cheima**tos**/ | *beautiful day to view from winter* |
| 7  **hod**oipo**r**oi dipson**ti** pegaion **rheos** | *to traveller thirsting spring's flow* |

1. After the heavy 'stathmôn', 'kúna' barks like a dog
2. three consecutive short syllables capture the tension of the boat's forestay
3. the plosives and repeated 'st' evoke the **st**ability of vertical pillars under external impact
4. short syllables and the echo of 'protonon' suggest the vulnerability of the heir
5. while liquids at the end create a sense of sailing on water, the initial 'ph' of 'phaneisan' captures the outburst of breath from astounded sailors
6. from a liquid implying beauty we move to the harsher 'k-ch' that brings in winter
7. Plato (who also noted the interiority of the 'n' sound and the outburst of breath in 'ph') comments explicitly on the root of 'rheos' to explain how the 'rh' sound is associated with movement[73] – the flow of water in the last word of the line contrasts with the plosives of lips desperate to drink

The job of the actor is to project this sequence of images onto the masked figure of Agamemnon. Forming these specific sounds in the mouth, and holding sufficient air, are already processes of the body. From vocalising it is a short incremental step to indicate a set of physical attitudes: the crouch of the dog, the tension of the rope, and the solid verticality of the pillar giving way to an attitude of seeing by father or sailor, and then to inhabiting an environment of spring or desert. These are tasks that we could imagine Lecoq giving to students in a neutral mask. While Harrison's language sustains the power and presence of the male actor playing Clytaemnestra, the Greek text invites the actor to surrender his body completely to the pictured image. This does not mean that the images had to be mimed or danced, merely that the whole body had to be engaged in finding the impulse which creates a fusion of sound and meaning. Freed by the mask from any requirement to present a character, or play his own gender against that of Clytaemnestra,

---

[73] *Cratylus* 426–7.

the Aeschylean actor could give his body completely to the creation of poetic speech.

In the Shakespeare extract we find a renaissance philosophy of the person. Agamemnon is compounded of three elements, the inert nerve and bone, the emotional heart, and the spiritual soul. Spirit in the form of God-given royalty modifies Agamemnon's physical substance. When Ulysses delivers his speech to the assembly, he laments that 'Degree being vizarded, / Th'unworthiest shows as fairly in the mask'. Achilles, he implies, has been usurping the part of king as if in a theatre. This is a Christianised world of revealed truth, where the qualities of the soul must be allowed to shine out, and a vizard or mask can only conceal the divinely ordained hierarchy. There is no such ideology in Aeschylus, where travellers, fathers and sailors inhabit the same experiential world as Queen Clytaemnestra. While Harrison introduces a discourse of personal feeling – 'I . . . no longer feel fettered, **I'm** free . . .' – Aeschylus displaces subjecthood onto a 'griefless *phreni*', the *phrēn* being a psychophysical centre of thought and feeling somewhere around the lungs. Ulysses in this extract adopts a social mask in order to secure himself a platform, and we are made privy to that playacting by his vapid rhetorical pairings, but in Clytaemnestra's language there is no identifiable sociolect, nor any calculating ego apparent behind the uttered words. Her dissimulation can be inferred only from the plot. The play of features that would be visible in the Athenian law-court is invisible in the theatre. The Greek mask, which obliterates any motive and personality *behind* the words, reveals the physical impulse that is *in* the words.

Hall is therefore right to insist that Shakespeare's iambic pentameter is his mask, and that mask on top of mask would be a redundancy. He was right to see the affinity between text and mask in Greek theatre when he brought together some remarkable talents to create the 1981 *Oresteia*. Harrison's text sat perfectly with Jocelyn Herbert's masks. Yet the project was also something of a cul-de-sac, with Hall going on to repeat the same strategies, while Harrison preferred to write and direct his own original material. Sadly, the Hall–Harrison collaboration, seeking a language for the mask, drew nothing from the Brook–Hughes collaboration ten years earlier, which had sought to root language in the body. Hall attempted a creative fusion of two different traditions, the improvisatory Copeau tradition of which his knowledge was superficial, and the Shakespearean verse-speaking tradition, of which his knowledge was profound, and in rehearsal there was a fracture between the two methods. Though Hall speaks of the mask as a tool for revealing, his production drew mainly upon the Brechtian principle of distancing. Harrison's conception of the mask also seems ambivalent when Brecht is modified by Nietzsche, and tragedians cross with Gorgons. A serious study of fifth-century iconography is something that neither Hall nor Harrison seems to have undertaken.[74]

---

[74] Hall (2000: 28) refers to Greek masks as 'probably made of thin leather'.

# 7 | The mask as musical instrument

In Chapter 6 I looked at the disjunction in Peter Hall's method between text work on the one hand, mask work on the other. Though Greg Hicks, helped by his personal pursuit of yoga, to which he later added Butoh and Capoeira, has achieved a high level of synthesis, this has been an individual achievement. The mask in Hall's *Oresteia* was an obstacle to be overcome by the voice, and thereafter a microphone in the nose of the mask negated the aural presence of the mask-object for the sake of textual clarity. My concern in this chapter will be with mask practitioners who have worked from the hypothesis that the Greek mask is a kind of musical instrument, and thus a means by which vocal and physical acting may converge.

In puppetry and in the *commedia dell'arte* tradition it is established that distinctive voices belong to particular puppets or masks.[1] When Dario Fo put on a classical slave mask carved in wood by Amleto Sartori, he was impressed by its sonority, and the way the mouth was formed into a megaphone, a feature which he related to the scale of ancient theatres. This led him to a conclusion about ancient masks in general:

> In terms of volume, the voice doubled itself, especially the low tones, allowing the hero-character to possess the deepest, richest voice. Every mask is a musical instrument that possesses a unique resonance. Employing various devices, it is possible to achieve a vast range of tonality, from falsetto to hissing and whistling noises, thus permitting one actor to portray several different characters.

Fo goes on to explain the difficulty for the actor when 'Your voice bounces back inside, distorting itself, and until you have got used to it, you can't breathe properly'.[2] The rigid helmet masks of antiquity inevitably created a more powerful resonance than leather half-masks. Turning this resonance from an obstacle (Hall's 'boxy' sound) to an asset requires a great deal of technical experimentation on the part of both actor and mask-maker, impossible under the normal conditions of mainstream theatre.

---

[1] Cf. Jarry's advice about the Ubu mask in Jannarone (2001: 248–9); Aslan and Bablet (1985: 285, n. 25).

[2] Fo (1989: 208–9).

Fo's proposition that each mask has a unique sound leads us at once to the question of characterisation. Hall was not interested in the notion of character, and Harrison's text made no attempt to create a different register for different characters.[3] We may contrast their production with a Swedish *Oresteia*, staged in a cylindrical gasometer in 2002. Masks were considered essential in a play which dealt with the relationship between humans and gods, and rehearsal masks were used from the start of the four-month rehearsal period. The masks for this production were made by Donato Sartori, son of Amleto and a close associate of Dario Fo. Sartori was politicised by the Marxist-oriented cultural climate in Italy in the 1960s and by participation in the Paris events of 1968, and his understanding of the mask is a materialist one. Just as *commedia* grew out of pagan practices and devil-worship, so he maintains that Greek theatre grew out of a popular, improvisatory Dionysiac cult, but became an autonomous form within the religious festival. In this context, the *Oresteia* tells the story of emergence into a rational world. Sartori explains how the size of the masked head required amplification of the body through costume, aiding visibility for those at the back, but he recognises also that masks do not just have a visual function. Experimentation in Greek theatres, with their excellent acoustic, convinced him that Fo was wrong to postulate a megaphone effect in ancient masks, but he remained struck by the 'characteristic acoustico-vibraphonic properties of this type of recitational instrument placed in exceptional Greek or Roman theatrical architecture'.[4]

Sartori envisages early craftsmen experimenting with different materials in order to follow indications of character provided by the poets. In the Hellenistic era he believes that masks acquired a higher level of artistry, so one character might have been given more than one mask as their dominant emotions in the play change. The physiognomic tradition of the Aristotelian era, as extended in the Renaissance, became the key to his own conception of the mask-maker's task (Plate 7.1). In 1984 he published a table of correspondences, indicating how core emotions and their opposites corresponded with different colours, shapes, materials, animals, ages, sexes and so forth,[5] and this ongoing research became the basis for his rich observation of human particularity. In *Masks of Menander* I related the materialist physiognomic traditions of antiquity to the masks of Greek New Comedy, where the links are very clear.[6]

---

[3] Underwood (1998: 79).    [4] Sartori (2003: 17–19).
[5] Sartori and Lanata 1984; Sartori (2003: 60–1).    [6] Wiles 1991.

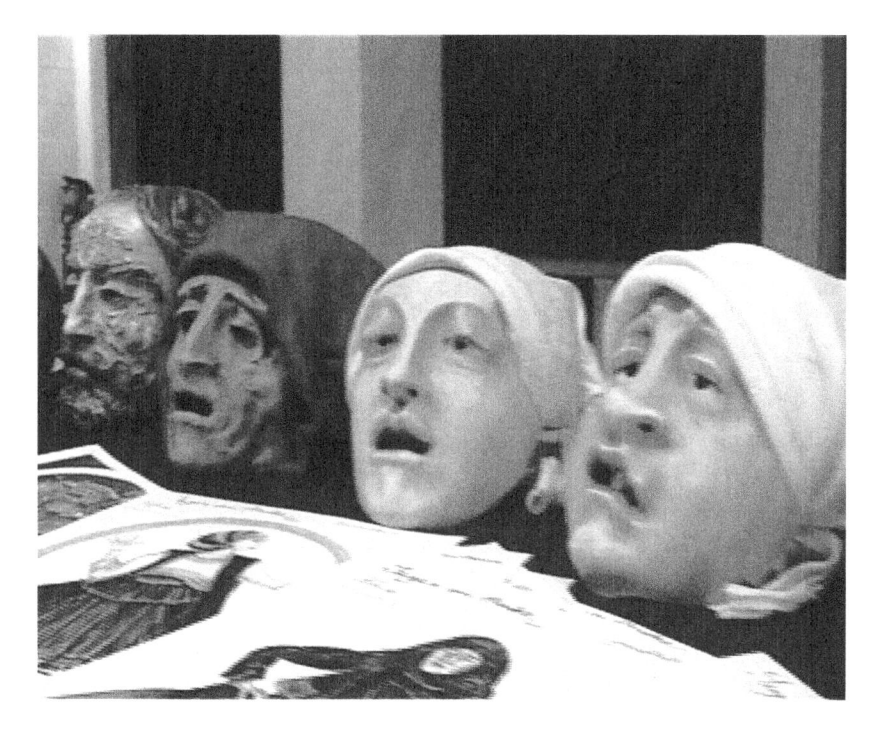

Plate 7.1  *Oresteia* masks by Donato Sartori.

What Sartori undertook in two years of work was to follow in the footsteps of his father who had made the leather masks for Barrault and create the 130 masks needed for the full *Oresteia*. He applied his physiognomic approach to Aeschylus, with a visual inflection from Nordic myth rather than Greek iconography. As the actors threaded through the crevices of the gasworks, each face communicated powerfully the sense of an individual character-type, and showed an ability to keep changing expression. The face of Agamemnon owed something to the lion, Aegisthus to the reptile; Orestes was conceived as essentially impulsive, Clytaemnestra as vengeful. This was a Nordic saga with a strong story-line. So far as I can judge from the video record, the scenes of stichomythia were most successful because the masks helped clarify psychological twists and turns. Choral speaking, however, raised the problem of perfect synchronisation that so troubled Peter Hall. Despite visits to Kerala and Mozambique, it was hard for the production team to find a ritual vocabulary that transcended the industrial environment, and the expressiveness of these physiognomies. It turned out to be a pair of actors from Lapland who found it easiest to produce the required ritual sound quality. In the manner of Thespis, Sartori experimented with a

**Plate 7.2** Michael Chase.

variety of found organic materials bonded with traditional eastern lacquers in order to make the masks for this production, but in the end was obliged to use a polyester resin that had an equivalent acoustic resonance because the production involved wading through water. His ideal of suiting the material of the mask to the character was not in this case achievable.[7]

While Donato Sartori sees himself as a sculptor who collaborates with directors, Michael Chase takes the view that the activities of mask-maker, performer, director and pedagogue should be integrated. He comes to the making of masks with an eclectic training in many forms of masked theatre including Balinese and *commedia*, and some of his skills were learned from Sartori (Plate 7.2). He is currently director of the Glasshouse Arts and Mask

[7] My source is a lecture by Donato Sartori at RHUL, April 2002, supplemented by written information from Paola Piizzi, and a lecture by Inger Ziefeldt. I am grateful to Anna Thelin for supplying a video of the performance. The *Sagan om Orestes* directed by Peter Oskarson was first presented by the Folkteatern in Gävle in February 2002.

Centre based in a college offering arts and crafts to students with special needs, and a few students are regularly absorbed into his productions, unified by help of the mask with professional and community actors. It was an interest in psychological archetypes that led him from themes like the 'four temperaments' into Greek tragedy. In a programme note for his 2003 *Antigone* he explained:

The masks for *Antigone* have been designed in as neutral a way as possible. I have tried not to bring too much in by way of character and emotion, focussing rather on their age, sex and archetype. These masks have been created specifically for the actors' heads, with resonance chambers in different parts of the mask. These support the actor's voice, and by doing so, assist in the overall transformation of the play from a psychological into an archetypal landscape.

When training masked actors Chase refers frequently to the head as a 'fifth limb', something that needs to have expression just like the hands and feet. If it is not articulated like a limb, then the mask becomes a blur, a meaningless object that simply intrudes between actor and spectator. Like Hicks he places much emphasis on the feet which provide a secure plinth for the body, and he attributes to Meyerhold a favourite exercise that massages the feet in order to animate them. Drawing on the same tradition as Barrault he refers to the actor's nipples as eyes, the belly as a mouth. He also distinguishes a 'thinking response of the movement of the head' from 'the feeling response of the chest and the will response of the arms and legs'.[8] This may remind the classicist of Plato's tripartite soul, hinting at ways in which the horses of Plato's metaphor could be translated into corporeal terms by the actor.[9] Chase's broad aim, common to many in the realm of physical theatre, is to create 'a technique of mask theatre where the body talks of emotions, ideas, intentions, not the face; in this way the communication becomes far more total and less psychological'. He finds that Greek masks are of particular value as a training tool because of their slower rhythm and tempo which means that there is space 'for thought processes to take place in the body'. Restricted vision in a Greek mask means that the whole body becomes a sense organ, and Chase uses a musical metaphor to explain what happens next:

The eyes can only see one thing at a time, they can see the feet, they can see the other actor, the audience, but only one thing at a time. The mask becomes linear, becomes like a melody rather than a harmony. The head moves in a melody, and the

---

[8] Chase 2000. Subsequent citations are from this interview.
[9] *Phaedrus* 245ff.; cf. *Republic* 436ff.

melody follows single notes of observation. These single movements that are drawn together more and more consciously create another sense of unity and harmony, with a bigger musical chord to be constructed.

In one crucial respect he is in accord with Peter Hall, namely an aesthetic distaste for the emoting human face. He describes how we can be 'presented with the soft still countenance of the face of the mask undistorted by raw emotion of the actor, and a degree of beauty and art sets in'. There are echoes of Hall when he explains that Greek tragedy involves a 'white hot emotion that the mask can contain' whereas 'without the mask we can become horrified by what the actor is doing. But within the mask we can accept it, it's palatable. We can go through a catharsis of watching the actor and their body and psyche move through such rich primal extremes of human experience' (Plate 7.3). In terms of technique, however, Chase works with different principles. Because he trains the actor to work with the spine and the centre line of the body, the actor is free to turn his or her back to the audience. Chase had no hesitation in staging the Senecan *Oedipus* in promenade style, or *Antigone* in traverse, because the masked body is expressive from any angle. Whilst Hall uses the mask, monotonously or mesmerically according to one's opinion, to eyeball the audience, Chase uses the mask as a device to tell the audience where to look. Because the eyes of the mask do not turn to left or right, the mask is like 'a miner's lamp on a dark night: wherever the lamp looks, the focus is'. This technique of projecting the gaze like a beam of light helps the audience to know who is listening, and offers a more fluid means of controlling the audience's attention in a theatre without stage lighting.

In terms of inner process, Chase does not speak of possession, but of the actor getting in touch with his own creative impulses, and a level of distance is always maintained. Avoiding use of the mirror, he has developed an exercise called 'charging the mask' whereby an unmasked actor 'teaches' a mask by moving and vocalising in a way that the masked figure has to mirror and echo. This efficacious device helps us imagine how the ancient poet, as *didaskolos* or 'teacher' of the play, must have taught the actors by direct demonstration, and breaks down Hall's binary divide between mask work on the one hand, text work on the other. The idea that the actor should learn by copying today seems characteristic of Asian traditions, while western actors expect to draw on their own inner resources. Chase's improvisatory method bridges these opposed principles, and helps the masked actor think outwards rather than inwards.

Plate 7.3 Actress wearing mask by Michael Chase.

The Glasshouse Project is an organisation inspired by the holistic philosophy of Rudolf Steiner, and Chase himself was educated in a Steiner school in South Africa. Steiner's wife Marie was an exponent of eurhythmy, a form taught today at the Glasshouse. Chase became interested in the acoustical properties of the Greek mask through reading about the work of Thanos Vovolis. The theory that the mask was an instrument for the voice made sense to him in relation to Steiner's remarkable lectures on drama given in 1924. Steiner was inspired by the possibilities of the Greek mask when he saw an oriental, probably Burmese, company at the British Empire Exhibition in Wembley. At last, he felt, he could see the true human being:

> For when you have before you the human being wearing a mask, the impression he himself makes upon you is due solely and entirely to the gesturing he performs with the rest of the body; and there's nothing to prevent you from letting the mask complete the beauty of the gesture above. One could not help thinking: Thank God, I have once again before me a human form, where up above arms and legs and body, which can express so beautifully what has to be expressed, sits not the dull human head, but the artistically fashioned mask, which with a kind of spirituality hides for the nonce the insipidity of the human countenance.[10]

Steiner's lecture was given in his theatre, the Goetheanum,[11] and his conception of the mask is inflected by Goethe's idealism. While Artaud's celebrated encounter with Balinese actors at a colonial exhibition led him to formulate the notion of 'spatial poetry' Steiner developed the idea that poetic speech was 'formed gesture'.

In order to develop 'formed gesture' Steiner turned to the discipline of Greek athletics, with its pure movements that recall Meyerhold's 'plastiques'. Running is a form of pacing the ground which helps articulate language, jumping gives emphasis to particular words, wrestling introduces hand and arm movements, discus throwing starts to make the face expressive, and throwing the javelin correlates with the act of throwing speech at an audience. Chase adopted these forms, linking the circular movement of the discus throw to the movement of the masked actor who addresses a circular Greek auditorium. In eurhythmy Steiner found the principle that, when repeated, specific vowels and consonants prove tied to specific emotions, muscular structures in the face, and gestures. He claimed that he had achieved 'a pure – let me say, a religious – understanding of what speaking really is . . . For such a conception of speech will, more than anything else, give you a strong and clear feeling of the place of man in the universe.'[12] On the Greek stage, a 'true feeling for poetry survived'. Steiner saw no such poetry in the fashionable Nietzschean productions of Max Reinhardt.[13] Chase took from Steiner an idealisation of Greek body techniques, a desire for poetry, and a sense that tying gesture organically to speech is part of the human search for cosmic harmony. Chase completed this conception by interpreting the Greek mask as an instrument designed to make sound and meaning converge.

---

[10] Steiner (1960: 79).  [11] See Wiles (2003: 54–7).
[12] Steiner (1960: 253).  [13] Steiner (1960: 78, 188).

When one works with Chase's Greek masks, as I have done on several occasions, the discipline he teaches is not to explore the exterior of the mask with one's eyes, but to explore the interior of the mask by bouncing sound off its different cavities. In this way the actor discovers the specific acoustic of an allotted mask, which can then be connected to other resonances from walls, the ground and (in the case of indoor performance) the ceiling. When the actor dons the mask, the mask is kept away from the head by wooden posts attached to an inner cap. Soft wadding would destroy resonance, and the posts are similar to those which separate the front and back of a violin. The actor now works with a partner, who puts fingers on different parts of the mask to test vibration. The pair learn the technique of directing sound into different cavities of the mask, creating a rich variety of tones. In order to make the possibilities of these masks clear, I shall transcribe some comments made by actors at the end of a day's workshop.

Julian Hanley, brought into the research project as a professional teacher of voice, was now convinced that the mask functioned as an instrument. He used the metaphor of 'surfing' to explain his feeling of

following a line of tone, or a line of music, into which you are dropping the vowel sounds and interrupting with consonants. It's about being able to . . . keep up a connection with the instrument you are working with – that was my reason for using that image. If it is too broken up, maybe it is more difficult to come back in at the right pitch, at the right level of the resonance of the mask . . . Within the rules of the mask there is actually a great deal of escape once you are riding the wave . . . There is a distinction to be made, I think, between the fundamental frequency of the mask, at which it resonates optimally, and . . . the different harmonics that the actor can bring to that, different tonal qualities . . . I think the masks do have a rhythm, each one has a separate rhythm. One mask can move quite effectively, quickly, simply, because of the way it is constructed: it's quite light, it's got a sharp nose, a particular kind of movement works. So the connection through that movement into the voice is kind of organic and obvious. Isn't it?[14]

Hanley identifies how actors have to find the specific frequency of the mask and then work their own harmonies, not simply imposing their own performance. Chase gave his Clytaemnestra mask a distinctly unhellenic pointed nose, and it was striking to see how this created a sharper sound and seemed to demand in turn sharper and more angular movements, in contrast for example to the rounded Apollo mask.

---

[14] This and subsequent citations are from a recorded discussion at RHUL on 16 April 2002. Transcript by A. Varakis. Part of an AHRB-sponsored project on 'the grammar of performance'.

Peter Bramley, trained by Lecoq, described the novel experience:

> I started to think about this idea of this thing being like a musical instrument . . . Some people who put masks on have a very spiritual approach to it, they think there is a spirit in the mask, and it's just interesting that the same kind of thing happens if you approach this thing technically . . . It needs to be played in a certain way, it kind of governs you . . . I kind of felt free, free to open up with the voice especially, that my need to feel that emotion wasn't necessary to perform it . . . It was all through sound. Normally my approach would be to study the dynamics of the mask, and how that moves, and to follow that physically – so this was very interesting for me to still feel physically something that I didn't have an idea of with the outside eye.

Bramley's technical, non-spiritual approach still involves being somehow governed by the mask. He responds not to the visible geometry of the mask, the planes and angles of which would normally shape his patterns of movement, but to the sound, which is ultimately a function of the same geometry. Another Lecoq-trained and also vocally trained performer, Erica Roberts, felt that in the universalising world of Aeschylus, which 'is about man of all men, the history of all histories, the goodbye of all goodbyes', the mask needs to receive the same charge and energy as Lecoq's neutral mask to make it radiate out into empty space. She found a suitable metaphor in

> those little diamonds that you touch and when you touch them the electricity in the diamond rises to meet your finger and they suddenly go ping! I feel so like that with those masks – and if you get the rules right about where you are sending your voice, about the movement, about the posture with it, about the dynamic of the voice, about the pitch, the whole sort of movement suddenly goes ping!

She discovered that moment of electricity when asked to move her whole body in the direction in which she was projecting her voice, which prompted questions about how the actor in stillness can make similar connections.

Angeliki Varakis, with an eclectic and more academic mask training, gave a vivid account of the performer's experience, with its inherent doubleness:

> I am a spectator of myself and at the same time I become an object . . . When I was rehearsing I said, 'okay, start mask, instrument play!' instructing myself – and then I start playing, I become an instrument along with the mask . . . and then when I am actually making the sounds they just come out and I am not conscious of it – but then I can criticise . . . I got lost in my 'Aaaa' and it just went, but I could also hear it at the same time and it's probably . . . because of the mask, in this shell, because of the resonance. I could hear my voice coming back to me, so that made it sound as if I was both an instrument and a live person.

The echo which the performer receives from a resonating mask, highly disconcerting to the novice, fosters a sense of divided identity. The mask seems to give the body instructions once the ego surrenders complete control, then gives the same ego feedback on what is happening. From the point of view of the performer, it is reductive to think of the mask as a mere tool for semiosis. One's sense of personal agency is challenged.

I have also worked with Michael Chase to explore the relationship between masks and outdoor performance.[15] Rudolf Steiner, though sceptical about the value of reverting to outdoor performance, underlined the connection:

On an open-air stage you will certainly not want human countenances; you will be constrained to go back to the mask. The mask, and the mask alone, will unite happily with nature's background. For the mask does not show man as he is, but makes him look rather like an elemental being; and elemental beings are at home in Nature. In order therefore to act in the open, we would have to return to times when man had as yet no desire to take his place on the stage as *man*.[16]

Modern holistic philosophies are less confident than Steiner about the separation of humankind from other forms of life. His point is nevertheless telling, that the mask creates a link between human beings and the natural world. The boundary between an inanimate environment and the flesh of the human subject comes to be experienced as permeable. A review of Hall's *Oresteia* in the *Guardian* was struck by the contrast of indoor and outdoor performance. 'London critics railed at the masks for obscuring words, and even the most enthusiastic spectator at the Olivier would concede that some lines were far from clear. At Epidaurus the problem was suddenly banished, and there was no need to justify the masks any longer. In an enormous open air theatre their role was important and obvious.'[17] We do not know what support Aeschylus obtained from the theatrical space where he played his *Oresteia*, but it is hard to doubt that greater acoustic support was required from the masks than would later be the case in the perfect conditions of Epidaurus. The *Guardian* reviewer, however, had more than clarity in mind when she referred to the function of the masks as 'obvious'. Perhaps she felt the same as the actor who found that, by contrast with London, 'in Epidaurus it really felt like ritual and not high art theatre'.[18] On a purely technical level, Peter Bramley observed that he could sense the precise

---

[15] An AHRB-sponsored project in 2000 on 'Greek masks and outdoor performance'. Documentation in Vervain and Wiles 2001.
[16] Steiner (1960: 319).   [17] Rosemary Burton in *The Guardian*, 24 June 1982.
[18] Jim Carter in a National Theatre platform discussion, 'National Theatre: twenty-five years on the South Bank', 10 May 2001.

resonances of the mask out of doors because there was no echo from the room. Chase confirms that 'in a big open field with no architecture for bouncing sounds off, the actor feels comfortable inside the mask, not to push, but to feel heard because they are hearing their own voice'.[19] The acoustic feedback which every actor relies upon in an indoor environment is supplied by the mask in an open outdoor space. Outdoor performance also tends to imply greater scale, and mask merges more easily with body when there is no insistent throbbing of an Adam's apple. Scale is related to pace, which needs to be slowed if the actor is to expand and fill the space. Thus, as Chase puts it, 'you turn your head slower, your gestures are deliberately slower, you walk slower ... and yeah it's just to give that other world the time to be there'.[20]

Michael Chase has a vision of the Greek mask which he lacks the resources to realise, either in vocal training or in having a trained company at his disposal. One of the difficulties of developing work in a Greek mask is that professional actors need to undertake a comprehensive retraining. Peter Hall took five months to rehearse the *Oresteia*, and Peter Oskarson in Sweden four. Thanos Vovolis is another visionary, whose aspirations for the Greek mask have yet to be matched by a production that satisfies him, though professional productions in Greece, Sweden and Iceland have shown the way. He has been working intensively on the Greek tragic mask since 1990, and this commitment has led him to move further than others, and ask more searching questions. Like Chase, he is unwilling to separate his work as a designer who builds Greek masks from the pedagogy that establishes how those masks should be used. For the freewheeling mainstream director who wants artistic control over the different production elements, this creates an impossible tension. Oskarson undertook two masked productions with Vovolis and drew inspiration from him, but preferred to work with Sartori when it came to the practicalities of realising a performance. Vovolis was no longer interested in Oskarson's traditional concept of theatricality. In a long-established partnership with the director Giorgos Zamboulakis, Vovolis has worked to develop an organic method of work that draws mind and body together. As a Greek, Vovolis has taken a far keener interest in the ancient cultural context and iconography than other European mask-makers, and he also benefits from an academic background in social anthropology. From the point of view of the modern classicist, his work represents a serious scholarly engagement with the classical past. Philosophically and culturally, we can trace a continuity from the work of Anghelos and Eva Sikelianos,

---

[19] Chase 2000.   [20] Transcript of discussion in 2002.

but not from Karolos Koun, whose tragic half-masks owed their genealogy to Brecht and to modern Greek folk culture.[21]

Vovolis starts from the premise that Greek tragedy was a choral form which continued to be defined in the fifth century by the memory of an original author/actor who separated himself off from the chorus and engaged in dialogue with it.[22] While Chase and Sartori assume that Greek masks defined contrasting character archetypes, for Vovolis the first purpose of the mask was to obliterate difference in order to make choral identity possible. He believes that in Greece: 'The human being was an organic part of the community without the psychological autonomy that marks modern man. The notion of the tragic is born when the individual being part of the community, begins to search for the truth outside the community.'[23] Vovolis contrasts the collective mentality of the Athenian world with an individualised, globalised and commercialised society where the opera singer for a million-dollar fee flies in already knowing the part, does the job in three days, and vanishes. The logic of the Greek form, as Zamboulakis puts it, is that each individual role is 'a deviational possibility of the chorus'. The protagonist is 'both his own destiny and part of humanity at the same time – he is never something different or extraordinary'.[24] The face of the mask may have indications of age and sex, and possibly ethnicity, but no physiognomic traits suggestive of character. Character does not exist *a priori* but is revealed through action.

When Vovolis describes the processes of the actor, his key term is *kenosis*, which translates literally as 'emptiness' but has a more active force than its English equivalent. The word has a theological ring in Greek, referring to Christ emptying himself of divinity at the incarnation, yet his usage seems more eastern than Christian, equivalent to the zen state of *mushin*, the 'no-mindness' that is a pre-requisite for total concentration in arts like acting and swordsmanship.[25] Vovolis differentiates *kenosis* from both the Catholic ecstasy which lies behind Copeau's account of possession, and the deep trance of Balinese *kris* dancers. Self-conscious thought has to be banished, he argues, if the actor is to inhabit the present moment in a state of total awareness and control, and there can be no question of a puppeteer manipulating the mask with deliberation. An 'empty' Vovolis mask communicates a sense of contained energy; it is a face caught up in some intense experience that evacuates rational thought (Plate 7.6). The eyes of a Vovolis mask like

---

[21] Wiles (2004b: 253–4).   [22] On origins of the actor see Pickard-Cambridge (1968: 130–2).
[23] Vovolis and Zamboulakis (2004: 112).
[24] From recorded discussions at RHUL 17–18 April 2002. Transcript and translation by A. Varakis.
[25] Suzuki (1988: 111–17).

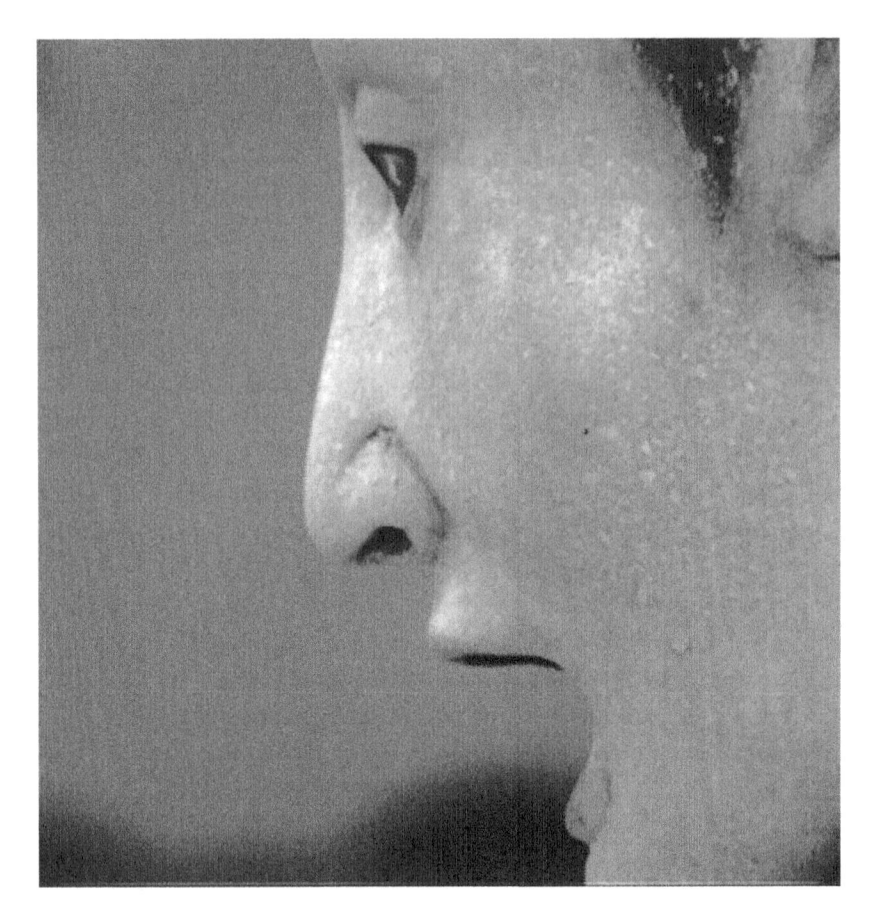

Plate 7.4 Rehearsal mask by Thanos Vovolis.

those of an Orthodox icon suggest a world that is inner but not psychological. The acquisition of *kenosis* is critical if the actor is to acquire physical presence in the mask, and surrender personal identity in order to become part of an extended chorus. The key to acquiring *kenosis*, as in yoga, is control of breathing, and chorality means the acquisition of a common breath. When Vovolis and Zamboulakis speak of the actor undergoing a metamorphosis, the term *vacheia* (the Bacchic) is often invoked, linking the mask back to the rites of Dionysos.

Vovolis' masks are objects of beauty, brought lovingly from a box and presented to the actor on a mat of black velvet. He shows his respect for the actor by presenting him or her with a mask that is no less beautiful and enigmatic than the face which is being covered, a mask that hints at 'other possible relations that wait to be developed, other worlds' (Plate 7.4).[26]

[26] Personal communication, 22 December 2005.

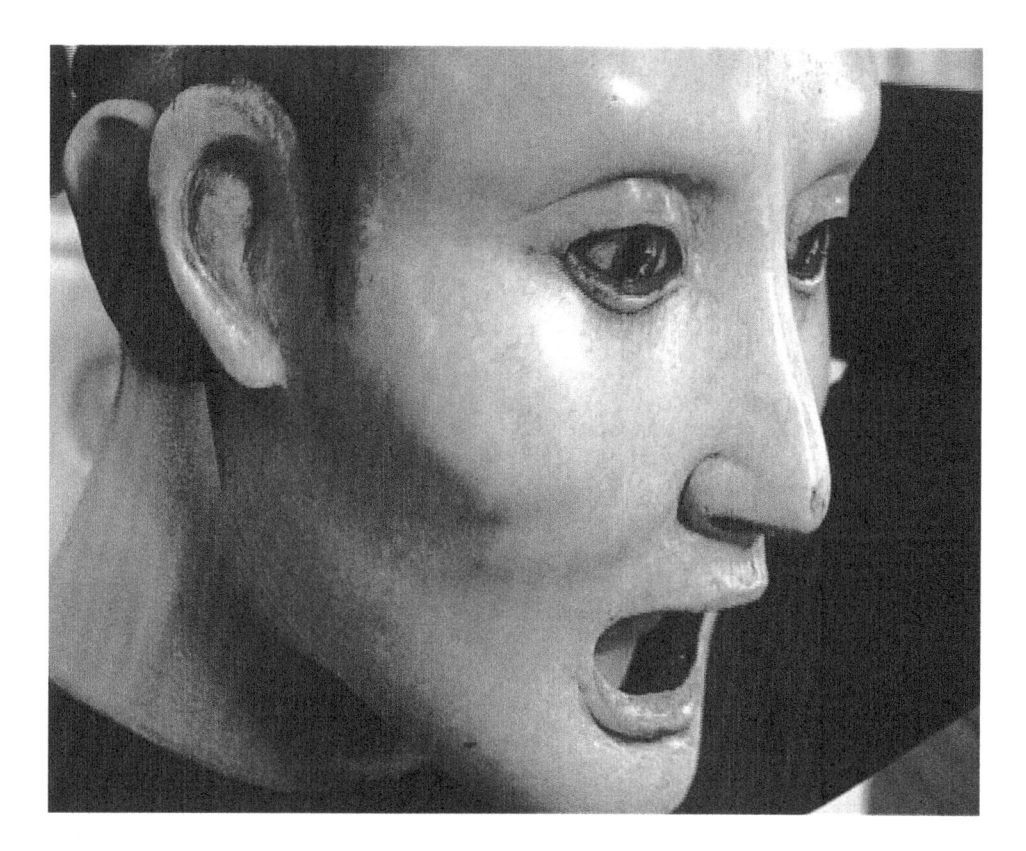

**Plate 7.5** Rehearsal mask by Thanos Vovolis.

The smell of beeswax helps to make these masks pleasurable objects to handle and wear. Like Noh masks of young women or old men, their expression encourages the intending wearer to gaze at them contemplatively. The masks are smaller than those of Michael Chase, and they lack Chase's dynamic lines which lead energetically outwards into empty space. They are sculpted with subtle planes, bulges and recesses that are imperceptible at first glance, designed to catch the light and create changes of expression when the spectator's angle of vision changes by a few degrees (Plate 7.5). The illusion of life is supplemented by a high level of asymmetry, which one only notices when taught to do so.[27] The mouth is smaller than in Chase's masks, and its form relates to the shape made by the human mouth in the utterance of ritual cries. The eyes are pierced at the iris, creating only a small aperture for the wearer. When the mask is tailor-made for the actor and the eyes precisely angled, the effect is to create a sense of vision through a central third eye. As in Noh masks, restricted vision is crucial to the creation of an

---

[27] I am grateful to Chris Vervain for demonstrating the extent of this asymmetry.

**Plate 7.6** Messenger in *Oedipus the King*.

appropriate mental state in the actor, freed from self and precisely focused, with the hearing and other senses sharpened. Turning to the point of view of the spectator, Vovolis likens his empty mask to a projection screen, onto which one can place emotions and an *ethos*, a moral character.[28] Its power lies in its potentiality.

Chase's acoustical technique is to direct sound from the mouth into the cavities of the mask, creating diverse moods and characterisations. For Vovolis, the mask becomes an outer layer of the actor's skull, separated by a thin gap. Actors are taught to develop the head resonator, so sound reverberating in the top of the head can by extension pass through the mask. In the experience of Patsy Rodenburg, Director of Voice at Britain's National Theatre, most actors overuse their chest and throat, and underuse the head resonator. She maintains that classic plays rooted in passion require exceptional use of head resonators because 'The higher the energy of the thought

---

[28] Vovolis and Zamboulakis (2004: 110–12).

and feeling, the more the voice rises into the head'. Her doom-laden tips to the actor on how to work in a mask, written at the time of Hall's *Oedipus Plays*, includes the advice that: 'The mask will probably respond to certain pitches and some resonances better than others. Generally speaking, placing the voice into the head resonators works better than the chest.'[29] Vovolis is thus not entirely at odds with the wisdom of mainstream theatre. Finding the head resonator is a slow matter of releasing tensions and learning to direct and control the breath.

Vovolis and Zamboulakis explain their acoustic ideal by citing Vitruvius' account of the Graeco-Roman theatre equipped with resonating vases embedded in the auditorium, and they are fascinated by the Pythagorean mathematics that define the proportions of Epidaurus. As in a perfectly constructed theatre, the sound created within the actor's head needs to find 'consonance' with the wall or shell that encircles it. 'The mask has to be considered as the first external resonance chamber, a link in a chain of sound that starts with the actor and ends with the theatron and its surrounding landscape.'[30] Since Plato in the *Timaeus* describes the head as a spherical microcosm, a historical case can certainly be made for surmising that some Greeks conceived the acoustics of the mask in metaphysical terms.[31] In technical terms, the attention to head resonance allows the mouth of the mask to remain relatively small. What is crucial is the moulding of the head, with careful calibration of thickness and distance from the actor's skull. Papier-mâché after years of trial and error has been refined to create a material with superior resonance.

Vovolis was inspired by Mirka Yemendzakis' 1988 production of *Persians* which explored the ritual cries incorporated in the text, and collaboration with her in the early 1990s led him to investigate the relation between sound and emotion, and the ability of the mask to enhance the vibration created by pure and intense sounds. In 2002 I had the opportunity of working with Vovolis and Zamboulakis on a short project that culminated in presentation before a conference of mask-makers of the scene from Aeschylus' *Persians* where Darius rises from the tomb,[32] a scene that is symbolic of the way the first actor emerged from the body of the chorus. The method, as in many eastern traditions, demanded that freedom should be found within a learned form, and this proved disconcerting for western actors. Learning the steps, the gestures, the metre and rhythm of the verse, and the breathing, while

---

[29] Rodenburg (2002: 95, 93, 329).   [30] Vovolis and Zamboulakis (2004: 129).
[31] *Timaeus* 44; on the Platonist logic underpinning Vitruvian acoustics see Wiles (2003: 181–3).
[32] AHRB-sponsored project on 'the grammar of performance' (2002).

placing the voice in the head resonator all in one simultaneous process, proved taxing. Zamboulakis taught the actors with masks removed, but awareness of the demands of the mask was a constant. In the event the actors felt they crossed an experiential threshold whereby shared speech inflections appeared to derive from a common breath and common movements, and not from keeping eyes upon an external conductor. It made sense to think of poetic metre as something measured in dance steps, and it was abundantly clear that the mind needed to be emptied of conscious thought if learned sequences were to be reproduced in perfect harmony with the group, whose co-presence could be sensed largely through vibrating sound. Michael Chase was a participant in the workshop, and when, in the role of Darius, his normal South African intonation vanished and a new pitch was found, the vocal transformation surprised those who knew him. Zamboulakis likens 'consonance' to the sound made when a singer breaks a wine glass through hitting the precise note, and this metaphor seemed appropriate to what many of us heard. I had the opportunity of seeing the exercise repeated in 2006 when a young Greek actress took the role of Darius, wearing a full bearded mask rather than a rehearsal mask. Playing with pitch, she demonstrated great vocal inventiveness, and I would never have known that this was the voice of a woman.[33] In the light of such experiences, one can imagine how Athenian audiences experienced a voice in the theatre as the voice of the mask activated by the actor, and not the voice of the actor mediated by the mask.

The task of presenting this work to a conference in an over-resonant studio exemplifies the difficulties characteristic of practice-based research. Vovolis was challenged to show how the same voice functioned masked or unmasked, but declined because proper acoustical experiment requires scientifically controlled conditions. Actors attuning themselves to the mask work organically, and cannot mechanistically turn themselves on and off. An instructive exchange took place when Vovolis was challenged by Malcolm Knight, a mask-maker devoted to Sartori's physiognomic principles who had been working on the scientific reconstruction of character-based New Comedy masks:

KNIGHT: How do we avoid the mystification? And get to the materialism in the methodology of the work? How can we ground it in such a way that we're not just endlessly talking about idealist abstractions like 'zing' and trance and so on . . . The methodology is inherent in the methodology and therefore you can't explain it.

[33] At the Athens festival: 8 July 2006.

VOVOLIS: What happened, with you, when you heard the actors talking?
KNIGHT: Not a lot.
VOVOLIS: Ahah. I wonder why?
KNIGHT: I do not mean to insult the actors, and I recognize greatly the value in taking people to a point of emptiness and then bringing them back in character.
VOVOLIS: 'Back in *character*?'[34]

Two approaches to the mask came into collision, one materialist and centred on character, the other identifying a political context but ultimately spiritual. Within the community of twenty-first-century mask-makers one saw here much the same tensions, based on deeply held beliefs, as those which divided Barrault from Barthes. Chase with his background in performance and in Steinerian mysticism found he could lose himself inside the Darius mask in a way that Barthes, the politically radicalised classical scholar, could not. The mental processes of the audience are harder to pin down, with Knight hearing one thing on the basis of one set of expectations, others hearing different and diverse things. Academic conferences are not good for generating collective audience experience. The arguments which emerged within this gathering of mask-makers were not in essence different from those which divide classical scholars, some of whom see tragedy as a function of the Athenian political system, others as an extension of the worship of Dionysos, while others again see tragedy in aesthetic terms as the art of imitating characters and emotions. Different premises about tragedy generate not only different historical interpretations of the mask, but also different ways of seeing the same actual mask in the present moment of performance.

Whilst I have much sympathy for Vovolis' project, it remains work in progress. Zamboulakis plans to direct *The Bacchae* in Iceland in December 2006, which may by the time this book is published have shown up new possibilities and difficulties. The work that I have seen has not yet sufficiently addressed the agonistic and rhetorical dimensions of Greek tragedy, that is to say the tendency of figures to engage in extended debates couched, at least superficially, in rational terms. The insights of Sartori and Chase still have their place as we seek to understand fifth-century performance. The special value of Vovolis' work for the historian lies in his demonstration of how masking could plausibly have functioned at a time when there was no clear boundary between tragic art and religious cult.

Vovolis' interpretation of the mask impacts on current debates about the nature of actor and role in Greek tragedy. In the remainder of this chapter

---

[34] The encounter was caught on *Personae*, the film record made by Renato Villegas (RHUL, 2002).

I shall move beyond the question of the mask as instrument, and address two issues of current debate, where Vovolis' approach seems illuminating: the rationale for doubling, and the 'metatheatrical' voice of the chorus.

In tragedy there were only three speaking actors, and for Vovolis and Zamboulakis this rule was a positive celebration of the actor's metamorphic skills. They argue that doubling created 'a field of interwoven relations and a unity that surpassed each individual role'.[35] Greg Hicks offers the point of view of an actor when he explains how he finds his mask before a performance:

> I go in. There is my archetype, there's my character, there's my performance in front of me – on that shelf, or wherever he's sitting. I put this on and I'm no longer me. I'm serving the archetype, I'm actually serving the mask, the mask is leading me on . . . Yes of course I have to be skilled in this and that, but actually it's taking me, my soul, on. At the end of the evening, when I take it off, it's over. It's finished. It's a clean psychological break.[36]

On this basis he loves the Greek principle of doubling, the 'clean cut off point. So remarkable. One can take one's world off. Liberating.'[37] He is able to release himself instantly because the character is in the mask, not in the text or in a body carefully chosen by the casting director. In Peter Hall's *Bacchai*, audiences were able to sense the excitement of the ancient convention. The doubling here, however, was strategic, and, at least for the audience, character was not completely a function of the mask. Hicks himself doubled the god Dionysos with the prophet Teiresias, and the Servant who describes Dionysos' miraculous power. Edith Hall in the *Bacchai* programme suggested that the original actor who doubled Agave with Pentheus was a specialist in youthful and female roles, and that the pathos of the infanticide is 'immeasurably heightened' when we are aware of the same actor playing both roles.[38]

Edith Hall's conception of the star actor as an assertive presence in late fifth-century tragedy raises important questions about the evolution of the mask convention. While she is centred on the actor, Vovolis prefers to emphasise the choral dimension of tragedy, and his interpretation of the three-actor rule implies that the person of the actor was less intrusive. It is worth pondering again what the vase painter of the 440s meant when he wrote:

PERSEUS

EUAION

BEAUTIFUL

OF AESCHYLUS

---

[35] Vovolis and Zamboulakis (2004: 117).   [36] Hicks 2002a.
[37] Hicks 2002b.   [38] Hall 2006 provides contextual support.

beside the head of Perseus, who is clothed in heroic rather than tragic costume and gazing at Andromeda.[39] The implication is that the actor Euaion was a sexually desirable youth, classically beautiful like the young man he played. In the image we see Perseus, we know this is Euaion, but we do not see Euaion-as-Perseus. In our complex bilateral brains, there is no single centre of consciousness where these two aspects of cognition are obliged to cohere. On the other hand, we cannot *see* the same image simultaneously as two different things, as demonstrated for example by Jastrow's duck-rabbit illusion, or Rubin's vase.[40] The theatrical spectator likewise could not form two perceptual hypotheses simultaneously and *see* both the mobile face of Perseus and the actor Euaion wearing an inert mask, but only one or the other at a given moment. Hall's account of Agave/Pentheus raises important questions of consciousness: was the Greek spectator consciously aware of the actor and pondering the patterned nature of destiny during the performance, or was he unconsciously responding to hearing the same vocal intonations? Was there any need to cast the actor according to type in order to achieve either of these effects?

The emergence of the star actor should not divert us from recognising the positive aesthetic and moral value which doubling had in the Greek theatre. When Demosthenes ridicules his opponent Aeschines as the 'third actor' charged with delivering an early speech of Creon in *Antigone*,[41] it is a logical inference that the 'protagonist', the leading actor seeking recognition of his skill, would have chosen to play the role of Antigone, and then after her disappearance would have switched to the role of Creon, who effectively assumes the role of chorus leader in the final lament. This would have demonstrated his skill to the maximum. One can imagine how Phaedra would have become her opposite, the manly Theseus, or the virile Ajax become his immature half-brother. An evil tyrant might become the noble Euripidean Heracles, while a demure wife becomes the violent Sophoclean Heracles. Just as Pentheus becomes his mother Agave, so the Persian queen would become her son.[42] We have seen a visual correlative on the Pronomos vase, where a female figure holds up a young woman's mask next to the head of the actor dressed as Heracles. In accordance with these principles, Helene Foley surmises from the *Oresteia* that trilogies characteristically demanded

---

[39] Krumeich (2002: fig. 174). See p. 15 above.
[40] On illusion see Gregory (1998: 205–8). Rubin's vase, illuminated so as not to distinguish foreground from background, allows one to see two faces in profile or a vase but not both simultaneously.
[41] *On the False Embassy* 247: cf. Wiles (2000: 159–61).
[42] Pickard-Cambridge (1968: 135–49) provides a useful checklist. Marshall 2003 offers a helpful discussion of technical issues involved in doubling.

versatility from a chorus.⁴³ While Edith Hall infers that the performer of Pentheus/Agave was a specialist in young/female roles, I draw a rather different conclusion, namely that the skill of the star actor lay precisely in his ability to switch from male to female and youth to age, as also from speech to song.

Without formulating the notion of a 'tragic hero', Aristotle nudges us towards that concept when he speaks (with all due gender bias) of how the best tragedies are founded around figures such as Alcmaeon, Oedipus, Orestes, Meleager, Thyestes and Telephus.⁴⁴ Clearly many plays, like *Medea*, the *Electras* or Sophocles' *Oedipus* plays, did require the 'protagonist' to measure himself against the demands of a single massive role. In playing such a part, however, the actor was free to play a scene of fear, a scene of anger, a scene of pain without worrying about consistency of characterisation. It was enough to find the movement and voice prescribed by the mask. Moving from the role of Antigone to Creon does not in essence differ from moving through the different personae of Medea: pained, scheming, anguished, vengeful. Awareness of doubling conventions helps us recognise that tragedies are not organised around the story of a tragic hero, but rather, as Vernant has suggested, around the tension between individual behaviour and collective behaviour.⁴⁵ Modern concern for the uniqueness of the individual tends to make us interpret the chorus either visually as a frame or temporally as an interlude in regard to the story of the hero. When he argues for the doubling of Antigone with Creon, Gregory Sifakis rightly observes that to 'wonder whether Antigone or Kreon is the hero of the play is posing the wrong question'.⁴⁶ Rather than construe the play in Hegelian terms as a contest of opposite individuals, the doubling of Antigone with Creon should encourage us to look at the play as an event in time. The protagonist may or may not switch roles and masks in the course of his journey from exceptional individual to playing to a common human being, akin to or assimilated by the chorus. Often, as in the case of Creon or Agave, this assimilation is expressed musically as the actor leads the choral lament.

Vovolis points to the unifying force of the mask. His masks create faces that seem identical, though each is in fact unique, and is modified further by the body of the wearer. For the actor, the isolated experience of working in a mask paradoxically requires an enhanced kinaesthetic and acoustic awareness of

---

⁴³ Foley (2003: 7–8).    ⁴⁴ *Poetics* xiii.5.

⁴⁵ In his seminal 1968 essay 'The historical moment of Greek tragedy': Vernant and Vidal Naquet (1990: 23–8).

⁴⁶ Sifakis (1995: 20, n. 32).

the other. The physical demands upon a tragic dancer were prodigious, and so were the moral demands, requiring a literally blind trust in one's peers. The tragic chorus could not simply be an extension of the poet's voice, like a chorus performing Pindar for example, for the voice is found in the mask, not transmitted through it. A colouring of Doric distinguished the voice of the chorus from that of actors speaking Attic Greek. We may hear the chorus as a Panhellenic voice which bound the singers into a wider collectivity, but we may also hear it as a more ancient voice, reaching back into collective memory.[47]

Vovolis' approach rules out naïve character-based realism of the type exemplified by the claim: 'it is most unlikely that the Council of Thebes would dance while pondering weighty problems of state'.[48] There is widespread critical appreciation today of the ritual basis of tragedy. Amongst would-be progressive critics, however, an interesting debate turns upon the supposed metatheatricality of *Oedipus the King*, at the point when the chorus responds to Jocasta's dismissal of oracles: 'why should I dance?' E. R. Dodds began the debate in 1966 when he stated boldly that 'In speaking of themselves as a chorus, they step out of the play into the contemporary world . . .' It is not mere pedantry to remark that Dodds refers to speaking rather than singing, stepping out rather than keeping step with the dance.[49] In response to Dodds, Albert Henrichs attempted a more nuanced formulation to describe the 'self-reflexivity' of this moment, suggesting that the chorus of citizen performers mediated between the past and present of the polis. Vovolis could have no quarrel when Henrichs explains how the mask 'transforms the self into the Other and integrates choral performance with the Attic cult of the "mask god" Dionysos', but difficulties arise when Henrichs refers to the chorus as a 'self-conscious performer of the Dionysiac dance'.[50] Self-consciousness cannot be a function of the performers, who must evacuate rational thought if they are to sing and dance in unison, so must be a projection of the audience. Sourvinou-Inwood endorses Henrichs' position, stating that the 'mask, while locating the chorus in the other world of the heroic past, at the same time draws attention to the fact that the *choreutai* are not in fact "other"' but are 'also underneath the mask, a chorus of male Athenians in the present'.[51] Calame agrees, pointing to the force of the first-person singular in 'why should *I* dance?' The characteristic slippage between singular and plural, he argues, may incorporate a virtual

---

[47] See Gould (1996: 219). [48] Gardiner (1987: 7). [49] Dodds (1983: 186).
[50] Henrichs (1994/5: 70). [51] Sourvinou-Inwood (2003: 51).

spectator or virtual poet within the choral voice.[52] This suggestion obscures what is most obvious and important about the first-person usage, namely that the chorus functioned simultaneously as fifteen bodies and as a single organism. Calame approves the way Dodds manages to 'unmask' the chorus members in order to reveal them as Athenian citizens.[53]

Vovolis distinguishes such Brechtian or 'schismatic' conceptions of the mask from his own holistic method which treats mask and body as a single organism.[54] Helen Bacon's exegesis of 'why should I dance?' is much better aligned with Vovolis' approach. Having emphasised the unifying effect of the first-person singular, she glosses: 'Their singing and dancing has no meaning unless it unites them in connecting the events of this evanescent world to the incorruptible, deathless world of the gods'.[55] Inspired by her observation of lament in Greek villages, she sees the binding force of music as part of a drive for cosmological unity within a mysterious universe. The unifying dynamic which Bacon describes is at odds with the familiar postmodern urge, expressed in criticism and performance alike, to fragment the world constructed by realist art.

This debate around four words of a Sophoclean chorus points up again the contrast between two intellectual positions. I return again to Claude Calame as my exemplar of the 'schismatic', Barthesian conception of the mask. In an essay on *Oedipus* revised in 2005, he maintains that:

The primary function of the classical Athenian mask is to dissimulate; only secondarily does it serve to identify . . . [T]he tragic mask of the classical period serves to distance a voice and a gaze that one might otherwise take to belong directly to the hero of legend represented as 'alive' on stage through dramatic *mimesis*. It serves to 'shift out' a voice and a gaze, for the mouth and the eyes are the two organs corresponding to the holes in the mask's surface; they allow the voice and gaze of the actor to appear to the spectators, beyond the hero he is miming.[56]

To juxtapose an opposite view, I shall cite the conclusion to Paulette Ghiron-Bistagne's essay on trance in ancient acting, where she distinguishes ancient from modern spectatorship:

The enjoyment of theatre today relies on distancing, on a constant awareness of fiction, which, at the very core of the dramatic event, allows us to maintain a critical eye on the interpretation. The spectator in Greek antiquity went to the theatre to involve himself completely in the performance. The less the distancing, the more

---

[52] Calame (1999: 135–7).
[53] Calame (1999: 136); on the mask as distancing device, cf. also Goldhill (1996: 250).
[54] Personal communication, 22 December 2005.    [55] Bacon (1994/5: 20).
[56] Calame (2005: 115).

effective is the *catharsis*, the 'purging' of the emotions. As we have seen, what is privileged by actors and spectators in the classical era is perfect illusion.[57]

She rounds off her essay with a citation from Artaud. Now it seems to me that Calame is demonstrably wrong in his account of the Greek mask. Although Jocelyn Herbert's masks, as seen by critics in the front row of the stalls or by viewers of the video record, may have betrayed the actor behind, the Greek masks of Sartori and Vovolis allow no such glimpses of the actor through the eye-holes and mouth, nor for that matter do the computer-generated replicas of New Comedy masks which Richard Williams has tested on professional actors.[58] Ghiron-Bistagne's position, though apparently naïve and traditionalist, is truer to the ancient evidence. The primary function of the tragic mask was not to dissimulate but, in Calame's terms, to represent the dead hero as 'alive'. Plato's famous statement that 'even the best of us', when listening to the laments of tragic hero and chorus, 'give ourselves up' to the experience, taking pleasure in our sympathetic emotions, does not exclude the possibility that part of ourselves remains aware of the pleasure being taken.[59]

To support Ghiron-Bistagne's case is by no means to undervalue the moral complexities generated by the action of Greek plays, but rather challenges the idea that cognition can be separated from emotion. When moral predicaments are viscerally felt, they are more likely to prompt a politically charged debate after the performance. The mask was always perceived as phenomenologically ambivalent, but it is reductive to think of that ambivalence in terms of actor and role, and to eliminate the religious dimension. We should think rather of the tension which Vernant identifies in sacred representational objects, where the aim was: 'to establish genuine contact with the beyond, to actualise it and make it present, and thereby participate intimately in the divine, but in the same process, to emphasise what divinity holds that is invisible, inaccessible, mysterious, fundamentally other and foreign'.[60]

John Jones, when surveying cross-cultural evidence for masking, in an aside to his main argument which he never pursued, noted that 'the mask very commonly associated with the cult of the dead is the epiphany of the departed ancestor, and its weird hooting in the night is called the voice of the dead (the root function of the so-called megaphone in the Greek dramatic

---

[57] Ghiron-Bistagne (1988: 78).
[58] In the AHRB-sponsored 'New Comedy Masks Project' based at the Institute for Art History, University of Glasgow: www.iah.arts.gla.ac.uk/masks. Some photos in Williams 2004.
[59] *Republic* 605D-E.   [60] Vernant (1990a: 342).

Plate 7.7 Mask made by Thanos Vovolis for *Oedipus at Colonus*.

mask is surely to change the voice, not amplify it)'.[61] Ghiron-Bistagne also wrote suggestively of the fear that could be engendered by 'a distinctive *sfumato* or *vibrato* due to wearing the mask, and to the person represented, the hero himself'.[62] The otherworldliness of Chase's voice was the dominant impression left on those who heard his performance as Darius, not louder or sharper but richer and more musical. It is not normal in the twenty-first century to imagine that our ancestors could rise from the tomb and speak to us, and our emotional responses to Greek theatre are conditioned accordingly.

In his account of the battle of Salamis, Herodotus includes a story that illustrates the power of a Dionysiac voice over the Greek imagination. A pro-Persian Athenian on the plain near Eleusis heard the sound of a processional song to Iacchus, a figure closely related to Dionysos, emerging from a cloud of dust. Knowing the Eleusinian festival to have been abandoned, the

---

[61] Jones (1962: 44). He had in mind William Ridgeway's theory that tragedy evolved from the worship of the dead.
[62] Ghiron-Bistagne (1989: 86).

Athenian inferred that this song emanated from the gods, but his Spartan companion urged him not to pass the news to Xerxes, for fear of being put to death.[63] It is clear that the Athenian, the Spartan and King Xerxes were all disposed to believe in the possibility of a disembodied divine voice. Despite the rationalism of philosophers, the emotions of the many were bound up with traditional religious belief. The world had not become an entirely different place by the time of *Oedipus at Colonus*, where Oedipus is said to have heard a voice from god, so fearful it made the hair stand on end, breaking the silence again and again with the words '*O houtos houtos, Oidipous...*'[64] The sound evokes Jones' weird 'hooting'. The question we have to ask is whether the hair of the spectators also stood on end, or whether the audience watched in cool postmodern scepticism. Given the genuine risk to those spectators of mass annihilation towards the end of the Peloponnesian war, and the play's focus on an actual Athenian cult which bore on the safety of the city, and in the context of what we know about Sophocles' own priestly activities, it seems reasonable to conclude that the voice of the messenger touched deep Athenian emotions.[65] How then should we understand the voice of the Oedipus mask as it resounded in the theatre, the voice of the hero who arrives to take his place in the underworld beneath the soil of Attica, a voice which held somewhere within it the voice of an actor? 'Hypokrites', the Greek term for an actor, implies an 'interpreter', as of omens and oracles.[66] The Greek mask was part of the cult of Dionysos, in some sense a sacred object, and just like omens it needed a skilled 'interpreter'. In the heightened emotional context of the festival of Dionysos, the voice of the mask was experienced as the voice of Oedipus, even though that voice was operated by a prize-winning actor.

---

[63] Herodotus viii.65. On Iacchus, see Parker (2005: 349).  [64] *Oedipus at Colonus* 1623–8.
[65] On the play, see Edmunds 1996; on Sophocles, Parker (1996: 184–5).
[66] Seaford (1994: 270, n. 153) disposes of Else's reductionist view that the term simply means 'answerer'.

# 8 | Masks and polytheism

It is helpful to turn the question, 'Why did the Greeks use masks?' back to front, and ask instead: what is it about our own culture that makes us so unwilling to use masks, and delimits the way masks are used? I use the term 'our culture' in confidence that almost all readers of this book will be united by a set of cultural assumptions remote from those of Greek antiquity – but there may be some Hindu readers, for example, to whom I should offer apology. When *we* hear the voice of Oedipus, *we* seem, by and large, to have no wish to hear that voice emanating from a mask. An understanding of Athenian religious belief is essential if we are to understand why Greek tragedy was once inconceivable without the mask. We must engage with the mask not just as a piece of theatrical kit, but in the context of a different metaphysics. Examining ancient masking through the lens of twentieth-century European theatre will not provide a sufficient set of reference points if we are seeking a fresh historical purchase on a subject that generations of scholarship have made all too familiar.

David Napier, at the start of an important monograph on the mask, remarks:

> Probably nowhere in the history of Western civilizations do we find more pervasive attention to masks than in the classical theatrical traditions of Greece and Rome. Though from these cultures the West inherited much of its philosophy and art, what it categorically does not inherit in its Judaeo-Christian tradition are their polytheistic preferences. This metaphysical difference is fundamental to a study of masks . . .[1]

The monotheistic traditions of Judaism, Christianity and Islam are, from a broad anthropological perspective, unusual in their reluctance to develop masked forms of performance. Monotheism has become hegemonic, and its principles need to be interrogated if we are to develop any sort of historical empathy with the polytheism of antiquity. Some key premises of monotheism relevant to the mask may be illustrated conveniently by the foundation myths of Adam and Moses.

---

[1] Napier (1986: 4).

1. *Idolatry is evil.* 'Polytheism' is a seventeenth-century coinage, and before then monotheists spoke of 'idolatry' – the worship of objects. It is a small step from the idea of statues being animated by the divine, to that of moulded or carved replicas of the face being animated by live bodies. Both statue and mask function as transitional objects, mediating between two worlds.[2] The second commandment given to Moses which states 'thou shalt not make unto thee any graven image' may in the Hebrew refer specifically to masks.[3] When Moses left his people to ascend the mountain, the women melted their earrings to make a golden calf whom they could worship as their god, and the backlash against idolatry which followed was both brutal and traumatic.[4] The idolising of the calf was effected through naked choral song and dance, and Judaism thereafter frowned upon dance that might induce a state of possession. For fear of inter-marriage, Jehovah's instruction regarding local polytheists was clear: 'ye shall destroy their altars, break their images, and cut down their groves'.[5]

2. *God sees through everything.* Adam and Eve use fig-leaves to mask their nakedness, but their sin cannot be hidden from God's gaze.[6] The guilt is theirs alone, and masking the body has no purpose when God sees everything. The face nevertheless offers a privileged access to knowledge, for when Cain becomes angry with Abel, God sees that his countenance has fallen.[7] There is no question of Adam or Cain performing a masked dance to placate this God, who is the unique source of moral authority. Those who have eaten from the tree of knowledge of good and evil know that the universe is shaped on ethical principles; there are no amoral cosmic forces susceptible to influence by symbolic performative gestures.

3. *The mask is a mode of deceit.* The subtle serpent is implicitly the devil in the mask of a reptile,[8] and the dominant mask in medieval theatre was that of the polymorphous devil. When the Judaeo-Christian mask is not a mode of deceit, it functions as pure sign. The mark that God put on Cain can be interpreted as the first semiotic mask, not changing Cain's identity but proclaiming the vengeance his killer would receive.[9] In racist interpretations, it was easy for this mark to be reconfigured as the black skin of the diabolic African.

---

[2] Cf. Emigh (1996: 7, 17); Holsbehe 1997.
[3] *Exodus* xx.3; I owe this information to Nurit Yaari. *REB* (1989) has 'carved image'.
[4] *Exodus* xxii.   [5] *Exodus* xxiv.13.   [6] *Genesis* iii.
[7] *Genesis* iv.5–6.   [8] Cf. *Revelation* xx.2, 10.
[9] *Exodus* iv.15. Hebrew interpretations include a letter incised on Cain's brow.

4. *Human and divine cannot be commingled.* The serpent promises that 'ye shall be as gods', and God has to act hastily to prevent Adam and Eve eating also of the tree of life so they may become immortal.[10] Once Adam and Eve have left the garden, an impenetrable wall separates divine and human worlds, and God withdraws the privilege of allowing his face to be seen. When Moses climbs into the clouds to receive the tablets of stone, he is allowed only a rear view of God as God moves away, but even this causes Moses' face to shine so it has to be covered with a veil.[11] While God's face cannot be imagined or represented, the face of the prophet testifies to the quality of his spiritual experience. Moses masks his face to conceal it, whereas in most polytheistic religions masks are a revelatory mode allowing free movement between human and divine states.[12]

5. *God is eternal.* The golden calf was a new creation, retrospectively identified with a plurality of gods who had led the Israelites from Egypt, but the words given to Moses on the mountain are written on stone so they will last for ever. The fluidity of polytheism, with its tendency to construct new representations of the divine in response to new circumstances, is alien to the great monotheistic religions which make their one god an eternal god, whose word is also eternal. The fifth-century historian Herodotus proposed a date of 400 years back when Hesiod and Homer gave to the Greek gods their current names, modes of worship, attributes and physical forms.[13] Reinterpretation of divine actions by the Greek tragedians exemplifies the way polytheistic religions renew themselves.

With these considerations in mind, I shall turn to three masked forms associated with different polytheistic traditions – Yoruba theatre, Topeng and Noh – so they may inform our view of tragic masking, and allow us to return to ancient tragedy released from a set of premises that derive from the Judaeo-Christian tradition. I begin with an eloquent evocation by the Nigerian poet Ben Okri of how the monotheistic tradition appears today in a post-colonial context:

They took the masks
The sacrificial faces
The crafted wood which stretches
To the fires of the natural gods

---

[10] *Genesis* iii.5, 22.
[11] *Exodus* xxxiii.22–3, xxxiv.30–5. In one interpretive tradition Moses acquires horns.
[12] Cf. Saraswati 2001.   [13] Herodotus ii.53.

The shrines where the axe
Of lightning
Releases invisible forces
Of silver.

Having seized these masks, carved from lightning-blasted trees, along with other sacred objects, the Europeans systematically burn them, disturbed by the apotropaic features of the mask, and unable to grasp a theology which binds gods to the environment:

They burned
All that frightened them
In the ferocious power
Of ancient dreams
And all that held
The secrets
Of terror
And all that battled
With dread
In the land
And all that helped the crops
Sprout
All that spoke
To the gods
In their close
And terrifying
Distance

However, a few images are saved from burning, to be stored in the basements of museums . . .

For the later study
Of the African's
Dark and impenetrable
Mind.
They called them
'Primitive objects'
And subjected them
To the milk
Of scientific
Scrutiny.

In this environment masks become dead things:

The images died in spirit
And contorted
Their faces
In the Western
Darkness . . .[14]

If we subject the Greek mask to the 'milk of scientific scrutiny', without making an effort to imagine the feelings of the polytheistic Other, we risk following in the footsteps of missionaries and early anthropologists, dismissing the mask as a 'primitive' means of making theatre and failing to understand what made the mask live. As the poem continues, Okri relates this violent repression of the spirits to the madness and violence of modern Nigeria. The monotheistic West is configured in this poem not as the land of Enlightenment but as the land of darkness, where rationalism cloaks a deep fear of death. Okri's poem portrays a lack of cultural understanding that remains a feature of the present. When Peter Brook went to Nigeria as a latter-day colonial explorer, he failed to achieve the same level of interaction that he observed in a Nigerian adaptation of *Oedipus*, where the audience seemed to ebb and flow with every second of the action.[15] His quest to purify the actor's work proved incompatible with the choral and the cosmic dimensions characteristic of African theatre. While African audiences laughed uncomprehendingly at his attempts to be serious, his own actors laughed equally uncomprehendingly when a Nigerian actor danced before them in a mask, representing different Yoruba gods.[16]

The Nigerian dramatist Wole Soyinka defines how an African world-view differs from that of the West by reference to a mask-drama which he witnessed in 1961 at the time of harvest, where a struggle against chthonic forces resulted in collective well-being. The audience plays a participatory but prescribed role, and 'contributes spiritual strength to the protagonist through its choric reality'. A history of loss lies behind the modern status of western drama as 'a form of esoteric enterprise spied-upon by fee-paying strangers'. Greek theatre space created an emotional power through simulating the cosmos, but in its subsequent history western drama has moved from cosmic to purely moral representation.[17] He attempted to

---

[14] 'Lament of the images' in Okri (1997: 9–10).
[15] Heilpern (1989: 297); cf. Brook (1998: 184–6).    [16] Heilpern (1989: 277).
[17] From 'Drama and the African world-view': Soyinka (1976: 38–41).

restore the cosmic dimension to Greek theatre in *The Bacchae of Euripides: a communion rite* (1973), an adaptation which owes much to Nietzsche. The play was a product of exile written for the British National Theatre, and seems to me a less powerful text than *The Road* (1965) which also culminates in a syncretic communion rite.[18] Here, in a perverted version of Christianity, the 'professor' culls the deadly road-side for symbols that will provide the definitive meaning of life, and in the final scene he 'resurrects' a masked Egungun dancer who has been run over by a lorry. This appropriation of traditional religion is halted when he is stabbed by a lorry-driver who is an animist and identifies with the spirits of the timber he carries. Inside the Egungun mask is a dumb palm-wine tapper who inhabits a liminal world between life and death, and vanishes in the final image of the play when the 'professor' dies.[19]

As a child Soyinka was forbidden by Christian parents to see Egungun dancers, but he refused to accept that the dance was evil, seeing Christianity and Yoruba polytheism alike as 'metaphors for the strategy of man coping with the vast unknown'. For him, the translation of the man within the Egungun mask into an ancestor is no different in kind from the idea of transubstantiation in the Christian communion.[20] In 1999 he recommended to African-Americans that they should use Egungun masks as a cure for the neuroses of American life, so dead ancestors appearing through actors' masks might counsel the living towards 'social reconciliation', via a therapeutic 'interpenetration of vitality' between the different worlds of the living, the dead and the unborn.[21] The boundary between these three planes of existence, fundamental to the Yoruba experience and alien to monotheism, is mediated by the mask.

The Egungun masquerade requires that the body of the wearer should vanish from sight completely so it may be assumed that a metamorphosis has taken place. An identical convention applied to Greek tragic actors, whose physical person was fully concealed. The elaborateness of the Yoruba costume bestows honour on the spirits, and the richness of Greek tragic costume can be explained in similar terms. It is a binding Yoruba rule that the wearer should be male. For Mircea Eliade, the great historian of comparative religion, this convention is almost universal: ceremonial nakedness 'increases the magico-religious power of woman' whereas 'Man, on the contrary, increases his magico-religious possibilities by hiding his face and concealing his body'.[22] Margaret Drewal, in her detailed study of Yoruba

---

[18] Texts in Soyinka 1973; on Nietzsche, see Soyinka (1976: 140–2).  [19] Soyinka (1973: 226–8).
[20] Soyinka 1976.  [21] Lecture cited in Pizzato (2003: 42).  [22] Eliade (1986: 64).

ritual sets out the basic anatomical logic whereby men enter while women are entered, with the result that: 'In masking, men cover and conceal their exteriors. But when women are "mounted" by a deity in possession trance, the spirit of that deity enters her "inner head," her interior.'[23] In Greece the same logic obtained: a woman may be possessed in corybantic rites, as a maenad or as a Pythian priestess, but it is the role of men to enter masks in the festival of Dionysos.

It is a guiding principle of Yoruba thought that the boundary which divides the living from the unborn and the dead is permeable, and the transformation of the Egungun dancer into an ancestral spirit depends on this permeability. Touring from house to house, the Egungun can become or represent different ancestors in different contexts. To penetrate the 'dark and impenetrable mind' of the fifth-century Athenian is even harder for a modern monotheist than coming to terms with Yoruba culture. The mysterious phrase *patrōioi theoi* or 'ancestral gods' covers a bewildering variety of practices, from ancestor cults within the family, to quasi-divine honours paid to the war-dead. Undifferentiated spirits of the dead emerged from the earth at the Anthesteria, when graves were opened along with wine. Athenian democracy was founded on the basis of ten tribes each notionally descended from an ancestral hero, and individual demes also had their heroes. Athenians learned from Euripides and other sources to trace their ancestry back via Erechtheus to the earth itself. The collective Eleusinian cult and select Orphic cults offered various promises about survival in the afterlife.[24] In these circumstances it is impossible to pin down what *the Athenians believed*; we can only generalise about what most Athenians *did*, and what they *did* presupposed that the dead were powerful. Like the Yoruba, the Athenians sensed that their ancestors had some ability to affect the present. In tragedy it was not the ancestors of the Athenians who came to visit but the heroic ancestors of the Greeks at large, animated by masks for the sake of their beneficent and instructive impact on the present. Eliade explains the centrality of anthropomorphic masks in Greek tragedy on the basis that 'the rigidity, the fixity, and immobility of feature do not belong to an ordinary man; only gods or the dead present such immobility of expression, while still being able to speak, to communicate their desires, and their thoughts'. He relates the actor's surrender of identity to the logic of masks, which is to transcend earthly time and reactivate the past. While death-masks 'reactualise

---

[23] Drewal (1992: 185).
[24] Parker (2005: 21ff., 296, 354, 446, etc.); Burkert (1985: 203–8, 289, 300, etc.).

historic time', primordial time is 'reactualised' and '*lived*' by means of ritual/theatrical masks.[25]

Egungun rites involve a continuous shift between categories that disconcerts the westerner. Peter Brook was struck by the way a Yoruba dancer could be simultaneously possessed yet fully conscious, so 'although it is the god and not the dancer who takes charge of the body, the dancer's movements are totally dependent on his own understanding of the nature of the god, or in theatre language, on his understanding of his role'.[26] Sometimes the Yoruba mask may be a sacred object, sometimes sacredness is a product of the ceremony and the wearer. Solemnity slips easily into entertainment, and myth into commentary on topical matters.[27] Commenting on mimetic and self-reflexive aspects of Yoruba performance, Margaret Drewal explains that it 'was as if the spirit realm materialized to show the spirit world to itself'. She goes on to discuss scholarly unease precipitated by the way Yoruba drama functions as 'ritual play *about* play and transformation'.[28] When classical scholars attempt to distinguish ritual from a 'theatre' characterised by metatheatricality, they do not pay enough attention to anthropological studies of this kind.

As in classical Greece so in modern Nigeria religious life is in flux, and many now seek to combine Muslim or Christian affiliation with traditional practices. The 'king' of one Yoruba town remarked in 1992: 'The way to preserve many of these cultural practices is to present them as "àṣà" [tradition] and not as "èsin" [worship]. The supernatural elements will have to be deemphasised to attract fellowship. If we present and sustain these customs as a mark of our identity with the past, with our ancestors, and as part of our history and heritage, not as a religious obligation, then they will survive.' The anthropologists (one Nigerian, one American) who recorded his words surmise that use of the English language encouraged the king to introduce dichotomies quite foreign to a Yoruba experience, for a distinction between 'culture' and 'worship' can only be made in the adopted language. In the presence of an Egungun, they argue, the Yoruba always have distinguished between mask and dancer, yet 'move beyond the dichotomy and discern a reality not otherwise observable'.[29] Margaret Drewal faced the same problem of evaluating data in relation to the Egungun dance. 'Sometimes spectators spoke of the person inside the mask, commenting on his performance. At other times they operated as if the mask was really a spirit.' She was driven to the conclusion that 'the spectator looked through multiple levels of reality

---

[25] Eliade (1986: 69–70).    [26] Brook (1998: 188).    [27] Picton 1990; also Strong 2000.
[28] Drewal (1992: 96–7).    [29] Pemberton and Aflayan (1996: 205–6), citing the Oba of Ila.

and moved back and forth between them at will. There was no puncture in illusion; there was no puncture in reality. There was only a reorientation of working assumptions.' This is possible because the 'spectacle dwells conceptually at the juncture of two planes of existence – the world and the otherworld'.[30] Drewal makes a valuable contribution here to the theory of mimesis. Within a framework of polytheistic thought, we need not limit our analysis of the Greek mask to saying that *either* the audience is lost in the experience *or* it must view in a state of Brechtian alienation; that *either* the actor vanishes into his role *or* the audience must constantly be rating his skill; that *either* the actor is possessed *or* he must be a master of technique.[31] The dichotomising logic of monotheism need not apply. A shift of working assumptions is sufficient to effect a bridge between human and divine realities.

From the chaotic fecundity of the Yoruba tradition, I shall pass to Bali and Japan, where an emphasis on a contemplative state of mind, inherited from the Buddhist tradition, links theatre to spiritual practices. Balinese Topeng is the product of a syncretic tradition that fuses Hinduism with indigenous animist beliefs. The performances are improvised, but like Greek tragedies are based on a well-known epic tradition. I shall concentrate on the best-known form, Topeng Pajegan, where one actor plays all the roles, doubling with the same freedom that souls have to migrate during the long journey of *samsara*. In Greek and in Noh masks, the actor looks through the iris, thus seeing with the same eyes as the being he has become, but in Bali the actor looks under the eyes, in a relationship that allows more separation of the actor's mind from the spirit of the mask, necessary when doubling is so rapid. As in Greece and early Japan, religious festivals provide the frame for a performance. At the end of the performance, the actor dons the demonic Sidha Karya mask and is said to become imbued with divinity, serving at once as emissary from the gods and intercessor for humankind.[32]

Peter Brook wrote an eloquent essay on the Balinese mask, inspired by his adoption of masks for the scripted version of *Conference of the Birds*, a Persian fable which played in Paris in 1979. In a determined break with naturalism, he avoided using masks simply to turn humans into birds.[33] Before celebrating the Balinese mask Brook begins with a diatribe against 'something disgusting, something really sordid, nauseating (and very common to the western art theatre) which is also called a mask'.[34] It is clear that he would not have been a sympathetic spectator of Hall's *Oresteia*, for

---

[30] Drewal (1992: 103–4). [31] See most recently Duncan 2006, esp. pp. 12–13.
[32] Emigh (1996: 151). [33] See Kustow (2005: 241–2). [34] Brook (1988: 217).

whilst Hall always starts from external form, Brook starts from within. The argument which Brook develops is essentially neo-Platonist, and rooted in his devotion to Gurdjieff, whose ego-centred but anti-egotistical philosophy holds that a central core of 'me' must be sought through the stripping away of falsehood.[35] We all wear masks in daily life, Brook argues, and the job of the artist is to remove masks, not impose them. His particular wrath is directed at the practice of hiring a designer to make masks so one is 'putting subjectivity onto subjectivity', and forcing the actor to start 'lying through the external image of someone else's lie', for these masks will derive from frustrations and hang-ups lurking in the designer's subconscious. Brook's theatrical ideals also owe much to Grotowski, who wrote that 'if we strip ourselves, and touch an extraordinarily intimate layer, exposing it, the life-mask cracks and falls away'.[36] *Conference of the Birds* was an allegory summing up Brook's mistrust of external form, showing how tears of genuine remorse can turn into unfeeling stones.[37] For Brook the frozen form of the mask in western theatre obscures an elusive and transient quality of authentic feeling that is only obtainable through the *via negativa* of stripping away falsehood.

Brook contrasts the dead mask of western art theatre with the 'traditional' mask which offers a 'soul-portrait', an 'anti-mask' portraying the inner truth of a man who has lost his social mask. It is a paradox, he claims, that 'the true mask is the expression of somebody unmasked'. Despite his horror of designer masks, he accepts the value of neutral masks used in actor training.[38] Balinese masks with their capacity for shifting expressions seemed to Brook 'true' masks because they reveal inner truths of human nature. He describes how his actors fell upon the masks and treated them like toys until they were sternly reprimanded for their lack of cultural respect; second time around, 'the masks looked different and the people inside them *felt* different'. It is instructive to note how different Brook's response was when confronted with non-naturalistic Kathakali masks. Before a nose 'like a white billiard ball', eyebrows that 'shot up and down like drumsticks' and fingers that 'spelled out strange coded messages', he experienced cultural alienation; when the dancer removed his make-up, explained everything and danced with his normal face, Brook found the performance preferable.[39] The anthropomorphic masks of Topeng were compatible with Brook's search for human universals in a way that most other eastern masks were not. When

---

[35] For this relationship see Kustow (2005: 246–51).
[36] Grotowski (1969: 23; cf. 46, 207).   [37] Brook (1998: 120).
[38] Brook (1988: 218–19).   [39] Brook (1988: 220, 160); cf. Bharucha (1993: 74–5).

he adapted *Mahabarata*, Brook rapidly abandoned an interest in masked Chhau dancers, and the thought of adopting an Indian dramatic form.[40] He used the elephant mask of Ganesh as part of the narrative frame to give his story mythic distance, and not as a device to explore the boundaries of the human, while his divine protagonists were resolutely anthropoid.[41] When Brook describes traditional societies as places 'where you have a thousand gods, each a face of the emotional potential inside each person', he psychologises polytheistic religion. He learned about Balinese masks from a Balinese actor living in Paris, and displays little interest in cultural context.[42] He perceived universal human nature in his set of Topeng masks at the cost of closing his eyes not only to the return of ancestors, but also to the Hindu ideology of caste. We can perceive Greek masks through the eyes of Brook, as universal human faces, or we can seek anthropological distance and accept that polytheistic beliefs engendered a different sense of the human.

John Emigh and Margaret Coldiron have both provided detailed accounts of a Topeng performance in its most common context, as part of a temple anniversary ceremony. In Emigh's account, the performance is given facing the sacred volcano from which ancestral spirits are called down during the temple ceremony. Before performing the ceremony the actor recites mantras over the basket of masks, addressing individual masks as 'honoured grandfather' or 'honoured grandmother', and asking them to wake up in order to dance. He then calls on the Hindu trinity, and burns incense for the masks to inhale, and after the ceremony the spirits are asked to return to their heavenly homes.[43] Emigh's informant explained to him that the masks are 'symbols of the ancestors, and it is my sacred duty to receive their magic, to allow it to enter me and animate the masks, one by one, until I am exhausted'.[44] Coldiron gives a similar account, adding that the actor calls on the god of *Taksu* or 'presence' to enter his body and the masks. She points to a link between the *taksu* of the performer and household *taksu* shrines dedicated to ancestors, significant since 'the masks themselves are idealised portraits of some of the most significant of these deified ancestors'.[45] In her analysis, the masks 'make present the deified ancestors and the legendary past in tangible form making the unseen (*niskala*) spiritual world discernible'. Theatre and efficacious ritual are intertwined because 'not only are the gods and ancestors invited to visit the temple unseen, in spirit, but they are also revealed and embodied through the Topeng drama. The performer is the

---

[40] See Schechner (1988: 134–5); cf. Bharucha (1993: 85).
[41] On the Ganesh mask see Saraswati 2001; also Emigh (1996: 50–1).
[42] The actor was Tapa Sudana: Kustow (2005: 239–40).   [43] Emigh (1996: 111–15).
[44] I Nyoman Kakul, cited by Ana Daniel: Emigh (1996: 153).   [45] Coldiron (2004: 176, 94).

**Plate 8.1** Hippolytus and Nurse. Thiasos Theatre Company.

link between the two worlds, a human being who, through the mask, gives form to the gods.'[46] (Plate 8.1)

There is little in this account of a Topeng performance that we could not apply equally well to a performance in the fifth-century sanctuary of Dionysos. There the god was a spectator through the medium of his wooden statue, and rites of purification established an appropriate context. The performance made divine or heroic (semi-divine) ancestors present in a recognisable form. The Balinese performance mixes sacred dance and speech, colloquial and ancient languages, narratives from the epic tradition and modern political commentary. The orthodox modern view is to see the ritual aspect of Greek theatre as an inert frame legitimating an essentially

---

[46] Coldiron (2004: 173).

political or interpersonal discourse, but it is equally legitimate to interpret the overall function of the Greek festival as a mediation between the spiritual macrocosm and the human microcosm, like Balinese theatre in the accounts of Emigh and Coldiron. The Sidha Karya ceremony, like the satyr play, provides a formal interface between two planes of reality.

Brook observed how the Balinese actor handled his mask:

> He looks at it for a long while, until he and the mask begin to become like a reflection of each other; he begins to feel it partly as his own face – but not totally, because in another way he goes toward *its* independent life. And gradually he begins to move his hand so that the mask takes on a life, and he is watching it – he sort of empathizes with it. And then something may happen which none of our actors could even attempt (and it rarely happens even with the Balinese actor), which is that the breathing begins to modify; he begins to breathe differently with each mask. It's obvious, in a way, that each mask represents a certain type of person, with a certain body and tempo and inner rhythm, and so a certain breathing.[47]

Because western actors cannot approach the mask through their breathing, or so Brook alleges, they are urged to treat the mask as if it were a classic role such as Hamlet. He maintains that the meeting of a Topeng mask with an individual actor, given due sensitivity and sincerity, will create a truthful performance that involves the actor being 'in the character'.[48] Brook does not entirely neglect non-naturalistic masks, but comments on one demonic Balinese mask that he tried out on his actors: such a mask 'contains forces in it and evokes stronger forces than the actor can evoke himself. I have never seen them used in the Western theatre in this way, and I think it is something very dangerous for us to approach without a lot of experimentation and understanding.'[49] Brook constructs an oriental Other who is empowered to enter masks by mysterious breathing techniques and surrender himself to 'forces' in a way that the western actor can never manage. The word 'dangerous' evokes the fear of which Okri wrote, a fear that once resulted in the burning of masks and other idols. In the post-colonial era we no longer burn masks, but we ignore them, or store them safely in museums.

Emigh and Coldiron do not comment on this breathing technique which Brook observed in the culture-free environment of a Parisian rehearsal room, but rather on the power of memory. The actor not only gazes at length in the way Brook describes, but also sleeps with the mask beside him on the pillow until the point where it enters his dream-world. Their Balinese informants emphasised the spirit inhabiting the mask, not the mechanics

[47] Brook (1988: 220–1).   [48] Brook (1988: 221).   [49] Brook (1988: 227).

of breathing. The procedures which Emigh and Coldiron describe, which seem partly about imprinting an image and partly metaphysical, are complemented by kinaesthetic learning of a movement vocabulary. This learning through replication is a mechanical procedure carried out unmasked, but the face needs to borrow the expression of the mask in accordance with the principle that the body is a unified organism.[50] Brook does not choose to relate such codes of movement to his inwardly oriented concept of 'soul-portraits'. The monotheistic mind-set makes sharp distinctions between self and external object, and Brook eliminates any notion of spirits within the mask. The idea that a spirit can pass from the mask-object into the person of the actor is incompatible with western vocabularies developed to explain the performance process.[51] Brook used masks in *Conference of the Birds* to allow free imaginative movement between the world of birds and the world of humans, but not any interface with the world beyond the aesthetic frame of the play.

John Emigh's analysis of the mask is uneasily poised between eastern and western conceptions of the world. He writes as a sympathetic interpreter of Balinese culture, but also seeks to extrapolate from his Balinese experience an account of the mask as a universal paradigm for the relation of self and other.[52] Emigh explains how, after manipulating the mask in his hand for a long time, his teacher starts to move his body, 'bringing the mask to life, making an amalgam of mask and self that, for lack of a better word, can be called character'. He defines this notion of 'character' in terms of 'congruence' between the actor's 'physical and spiritual resources and the potential life of the mask', endorsing Brook's equation between the Topeng mask and roles such as Hamlet.[53] The vocabulary to which Emigh resorts seems to me treacherous, for it is unclear what notion of the Balinese 'self' survives in the 'amalgam'. The Balinese actor who maintains that his soul is in fact the soul of his grandfather has a very different sense of selfhood to the western actor.[54] In the final chapter of his book, Emigh seeks to assimilate his understanding of Balinese theatre with universal processes of acting applicable to his students at Brown University. The metaphysical domain is eliminated in favour of a meeting between self and mask 'located within the actor's own body'.[55] Balinese theatre is absorbed into the ideal of

---

[50] Emigh (1996: 116–18); Coldiron (2004: 189–91, 197–9).
[51] On spirit and mask, see Eiseman (1990: i.132, ii.208, 218). [52] Emigh (1996: xvii).
[53] Emigh (1996: 116, 275, 251). Cf. pp. 282–3 for a reserved appreciation of Brook's *Mahabarata*.
[54] Hooykas (1973: 23), Emigh (1996: 80, etc.); Emigh (1996: 200) pays lip-service to postmodern conceptions of the self.
[55] Emigh (1996: 275).

194    *Mask and performance in Greek tragedy*

Plate 8.2  Actor and mask. Würzburg.

'physical theatre' which as we have seen drives much modern western work on the mask, and the relationship between microcosm and macrocosm is surrendered in this deeply ideological procedure. The fundamental Hindu concept of *dharma*, the adjustment of 'me' to the order of society and the cosmos necessary to gain *karma*, is abandoned in favour of a western ethical and philosophical system which seals the human individual into his or her psycho-somatic micro-universe.

Emigh gains cultural authority for his position by drawing the Greek world into his paradigm. He evokes the Aristotelian concept of *ethos* as a synonym for character, and reproduces as his frontispiece a well-known south Italian vase fragment of *c*.340 BC in Würzburg (Plate 8.2). The vase portrays a 'paunchy, balding actor' with stubble on his chin, holding a heroic bearded mask, and used a new technique of colouration. Emigh alleges that the 'seemingly miscast provincial actor gazes intently upon that unlikely image of a self that he must lay claim to with voice and body'.[56] In fact, the artist has been at pains to represent the eyes of the actor as upturned,

---

[56] Emigh (1996: 277).

conspicuously *not* gazing at the mask. The mask in turn is gazing at something in the distance, having an autonomous life-force of its own. The actor's hair indicates that the performance is now over and there is a complete separation of actor from the spirit of the mask. Paulette Ghiron-Bistagne identifies this as the first iconographic image which differentiates the real actor from his mask, and comments on the error that we make when we are fascinated today by the realistic portrait at the expense of the mask. We have only the bare names of the greatest fifth-century actors, she argues, a sign of how far their identity was effaced by the mask. 'It was the mask, not the actor, that created the *personnage*'.[57] Pat Easterling notes the iconic status of this image on the covers of modern publications.[58] Even in this fourth-century representation, it is hard to see where we should locate the selfhood to which Emigh clings. The stubble is not a sign of individualistic bohemian decadence, but a generic sign of the profession, because one needs to trim the beard in order to wear a mask comfortably.[59]

The Würzburg fragment demonstrates a principle that is quite the reverse of Emigh's contention: there can be no 'amalgam' of self and other in the mask. Emigh might have drawn different conclusions if he had reproduced the grave relief from Salamis,[60] or this vase from Brindisi, dated some two decades earlier than the one he chose (Plate 8.3). An actor – or perhaps one should infer from the stick a playwright or chorus-trainer – manipulates a maenadic mask, while a woman holds a similar mask at arm's length to gauge its profile. The human faces are intent, serious and expressionless, and the masks are in no way individualised. The female attendant seems to be looking at the mask, but the man's gaze as in the Salamis relief is more abstracted and fixed on the hand above the mask. The features of the mask are known and familiar to the actor, and it is the transformation effected by the mask that matters. There is nothing in this vase image to express the notion of a unique *ego* that will survive once the mask is worn in a choral dance. Emigh's idea that the actor's 'self' does not vanish but amalgamates with another 'self' immanent in the mask is a necessary construct if one believes that the loss of self is equivalent to the loss of meaning in existence, but it is a dangerous extrapolation from the Balinese source material, and an untrustworthy guide to fifth-century Greece. Greece can all too easily be assimilated as the root of 'our' western theatre, when the evidence is interpreted incautiously with the aid of modern visual schemas and psychological vocabulary. The hermetic

---

[57] Ghiron-Bistagne (1989: 86).
[58] Easterling (2002: 328). In addition to these four, add now Vasseur-Legangneux 2004. The generosity of the Museum in seeking no reproduction fee is a contributory factor.
[59] Green (2002: 99).   [60] Drawing 3.3 above.

Plate 8.3 Actor with masks. Brindisi.

western 'soul' or 'self' is as a function of monotheism, and the plurality of spiritual forces in a polytheistic universe requires other modes of describing human experience.

Noh theatre offers perhaps the most attractive of all analogues for Greek tragedy. The tragic theme of loss, the poetic text, the participation of a chorus and the distinctive role of a leading actor make the comparison apposite. Modern myths of oriental timelessness, however, complicate most discussions of Noh, which has evolved in subtle ways over the centuries. I shall focus on the age of Zeami (1363–1442) when the classic texts were written, and the canonical system of masks took shape. In that period the audience was often arranged in a circle, the repertory was more fluid, and plays were performed with much more rapidity. One of the most fascinating historical shifts, it has recently been suggested, may be the increasing size of the human body. It is possible that masks of constant size now set in the midst of the face and framed by the jowls of the actor would in Zeami's day have covered the face, even though oral tradition holds that a mask:body ratio of 1:8 has obtained since the age of Zeami.[61] Kanze Hisao described the visible jowls as a means of avoiding the realism of a doll. The mask becomes one with his flesh, but at the same time is something he struggles against; it provides disguise, but also has a role of its own. The mask is a companion that provides entrance to another world, which the audience must also enter, and it must under no circumstances be seen as a mere fabrication. Kanze Hisao often acted in Japanese versions of Greek plays before his death in 1978, and his account of the mask helps the classicist set aside familiar western dichotomies between illusion and alienation, possession and technique.[62]

Zeami interpreted the prior history of Noh in writings transmitted to his successors.[63] His foundation myth, which roots Noh in Shinto folk religion, tells of a woman dancing obscenely to lure the Sun Goddess from her cave, and recalls the Greek story of Baubo entertaining Demeter, placing the female as both thematic focus and taboo in Noh performance. The next phase is set in India, where sixty-six plays were performed by disciples as a prophylaxis or diversion, so the Buddha could perform his ceremonies in peace. From here, Zeami traces a route via Bactria and China to the sixth-century court of Japan, where a quasi-divine foundling performs these plays publicly in the palace, bringing tranquillity to a restive population. The sixty-six masks were made by the Japanese Prince, lending a high status to the art of mask-making. An obvious purpose of this historical sketch is to create a precedent for Zeami's newly elevated status as an actor in receipt of court patronage. Zeami now takes the 'sarugaku' performance tradition through to the tenth century, when the sacred repertory is stripped down to three plays of special Buddhist significance. These include a version of the shamanistic ritual still regularly performed as preface to a Noh programme. In the Okina ceremony the actor publicly dons the sacred mask of an old man to enact the descent of a god into the player, thereby sacralising the performances which follow.[64] Zeami tells the story of how an Okina mask dropped by a

---

[61] Coldiron (2004: 265–6); Pulvers (1978: 5) citing the mask-maker Susuki Keiun. 1:8 is the Hellenistic head:body ratio of Lysippos, in contrast to the canonical 1:7 fixed by Polykleitos.
[62] Kanze Hisao 1984. See also p. 234 in that volume.
[63] 'Style and the flower' in Zeami (1984: 3, 31–7).
[64] Komparu (1983: 3–4); Pulvers (1978: 166–71); Martzel (1982: 109ff.); Thornhill (1993: 196).

crow once persuaded a samurai to become an actor, and his own company's Okina mask was 'discovered' at a shrine.[65]

There is no evidence for regular use of masks in *sarugaku* at this period,[66] so Zeami seems to have written his plays in the wake of a developmental leap similar to that which must have occurred in early fifth-century Athens. When he reaches his own generation, Zeami emphasises the affiliations that tied troupes to particular shrines, listing a series of performances at religious festivals designed to pacify devils and calm unbelievers. His broad theme is clear: performance is bound up with the complex interaction of Shinto and Buddhism, and aspires to create a mind that is at peace. Zeami imbued his plays with Zen-related qualities cherished by the nobility, beauty, nostalgia and the subordination of passion in favour of duty, and this political context encouraged him to develop the potential of anthropomorphic masks. To interpret this trajectory as a simple transition from the sacred domain of ritual to the secular domain of art would be simplistic, and it must be remembered that Zeami ended his days as a monk. Zeami's historical sketch emphasises at every point the religious nature of his activity.

From the fourteenth century, masks of young women in particular are characterised by the quality of *yugen* or 'grace', an important aesthetic/ethical term that can be likened to the Greek *sōphrosynē*.[67] The indeterminate mood of these beautiful masks, poised between tranquillity and grief, recalls the Greek ideal of mental balance, an equilibrium bound up with the perfect proportionality of classical beauty.[68] There is, however, a stronger sense of emotion in these Noh masks than in the classical face. Eliade's account of how masks transcend earthly time and reactualise the past helps explain the power of *yugen* in these female masks. Noh plays are set in the past with their principal characters identified as ghosts who yearn for something unfulfilled in life, and masks further the feeling that time has stopped. The cyclic sense of time characteristic of Buddhism, with its wheel of life and rounds of rebirth, sits more comfortably with the theme of ghosts than the progressive, linear temporality of monotheism. There is a tension in Noh drama between the beautiful 'intermediate' or 'neutral' mask, with its ethical roots in Zen Buddhism, and the demonic mask, with its associated ideas of possession. In Shinto tradition the *kami* or spirits immanent in

---

[65] Zeami (1984: 239–40, 237).   [66] Pulvers (1978: 52–3).

[67] Pulvers (1978: 72–6); Komparu (1983: 12–14); cf. Johnson (1992: 26–7). Translations of 'yugen' include 'subtle profundity', 'profound sublimity', 'mysterious elegance' and 'subtle revelation of beauty'.

[68] See Green (2002: 99).

nature have no form, but use the mask as a receptacle in order to become visible, and a legend centred on an extant demon mask tells how Zeami used its magic power to bring rain during a drought.[69] Demonic masks were the earliest types, followed by old men, and only later by heroic warriors and women.[70] Because the *shite* or leading actor moves between the two modes and changes masks when a woman is revealed to be demonic, *Medea* has proved an obvious choice for adaptation into Noh form.[71]

In Zeami's secret writings, the subject of mask technique is conspicuous by its absence. In fact, his only sustained advice relates to the problem of playing without a mask: when acting a lowly character with no mask, the actor must keep his facial muscles in complete immobility, and it is particularly hard to play a mad woman unmasked since the face needs to be descriptive but can all too easily become ugly.[72] Zeami's son recorded his father's comments on the specialisms of particular mask-makers, but no advice on performance beyond the generalisation that masks should be chosen in relation to the specific actor. We hear of a tight-lipped demonic mask that Zeami's successors proved unable to wear, requiring something lighter and less intense.[73] The silence of Greek literary sources about masking becomes more explicable when we look at Zeami's failure to identify masked acting as a topic needing analysis. Zeami passed on his writings to Zenchiku, who explained how a quality of mind is embedded in the mask, yet needs to be awoken by the actor.[74] We first glean a sense of technique from Komparu Zempo (1454–1532), who advised that masks of women and demons should both be worn in a bowed position, but strength must be put into the demon's mask, none into the woman's.[75]

Komparu Zempo also advised on the angle at which masks should be held in the hand when shown to others. There is nothing in our early sources, however, to anticipate a modern understanding that the mask when lowered is 'clouded', i.e. sad, while the raised mask is 'shining', i.e. joyous.[76] This optical phenomenon is enhanced by white stones around the Noh stage which reflect natural light up onto the mask. A recent psychological experiment which showed photos of disembodied Noh masks to Japanese and English subjects succeeded in eliciting the opposite response, namely that

---

[69] Nearman (1984: 38).   [70] Pulvers (1978: 52, 59).
[71] Pulvers (1978: 193) analyses a mask from a Tokyo production of 1975. On Ninagawa's kabuki-based *Medea* see Smethurst 2000.
[72] Zeami (1984: 12, 14).
[73] Pulvers (1978: 184–5). His translation seems more coherent than the Princeton version: Zeami (1984: 238).
[74] Nearman (1984: 43–4).   [75] Pulvers (1978: 62).   [76] See Wiles (1991: 108).

the lowered mask looks 'happy', the raised mask 'sad'.[77] The experiment demonstrates through its perverse result that behind every nuanced expression there lies a counter-expression. The crucial relationship, one discovers, is not that of the spectator's eye to the mask, but that of mask to actor's body. Margaret Coldiron interviewed a Noh actor who seemed to have used the technique of raising and lowering particularly well. The performer (who happened to be a woman) had absorbed technique to the point where manipulation of the mask was intuitive, and she professed only to be conscious of her feelings for the character she was playing.[78] We may well imagine that in Zeami's day a similar absorption into the other meant that the mask in performance was always experienced as the face of the other, not as an object out there to be manipulated. In those days there was no question of wadding to keep wood and flesh apart.[79] The same absorption into the mask must have obtained in classical Athens. The fifth-century actor, I suggest, having once assimilated his technique, was like Zeami more concerned with a mental transformation.

Nowadays the mirror room is where the actor ritualistically enacts his encounter with the mask-object. Both Peter Hall and Peter Brook stumbled into mask work by asking actors to stare at their own masked faces, a procedure which breeds externality and self-consciousness.[80] In fact, the Japanese actor strategically avoids eye contact with his own image in the mirror, and simply gains a sense of his overall physical presence, while adjusting to the restricted vision and breathing imposed by the mask.[81] The modern Noh actor sometimes uses the female *ko-omote* as a neutral rehearsal mask, and then dons the appropriate mask for a one-off performance, engaging before the audience in a live encounter with the presence contained in the mask.[82] In Zeami's day the mask was not laden with centuries of cultural memory and the plays were new, so the same meeting of self with object was not required to generate theatricality. The mask was a function of a broader task, finding the essence of the character, and the perpetual enemy was externalisation. Some plays, Zeami maintains, succeed through the visual aspect, some through sound, but the highest experience is achieved in plays that succeed through the heart.[83] The sensory deprivation imposed by the mask enhances that inward focus.[84]

---

[77] Lyons *et al.* 2000.  [78] Coldiron (2004: 256–7).  [79] Coldiron (2004: 263).
[80] Abd' Elkader Farrah described Brook's attempt to rehearse a masked Ubu in front of a mirror for *Ubu aux Bouffes* (1977): lecture at the APGRD, Oxford, 30 January 2002.
[81] Kongo Iwao (1984: 78–9); Coldiron (2004: 250–1, 298–9).
[82] Coldiron (2004: 244–6).  [83] Zeami (1984: 99–102).  [84] Coldiron (2004: 200–1).

Zeami was less concerned than the modern Noh actor with the closed relationship between himself and the mask-object, but more highly sensitised to his audience. A performance had to be adjusted to the mood, time of day and social status of the spectators, and it was a protocol that the actor should face the aristocracy but not fix his eyes upon them.[85] Like actors in classical Greece, Zeami regularly performed in the context of a competition, which was an incentive to develop responsiveness to those who judged.[86] He writes repeatedly in terms of advancement, both of skill and understanding, and conceived this in terms of 'nine levels'.[87] Though the criteria for awarding a prize related to success in playing distinct role-types according to their requirements, we find no concept of characterisation in Zeami, or any idea that he had to impose a unique personal stamp on his performances. This was a theatre that celebrated versatility, and Zeami praises his father for his ability to play demons, old men, young women and priests, whilst also able to move between popular and aristocratic audiences. There is a small caveat about age, however, for although 'the art of *no* involves nothing more than putting on a mask and adopting an appearance appropriate to the role', the audience will remain unconvinced when an old man tries to play a young girl, so roles must in some measure be accommodated to bodies.[88] The complexity of the Japanese experience offers a salutary warning should we ever be tempted to construct a theory of Greek acting on the basis of some glancing reference in Plato or Aristophanes.

Zeami helps us conceive how the Dionysiac mask functioned as a sacred object. Whilst the Shinto tradition supported the idea that spirits were embedded in the wood of the mask and transmitted by the spirit of the carver, the Zen tradition implied that spirituality must lie in the mental processes of the carver and actor. The Noh mask was a complex phenomenon. Against folk tales of masks dropped by crows or magically bringing rain, we must set Zeami's advice on inner mental processes and Zenchiku's cosmologically oriented account of looking through the orifices of a mask. An obvious parallel with Greece lies in the way masks were given to shrines as votive offerings. Richard Green infers the existence of this Greek practice from images of masks hanging between temple columns.[89] In medieval Japan pious gifts are well documented. Zeami's son, for example, gave to the Tenkawa shrine a distinctive old man's mask that his father no longer used, a votive offering to Benzaiten, a goddess associated with the arts. It is clear that

---

[85] Zeami, cited in Raz (1983: 102).   [86] Zeami (1984: 60–3).
[87] Zeami (1984: 20–5).   [88] Zeami (1984: 179–80, 160).
[89] As in the Samothrace krater: Drawing 2.8 above; cf. Wilson (2000: 239–42).

this was a genuine votive offering by a man in difficulties, and not simply the discarding of redundant equipment.[90] Noh masks today are sacred in the same way as antiques or works of art, with the special exception of Okina, but Zeami's attitude to masks is more mixed. The line of mask-makers known to him does not extend back much more than a century, and carvers were just beginning to identify themselves as artists by signing (in the position of the third eye) masks which they presented to shrines.[91] There was a sense of aesthetic innovation, yet some demon masks were very ancient. Zeami mentions a demon mask in his possession that was withdrawn from use and treated as sacred on account of a dream, then restored to use on the basis of a second dream.[92] A young female mask would not have induced similar dreams and treatment, but Buddhist spiritual practices would still inform his use of it. The slippage between ritual and art, the sacred and the functional that we sense in Zeami must also have characterised the complex world of polytheistic Greece.

I have argued in this chapter that the Greek mask belonged to a polytheistic culture, and comparison with other such cultures helps us see that its use relied on propositions or experiential truths alien to monotheism.

1. The mask was a sacred object, an aspect of the worship of Dionysos. This linkage is clear in our vase representations.
2. There was no secret reality *behind* the mask. Truth was made visible by the mask, and the actor's hidden face was of no consequence.
3. The mask served not for deception but revelation. It brought about a metamorphosis of the wearer, and the epiphany of an ancestral world.
4. The mask, at once animate and inanimate, was a means of commingling human and spiritual worlds.
5. A new creation of the proto-democratic period, the mask belonged to a fluid religious system that, whilst cherishing tradition, also thrived upon change.

Greek religion rested upon ritual practices associated with myths, not upon codes of belief, and asking what Greeks *believed* about the mask is a doomed enterprise. Our task is to make sense of what the Greeks did. We can either slot Greek tragedy into a received explanatory framework that we use to make sense of *our* theatre, *our* fellow human beings, and *our* cosmos, or we can go in search of the cultural Other. If we adopt the first course, we shall

---

[90] Pulvers (1978: 70–1; cf. 87).   [91] Zeami (1984: 236–8); Pulvers (1978: 66–7, 94).
[92] Zeami (1984: 35–6, 237–8).

end by concluding that the mask was a mere accessory, a minor element of *opsis*, of little hermeneutic value to the historian or practical use to the modern performer.[93] If we adopt the second and more difficult strategy, we shall find that the mask offers us a uniquely helpful point of access. It has been my argument throughout this book that masking is a device which transforms mental states. Devotion to or rejection of the mask is tied to ways of understanding the world. The spiritualism of Copeau, Sikelianos and Barrault is bound up with their devotion to the mask, while the autonomous decision-making ego of Sartre, like the individual stripped of social masks celebrated by Grotowski and Brook, cannot be accommodated to the ancient and widespread human habit of masking.

I shall end with a thought-experiment based on an anecdote recounted by Greg Hicks. As Orestes, at the start of the *Libation-Bearers*, he had to invoke the god Hermes:

This is not fanciful. This did happen to me. I felt a bolt of electricity go absolutely right up through my body, through my spine, and sit right there [*gesture to head*] as I arrived at that centre spot at Epidaurus. Inside the mask we had this chamois leather to take the sweat. You're not going to believe this but when I took the mask off there was a brown stain on it.[94]

The task is to imagine how, if this text had appeared in the *Histories* of Herodotus alongside other records of divine epiphanies, our whole conception of ancient theatre performance would have been changed. Generations of critics would have worked over this specimen of 'popular belief', so it became the privileged key to our interpretation of the ancient actor and his mystical views. But in fact, this text derives from 'our' agnostic and scientifically oriented world, which possesses ample techniques of rationalisation. 'This did happen to me' can be explained away as fanciful actor talk, and it is certainly not my purpose here to argue for divinely powered electromagnetic energy fields. I have reproduced Hicks' words in order to signal how differently artists and academics tend to describe the world, and also to suggest that Hicks' devotion to the mask cannot be dissociated from a metaphysical conception of reality. Academics have no professional tools for analysing a thing called 'spiritual energy', but have a duty to be objective in recording how others use such terminology. When Ted Hughes praises Peter Brook for teaching the actor to 'become the vehicle for a spirit', we run

---

[93] On *opsis* see Wiles (1997: 5).    [94] Hicks 2002a.

into a similar impasse.⁹⁵ How is one to translate such expressions by artists into the language of academia, without destroying a core of belief and felt experience? If it is hard to deal with such language when it emerges from one's own country and one's own times, it is all the harder when studying the remote world of fifth-century Athens. That effort must nevertheless be made if we are to understand the other, and not endlessly project onto the Other a replica of oneself.

⁹⁵ 'Orghast: talking without words': Hughes (1994: 125).

# 9 | The mask of Dionysos

As in Asia and Africa, so in classical Greece the dividing line between artistic and religious practices is a blurred one. I shall argue in this chapter that no sharp distinction can be made between the theatre mask and the mask of Dionysiac cult. As always, it is helpful to start with semantics and note that none of our three terms, *theatre*, *cult* and *mask*, had a direct conceptual equivalent. In order to engage with ancient understandings of the 'mask', I shall begin by examining how masks feature in a Greek dramatic text, and then pass to a well-known set of vase images depicting a mask-based 'cult'. On that basis I shall clarify how, within the framework of Athenian religion, theatrical masking relates to the god Dionysos. In a coda to this chapter I shall imagine by means of a historical comparison what the notion of a theatrical 'epiphany' might have meant in antiquity.

A satyr play by Aeschylus called *Isthmiastai* or *Theoroi* offers us our best evocation of the theatrical mask.[1] In this play Dionysos brings his chorus of satyrs to the Panhellenic festival of Poseidon at Isthmia, where he expects them to participate as 'theoric' dancers, an official visiting delegation. There can be little doubt that Athens would have sent a regular choral *theōria* to serve as its representative.[2] The satyrs, however, have developed a passion for athletics, the major focus of the biennial festival, and have decided to become Isthmiasts, rather than *theōroi* representing Dionysos. They have abandoned their patron and turned to Poseidon, whose temple dominated the sanctuary and stadium before its destruction by fire in around 480 BC. In our surviving papyrus fragment, the satyrs are given images of themselves, which they elect to hang in the temple as a sign of their devotion to Poseidon. As Richard Green has argued, these images can only be masks, and I shall refer to them as such in my account of the papyrus fragment.[3]

When our fragment begins, Silenus or some other representative of Dionysos has just presented 'likenesses' (*eikous*) to the satyrs, ending with

---

[1] Text in Radt 1985; there are no significant changes in Diggle 1998. Translation and commentary in Lloyd-Jones 1957. Metrical analysis in Webster (1970: 119).
[2] See Rutherford 2004.
[3] Green (1991: 48), citing earlier literature, including Ferrari 1986 and Sutton (1984: 29–33). Green (1995: 45–6) is a shorter version of the same text.

the words: 'However you act, all will be in reverence [*panta soi tad' eusebē*]'. These likenesses or masks are thus sacred objects. The chorus leader asks the excited chorus to gaze in silence at his mask and consider how 'this phantom [*eidōlon*] could be more like my form, a simulation [*mimēma*] by Daedalus. It lacks only a voice.' The chorus jostles excitedly singing: 'Look! See! Move! Move again!' until the leader's song becomes more solemn: 'These offerings as an adornment [*kosmon*] I bring to the god, a beautifully painted votive'. Holding up the mask prompts a different reflection: 'For my mother what a matter this would be. If she saw him, then certainly she'd turn and [wail], imagining the presence of me whom she nurtured. He is so alike [*empherēs*].' The metre now becomes trochaic appropriate to ritual action: 'Come, look on the house of the Sea-god, Earth-shaker! Fasten up, each of you, the declaration of a beautiful form, voiceless herald, bar to the traveller [that] will hold back strangers on the path with its f[earful expression]. Hail, king! Hail Poseidon, ruler . . .!' During these lines the satyrs must affix their masks around the temple of Poseidon to serve as apotropaic images, at once declaring this a sanctuary and warding off danger. Ralf Krumeich maintains that the objects hung on the temple are votive tablets of wood or clay, with images painted on them,[4] but his case relies solely on the word 'kalligraptos' (beautifully painted), even though masks were also painted objects, and he glosses over the tradition that Daedalus was the inventor of sculpture rather than painting.[5] Votive tablets did not have the same apotropaic function as masks, and the painting on them was in fine detail, not legible by a theatre audience.

At this point a figure who must be Dionysos makes his surprise entry, catching the satyrs in their treacherous homage to a rival god. His jest turns upon the hanging masks which announce the satyrs' presence in the sanctuary of Poseidon. These masks have seeing eyes which should have noticed the new arrival coming along the path: 'I was bound to find you, gentlemen. I will not say to you, "the traveller came unseen," for the path itself informed me.' After three corrupted lines Dionysos looks at the satyrs' genitalia, which they have infibulated in the manner of athletes: '. . . short phalluses like mouse tails, as if you've worn them out in Isthmian pursuits. You haven't slacked, but are beautifully gymnastic (i.e. naked). Had you kept to the old way of drunkenness, it's more likely I should have seen you dancing.' The abandonment of wine is part of the satyrs' new way of life.[6]

---

[4] Krumeich 2000.   [5] See Morris (1992: 220–1).

[6] I offer here this book's one contribution to traditional philology. Diggle and Radt follow all earlier editors in printing 'paro[imia]n', implying reference to some 'proverb' which the audience is supposed to supply. I propose 'paro[inia]n', which means excessive wine-drinking. Wine is naturally linked to dancing in a Dionysiac milieu.

Dionysos goes on to accuse them of exercising the arm, and of wasting his money, alluding to his expenditure as a choregos. Amid accusations of a broken oath, the text disintegrates. When the papyrus resumes, Dionysos complains of being slandered on the grounds that he is no worker in iron, but a feeble effeminate (*gynnis*), and he resumes his complaint soon after. 'No one young or old willingly abandons the two rows [of my chorus], yet you are Isthmiizing'. He laments that the satyrs have marked their change of allegiance by wearing wreathes of pine in lieu of ivy. The chorus responds obstinately that it will never leave Poseidon's temple. A new character appears and, as emblems of the satyrs' new metier, presents them with metal objects fresh from the anvil. The satyrs do their best to decline the gift, but it seems they are now obliged to leave the temple and 'Isthmiize' before being allowed to sail home. The satyrs, clearly, have received their comeuppance in accordance with the rule that those who spurn the worship of Dionysos always receive as their reward some violent and unexpected punishment. The nature of these frightening metal objects has been much debated. The logic of the plot suggests, in my opinion, that the satyrs are about to engage in the new and physically taxing sport of racing in hoplite armour, which we know was introduced at Olympia in 520 and Delphi in 498 BC.[7] Dionysos refers to a satyr hiding behind a shield before speaking of the accusation that he is himself no worker in iron, and he refers also to the satyrs exercising the arm (not both arms), so we may infer that the satyrs have been learning to carry a hoplite shield. Since there is no evidence that contestants carried swords, the frightening metal object is in all probability a hoplite helmet, which is of course a kind of mask. A late sixth-century wine cup illustrates the connection of thought between the fierce eyes of a running hoplite and the prophylactic eyes of Dionysos (Drawing 9.1).[8] My hypothesis reinforces the symmetry between the Athenian festival of Dionysos centred on choral dancing and the Panhellenic festival of Poseidon centred on athletics, both of which made extreme physical demands on young Athenians, within a competitive culture. The humour of Aeschylus' play would find a parallel in an early fifth-century storage jar, where Dionysos, constrained by a military cuirass worn over his feminine chiton, is presented by a satyr with a helmet and with a thyrsus in lieu of spear (Drawing 9.2).

Though Richard Green makes a strong case for masks in Aeschylus' satyr play, I cannot follow him when he argues that the humour turns on the audience's 'recognition that the dramatic illusion is being stretched to near

---

[7] Golden (1998: 27). Lloyd-Jones (1957: 545) suggests javelins; Taplin (1977: 422), following Reinhardt, prefers shackles.
[8] On the cup see Ferrari 1986.

**Drawing 9.1** Hoplite on an eye-cup. Bryn Mawr.

breaking point'.[9] Like so many, Green is haunted by the real citizen actor lurking beneath the false theatrical mask. Such talk of 'dramatic illusion' depends upon inappropriate modern notions of the real, and belies the fact that the citizen actually *was* a servant of Dionysos when he danced in a satyr chorus. The fourth-century Apulian vase which depicts a masked comic actor dressed as Antigone and carrying Antigone's theatrical mask offers us a useful analogy (see Drawing 2.9).[10] The scene refers the viewer to tragedy, and the visible phallus signals that this is a comic performance, but there is nothing in the vase painting which refers us to the actor, who remains invisible and irrelevant as ever, or which stretches conventions to 'breaking point', since comedy regularly deals with how tragedy is made. By the same token, there is nothing odd in the way Aeschylus introduces the mask into a satyr play, for the genre is defined by the fact that members of its chorus are servants of Dionysos, and masks were parts of the god's cult. In Sophocles' *Trackers*, the satyrs are temporarily servants of Apollo, and the play deals with the origins of Apollo's lyre, while another satyr play deals with the invention of the *aulos*,[11] and in the Pratinas fragment, the music of the theatrical *aulos* is at issue.[12] Euripides' *Cyclops* brings wine-drinking ceremonies to an uncivilised world. The business of satyr plays is to deal

---

[9] Green (1991: 48). He draws on Bain and Taplin for his conception of dramatic illusion.
[10] Discussion in Taplin (1993: 84).  [11] Seaford (1984: 36).
[12] See Pickard-Cambridge (1962: 17–18); Seaford (1984: 15). It cannot be proven that this fragment is from a satyr play, but the likelihood is strong.

Drawing 9.2 Satyr arming Dionysos. Paris.

with all things Dionysian, creating a bridge between the wide-ranging epic world of tragedy and a more specific mythology tied to the patron deity of the festival.

Aeschylus' play, if my interpretation is correct, did not simply incorporate masks but provided a comic aetiology for the restrictive head mask of Athenian theatre. Dionysos presents the satyrs with masks, perfect products of mimetic art, which the satyrs then offer to Poseidon, and the pay-off is that the rebel satyrs are forced to wear heavy helmets in order to 'Isthmiize'. Their long-term punishment, I surmise, is that they will have to wear masks like helmets whenever they dance in a chorus of Dionysos. As I suggested in Chapter 3, tolerance for wearing uncomfortable theatrical masks may well have derived in practice from the need to wear hot metal helmets in hoplite training. Such an aetiology is paralleled by that of the satyric phallus. Dionysos is supposed to have inflicted the genital affliction of 'satyriasis' on the Athenians as a punishment when they failed to receive with due respect the statue of Dionysos that would later sit in the auditorium during theatre performances.[13]

The satyrs of *Isthmiastai* who hang up their masks on the temple have abandoned their phallic erections for the sake of athletics. Wine, dancing and masking are all tools for changing mental states, and Eric Csapo points out that the erect phallus is also an instrument of possession.[14] Student workshops suggest to me that the psychological effect of donning ithyphallic shorts was not so very different from that of donning a mask, liberating the wearer from prior constraints. Vases in Athens and Bonn depict satyr briefs as a form of mask, suggesting a precise parallel between the two theatrical functions (Drawing 9.3).[15] There is an interesting binary relationship between satyric dancing, with its unrestrained virility, and tragic dancing, with its requirement of cross-gender dressing and surrender to feminine modes of lamentation. When Dionysos finds himself condemned as a 'gynnis', the original audience may have been reminded of how that same term was used in Aeschylus' Lycurgan trilogy, where an effeminate Dionysos punished the Thracian king by driving him to murderous madness.[16] For the dancer who had performed in three tragedies, the satyric dance was in some sense a rite of emergence, a quitting of the female psycho-physical state. The nature of the satyrs' masculinity is at issue in this play.

When Dionysos finds the satyrs thanks to their images outside the temple, he gains his bearings just like a visitor to Athens in a play by Aristophanes. The visitor wants to find the temple of Dionysos, and is told that this is where the *mormolykeia* have been hung.[17] The term *mormolykeion* refers to the demon Mormo used to scare children, and the joke may be that theatrical masks of all kinds were hung on the temple as dedicatory offerings.[18] Alternatively the satyr masks may be hung as antefixes or gargoyles, with the idea that rainwater should run through their open mouths.[19] A small jug in Eleusis shows a child, perhaps in connection with the Anthesteria, holding out a

---

[13] The aetiology is recorded by a scholiast on Aristophanes' *Acharnians* 243.
[14] Csapo (1997: esp. 260, 266).    [15] Pickard-Cambridge (1968: figs. 45, 46).
[16] *Edoni*: fragment 31 (Lloyd-Jones).    [17] Aristophanes *Geras*: fragment 130 (Kassel-Austin).
[18] Wilson (2000: 238–42) reviews the evidence.
[19] The suggestion was first made by Fraenkel: Lloyd-Jones (1957: 543). The National Archaeological Museum in Athens has a fine collection from the temple of Apollo at Thermon.

Drawing 9.3 Satyr. Athens.

satyr mask to scare a playmate,[20] and Aeschylus plays upon this primitive fear-inducing aspect of the mask, yet the masks are also experienced as beautiful. Aeschylus' text helps us understand why we must conceive the tragic mask as in some sense a sacred object, for in a society that lacked our pervasive technologies of reproduction, the phenomenon of perfect likeness was a magical one, and its achievement was a means of accessing the divine. Today we may think of 'realistic' art in terms of scientific nineteenth-century naturalism, but for the satyrs a perfect likeness is 'ou kat'anthrōpous' – 'not according to the human'. The masks become a source of 'reverence' shown to a god. Aeschylus' reference to the mask as a *mimēma* of Daedalus finds an echo in another satyr play by Euripides, where an old man is told not to be afraid because 'all Daedalus' statues [*agalmata*] seem to move and look'.[21]

---

[20] Green (1994a: 79). The image is catalogued by Webster (1967: AV 26). Cf. the comic mask used by children in a Leningrad chous: Pickard-Cambridge (1968: fig. 780).

[21] *Eurystheus*: fragment 272 (Kannicht). On Daedalus' living statues in Athenian tradition, see Morris (1992: 222–3).

The primary emotion which Daedalus' statues aroused in the Athenians is said to have been 'wonder'. The miraculous nature of Daedalic realism is illustrated by the story of how he made a hollow cow for Pasiphae, so a bull could copulate with her and beget the Minotaur, and we may think of this cow as a giant mask, so real in its aspect that it allowed the wearer to transcend the boundaries of the human.[22] Of all Daedalus' innovations intended to make images lifelike, perhaps the most crucial was to represent open eyes, not the closed eyes of the dead.[23]

As I noted at the start of this book, there is no fifth-century word for 'mask', which in our language has connotations of concealment inappropriate to the Greek context. The comic poet Cratylus apparently coined the exotic term *brikeloi* (a corruption of 'mortal-likes') when he wanted to refer to tragic masks.[24] Once we nominate the 'mask' as an object (as I have done, for example, in the title of my book), then as Alfred Gell points out we shift attention away from the agency of the object, and the act of masking, in what seems a common-sense procedure but is actually a function of our desire to pass objective judgements. In this Aeschylean text, aesthetic discourse turns on relationships, different modes of likeness, and different emotions generated,[25] while the thing itself is never explicitly named and thus contained. We may recall again Okri's lament for Nigerian masks removed to the British Museum:

They called them
'Primitive objects'
And subjected them
To the milk
Of scientific
Scrutiny.

It is all too easy for scientific catalogues of classical masks to become versions of Okri's museum basement. For Aeschylus' satyrs, the power of the mask is related to the power of an *eidōlon*, a ghost or spirit, whence our word 'idol'. Without a sympathetic understanding of 'idolatrous' religion, we shall never explicate the ancient mask except by means of a circular reasoning that is a function of our own vocabulary. Our need to reify is part of a desire to control.

---

[22] Diodorus 4.77; cf. Morris (1992: 186).   [23] Diodorus 4.76; cf. Morris (1992: 241–2).
[24] According to Didymus: Cratylus frag. 218 (Kassel-Austin).
[25] The language is not untypical of other aesthetic discussions: cf. Hallett 1986, Stieber 1994.

August Frickenhaus in 1912 first gathered together a group of vase images representing Dionysos in the form of a pillar dressed with robes and a mask, and he associated these images with the Lenaia, on the basis of supposed maenadic rites celebrated at that festival. In Chapter 2 I pointed to the presence of 'nymphs' on one of these vases (see Plate 2.9). The romantic picture of Athenian women cavorting with the freedom of Isadora Duncan gradually lost its appeal during the twentieth century, lending credibility to the counter-view, argued by Nilsson, Burkert and others, which associated this mask cult with the oldest festival of Dionysos when the new wine was opened, the Anthesteria.[26] Carpenter evades the controversy by asserting that the mask-idol is simply a commonplace of 'popular religion'.[27] Firm evidence is missing because vase painters play imaginatively with a repertory of motifs and did not work as documentary photographers. In *Le Dieu-masque*, a comprehensive re-examination of the vases, Françoise Frontisi-Ducroux located the mask as key to this corpus of vases, and concluded that some sort of mask cult must have emerged in Athens in the late sixth century.[28] Her main interest, however, lay in decoding the language of images, and developing a structuralist conception of Dionysos rather than attaching the images to a specific festival. The consensus remains as Parker describes it: 'No one has yet deconstructed the mask of Dionysus hung on its pole: this, it is agreed, is so specific and singular an image that we may be sure of its real existence out there'.[29]

Frontisi-Ducroux sees the pillar mask as the logical outcome of a dissociation between face and body characteristic of the worship of Dionysos, but offers no hypothesis about its origins. Frickenhaus identified two epithets of Dionysos that may be relevant. In the Theban cult of Dionysos *Perikionios* ('Around the pillar'), the pillar seems to be clad in ivy, not robes and mask,[30] but a clay mask of Dionysos from the mid-fifth century with tie holes on the side, found in the Theban area, could nevertheless belong to such a cult,[31] which could have been adopted and adapted in Athens, like the cult of Dionysos Eleuthereus whose statue was imported from Theban territory.[32] The cult of Dionysos *Orthos* ('Vertical') was related to the mixing of wine in Athens,[33] and the epithet is suggestive because of its analogy to

---

[26] Helpful summary of the debate in Pickard-Cambridge (1968: 30–4); see subsequently Burkert (1983: 236–7). Osborne 1997 restores some credibility to the old notion.
[27] Carpenter (1997: 97).     [28] Frontisi-Ducroux (1991: 213).
[29] Parker (2005: 310); the same point is made in Carpenter (1997: 94).
[30] Pickard-Cambridge (1968: 32, n. 2); *Orphic Hymn* 47.     [31] Frontisi-Ducroux (1991: 208–9).
[32] Zeitlin (1993: 148) points up the political significance of the transfer.
[33] Philochoros in Athenaeus 2.38.

the Spartan cult of Orthia. In the sanctuary of 'Orthia', later assimilated with Artemis, excavators uncovered some 600 often wearable clay masks, which depict heroes as well as grotesques, part of the only Greek ceremony we know that could in the course of the sixth century have inspired an Athenian use of performance masks.[34] A world of activity has left few traces in the written record, and 'could' is the dominant word in this paragraph. Frickenhaus' vases prove more informative.

Different categories of vase, according to their function, offer different accounts of the mask-idol. One Athenian workshop in the early fifth century produced a batch of oil-flasks with crudely drawn maenads and male companions dancing around a column, to which a bearded mask is attached, sometimes two masks back to back. Since these flasks were used to pour libations, normally on graves, and not for drinking, there is no allusion to wine (Drawing 9.4). On the exterior of a wine cup by Makron from this earlier period a maenad carries wine, and the god is more lifelike, fully clad though still without arms, while the column has started to melt away. To drain the wine and become inebriated was to pass from worship to the real presence of the god, and thus the drinker who emptied his cup saw at the bottom Dionysos fully alive and endowed with arms and feet.[35] In the middle of the century a workshop specialised in exporting *stamnoi*, vessels used for mixing wine. In this group we do not see maenads in self-induced trance, but sober women engaged in dispensing wine from a *stamnos* in front of a masked and clothed column. I illustrate with an example from Boston, where a fabric beard has been draped over what might be the authentic and miraculous face of the god (Plate 9.1). Frontisi-Ducroux has pointed out how, on these *stamnoi*, the idol of Dionysos commonly faces the viewer, who is offered a direct engagement with the divine presence, while on the oil-flasks we look at the masks in profile, and it is entranced maenads who engage with the mask. In both cases, the religious efficacy of the mask's gaze changes the mental state of those transfixed by it. Frontisi-Ducroux placed theatrical masks outside her remit, but her discussion has obvious implications for theatrical performance. In Chapter 6 I contrasted Peter Hall's technique of mesmerising the audience by confronting them with the mask with the Sikelianos technique, which was rather to create mesmerised performers. When Eric Csapo writes that 'actors in masks are not only possessed by Dionysus; they share the god's power to take possession',[36]

---

[34] Carter 1987 traces a Phoenician genealogy for the practice. Frontisi-Ducroux (1995: 5–6) discusses a mask from Megara Hyblaea in Sicily that points to other possible traditions.
[35] Kylix by Makron, reproduced in Pickard-Cambridge (1968: fig. 17); Osborne (1998: figs. 80–1).
[36] Csapo (1997: 257).

Drawing 9.4 Mask-idol. Brussels.

he points to the double force of the mask that is looked upon but also looks. Frontisi-Ducroux's structural approach leads her to emphasise distinctions of gender, arguing that every woman is a 'virtual maenad', immutable in her condition of alterity, so women do not need wine in order to enter a trance state, while men undergo fundamental transformation through the agency of Dionysos, becoming inebriated, or turning physically into satyrs.[37] She could have added tragic masking as a related mode of male transformation.

---

[37] Frontisi-Ducroux (1986: 175–6). Osborne 1997 addresses issues relating to the corpus that underlies her analysis. Peirce 1998 argues that these bacchants do drink, and have been transposed into a male role in a purely iconographic convention.

Plate 9.1 Idol of Dionysos. Boston.

Jugs offer a different category of information. Beneath the pouring spout of one *oinochoe*, a woman pours wine which either honours or has turned itself into a ceremonial head of Dionysos, adorned with foliage and a flower-shaped cake (Drawing 9.5).[38] Most interesting are two jugs of the chous type specifically made for the solitary drinker at the Anthesteria. A chous in Athens depicts a lifelike mask of Dionysos set in a *liknon*, a basket or vane used for winnowing corn. On one side of it a woman holds grapes, on the other wine, suggesting the transformative power of the god in this celebration of the vintage. The mask is crowned and decorated with ivy, and a cloth hangs from the base (Plate 9.2). Bérard and Bron, calling attention to the discarded cloth, surmise that this jug referred to an unveiling ceremony whereby the mask would be revealed before being set on a pillar.[39]

A recently discovered chous seems to inhabit the world of myth (Drawing 9.6).[40] It depicts a vane on an identical table, with its contents now concealed by a cloth. On the left, attached to a monumental structure and commanding a krater of wine beneath, we see a mask of Dionysos, crowned

---

[38] Frontisi-Ducroux (1991: L 61 = plate 87).  [39] Bérard and Bron 1990.
[40] Published in Tzachou-Alexandri 1997.

*The mask of Dionysos* 217

**Drawing 9.5** Libation for Dionysos mask. Berlin.

**Plate 9.2** Mask in a *liknon*. Athens.

**Drawing 9.6** Epimetheus and Prometheus. Athens.

not with Dionysiac ivy but with the laurel of Apollo, which also decorates the vane. Between the mask and the vane stands a beautiful young man, drinking. He is crowned with the ivy of Dionysos, which also hangs round the krater, and adorns the attendant on the right. Over the vane stands a scrawny older man adorned with a less luxuriant version of laurel that might rather be osier. To unlock the riddle of this vase, we need to recognise that, as in the first chous, the vane contains the mask of Dionysos. Concealed by a drape, the mask is angled so its hidden gaze confronts its double on the monument opposite.[41] The painter wrote in the names 'Epimetheus' (Afterthought)

---

[41] A similar vane is placed beneath the mask-idol on two of the *stamnoi*, confirming a familiar link with the idol. We might also recognise the draped mask of Dionysos in a vase in Ferrara, concealed in a vane and carried as a processional offering to a Dionysos who has been assimilated with the eastern Sabazios, as here he is assimilated with Apollo. Discussed at length in Carpenter (1997: 70–9), plates 28–9; cf. *LIMC* 'Dionysos' 869.

above the young man drinking and 'Prometheus' (Forethought) above the older man, and their linkage alludes to the myth of Pandora's jar.[42] 'Epimetheus' broaches the new jar of wine at the Anthesteria, drinking without heed for the future, while his brother 'Prometheus', endowed with eternal foreknowledge, eschews wine and honours the mask of Dionysos in its safe and veiled condition. Adopting the prophetic persona of Apollo, this Prometheus perversely treats Dionysos as though he were Apollo. The Dionysiac Epimetheus confronts the viewer, while the Apolline Prometheus is in profile, offering himself to a more rationalistic mode of viewing. The vane and its hidden mask is the focus of the image, placed centrally beneath the pouring spout of the jug, and the slave on the right holds a jug to remind the viewer of the real-life object. As this wine pours over the vane, it will bring the hidden Dionysos to life so the viewer/drinker can meet him face to face, celebrating the restorative value of drinking, and shunning inappropriate care for the future. This image is 'self-referential' in the same terms as Aeschylus' satyr play, reinforcing the power of the ritual in which the viewer is engaged.

Bérard and Bron make a convincing case when they suggest that the traditional first step of the cult was to bring in the mask under a drape so it could be unveiled in a moment of epiphany. Such a revelation of the mask recalls not only the Japanese Okina ceremony, but also one of the myths which speaks of how Dionysos induces madness. After the fall of Troy, a Greek hero obtained a chest containing the image of Dionysos, but when he opened it the sight sent him mad, and he was only cured when the people of Patras accepted him and his chest, making the chest the centrepiece of their worship.[43] The gaze of the mask is dangerous in what it does to the human mind, just like wine. In Athens, it seems that the dangerous face was revealed and attached to a pole or column, then draped with clothing and decorated with foliage and cakes, remaining all the while a construct, a mimesis of the human form that could safely be dismembered. Marcel Detienne describes the mask as the 'insignium' of Dionysos which 'affirms his epiphanic nature as the god who never ceases to oscillate between presence and absence'.[44] There is a tension in these vase images between the power of the eyes to live and possess, and the pillar that is only a pillar. Unlike Herms, the column of the Dionysos-idol has no gender, consistent with the sexual ambivalence of a god who makes men behave like women.

We should not reify the 'jug' any more than the 'mask', but think of it as a 'pourer', with the emphasis on its agency. The viewer engages in solving the

---

[42] See Hesiod *Theogony* 565–616.   [43] Pausanias vii.19–20.   [44] Detienne (1986: 60).

riddle and in pouring the wine across the painted mask, and the mask itself is seen to be in process. The playful nature of Athenian vase painters can be a source of frustration to the scientific historian. When we see idols variously clothed and unclothed, dressed in a simple drape or fine robes, with a fake or integral beard, life-size or larger, adorned with cakes or given twigs to make them tree-like, we may find ourselves yearning for a definitive photo. We must, however, resist this temptation and allow the vase painter's creativity to instruct us, helping us see that Greek rituals were never frozen in time but were acts of transformation. The power of the mask-idol was related to the worshipper's ability to keep modifying its nature. If we think now of cult as static, theatre as innovative, then we set up a false dichotomy which belies the parallel creative processes involved in ritual. More insidiously, when we think of theatre growing out of ritual, then we are likely to think of 'ourselves' who today have 'theatre' as being more 'advanced' than those who only have 'ritual'. Both cult and tragedy were subject to fixed parameters, but within those parameters there was room every year for participants to innovate. Masking the idol and masking the actor were both tasks of the human imagination. Viewing those masks was neither illusion nor delusion, but a creative act.

Both the satyr mask, complemented by phallic briefs, and the bearded mask-idol, complemented by its robes, must be placed in the context of the many anthropomorphic images belonging to the worship of Dionysos. Representations of the god included the wooden idol of Dionysos Eleuthereus which watched the theatre performance, perhaps plated in gold with a painted wooden face like idols at Corinth made from the wood of Pentheus' tree.[45] Then there was the hollow statue of gold and ivory housed in the new temple of Dionysos, the work of the late fifth-century artist Alcamenes, an art-work but at the same time an object of religious contemplation;[46] whether this statue gave the god his new androgynous face, or his traditional face with a rough beard is unknown.[47] Then again we have paintings in the temple, which included Dionysos, Ariadne, Lycurgus and Pentheus.[48] Tragic masks belonged with this array of sacred representations, and I shall consider their ontological status further in the next chapter. It seems plausible enough that tragic masks would have been placed in the temple after a victory, adding to the display of sacred images. For now, my concern is limited to the mask of Dionysos himself.

---

[45] Pausanias ii.2.6–7.   [46] Pausanias i.20.2.
[47] Carpenter (1997: 89–91) argues that the Parthenon was decisive in fixing the new portrayal.
[48] Pausanias i.20.2. Green (1982: 243, n. 24) suggests the paintings may have been on movable panels.

Three major studies in the early 1980s threw a spotlight onto the mask of Dionysos in Euripides' *Bacchae*, a play that had particular resonances at the end of a period preoccupied with political and sexual liberation,[49] and the way these studies conceived the Dionysos mask has implications for the mask at large.

In an essay published in 1980 Helene Foley assumed that Dionysos wore a 'smiling' mask. This smile was an ambiguous one, serving to differentiate the fixed face of a mortal from the double-faced nature of the god. While suggesting that Dionysos and Pentheus departed for Cithaeron wearing identical saffron costumes, Foley insisted that the pair were visually distinguished by their masks, which were 'expressive of the gulf between god and man'. In the final scene, the severed head of Pentheus is seen as the actor's mask, which leads us on to 'consciously see the god's face as a *mask*, that is, a theatrical or symbolic rather than a direct or "real" manifestation of the many-faceted divinity', and the last scenes of the play are said to 'clarify precisely why the god was worshipped as a mask'.[50] Foley's conception of the mask encouraged readers in the 1980s to conceive a tragi-comic and ironic Euripides, and her reading appealed because it could be aligned with the monotheistic assumption that god is invisible, only apprehended through symbols. When she incorporated the essay in her book *Ritual Irony* (1985), she emphasised that 'the play thoroughly debunks the traditional anthropomorphic assumptions about Greek divinity'.[51]

To understand masking in Euripides, Foley put her trust in earlier scholarship. E. R. Dodds in his 1960 edition of the *Bacchae* assumed that Dionysos 'no doubt wore a smiling mask throughout', a smile which he described as 'enigmatic'.[52] And John Jones in 1962 identified in Euripides 'a whole range of mask-piercing and even, at the end of his life, mask exploiting effects', adding that 'the smiling mask of the stranger in the *Bacchantes* is meant to be inscrutable; it is a modern mask'.[53] Foley followed him in seeing the Dionysos mask as 'a mask in the modern rather than in the ancient tragic theatrical mode'.[54] This smiling mask was, however, a chimera, for the Greek term *gelan* indicates laughing rather than smiling.[55] In lines 438–9 the messenger ascribes to the laughing Dionysos a wine-coloured cheek that is not

---

[49] See Zeitlin 2004; Sampatakakis 2004.   [50] Foley (1980: 132–3).   [51] Foley (1985: 245).
[52] Dodds (1960: 131 – note to l. 439; 205 – note to 1020–3). The genealogy of Dodds' smile can be traced back to Winnington-Ingram (1948: 19).
[53] Jones (1962: 270).   [54] Foley (1980: 133) = Foley (1985: 253).
[55] Seaford (1996: on ll. 439, 1021). Foley also cites Rosenmeyer who translates 'laughing' but imagines a smile, while lamenting the 'awkward requirements of a physical production' – Rosenmeyer (1963: 105–6, 112).

pallid, but Pentheus twenty lines later refers to his white skin, so there is no stability in the god's features. The second reference in 1020–1 is specifically to an *animal* hunting with a laughing *prosōpon*; we can picture an animal with bared teeth creating the semblance of laughter, but not smiling. Faces in tragedy are not stable, and there are many references in tragedy to masked faces which supposedly weep.[56] Foley has subsequently become a powerful advocate of performance-based approaches, but in the 1970s, before Hall's *Oresteia*, classical scholars were in no position to investigate the dynamics whereby an audience projects expression onto a neutral mask. The enigmatic smile which can be a powerful signifier in Hollywood, or indeed in avant-garde productions like Schechner's *Dionysus in 69*, was never tested against the practicalities of masking.

In a monograph on the play published in 1982, Charles Segal developed a conception of the mask with roots in psychoanalysis. He tells us that: 'Euripides was fond of speculating about the veil that conceals inner thoughts and feelings from the face we show to others or see in others. It is not hard, then, to recognize the implication that the stage mirrors life. All of us wear masks . . .'[57] From his conception of an individual endowed with an inner life that is in tension with facial expression, Segal moves naturally to the theatrical mask as a mode of disguise. While Foley assumed that Dionysos wears one smiling mask throughout, Segal postulates a bearded cultic mask for the opening and closing scenes when the god speaks as a god 'in propria persona', and a youthful mask for the disguised Lydian stranger. Classing the play as a 'metatragedy', he argues that the head of Pentheus is finally revealed as 'but an empty mask', a 'man-made artefact that embodies the human power to create and use symbols'. The psychological unmasking of Pentheus correlates with his literal unmasking at the hands of a Dionysos turned stage director.[58] The power of this metatheatrical empty mask depends on spectators previously 'identifying' with figures on stage.[59] In a 1997 postscript, Segal justified his metatheatrical reading as an escape from sterile debates about belief or disbelief in the gods.[60] Jettisoning ethically driven readings in favour of post-structuralism, Segal envisages a mask which functions as a pure theatrical sign. As in the case of the 'smiling' mask, linguistic and archaeological evidence for a self-referential 'empty' mask is scant. We have no reason to think that the audience in a large Greek auditorium would have viewed a disembodied head differently from the

---

[56] References in Pickard-Cambridge (1968: 171–2).   [57] Segal (1997: 236).
[58] Segal (1997: 240–7).   [59] Segal (1997: 215–16).   [60] Segal (1997: 375).

viewer of a vase painting.⁶¹ Segal's construct, like Foley's, offered a reading of Euripides that spoke to the 1980s.⁶² Less politically driven than Foley, his independent conclusions reflected the same Zeitgeist. If the tragic mask does not belong to Athenian ritual, but to an ironic perversion of ritual, then its place is to be a metaphor.

For Jean-Pierre Vernant in Paris, a study of the *Bacchae* was the culmination of a research project into the Greek mask, a project which benefited from collaboration with Frontisi-Ducroux.⁶³ He identified three distinct spheres of masking. (1) The Gorgon, the decapitated head of Medusa, was a ubiquitous face that captured the gaze of the viewer, causing a confusion of identities and inducing terror of death. (2) Artemis had charge of initiating youth, and masking ceremonies helped boys and girls locate their place in the community. (3) Dionysos, concerned with life rather than death, and adults rather than children, was god of the mask; his masks break down categories of difference and allow the worshipper to experience the god's presence. Different philosophical traditions converge in this analysis. Sartrian existentialism showed how identity was a function of the gaze, the structuralism of Lévi-Strauss explained culture in terms of the binary oppositions that Dionysos dissolves, and Nietzsche pointed to the power and collectivity of Dionysiac possession. Less committed to the literary text than Foley and Segal, Vernant communicates more sense of the power of the mask. Indeed, he is quite lyrical when describing what it is to put on a ritual mask:

Possession: to wear a mask is to stop being yourself and to embody, while the masquerade lasts, the Power from another world that has taken hold of you, for you to mimic the totality of its face, its movements, its voice. The replication of face by mask, the imposition of mask onto face to leave it unrecognizable, implies derangement [*aliénation*] in respect of self, as you are taken in charge by the god who throws bridle and reins over you, straddles you and takes you off at a gallop – and established in this way is a contiguity of man and god, an exchange of status that may result in complete confusion, and identification.⁶⁴

Vernant goes on to argue that one who sees the Gorgon may have an experience of the same nature as one who wears the mask.

---

[61] Cf. the decapitated head held by maenads in *LIMC* 'Pentheus' 66 (late fifth century) which offers no hint of the theatrical mask.
[62] Cf. for example Oranje (1984: 132–3) for a similar distinction of god from Lydian stranger, and epiphany from mimesis.
[63] Seminars from 1978–84 are recorded in Vernant 1990b.     [64] Vernant (1990b: 116).

The *Bacchae*, however, belongs to the domain of theatre, and Vernant addressed this distinction in his seminal 1968 essay 'The historical moment of tragedy in Greece': 'By its very nature and function the tragic mask is something quite other than a religious costume. It is a human mask, not an animal disguise. Its role is not a ritual but an aesthetic one.'[65] He refined these ideas in 1981, defining the relation between tragedy and Dionysos in terms not of origins but of Dionysos' function as god of illusion. The spectator, he maintained, was always aware of the mask as a sign, visibly a work of mimesis. 'Tragedy thus opened up a new space in Greek culture, the space of the imaginary, experienced and understood as such, that is to say a human production stemming from pure artifice'.[66] Three years later, in an essay written with Frontisi-Ducroux, he commented that, given the context of performance in a festival of Dionysos, a distinction between tragic and ritual masks 'may at first sight seem surprising'. Nevertheless, he insisted, the function of the theatrical mask was 'to resolve certain problems of theatrical expressivity' – in contrast to masks like those in the sphere of Artemis in which 'the faithful disguised themselves for purely religious purposes', or a cult mask of Dionysos which, 'through its countenance with its strange eyes, expressed certain characteristics peculiar to Dionysus, the divine power whose presence seemed ineluctably marked by his absence'.[67]

It is a sign of how Vernant experienced theatre-going in twentieth-century Paris that he assumes such a sharp divide between the contained aesthetic experience of theatre, and the intensity of the religious encounter with Dionysos. Though not subscribing to their tragic-comic reading of the play, Vernant read Foley and Segal with appreciation. He accepted without query Foley's 'smiling' mask of Dionysos, though he was more concerned to stress its staring Gorgon eyes,[68] and he accepted Segal's vision of Dionysos as a stage illusionist.[69] Like Segal, he spoke of the mask being 'hollow, empty', but he gave more credit to the power of the empty mask to tear you from yourself, to disorientate, and possess, so you feel 'as if the mask is applied to your own face, to cover it and transform it in its turn'.[70] He refers in this discussion to the power of Dionysos over Pentheus, not the power of the play over the audience, and takes it for granted that there is a difference in kind between the cult mask, whose fascinating and invasive gaze realises the

---

[65] Vernant and Vidal-Naquet (1990: 23–4).
[66] 'The god of tragic fiction': Vernant and Vidal-Naquet (1990: 187).
[67] 'Features of the mask in ancient Greece': Vernant and Vidal-Naquet (1990: 189–90).
[68] Vernant (1990b: 217, 232). The essay is translated as 'The masked Dionysus of Euripides' *Bacchae*' in Vernant and Vidal-Naquet (1990: 381–412).
[69] Vernant (1990b: 234).    [70] Vernant (1990b: 232).

presence of an absence, and a theatrical mask 'that seals the identity of a *caractère*, that puts forward the stable identity of a *personnage*'.[71] While agreeing with Segal that Dionysiac experience and the experience of tragedy are 'homologous', he describes the magic of the god as transmuted 'in accordance with the procedures of dramaturgy and the charms of poetic expression'. For an ecstatic encounter with the god, he substitutes a time-honoured Aristotelian catharsis.[72]

My thesis in this book runs in the opposite direction. I have argued that the primary function of the tragic mask is not to seal and fix a character type, but to transform a wearer, and to take power over an audience within the context of a culture where the aesthetic domain did not separate itself off from the religious. I have shown how often the mask has been thought to 'possess' twentieth-century actors, both outside and inside the western tradition, and we should consider now in what terms the experience of the fifth-century actor was described. Though neither of our two best sources refers to the mask, they give us a glimpse of the creative process. In Plato's *Ion*, Socrates interrogates a professional reciter of Homer, who believes that he performs on the basis of inspiration.[73] When Ion performs Achilles or Odysseus, he is physiologically changed, his hair standing on end in fear, or his eyes filled with tears of pity. Socrates suggests that the force of a magnet passes from the Muse, via the poet to the performer, and then on to the audience. According to this metaphor, the performer hangs suspended within a chain of iron rings, held together by magnetism. Plato develops a rich vocabulary to describe Ion's state of possession, which he links to that of an actor, choral dancer or lyric poet. The performer is *ekphrōn* (out of his senses), *entheos* ('in-god' or 'god-in'), *enthousiazōn* (enthusing, inspired), *katechomenos* (held, occupied), *hermēneus* (a hermeneut, like Hermes messenger of the gods). While in this state of inspiration, Ion simultaneously observes the audience and evaluates the success of his inspired performance, free to cast his eyes about him because he recites Homer unmasked. Plato's analysis of two psychic levels helps us understand how a masked actor might have experienced possession with his full physical being while remaining in technical control of his performance, and Stanislavski described something similar in relation to Kostya.[74] Plato refers elsewhere to the inspired poet whose skill or *technē* is *mimēsis*, rejecting simple dichotomies between ecstatic experience and craft.[75]

---

[71] Vernant (1990b: 217).   [72] Vernant (1990b: 246; cf. 226).
[73] Translation in Russell and Winterbottom (1972: 39–50); commentary in Murray 1996.
[74] Pp. 79–80 above.   [75] *Laws* 719c.

Actors are largely absent from the world of Aristophanic comedy, for they did not put a personal stamp on their work in the same way as playwrights.[76] However in Aristophanes' portrayal of Agathon the tragic playwright we see how inspiration relates to craft.[77] Agathon is described by his servant as a craftsman who needs to mould his strophes and soften them in the sun, but he is shown to the audience as one who finds inspiration by acting out the parts he writes. Agathon's method is to work from external form, taking on the visual attributes of the heroine's role, costume, props and a shaven face, and a fashionable allusion to *mimēsis* accompanies a visual joke which involves Agathon hiding his masculinity between his legs. The insult thrown at Dionysos in Aeschylus' Lycurgan trilogy – are you a *gynnis*? – is now thrown at Agathon, who becomes a version of the androgynous god, wearing the same saffron dress that Dionysos would wear in *Frogs*.[78] In Agathon's cameo performance we see possession and mimesis bound up together in the creative process: Agathon as chorus leader invokes different divinities, and in an antiphonal response Agathon as choral group provides an extemporal (*di'aiphnidiou*) response in song and dance, in a crescendo of religious enthusiasm. The antiphonal technique reminds us of how actors must have learned their parts, echoing the words and movements of their teacher in a way that modern actors might dismiss as mindless. There is no mask required as a prop in this scene because Agathon shares the beautiful androgynous features of the god.

If we conceive tragedy not as a mode of bringing scripts to life that happens to use masks, but as a mode of bringing heroes to life that happens to use scripts, then many conceptual difficulties evaporate, and tragedy will no longer seem an embarrassing appendage to religious cult, tacked on for reasons of convenience or tradition. Albert Henrichs traces a clear and mostly judicious path through the morass of scholarship on the god, and I shall call on him as a convenient guide.[79] He addresses the question of whether we may define the god as 'one coherent divinity', given his four distinct provinces of wine, theatre, maenadism and the underworld. Henrichs describes how Dionysos straddles the mortal and immortal worlds, often disintegrating physically before being restored in an epiphany. Sketching the history of scholarship on the god, he points to the seminal importance of Nietzsche, whose influence was transmitted in a book of 1933 by Walter

---

[76] Ghiron-Bistagne (1976: 146) cites scattered references.   [77] *Thesmophoriazousai* 39ff.
[78] *Thesmophoriazousai* 136. Cf. my discussion of *Isthmiastai* above. The scholiast confirms that the question was put to Dionysos: Oranje (1984: 117). For the robe mentioned at l. 138, cf. *Frogs* 46. In Aeschylus, Dionysos wore a long Lydian chiton: frag. 29 (Lloyd-Jones).
[79] Henrichs 1993a.

Otto,[80] and he applauds Otto for emphasising that Dionysos was not just a psychological category, but was experienced in personal and absolute terms as a divinity. Otto's emphasis on the dual nature of Dionysos stimulated Vernant and fellow structuralists to interpret Dionysos in terms of unifying binary oppositions. However, Vernant's 'alterity', involving distinctions of self and society, separates us from what Henrichs thinks crucial: the phenomenological immediacy of the Greek encounter with a god.

Henrichs is right to challenge modern tendencies to secularise and psychologise. He insists that the devil is in the detail, and that one cannot separate the experience of Dionysos' divinity from specific physical manifestations in specific cults. His difficulty in formulating any overarching sense of the god, however, is exacerbated by a determination to see the theatrical mask in terms of alterity rather than epiphany, in accordance with tendencies that he elsewhere resists. He lines up a formidable array of modern scholarship, including Zeitlin, Goldhill, Calame, Segal, Foley, Vernant and Frontisi-Ducroux, to support the view that masking is 'tantamount to "playing the other"'.[81] On the practicalities of masking he relies on Melchinger, who was clear that the tragic mask had lost all link with ritual magic, and Pickard-Cambridge, where the revisers express concern about how the 'unchanging expression of the mask' could possibly deal with fluctuations of mood and emotion.[82] For purposes of visualisation, he cites not Peter Hall but earlier productions by Karl Gotthilf Kachler in Basel, which used masks aspiring to archaeological authenticity.[83] Looking at photos of Kachler's masks, one detects a certain energy that derives from the inspiration of the Basel carnival, but these masks offer simple fixed expressions with staring eyes and no sense of classical neutrality. They are larger than life, and there is no indication that they helped connect the actors with their bodies.[84] The staging of the mask in these performances reinforced the message of progressive scholarship that masks call attention to their own artifice. Their effect was necessarily alterity rather than epiphany.

In respect of the *Bacchae*, having stated that 'the transformative power of Dionysus is inseparable from his epiphanies', Henrichs follows prevailing scholarship in explaining how 'epiphany becomes theatre'.[85] He treads a

---

[80] Translated as Otto 1965.   [81] Henrichs (1993a: 38, with n. 66).
[82] Pickard-Cambridge (1968: 174).
[83] The technique of placing stiffened linen in moulds is described in Kachler (1991: 22).
[84] Kachler's first tragedy was Sophocles' *Electra*, presented in the museum courtyard in 1939, while later productions would use the ancient theatre at Augst. Documentation in Kachler 1986; I am grateful to Chris Vervain for her observations on the photos.
[85] Henrichs (1993a: 19–21).

familiar route, discussing how identities are 'simultaneously revealed or concealed by the mask', so the mask becomes a metaphor, and he tells us that Dionysos 'masks his "true self", his divinity, behind a deceptively human face'.[86] Dionysos does indeed state in his prologue that he has changed his divine form to that of a mortal, and the purpose of his rites is that he as a god can be visible to mortals,[87] but there is no indication that mortals in the audience were going to be offered a view of the 'real' god, because there was no alternative way of visualising the divine. Accepting the premise of the smiling mask, Henrichs floats his own staging theory whereby Dionysos wore a different 'god mask and divine costume only for his elevated deus-ex-machina appearance in the closing scene'.[88] As so often in classical scholarship, the practical questions are not addressed. Tragic costume, so far as we can tell from vases, was always decorative and sacral, so there was no obvious divine costume to call upon. And what constitutes a god mask? A bearded anthropomorphic image, colossal in scale, or something more radical? In the prologue of his 2002 *Bacchai*, Peter Hall imposed on top of the Dionysos mask a distinctly cumbersome bull mask, which sat awkwardly with the ironic tone of the translation, but satisfied a modern desire to differentiate god from human. By the time of *Bacchae*, Dionysos was consistently portrayed on vases as a beautiful young man with feminine features, so the idea that this face is a disguise to be shed in the final scene makes little sense.[89] The finale up on the crane was a demonstration of the god's power, not a formal unmasking.

Henrichs cites the Pronomos vase as evidence that the dramatic mask was 'a means of creating distance between the fictional characters and the civic identities of the actors and audience'.[90] I argued in Chapter 2 that quite the reverse is the case, since the vase shows citizen identity dissolving into that of the satyr, and in my next chapter I will interrogate further the notion of 'fictional characters'. Vase painting provides our richest source for understanding how the Athenians experienced Dionysos, because the mask could be represented pictorially in a way that language did not allow. We see in vases that the mask was fully part of the god's domain, a means of experiencing divinity. Two further representations of Dionysos from around the period of *Bacchae* will serve to reinforce my argument in this chapter,

---

[86] Henrichs (1993a: 38–9).
[87] *Bacchae* 4, 53–4, 22.     [88] Henrichs (1993a: 19, 38, n. 67).
[89] *LIMC* 'Pentheus' 65 offers a late fifth-century example of how divine and human faces were iconographically identical. The long hair of Dionysos echoes that of his decapitated victim (probably Dryas not Pentheus) on the other side of the vase.
[90] Henrichs (1993a: 20, n. 15).

**Drawing 9.7** Mask and wine. New York.

that theatrical masks were Dionysiac masks, and the ritual/theatre divide is a modern imposition.

The first is an Apulian krater from the early fourth century, the form of which is replicated self-referentially in another krater at the centre of the image (Drawing 9.7).[91] On the left Dionysos, identified by his thyrsus, gazes at a feminine mask, whose hair and complexion replicate his own; on the right, a young man with the head of a satyr pours wine into the mixing-bowl. On this vase-within-a-vase two satyrs are dancing, representing the Dionysiac state into which the drinker will pass. The physical relationship of mask and krater makes it clear that the two conditions are akin, performing in a mask and intoxicating oneself with wine. Mixing water with wine is like mixing human with divine in the mask. The mask is not pictured here as a mere metaphor but as a physical tool for transformation. The painter has not attempted to represent emptiness or artifice in the mask, or a distinct expression such as a smile, but the mystery of seeing a face that is doubled, a face that will be alive as soon as it is placed on a body. The left-hand figure is not Dionysos *in disguise* as a human being, but simply the god in human form. We can usefully borrow the language of Margaret Drewal and think

---

[91] Attributed to the Tarporley painter. See Trendall and Cambitoglou (1978: 46).

**Drawing 9.8** Actor with Dionysos. Ferrara.

of how the viewer may reorientate working assumptions at will, moving between seeing a god and seeing a beautiful human actor holding the tool of his trade. Renate Schlesier has pointed out how many tragic figures are likened in the text to maenads, and are therefore effectively 'doubled' and, as she puts it, 'seen with a Bacchic mask'.[92] The femininity of the mask is a trope in vase painting, because to don the mask of Dionysos is to join his thiasos and surrender to female emotion. In the vocabulary of the vase painter, the mask of the maenad became the essential tragic mask.

My second example is an Athenian vase in Ferrara, from the end of the fifth century (Drawing 9.8).[93] In the centre a woman looks out at the viewer and holds up two masks, which dominate the vase on account of their white pigment, and echo a pair of balls with which women play on the reverse. On the right, a bearded actor in theatrical costume meets the gaze of an ivy-crowned female mask. The crown, tragic costume and central position of the woman suggest that this is the figure whom the actor will play, or

---

[92] Schlesier (1993: 94–6, with nn. 25–31).
[93] Olivia Ghiandoni describes the vase in Berti and Gasparri (1989: 132). I am grateful to Dr Berti for allowing me to inspect the vase.

rather become, when he wears the crowned mask. The mask replicates the feminine facial features and hanging locks of Dionysos, allowing the actor via the mask to engage vicariously with the god. The relationship of the actor to Dionysos, seated on the left beneath a spray of ivy, is established by the symmetry of his pole or sceptre with Dionysos' thyrsus, and both have attendants adjusting their attire. Another binary opposition is set up when we notice how Dionysos faces in the direction of a satyr, who mimics the god's gesture, and reclines on a fawnskin, in contrast to the rich cloak of the god. While the actor contemplates a beautiful female mask, the satyr is gazing at a shaggy female mask which mask gazes in turn at the viewer.

The interplay of gazes, symmetries and oppositions indicates how subtle Athenian thinking about the mask had become. It is only by meeting the gaze of the mask that the actor can encounter the face of Dionysos, who manifests his embodied self only to the satyr. The satyr, however, is a ridiculous thespian crowned in ivy, who can only aspire to a wild, ugly mask with vacant eyes, and the complicated relationship of nature to culture echoes that of divine to human. The raw instinct of the satyr generates a bogey mask of no aesthetic value, and the artifice of the actor is needed to create tragedy, beauty and mimesis; yet without the presence of Dionysos in the tragic mask, its power to live would be missing. The function of a krater is to mix wine with water, and the raw power of instinct needs to be cut with artifice in just the same way. Found in a tomb, this vase also speaks about loss of self in death. The wild mask terrifies because it is devoid of its *psychē*, but the beautiful mask speaks of how new life can be created. This remarkable vase has no interest in portraying 'real' citizen actors semi-visible beneath their theatrical attire, but uses theatre to speak of how humans engage with the divine.

The double aspect of the mask is laid out for us. We look at the beautiful mask in profile, to see how the actor is absorbed in it, but we are also looked at by the wild mask, to find our own equilibrium disturbed by its gaze. These are the opposed principles of Artemis and Gorgo in Vernant's theoretical model. Henrichs' four provinces of Dionysos are united in this vase: a container for *wine*, found in a *grave*, it shows how the actor will become akin to a *maenad* by virtue of the *theatrical* mask. Understood as a vehicle for mental and physical transformation, and a sophisticated technique for encountering the divine, the tragic mask sat securely amid all those other activities which honoured the god.

As a coda to this chapter, which has been concerned principally with the wearer of the mask, I wish to consider how the effect of Dionysiac masking on a massed audience may also be conceived in religious terms, and for that purpose Nietzsche provides a useful starting point. In Nietzsche's account of early Greek tragedy, the song and dance of the tragic chorus so enraptured the audience that when an awkwardly masked hero came onto the stage the audience saw not his theatrical accoutrements but a vision. Seeking to describe this epiphany of Dionysos in the theatre, Nietzsche cited the plot of *Alcestis* as an analogue for the theatrical experience. Admetus, having lost his wife, is consumed by a vision of his wife when:

> suddenly a woman with a similar form and gait is led towards him in disguise; if we imagine his sudden tremor of unease, his impetuous comparison, his instinctive conviction – then we have an analogy to the emotion that the spectator felt when, in a state of Dionysiac excitement, he saw the god, with whose suffering he had already identified, walking on to the stage. He involuntarily translated the entire image of the god that was trembling before his soul to that masked figure, and dissolved its reality into a ghostly unreality.[94]

Though we must discount Nietzsche's idea that Dionysos underwent a proto-Christian martyrdom before being reincarnated under the mask of Alcestis, something of value remains in this evocation of a theatrical epiphany, encouraging us to reconstruct the emotions of a crowded audience exposed to the new visual and musical medium of tragedy.

Nietzsche's vision of Greek tragedy stemmed not so much from a fevered imagination as from the theatre that he knew. Shakespeare's statue scene in *The Winter's Tale*, where a woman supposed dead returns to her husband, has often been likened to the ending of Euripides' play, and the analogy is worth pursuing further, in order to clarify what a 'theatrical epiphany' might mean in terms we can more easily understand. This comparative exercise will make it easier to grasp the propositions about fifth-century spectatorship that I shall advance in my next chapter. The performance of Helen Faucit, who first played the role of Shakespeare's Hermione in 1837, helps us put Nietzsche back in his mid-nineteenth-century context, when theatre had the capacity to excite a massed audience in a way that became almost impossible in the sophisticated theatres of late twentieth-century Paris, London or New York.

When Faucit played in Scotland in 1847, *The Scotchman* wrote of 'the thrill that passed through the audience on the first raising of the curtain from the seeming statue', and continued: 'What statue ever breathed out the soul that modulated that face? It was the realizing of the sculptor's hopeless dream . . . The spectator became an actor in the scene, and all "Held their breath . . ."' For

---

[94] Nietzsche (1993: 45).

this reviewer it was 'as if we looked upon a being almost too pure to be gazed on with unveiled eyes . . . Poetry, painting, sculpture, – the best of each . . .' *The Glasgow Herald* hymned: 'So complete was the illusion, so still the figure, so sightless the eyeballs, that you seemed insensibly to forget it was a living being who stood before you; and when amidst the melody of the music she turned her head towards the king, the whole house started as if struck by an electric shock, or as if they had seen the dead arise.' *The Glasgow Citizen* described the scene as 'the most entrancing thing we ever remember to have seen, – actually suspending the blood, and taking the breath away. It was something supernatural almost; and till the descent was fully accomplished, and the stone turned to palpable woman again, something of a fine fear sat upon us like a light chilliness.' The emotions of the performer seem to have been equally intense. In Edinburgh, Faucit learned that the whole audience instinctively rose as she descended from her pedestal, and accounted for this by 'supposing that the soul of Hermione had for the time entered into mine', so that 'my "body thought"'. She only heard tell of this reaction, for her eyes were on Macready's Leontes. 'You may judge', she concludes, 'of the pleasure it was to play to audiences of this kind'.[95] I have already noted Brook's shock at encountering a Nigerian *Oedipus*. The challenge for the historian of ancient theatre is to imagine the emotions of a Greek audience. If it is not too whimsical to imagine the Greeks writing theatre reviews, we might guess that these would have sounded more like the Scottish reviews of 1847 than reviews of today. We must not project onto antiquity the reactions of modern western spectators, saturated by technologically generated images, and subscribing to a metaphysics far removed not only from the Greeks and Yoruba, but also from the European romantics.

Faucit had read Schlegel who defined the Greek style for the nineteenth century in terms of the statuesque. When she took the role of Antigone in 1845, John Coleman had praised her face of Artemis, while De Quincey celebrated her as 'the most faultless of Grecian marbles'.[96] As Shakespeare's Grecian statue, Faucit gave a perfect classical performance, informed by her renderings of Antigone and Iphigenia, and by visits to study classical statues in the Louvre. Faucit provides an object lesson in the power of the sculpted face in the theatre, and the effect of a single movement of the head. There is a close analogy between the way Paulina draws back the curtain to reveal Hermione's statue, and the way Admetus draws back the veil to reveal the

---

[95] Furness (1898: 299–300, 391–5).
[96] Carlisle (2000: 172, 159). Cf. Hall and Macintosh (2005: 326–35). Fiona Macintosh's forthcoming stage history of *Oedipus the King* will contain valuable material on statuary and acting.

mask of Alcestis returned from her grave, creating a 'marvel' or 'thauma' for stage figures and audience alike.[97]

In Shakespeare's own day, the lifelike statue of *Winter's Tale* articulated a tension between material and immaterial, and drew inspiration from the medieval paradigm of Christ stepping from his tomb. Paulina's commentary is packed with references to magic, conjuring, 'superstition', 'wicked powers' and 'unlawful business', for Shakespeare was touching on a taboo area of experience in a Protestant England that had learned mistrust of icons and transubstantiation. In the nineteenth century, when cultural anxieties turned more on sexuality than religious creed, Faucit presented herself as the actress incarnate yet untouchable, offering to the male gaze the opportunity to evaluate not only her body but also her moral probity. She created the illusion of marble, so the audience might take pleasure in seeing her sculpted features melting into human ones, as the soul within the body became apparent. In Jacobean and nineteenth-century productions alike, the statue created a frisson because a pagan celebration of the flesh was in tension with the Christian theme of guilt and redemption. In the masked theatre of Euripides, there was no such voyeuristic fascination with the embodied actor. The body of the performer was invisible, and the speaker of Alcestis' lines had probably now taken the part of Heracles, leaving an unknown player to animate the silent mask in the finale. The context of the final scene was overtly Dionysian, for Heracles had intoxicated himself with wine before wrestling with the god of death, and Euripides' play had taken the place of a regular satyr play.[98] The tensions in this Dionysian world were not between flesh and marble, but between the human and divine worlds. The mask was a tool for mediating that divide, breaking the boundaries that delimit the human body. Alcestis in the final scene replicates the statue envisaged by Admetus,[99] intended like most Greek statues to create a bridge to the divine world. In the opening of the play Apollo manifests himself in the human form that he took as a serf, but it transpires that he is powerless to rescue his friend's wife from a stronger god. The chorus concludes that neither Orphic mystery religion nor Apolline wisdom controls events, but only the aniconic deity Ananke, 'Necessity'. Alcestis has fallen into the hands of this goddess who lacks idols or sacrificial rites, and in this religious limbo, they advise that Alcestis' tomb should become the focus of a cult, so she can be worshipped as a divine *daimōn*.[100] In the finale, the Alcestis whose mask

---

[97] *The Winter's Tale* v.iii.100; *Alcestis* 1123.   [98] Cf. Segal (1993: 40).
[99] Cf. Segal (1993: 46, 49).   [100] *Alcestis* 962–1004.

is unveiled before the audience may be seen either as human or as *daimōn*. The mask was the key to this ontological ambivalence.

The well-sculpted mask has a power to arrest and focus the gaze of a large audience under natural light in a way the naked face lacks. When Admetus takes the hand of the veiled woman while avoiding her gaze, he likens his act of betrayal to executing the Gorgon.[101] Real salt tears in an outdoor theatre would be lost, but the mask pulls attention to Admetus' face, helping the audience imagine that 'well of tears that springs from my eyes', and in its 'Gorgon' aspect the mask of Alcestis would have arrested the audience as well as Admetus.[102] Outdoors at the Globe, the necromancer Simon Forman was more interested in the chicanery of Autolycus than the magic of the statue,[103] and we may guess that the statue was most potent when *Winter's Tale* was performed at court, evoking the new painted effigy of Mary Queen of Scots, designed for the new tomb in Westminster Abbey to which her bones would soon be transferred.[104] The impending ceremony was important because James' divine right of succession passed through Mary, his wronged Catholic mother. Shakespeare's play derived its power from allusions to the magical world of bones, tombs, sacred spaces and divine bodies, but its Grecian references placed it more safely in the secular sphere. When the statue by Giulio Romano is said to be nature's ape,[105] Shakespeare's play defines itself formally as artistic mimesis. Euripides' play, by contrast, was performed in a religious sanctuary, and in a polytheistic world there was no formal distinction between religious and secular spheres.

In an annual drama, the wooden statue of Dionysos was taken from its hiding place and progressively invested with agency as it returned to Athens in a re-enactment of the god's original entry into the city, bringing potential rewards and potential danger. Its final task was to watch a set of images animated and paraded before it. There was a difference of degree between the ancient wooden image of Dionysos and the freshly painted face of Alcestis, but not a difference in kind. Making images in a polytheistic culture is a means of managing the world, for when divine forces are given lifelike form, they can be apprehended and experienced. Having lost control of his world, Admetus wants to make an enduring image of Alcestis, and miraculously her image appears endowed with movement, though not yet with speech. As Nietzsche perceived, there is an equivalence here to the theatrical process at

---

[101] *Alcestis* 1123. Cf. 509, where Admetus greets Heracles as a descendent of Perseus.
[102] *Alcestis* 1068, cf. 986, 1041, 1047.   [103] Orgel (1996: 62).
[104] Bullough (1975: 116–17).   [105] *The Winter's Tale* V.ii.99.

large. When bidden to speak, Admetus addresses his unveiled wife as: 'O eye and body of a dearest woman!' pointing to the primary miracle of a mask, which is its ability to see. It is the possibility of ocular exchange that makes the mask seem alive, and not a mere actor's prop. In a polytheistic culture it was not the glimpse of Helen Faucit's private God-given soul that stirred spectators, but the glimpse of a different beyond, the world of the gods. Like all fifth-century sculpted works of beauty, masks provided access to that world, not as objects in themselves, but through the epiphanic process of their unveiling.

# 10 | Sacred viewing: 'theorizing' the ancient mask

'For contemporaries it must have been dazzling enough, especially in the early years, when each Dionysia might reveal to the audience for the first time ever an Orestes, say, or a Memnon, or a Niobe, or an Oedipus, who was no longer a mere mechanical component in a famous story but who breathed, walked, and, above all, spoke for himself.'[1] John Herington invites us to imagine what it must have been like to witness the fifth-century Dionysia, when figures of myth were given a human form they had never possessed so fully. Whether he is right to place speech at the forefront of the experience is, however, another question. The monotheistic traditions of Christianity and Islam base themselves on the word, but Greek religion had no equivalent textual point of reference, and its sense of the sacred was rooted rather in objects and places, and in actions tied to those objects and places. Religious experience turned upon what was seen with the eyes, as for example in the famous and secret *drōmena* of the Eleusinian Mysteries. Seeing was the primary way to access the divine, and my subject in this chapter will be the collective seeing of masks in the context of a religious festival. My argument will be that the viewing of masks was akin to the viewing of sculptures and other images in sanctuaries. When Plato describes the shivering, sweating and prickling induced by a beautiful *prosōpon* in a man who has recently experienced the Eleusinian Mysteries, we note the importance of context in determining how and what we see.[2]

In Chapter 9 I read Aeschylus' *Isthmiastai or Theoroi* as a comic aetiology for the theatrical mask. The word *theōroi* evokes the activity of the chorus, which had come to the Isthmus to watch an athletic contest held in honour of Poseidon. With its ambiguous etymology in the words *thea* ('spectacle') and *theos* ('god'), the word *theōria* is critical to any ancient understanding of spectatorship.[3] Jas Elsner explains what distinguishes *theōria* from illusionistic modes of viewing within antiquity:

---

[1] Herington (1985: 136). [2] *Phaedrus* 251.
[3] See Rutherford 2000; also Goldhill in Goldhill and Osborne (1999: 5–7); Nightingale (2004: 44–6).

The difference from the visuality of naturalism is fundamental. For in mimesis, the viewer stands apart from the world of the image, which operates illusionistically in its own space . . . Ultimately, because there is no contact in the regime of naturalist representation, there is only longing, nostalgia, and frustrated erotic desire. By contrast, in ritual-centred viewing, the grounds for a direct relationship have been prepared. The viewer enters a sacred space, a special place set apart from ordinary life, in which the god dwells. In this liminal site, the viewer enters the god's world and likewise the deity intrudes directly into the viewer's world in a highly ritualized context. The reciprocal gaze of this visuality is a kind of epiphanic fulfilment, both of the pilgrim-viewer, who discovers his or her deepest identity in the presence of the god, and of the god himself, who receives the offerings and worship appropriate to his divinity in the process of the pilgrimage rites.[4]

The so-called 'theoric fund' allowed Athenian citizens to participate in a rite of *theōria*.[5] Viewing the Dionysia was a theoric activity in Elsner's terms, with spectators caught up as participants and not as mere spectators contemplating an illusion. They wore garlands to certify their status as active *theōroi*,[6] and they did not just view the statue of Dionysos Eleuthereus as it passed through the streets, but were viewed by it. Likewise they did not simply see masks as mimetic objects, but were seen by them and thus in turn became the objects of spectatorship.

Aristotle's *Poetics* has had a huge influence in perpetuating logocentric accounts of Greek tragedy. Theatre historians mostly encounter Aristotle in the context of his *Poetics*, where the visual element or *opsis* is relegated to a humble position. It is salutary, therefore, to notice how Aristotle refers to the Dionysia in the *Protrepticus*, a work of his youth where he defended the contemplative or 'theoretical' life of a philosopher. Within the hierarchy of the senses, the young Aristotle takes it for granted that sight is the sense most valued and honoured by everyone – and should be second only to contemplative thought, which like sight is to be valued for its own sake. Festivals provide him with a useful analogy:

Just as we travel to Olympia for the sake of the actual spectacle [*thea*], without any further benefit, since the *theōria* is in itself of more value than wealth, and just as we watch [*theōroumen*] the Dionysia with no aim of taking something from the actors, since we actually pay them a fee, and just as we go to many other spectacles [*theas*] in exchange for money: so *theōria* of the universe is to be esteemed over all that is of seeming value. We ought not make such an effort to travel and watch [*theasasthai*] men who imitate women and slaves, or who engage in fighting and

---

[4] Elsner (2000: 61).   [5] See Csapo and Slater (1995: 287–8, 293–7).
[6] Philochoros, cited in Pickard-Cambridge (1968: 272); cf. Elsner and Rutherford (2006: 12–13).

running, and then deem it wrong to contemplate [*theōrein*] gratis the nature and truth of things.⁷

Drama and sport are cognate activities. The mimetic activity of playing women and slaves in dramatic performances resembles racing and martial arts at the Olympic Games in being, essentially, an event to be watched. Spectatorship is not something we feel to be instrumental, Aristotle suggests, but an activity that we value as an end in itself.

This ocular account of theatre-going derives from Aristotle's teacher, Plato, who privileged sight both in the *Republic*, where the eye is related to the divine light of the sun, and in the *Timaeus*, where sight allows men to contemplate the heavens. In the *Theaetatus* Plato develops an interactive theory of vision whereby the seeing eye and the white stick can have no existence except when the active force conjoins with the recipient.⁸ In the *Timaeus*, following the fifth-century philosophers Empedocles and Alcmaeon, Plato describes how a fire burns behind the eye, from which it follows that the eye is a source of light, emitting some sort of rays in order to see.⁹ This extromissive theory of vision, which we can trace back to Homer,¹⁰ allows us to conceive how viewing in the fifth-century theatre might have been imagined as an active engagement, consistent with the reciprocal processes of *theōria*. However, when we turn to Aristotle's mature treatise on the senses, we recognise the author of the *Poetics*, for Aristotle now declares that hearing is the most important sense for acquiring philosophical wisdom. He firmly rejects Plato's extromissive theory, and declares that the eye's basic element is not fire but transparent water.¹¹ Vision thus passes inwards to the soul through the eye. In Aristotle's scientific account of the world, the spectator has become the passive recipient, not the interactive agent.

Greek tragedy was viewed as part of the Dionysia. Amongst many recent attempts to understand what this might mean, Simon Goldhill's essay 'The Great Dionysia and civic ideology' has been especially influential, republished in the collection *Nothing to do with Dionysos?*¹² In that volume, his essay proved the most comprehensive attempt to locate tragedy within its festive frame, an intellectual project that needed rescuing in the wake of

---

⁷ *Protrepticus* B.44 (Düring). On the primacy of sight, see fragments 72, 75, and cf. Aristotle *Metaphysics* 980a.
⁸ *Timaeus* 46–7; *Republic* 507–8; *Theaetatus* 156.
⁹ *Timaeus* 45. Cf. Empedocles frag. 88 (Wright); Theophrastus *On the Senses* 26.
¹⁰ Prier (1989: esp. 69, 74).
¹¹ *On Sense and Sensible Objects* 437–8. Later authorities such as Galen and Euclid retained the extromissive theory.
¹² Goldhill 1990b – first version published in the *Journal of Hellenic Studies* in 1987.

Nietzsche, whose name had been tainted by fascism, and of the Cambridge ritualists, who had placed excessive trust in Frazer. Goldhill called attention to events that took place on the day of performance and defined what he saw as an ideology of the *polis*. To the military parade of orphans reared and honoured by the Athenian state, Goldhill could tie Neoptolemus in *Philoctetes*, the gallant son of a famous dead father. Reading Sophocles' plays in relation to such pre-play ceremonies, he argued, 'makes his dramas considerably more radical and questioning than the image of "pious Sophokles" sometimes allows'. While pre-play rituals reinforce a code of civic values, tragedies focus on a hero whose commitment is directed to family or personal achievement. Taking a loose view of Dionysos as a god who transgresses boundaries, Goldhill concludes that: 'It is the *interplay between norm and transgression* enacted in the tragic festival that makes it a Dionysiac occasion'.[13]

The argument is a powerful one, and communicates a sense of tragedy's importance within Athenian society. It has, however, three major limitations. The first lies in its determined secularisation of the 'pious Sophokles', even though Goldhill notes in passing that 'Sophokles himself was actively involved in the cult worship of the heroes – a religious phenomenon of growing importance in the fifth century'.[14] In a vigorous polemic entitled 'Creative euphoria: Dionysos and the theatre', Synnøve Des Bouvrie argues that the relation between tragedy and Dionysiac religion has been bypassed in volumes such as *Nothing to do with Dionysos?* She comments on the arbitrary way in which Goldhill focuses on certain civic ceremonies immediately preceding the performance while ignoring all the ceremonies with the statue of the god on the days preceding. Goldhill's vision of tragedies as essentially vehicles for 'questioning' norms of behaviour reflects his personal taste for intellectual and ultimately moralistic theatre.[15] Her alternative is a Turnerian account of festival as a liminal occasion during which the emotions engendered by tragedy draw everyone into a state of communitas, a process whereby communal values are renewed. She places masks alongside dancing and the mass consumption of wine at the festival as an 'exotic' element 'affecting the senses, emotions, and phantasy of the participants'.[16] Her Dionysia is a participatory event for: 'Even if only some, the actors, were engaged in the performance, the audience participated equally in reviving the primordial past, celebrating the larger-than-life actions of the heroic race'.[17] An unspoken politics of gender may lie behind the way Des

---

[13] Goldhill (1990b: 117, 127).  [14] Goldhill (1990b: 116).
[15] Des Bouvrie (1993: 80 n. 3, 110 n. 161).
[16] Des Bouvrie (1993: 88, cf. 93); on wine and music cf. Stanford (1983: 13).
[17] Des Bouvrie (1993: 92).

Bouvrie privileges emotion, participation and collective experience over intellect, detachment and individualised experience. From the perspective of the twenty-first century, one can see how Goldhill's evident distaste for religious or mystic accounts of the world leads him as a historian to play down the power of religion as a motor of human conduct. In time-honoured fashion, his view of ancient theatre becomes a utopian vision of how theatre should be within his own culture.

The second difficulty in Goldhill's account is his postulate of an essentially citizen audience. One of his key texts is a statement by Isocrates that the Athenians paraded tribute and orphans because they were 'seeking thus to display to our allies, on the one hand, the value of their own property which was brought in by hirelings, and to the rest of the Hellenes, on the other hand, the multitude of the fatherless . . .'.[18] The addressees of the pre-play rituals are thus crucially non-Athenians. We recall how Aristotle brackets the Dionysia alongside the Olympic Games as a spectacle that one might travel far to see. When Martin Nilsson in 1925 interpreted the Dionysia as part of 'civic religion', he anticipated Goldhill in noting how the plays gave a 'lesson in citizenship', but he added that 'foreigners were given a healthy lesson in the greatness of Athens'.[19] The propagandist or 'public relations' aspect of Greek tragedy needs somehow to be reconciled with Goldhill's 'troubling' and 'transgressive' account. The tensions which Goldhill rightly identifies between household and *polis* should not be allowed to obscure other tensions between local and pan-Hellenic values.

My third reservation about Goldhill's argument concerns his logocentric account of tragedy as a form which 'takes key terms of the normative and evaluative vocabulary of civic discourse, and depicts conflicts and ambiguities in their meanings and use'.[20] Tragedy effectively reduces itself to text, and elements such as music, dance and mask become of small account. Criticism is as always a function of institutional context, and in a Cambridge classical literature seminar back in the 1980s music, dance and mask were not deemed crucial topics. Language loses its former hegemony within the academic perspective of contemporary Theatre Studies, where the intellectual quest is for how tragedies 'work', both historically as performance events, and in the present when brought to life again by modern actors and audiences. Given this perspective, we are forced to take more seriously Plato's

---

[18] Isocrates *On the Peace* 82, cited from Goldhill (1990b: 101); cf. the broad argument in Rhodes 2003.
[19] Nilsson (1925: 256).  [20] Goldhill (1990b: 126). Cf. the debate in Wiles 1987, Goldhill 1989.

view that sight is the most important of the senses, and the best route to philosophical wisdom.

In order to conceive how the Dionysia functioned as a locally generated pan-Hellenic festival, and to challenge again the conceptual boundary which separates art from ritual, let us as a stimulus to the historical imagination consider the terms of the peace treaty which temporarily halted the Peloponnesian war in 421 BC. It was agreed that the Spartans would send an annual embassy to the Great Dionysia to reaffirm the treaty, and the Athenians would send an embassy to the equivalent Spartan festival, the Hyacinthia.[21] These festivals were anniversaries of the original oath-taking, and natural occasions for representatives of different allied states to converge. The performance of Aristophanes' *Peace* must have played some part in easing the mood of negotiators on both sides in 421, and the presence of an allegorical character called Theoria reflects the fact that a Spartan legation was engaged in a *theōria* of the Dionysia, ritualised viewing as a kind of pilgrimage.[22] In Aristophanes' play the Athenians are joined by members of other warring Greek states to set up a giant statue of Peace, anticipating the permanent columns set up on the Acropolis and at the scene of the Hyacinthia soon afterwards to mark the peace treaty. One would love to be certain which tragedies were performed in 421, contributing to the political mood.

If the Dionysia centred, albeit only for the duration of one comedy, on a colossal statue, so too did the Hyacinthia. The tomb of Hyacinthus was the pediment for an ancient forty-foot bronze statue of Apollo surrounded by some sort of architectural 'throne'. According to the myth, Hyacinthus was accidentally killed by a discus thrown by Apollo. The three-day cycle of the festival took participants through an emotional trajectory closely akin to that of the Dionysia. First there was a period of mourning for the dead hero, when no crowns would be worn, no paeans sung to Apollo and little food would be eaten. On the second day there was a *thea poikilē* – literally, a 'variety show', with songs and dances, and processions passing through the 'theatre'. The statue of Apollo was an immense column endowed only with feet, arms and a helmeted head,[23] and it is generally believed that on the final day the women of Sparta draped Apollo with fabric, bringing the illusion of life to the immense bronze shaft in a manner that recalls how Athenian women dressed and masked a column in order to animate a Dionysos. The processions ended with the sacrifice of animals and feasting on their meat,

---

[21] Thucydides v.23.  [22] See Kowalzig (2006a: 60–1).
[23] Pausanias iii.19; cf. Martin 1976, Petterson (1992: 129).

much like the finale of the Dionysian procession, and Hyacinthus would in some form have been an honoured guest.[24] Since the Spartans had no pretensions to 'democracy', their ceremonies were more inclusive of young women, who paraded in decorated carts and chariots, and of slaves, who were allowed to join the feast.[25] The festival passed from collective grief to collective celebration just like the Dionysia, where tragedies calling for displays of grief at the death of mythic heroes were followed by celebratory satyr plays.

The Spartan ceremony honoured the bronze Apollo by placing before him ornamented vehicles, music and dances, whilst the Athenian ceremony honoured the wooden Dionysos by placing choruses before him, performed as in Sparta by young men. There is an obvious difference, of course, in that the Athenian dances were new, and accompanied by dialogue, whilst the Spartan dances were *archaikên* or 'traditional'. Gregory Nagy believes that the poems of Alcman would have been amongst the works reperformed in the festival.[26] In local terms, both events were ceremonies of aggregation. Just as the cult of Dionysos Elethereus related to the annexation of the Theban town of Eleutherai, so the Spartan ceremony commemorated the annexation of Amyklai, the outlying Spartan community which housed the cult. The display of a breastplate worn by a Theban warlord who assisted in the invasion commemorated the latter event.[27] Though all of Sparta decamped to the festival, it must also have served to impress outsiders, such as the embassy from Athens, or Theban allies.

The altar-cum-tomb at the base of Apollo's statue represented Hyacinthus and his sister being carried to heaven, whilst a bronze door gave access to the bones supposed to lie beneath. Like the Dionysia, we may assume that the Hyacinthia did not confine its mythic frame of reference to a single Apolline myth, for the same altar also depicted Heracles being taken to heaven, and many other divine figures including a grouping of Dionysos, Semele and her sister Ino.[28] The songs and dances must have incorporated a similar breadth of mythic reference. The festival as a whole can be described as epiphanic, a means of making gods and heroes live for the participants, and thereby honouring those divine forces. We can readily imagine how robing the image of Apollo and addressing him would achieve that aim, but it is

---

[24] Cf. Burkert (1985: 205).
[25] Polycrates in Athenaeus iv.139. Literary sources are gathered in Petterson 1992. On dressing the statue see Petterson (1992: 11); also Piccirilli 1967.
[26] Nagy (1994/5: 42–3).
[27] Aristotle frag. 532: see Petterson (1992: 110). On Eleutherai, see Connor (1990: 10).
[28] Pausanias iii.19; cf. Petterson (1992: 110).

less clear what procedures created the sense of a heroic Hyacinthus able to transcend death in order to join the feast. Somehow, the intense emotions invested by participants in Hyacinthus' death and resurrection must have related to their feelings about personal death. The Athenian *theōroi* who came to renew the oath of peace would have known that their personal and collective lives turned upon this oath, as did their Spartan counterparts watching tragedy in Athens.

Richard Seaford points to the 'inherently mimetic tendency of lamentation in Greek hero-cult'.[29] The mimesis or re-enactment involved in mourning and celebrating Hyacinthus is related to that other form of mimesis or re-enactment involved in mourning and celebrating a tragic hero in the Dionysia. A historical link between tragedy and hero cult is attested by Herodotus when he describes the reforms of Cleisthenes in sixth-century Sikyon. An important hero cult in that city centred on the tomb of Adrastus, Argive leader of the 'Seven' who attacked Thebes, and later acquired the throne of Sikyon by marriage. Sikyon was now at war with Argos, but the Argive's tomb was too sacred to touch, so Cleisthenes approached his Theban allies and secured permission to translate some relic of Melanippos, one of the Theban champions in the war against the Seven, to a shrine in Sikyon. Herodotus goes on to explain that 'tragic choruses' in Sikyon had hitherto been performed in relation to the sufferings of Adrastus, and not in honour of Dionysos, who was of course of Theban birth. With the advent of the new relic, placed in a position of strong political symbolism, the tragic choruses were transferred back to Dionysos, and the other rites formerly offered to Adrastus were now dedicated to the Theban Melanippos.[30]

This comparison of the Dionysia and Hyacinthia can be explored on two levels. Firstly we can compare different formal means of honouring a supernatural being through mimetic enactments involving lamentation. Rites in honour of a hero may involve 'tragic choruses' in just the same way as the re-enactment of a heroic death at the Dionysia. And second, we can try to interrogate different beliefs about efficacy and illusion. In what sense did the Spartans 'believe' that Hyacinthus emerged through the bronze aperture to join them at their feast, or the Sikonians 'believe' that Melanippos would now help them in their fight against Argos? When Robert Parker writes about the interpenetration of tragedy and hero cult, and asks himself whether Athenian claims about the return of the dead are simply 'enabling fictions', he arrives at the formulation that the Athenians

---

[29] Seaford (1994: 142).  [30] Herodotus v.67; cf. Seaford (1994: 112–13, 142).

acted *as if* the dead can influence events, they perform rituals *as if* they are efficacious.³¹ The theatre historian may be reminded of the famous Stanislavskian 'if' formulated to account for the ambivalent combination of belief and detachment experienced by the actor, and ultimately by the audience.³²

The heroes who peopled Greek tragedy belong to a crucial category in Greek religion, located mid-way between gods and common mortals. Unlike gods, heroes have tombs and mortal remains, but like gods they escape the normal confines of death. Just like gods they must be honoured because they have power to influence human affairs, but they can only exercise this power within limited environs defined by their physical remains. Heroes are connected by a secure yet vaguely defined time-line to the present world of their descendents, and actors in Greek tragedy were thus charged with *re-enacting* events that once happened, as distinct from merely *acting* in fictions. Hero cult is associated with the rise of the city state, providing a substitute for the aristocratic cult of familial tombs and ancestors. All members of the community defined by the cult could participate on equal terms, and feel united through their collective outpouring of emotion.³³ In democratic Athens, where strict limits were placed on mourning at funerals and on the erection of grave monuments, and where those fallen in war were honoured by an austere funeral speech delivered on behalf of the state, it is easy to see how tragedy provided a cathartic outlet for suppressed private grief.³⁴

The particular form taken by choral dancing and collective lament in Athens is of course a remarkable one. Plato regrets the merging of traditionally distinct genres such as lament and the dithyramb under the pressures of democracy,³⁵ and Spartan traditionalism contrasts with Athenian love for innovation. Barbara Kowalzig offers a compelling interpretation of what transpired in Athens. In terms of age and gender, she explains, choruses were traditionally akin to the god or hero they celebrated and in some sense represented. Within the worship of Dionysos, dance was a prime means by which ecstasy and experience of the god could be achieved. In democratic Athens, Dionysos acquired an effective monopoly of public choral dancing, and displays by women or elite social groups were eliminated. An analysis of tragic choral odes shows how the status of the chorus is regularly modified,

---

³¹ Parker (2005: 143–5).    ³² Cf. Stanislavski (1967: 49–54).
³³ On hero cult see Burkert (1985: 203–7); Kearns (1989: esp. 1–4, 135–8); Seaford (1994: 109–20); Parker (2005: 445–51); Kowalzig 2006b.
³⁴ Seaford (1994: 137–42), esp. n. 153 on the emotional expressivity of audiences. cf. Loraux (1986: 44–7); Foley (1993: 105–7).
³⁵ *Laws* 700.

under pressure of tragic emotion, to yield a Dionysiac dimension. When tragedy provided simulations and aetiologies of non-Dionysian ceremonies, it did so as a ritual form that subsumed other modes of choral expression, in a take-over that echoes the fate of Sikyonian dances for Adrastus.[36] The diverse mode of tragedy paradoxically allowed a homogenisation of choral dance, consistent with democratic ideals of uniformity. Homer and the epic tradition provided Greeks with their common frame of religious reference, yet the Athenians were of little account in those poems, and Athens possessed, for example, nothing equivalent to the cult of Helen and Menelaus at Sparta. Tragedy constituted a quasi-imperialist appropriation of Greek myth and cult, allowing the Athenians to establish the Dionysia as a pan-Hellenic festival that would bring glory to the city consistent with its political power.[37] The theatrical mode of tragedy allowed mass involvement in accordance with the democratic ideal of inclusivity. Analysis along Kowalzig's lines helps breaks down the binary opposition between theatre and ritual, showing why the Dionysia and Hyacinthia were commensurate events, both in their psychological effect upon participants, and in their political efficacity.

The figures who people Greek tragedy were regarded as ancestors in a way that transcended pure symbolism, even if precise genealogies were elusive. If we return for example to the peace treaty of 421, we find that the Spartan king wanted peace because of political pressure at home. His position rested on the way he had used his descent from Heracles and support from the Delphic oracle to redeem past disgrace, and some manipulation of the oracle was now alleged.[38] Individual aristocratic claims to descent from heroes were increasingly counterbalanced by collective claims on behalf of the state to which heroes physically belonged. The bones of Theseus were solemnly brought to Athens in 476/5 and placed in a shrine, just as the bones of Orestes had once been carried to Sparta.[39] In a defence of Athens' imperialist past, Isocrates declares that he needs to begin with the excellence of his race. He lists a series of crimes associated with Thebes – matricide, fratricide, incest, feasting on children, exposure of children and so forth – describing them as 'such a mass of ill-doings that supply has never lacked for those who by annual custom bring into the theatre the events that once took place'.[40] Turning to Argos, he asks: 'Who does not know, who has not heard from the tragedians [*literally: tragic teachers*] of the events that once befell Adrastus

---

[36] Kowalzig 2004; Kowalzig 2007.   [37] Cf. Kowalzig (2004: 64); Kearns (1989: 137).
[38] Thucydides v.16.   [39] Parker (1996: 168–70); cf. Herodotus i.67–8.
[40] Isocrates *Panathenaicus* 121–2. Cf. Zeitlin 1990b.

at Thebes?' In that instance the Athenians ensured burial of the Argive dead in accordance with custom immemorial, laid down by divine powers.[41] He adds that the Thebans came to their senses through negotiation, and notes how this modifies his account of the incident in a speech he delivered when relations with Thebes were more difficult. For Isocrates there was no doubting that Greek tragedy dealt with 'progonoi' or 'ancestors', and with 'events that once took place'. The famous heroic deeds were certainly done, but their details need constantly and creatively to be re-evaluated. Euripides' *Suppliants* was one such nuanced re-evaluation of what befell Adrastus at Thebes.

If we are to understand what the Dionysia meant to participants, we must start by finding the right historical vocabulary. Edith Hall points out that there is no classical Greek term to express our notion of a 'part', 'role' or 'character' in a play. The terminology found in Aristophanes 'describes a direct and binary relationship between the actor and the concrete individual he actually "becomes", rather than a more complex triangular relationship including the mysterious, abstract additional entity we now call the "role" of the impersonated individual'.[42] There was, moreover, no generic word meaning 'to act' that embraced both speaking actors and chorus. The task of the actor or *hypokritēs* involved 'responding to' and 'interpreting' the mask, which was in turn the 'face' of the ancestral hero. For Ghiron-Bistagne, the force of the term *hypokritēs* lay in the merging of actor and incarnated hero effected by mask and disguise.[43] And as Frontisi-Ducroux observes, there was no way of speaking about a face under a face.[44] The purpose of the tragic mask was to bring the face of Adrastus or Theseus into the theatre, for purposes of *theōria* in honour of a god.

Masks brought into the theatre dead people from the heroic age *as if* they were alive, for purposes of what Elsner terms 'ritual-centred viewing'. Athenians in the later fifth century preferred to memorise the dead by means of stone images carved in relief, but in the Mediterranean world around them masks had long been used, for the mask is a simple and obvious device to make a face permanent, overcoming the decay of the flesh. The Pharaohs were embalmed and decked with funeral masks so they would survive in the afterlife, transformed into the god Osiris whom Greeks conventionally identified with Dionysos, and in Egypt unlike Greece, a transfer to the world of the gods was available to all. Until portrait masks appeared in around 300 BC, the dead were always buried with idealised faces that linked them to

[41] Isocrates *Panathenaicus* 168–9. [42] Hall (2006: 37). [43] Ghiron-Bistagne (1976: 116).
[44] Frontisi-Ducroux (1995: 41; also 14ff. for mask terminology).

Drawing 10.1 Death-mask from Sindos.

divinities.⁴⁵ The best-known Greek death-mask is of course the gold 'mask of Agamemnon' that once covered the face of a Mycenean king in his tomb, but the custom of placing gold masks over warriors' faces continued in the Balkans through the classical period, sometimes adjoined to helmets in a rite that must have conferred some sort of divine status (Drawing 10.1).⁴⁶ Recent excavations at Pella have shown that Macedonians in the later sixth century maintained a similar custom.⁴⁷ The Etruscans placed masks or model heads

---

⁴⁵ Griffiths (1980: esp. 69–74); Hornung (1992: ch. 9); Taylor 1994; Walker and Bierbrier (1997: 14, 77, 131).
⁴⁶ Theodossiev 1998.
⁴⁷ *Kathimerini*, 26 August 2003. I am grateful to Yana Zarifi for this cutting. The Mycenaean masks are in the National Archaeological Museum in Athens.

on canopic urns in the sixth century, while the Roman republic developed the cult of the *imago*, the wax mask of the nobleman that would be worn in parades by his descendants.[48] The Athenians did not place masks over their dead to give them life everlasting, but in the theatre the mask had a job to do that was not unrelated. Heroes who had transcended mortality were kept alive in the public memory.

For Simon Goldhill the *Ajax* provides an important case study because it allows him to demonstrate an affinity between the war orphans of Athens and the plight of Eurysaces after his father's death. The ideals which Ajax imparts to Eurysaces before committing suicide are in flat contradiction to 'the dominant ideology of the city'. Goldhill identifies as 'an essential dynamic of Sophocles' tragedy the way Ajax becomes both an outstanding hero and unacceptable to society'.[49] Peter Rose, having analysed the difficulty faced by historians who try not to impose their modern paradigms on the past, takes issue with parts of Goldhill's account. On the level of emotion, for example, he suggests that war orphans would have heightened the pathos of the performance. He describes an Althusserian process of 'interpellation' whereby ideology operates through the positioning of the audience, but this useful method of analysis does not pass beyond text to incorporate the gaze, which may also interpellate.[50] A pupil of Goldhill writes of 'tragedy's capacity for prompting self-reflexivity through dissent',[51] and the civic status of Teucer has been flagged as a topical political issue by Ruth Scodel.[52] Political, issue-based readings of this kind are an improvement on Bernard Knox's post-war account of heroic characterisation, which interests itself in what lies behind Ajax's 'mask of a brutal soldier',[53] for they do not stumble on the disappearance of the hero half-way through the play.

The problem with modern political readings is not that they are wrong, but that they are partial. Goldhill excludes from his contextual frame the religious apparatus around the processing of Dionysos' statue, and by the same token he marginalises religious issues in his discussion of the text. He has no apparent interest in the seer's pronouncement, relayed by the Messenger, that Ajax is punished by Athena because he has denied any need for her assistance.[54] The plot at this point reveals the consequences of an ethico-religious failure that is of no direct relevance to modern secular society, and critics reslant the play accordingly. Likewise, the second half of the play focuses on the burial of a corpse, an issue that was of profound

---

[48] Haynes (2000: 106); Flower 1999.   [49] Goldhill (1990b: 116–18).   [50] Rose 1995.
[51] Barker (2004: 20).   [52] Scodel 2003.   [53] For example Knox (1964: 9).
[54] See Pucci (1994: 30).

moral concern in antiquity because of its different tenets about the afterlife, and more specifically because burial was essential if Ajax was to figure as the object of hero cult. To make the play *relevant* for a modern reader or spectator is a project that all too easily engenders denial of the play's cultural otherness. Dionysian masks are part of that problematic but interesting otherness since they are no longer part of our everyday theatrical culture.

Ajax was a hero of great importance to the Athenians because he had become their surrogate representative in the *Iliad*. He hailed from the island of Salamis, and when Solon invaded the island with an Athenian force, Spartan arbitrators declared Athens entitled to ownership on the basis of how Ajax related to Athens. His two sons, Eurysaces who is the focus of Sophocles play, and Phlious, who is omitted, were already the object of Athenian cults.[55] Some Athenian aristocrats traced their lineage to these men – Cimon and Miltiades to the first, Alcibiades to the second[56] – but in the democratic reforms of Cleisthenes, Ajax was, with the approval of the Delphic oracle, made the titular hero of one of the new tribes designed to transcend class and geography. At the battle of Salamis the Athenians not only called upon Ajax and his father Telamon on the island of Salamis, but also brought in a boat from Aegina the 'sons of Aeacus', i.e. relics or effigies that must have included Telamon. In Plutarch's version, these figures were seen as phantoms. After the battle a captured Persian ship was dedicated to Ajax.[57] Ajax was thus an important religio-political presence in Athenian life, and it is clear from Herodotus' account of Salamis that heroes within their sphere of influence were felt to have genuine power to influence events.

We have thus to consider what it meant, within the religio-political environment of the Dionysia, to bring this Ajax into the theatre, and make him speak and walk and cast his gaze over the audience. Presentation of the tragedy clearly added to the honour and fame of this semi-divine being.[58] Barbara Kowalzig has shown that Ajax's association with Athens was still contested by her neighbours.[59] When Sophocles brought Ajax to life, emphasising the hero's Athenian credentials, and casting the Spartan king as principal villain, we need see no contradiction between Sophocles'

---

[55] Plutarch *Solon* 10. On the Ajax cult see Shapiro (1989: 154–7); Wickersham 1991; Vandiver (1991: 108–9); Henrichs 1993b; Seaford (1994: 136).
[56] Shapiro (1989: 155); Plato *Alcibiades I* 121.
[57] Herodotus viii.64; cf. Plutarch *Themistocles* 15. [58] Cf. Antonaccio 1994.
[59] Kowalzig (2006b: 85–91).

three roles as poet, as collector of revenues from a *de facto* empire, and as priest.[60] If the speeches given to his stage figures reflected contemporary debates about aspects of citizenship, that very topicality served to enhance the audience's sense of a living, breathing human being standing before them. To make Ajax the Homeric hero engage with the world of the present was not to construct an aesthetic of alienation, or a politics of dissent, but to create a living encounter with a figure from the past.

Christiane Sourvinou-Inwood offers a useful corrective to Goldhill's secularism by placing tragedy within the frame of its religious apparatus. She aims to see Greek tragedy through the 'perceptual filters of the past' and favours a metaphor from cinema whereby the camera 'zooms' in and out, showing spectators the wide-angle world of Homeric myth at one moment, at another zooming in on a particular contemporary cult.[61] Her account of audience perception in terms of 'schemata' is informed by structuralism with its emphasis on cognition, and the possibility that one's senses may be directly touched by the music of the *aulos*, or by the revealed image, seems disallowed by the hypothesis of 'perceptual filters'. Her cinematic metaphor allows little space for the reciprocal processes involved in live experience in an open-air theatre: I see myself reflected back in the eyes of the mask, I find my tears reflected in the eyes of my fellow spectators. Her approach is a minority one, and I have focused on Goldhill because he represents a more mainstream current in late twentieth-century thought, one which interprets all human thought and communication in terms of language. My own argument in this book is for the autonomy of visual experience. I want to shift our paradigm for understanding Greek tragedy in order to place visual experience combined with sound at the forefront. In place of the notion that Greek tragedies are texts which happen to be acted, I regard tragedies as images which happened to move, sing and speak. As Ibsen explained to Norwegian students, 'It was a long time before I realised that to be a poet means essentially to see',[62] and as Peter Brook famously remarked, it is the play's central image or silhouette that burns into the mind after the play is over.[63]

The audience did not of course need any reminding that tragedies were written. When Florence Dupont considers the relation between the material practice of writing and ritual performance, she turns to Svenbro's meditations on tomb inscriptions. These suggest to her that writing

---

[60] On his stewardship, see Bradshaw (1991: 124); on his priesthood of Asclepius see Parker (1996: 184–5).
[61] Sourvinou-Inwood (2003: 15, 22–5).   [62] Ibsen (1961: 3).   [63] Brook (1968: 136).

serves essentially to give voice to what has none: objects, the dead, groups, or indeed theatre masks. The actor lends his vocal capacities to the character [*personnage*], but does not incarnate it; he sounds [*sonorise*] his mask on the basis of words that are not his own. So the mythical hero and the mask associated with him in the theatre have the quality of permanence, like the technique of the actor, while the words, those written by the poet, are ephemeral and disappear once uttered.

The theory of mimesis, which takes a *personnage* to be the representation of a human being, fails to engage with this mix of the permanent and impermanent...[64]

Broadly speaking, in Greek tragedy as in Roman tragedy, text and actors serve to animate timeless masks, that is to say, to integrate them within the transient, linear, irreversible time of a performance; otherwise these masks would retain the fixity of a statue or a corpse. The words of the poet and the bodies of the actors, always different, help bestow that aspect of impermanence which characterizes human life. So nothing allows us to regard multiple 'interpretations' of a tragic character by different poets as a meaningful concept. Multiplicity is a condition of the ritual itself.[65]

Though the association of particular masks with particular tragic heroes is a feature of Roman rather than Greek tragedy, Dupont's formulation is helpful for our understanding of the Dionysia. To find new words for traditional heroic figures was precisely the ritual requirement. It was the mask which gave to the tragic figure its quality as a monument.

At the end of the *Ajax* the chorus is told that Ajax was the noblest of mortals, and concludes: 'Many things, to mortals when they see, are known. Before seeing, no one is a prophet of the future, for what will happen.'[66] Starting from the principle that seeing is knowing, let us re-examine the *Ajax* as a script written to be the basis of an ocular experience, designed to animate and 'sonorise' masks. The first thing the audience saw was the goddess Athene, and it is indicative of Ajax's future in Athenian cult that he can see her, whilst Odysseus can only hear her voice resonating like a bronze trumpet. When Athene promises Odysseus that she will turn the 'rays' of Ajax's eyes away from him,[67] we are reminded of the extromissive Greek theory of vision, and the active power of the gaze that will spring from Ajax's painted mask. She summons the maddened Ajax, and asks Odysseus if he sees now the power of the gods. Odysseus responds to this vision with pity, saying that he sees his own situation in that of Ajax, and continues: 'I see

---

[64] Dupont (2001: 78); cf. Svenbro 1993.  [65] Dupont (2001: 80–1).
[66] *Ajax* 1418–20.   [67] *Ajax* 69–70.

us as nothing but phantoms [*eidōla*], though alive, or an empty shadow'.[68] A modern masked production might choose to emphasise at this point the reassuring material presence of the actor beneath the ghostly mask, since modern spectators have no vision of their own future as shadows in the underworld.

The *parodos* or opening choral ode is devoted to the inadequacies of speech as a means of conveying truth. Rumours are everywhere. By keeping his 'eye' within the tent, Ajax is provoking evil talk.[69] When the chorus calls Ajax out, it is Tecmessa who appears, to give a precise description of what will be seen, namely Ajax surveying the slaughtered animals. A long build-up prepares for the extrusion of the *ekkyklēma*, and the sight that will confirm oral accounts. The *aulos* heightens the emotionality of what is now revealed. Ajax sings his first strophe on the theme of what 'you see', and the antistrophe on what 'I see'. His second strophe begins again with 'you see', and the antistrophe turns to what 'he', Odysseus, sees. In his third strophe Ajax extends his account of the reciprocal gaze beyond the domain of human interaction, for he cannot 'look upon' the gods; and in the antistrophe, though he was the best man 'seen' by Troy, he concludes that he will not again be 'seen' by his native Salamis. When Ajax calms and reverts to speech, he explains that his 'eye' and his 'mind' (*phrenes*) were set whirling by Gorgon-eyed Athene.[70] This ability to see the goddess, and the madness that results from the meeting of gazes, equip him for semi-divine status. Ajax demands to see his son, who proves his mettle by casting his gaze (*prosleussōn*) silently over the carnage.[71] Without a mask, the actor would have no means of rendering the power of the gaze that Sophocles' text demands.

In the next choral ode, the chorus directs its gaze forward as if across the water when it addresses the island of Salamis. As recipients of this gaze, the audience recognise themselves, for Salamis is part of the Athenian *polis*. Ajax returns for his emollient 'deception' speech, where he promises in ambiguous language to hide his sword in the earth. In modern theatre of the naked face, it would be easy to play this speech for a psychological subtext, but in the Greek theatre of masks it is simply an object lesson in the opacity of language. The chorus responds in its next ode by dancing to Pan, celebrating light, and declaring that Ares has lifted his hurt from its eyes.[72] Ajax concludes his suicide speech by interpellating the audience as Athenians, for when the audience heard the address to 'famous Athens!' they must have seen themselves reflected back in the eyes of the mask.[73] There is

---

[68] *Ajax* 125–6.   [69] *Ajax* 191–2.   [70] *Ajax* 447, 450.   [71] *Ajax* 546.
[72] *Ajax* 693ff.   [73] *Ajax* 861.

no critical agreement on how the suicide, the disappearance of the body and its subsequent revelation were effected,[74] but we may be sure that realistic nineteenth-century stage bushes would not have given due magnitude to Tecmessa's declaration that 'Ajax this our recently new-slain lies'.[75] Hector's sword is planted in the earth at the start of the suicide speech, but self-impalement in front of the audience would stray far from the practice of any other Greek play, and there are no lines to cover Tecmessa's discovery of the body. Technical difficulties disappear if Ajax is wheeled in on the *ekkyklēma* for his suicide speech to signify a new location, then removed on his final lines, and brought forward again when Tecmessa commences her lament, impaled on his sword. The only objection to this staging, requiring three uses of the *ekkyklēma* within a single play, is an aesthetic one, arising when we conceive the *ekkyklēma* in negative terms as the solution to a difficulty, Sophocles' way of reconciling the story he needs to tell with the awkward constraints of dramatic illusion.[76] We must turn this way of thinking around, and see the tragedian's art as one of unveiling images, each carefully prepared. If we think of the tragedy as being, in the first instance, a political discourse intended to provoke ethical debate, then the physical business of the rolling trolley will seem an intrusion, but if we think in terms of *theōria*, of a religio-political spectacle that is meant to astound and work on the emotions, then the technique needs no defence.

The second half of the play is dominated by the sight of Ajax's corpse. Charles Segal, in accordance with his metatheatrical conception of Greek tragedy, sought to contrast the heroic image of Ajax in Homer with the physical ugliness of the corpse, but his theatrical imagination led him to visualise naturalistic bodies rather than masks.[77] In friezes and heroic vases, dead bodies are horrifying, but never ugly. In theatre of the naked face, corpses are usually something of an embarrassment, rapidly hauled off the stage in the final scene, and an audience will tend to be fascinated by the self-discipline of the actor, who may or may not possess Helen Faucit's ability to hold still for ten minutes. In Greek theatre, such difficulties vanish. The actor can withdraw to take the part of Teucer, and be replaced by a dummy, but Ajax remains ever present, inherent in his mask. The suicide of Ajax half-way through the play also provides a structural difficulty for those who, nourished on Shakespeare or Racine, would see the play as the life-story of a Sophoclean hero, but for the audience at the Dionysia the suicide was merely a critical moment upon Ajax's journey to becoming a cultic hero. It

---

[74] Garvie (1998: 203–4).  [75] *Ajax* 898–9.  [76] See Wiles (1997: 162–5).
[77] Segal (1995: 24–5).

is only with his burial that his death is complete and heroisation can begin.[78] The mask lends its power to the next epiphany of Ajax when Teucer has the veil removed to reveal the face. As the mask appears, Teucer addresses it: 'O *dustheaton omma* even of courage bitter', and the Greek phrase (literally 'ill-to-look eye') captures the ambiguity that a mask's gaze possesses, at once looked at and looking.[79] In Mycenae, Egypt and Thrace, masks covered the face of the dead in order to dissolve the boundary between life and death, and it is a characteristic of masks that, when deprived of mobility, they take on the quality of death. The phenomenological ambiguity of the mask, what Otto called 'the fraternal confluence of life and death',[80] is crucial to the second half of the play, when Ajax is inanimate yet also an agent with the power to help friends and harm enemies.

The final epiphany of Ajax is the moment when Eurysaces, with three locks of hair, formally positions himself as a suppliant clinging to a body that has now effectively acquired the functions of a sacred relic. Tecmessa and Teucer at some point add themselves to the tableau.[81] Meanwhile, the chorus in its final ode draws the world of the audience into that of the play. The first strophe ends with what war does to the Greeks, the antistrophe with what war does to humans. The second strophe starts with Ares, and ends with Troy; the antistrophe starts with Ajax and ends with Athens. The masks of the chorus, and probably also the mask of Ajax, confront the audience, inviting them through an exchange of gazes to view themselves in what Elsner called 'ritual-centred viewing'. Agamemnon arrives to dismiss Ajax as a mere shadow, but Teucer addresses Ajax by name as if he still lives,[82] and it is the mask which allows Ajax to seem at once and so strongly both dead and alive. Like Isocrates, Teucer regales the Argive Agamemnon with the horrors of Argive myth, pointing implicitly to how the story of Ajax will glorify Athens. Identity in the ancient world was a function of how one appeared in the eyes of others, and Ajax had to be *seen* as a hero. Sophocles' purpose was to represent Ajax in a manner so compelling that any visitor to the Dionysia would surrender to his power, even though intellectually they might be aware of the political manipulation involved.

In this account of the *Ajax*, I have sought to demonstrate that viewing the play at the Dionysia was a *theōria*, an encounter with sacralised images. The play is organised in a sequence of epiphanies to maximise the power of the masked figure. Everything turns upon the gaze, which the mask magnifies. We need to distinguish the understandings of a modern book-based society,

---

[78] See Bradshaw 1991; Henrichs 1993.   [79] *Ajax* 1004.   [80] Otto (1965: 209).
[81] *Ajax* 1309; cf. the logic of the three locks.   [82] *Ajax* 1257, 1269.

whereby the visual illustrates or fleshes out the written text, from the practices of an oral society, where language served to animate the visual image. Words and pictures had different functions. The language of Ajax tells us that he would be a problematic citizen in any democracy, but only vision, supported of course by music and speech, could communicate the aura that belonged to a demi-god. This was a culture where myths were fluid and uncertain, but religious experience was based upon encounters with visible and tangible objects. Athens could not obtain the actual bones of Ajax, but at least she could, through masks and sumptuous costumes, combined with song, dance and skilful storytelling, create a feeling of certainty that this ancestor was once safely buried at Troy.

The idea that plays are essentially acts of deception goes back to Plato. Plutarch, a devotee of Plato, tells the story of how Solon in his old age, as a lover of *paidia* (childish play) along with wine and music, goes to 'watch' Thespis acting, a novelty that is attracting the many. After the performance the appropriate Platonist question is placed in Solon's mouth: is not Thespis ashamed to falsify so much before so many? The point of Plutarch's tale lies in the story that follows, when Pisistratus the future tyrant enters the Agora in a chariot, claiming to have been wounded by his political opponents, and evidently covered in blood. Solon accuses him of 'acting the Homeric Odysseus' who deceived his enemies by a similar trick.[83] In Plato's theory of mimesis, there was a correlation between the falsity of tragedy and the falsity of a performative political system. If we turn this model around, and think how hard democracy actually worked to eliminate spectacle and demagoguery, then we should also turn the theatrical model around and see how hard tragedy worked to be the vehicle of divine revelation. When Plutarch links *hypokrisis* with music and wine, he takes the Dionysiac context for granted. It is the term *paidia* that we need to interrogate most carefully in this passage, for a child's imagination like the Dionysiac imagination transcends logical categories of true and false.[84]

In what sense, then, did Sophocles *bring Ajax into the theatre*? What was the ontological status of the masked figure? Françoise Frontisi-Ducroux sets out some of the assumptions that underlie my argument:

We should understand that when worn the mask does not have the function of hiding the face which it covers. It abolishes and replaces it. In the theatre, beneath the dramatic mask, the face of the actor does not exist, and his individuality, as revealed

---

[83] Plutarch *Solon* 29. Cf. Pisistratus' other famous theatrical trick in Herodotus i.60. I find no evidence for the audience complicity proposed in Connor 1987.
[84] Kowalzig (2006b: 79) shows how the term here links politics to a ritual context.

by his own face, disappears and is replaced by that of the incarnated *personnage*. He is henceforth Clytaemnestra, Medea, or Hippolytus . . . The tragic actor, like the celebrant of a ritual, fulfils a liturgical function; he is the animator, silent or speaking, of the costume he dons and the hero he brings back to life . . . The mask does not hide, but designates and signals the hero to whom voice has been restored.

She adds that the institution of a prize for acting is no obstacle to her account, since victory went to the actor best able to submit himself to the *personnage* whom he incarnated.[85] There remains nevertheless a tension between Frontisi-Ducroux's phenomenological language which declares that the actor incarnates and *is* Clytaemnestra, and her semiotic vocabulary which declares that the mask *signals* the hero. In the same discussion she denies that 'the wearer of the mask thinks he has really become the *personnage* or mythic creature whom he represents. Rather his own identity has not been taken into account.'[86] And she thus side-steps the issue of change in the mental state of the actor, which, I have argued, was central to the association of tragedy with the wine-god.

We have very little evidence for the ancient reception of tragedy, and what we have derives in the main from a philosophical elite, or from comedy which was itself part of a Dionysian festival. The third-century historian Diodorus, though he belongs to a later age, provides a more representative view when he considers how to incorporate the mythic Heracles into his historical narrative:

People view [*theōrousin*] the might of Heracles from the feebleness of today's men, and so mistrust writings about the extreme scale of his Labours. Generally, in myth-based history, one cannot establish truth with exactly the same rigour. Likewise in the theatres we do not believe [literally: are not persuaded] in the existence of hybrid Centaurs with bodies of double origin, nor in Geryon with his three bodies, yet we accept such myths, and by our applause enhance the honour of the god. It would be strange if . . . our forefathers should have agreed to accord him immortality on account of his extreme feats, and we then failed to maintain this ancestral piety towards the god.[87]

This passage gives a wonderful glimpse into the ambivalence of the polytheistic mind. On the one hand, the stories are incredible, yet on the other hand the status of the tragic performance as sacred rite is beyond question. The audience is not persuaded that centaurs were ever a reality, yet

---

[85] Frontisi-Ducroux (1995: 40).    [86] Frontisi-Ducroux (1995: 40).
[87] *Diodorus* iv.8.4–5; cf. Veyne (1988: 48).

there is no doubting that Heracles is really a god. If Heracles was somehow made a god by human ancestors, piety is owed to ancestors and their ways must be followed. Fifth-century Athenians would no doubt have come up with equally ambivalent language if interrogated by a modern scientifically minded anthropologist.

Jean-Pierre Vernant has written with great subtlety about Athenian religious images. He has analysed, for example, the relation between an idol and an *eidōlon*, conceived as the intangible double of one's vital being. He has contrasted the mesmeric and interactive power of open eyes in images of the Gorgon or Dionysos with the experience of 'absence in presence' imparted by closed eyes in stone *kouroi* (youths) representing the dead. He has explored the binary opposition which ties the material stone of the indestructible *kouros* to the eternal but insubstantial psyche or *eidōlon* of the dead.[88] Yet, as I noted in the last chapter, when he turns to theatre masks his account of performance becomes reductive. He rightly reads Plato's theory of 'mimesis' as a response in part to the experience of theatre, but he then interprets theatre retrospectively through the lens of mimesis:

In the accurate meaning of *mimeisthai*, to imitate is to simulate the effective presence of an absent being. In face of such a representation, there are only two possible attitudes, one of which is ruled out in advance: either, putting yourself out of play [*hors du jeu*], you take the spectacle for reality itself; or else, entering into play, you grasp that it constitutes its own domain, which must be defined as that of theatrical illusion. Awareness of the fiction is what constitutes a spectacle as dramatic. It appears to be at once its condition and its product.[89]

Most intelligent Greek polytheists, it seems to me, were like Diodorus quite happy to get along with 'both/and', experiencing no need to sign up to Vernant's rationalistic 'either/or'. The actor both *is* Clytaemnestra and *represents* Clytaemnestra, just as Ion the rhapsode both *is* possessed *and* pursues his craft in a calculating fashion. In respect of Ajax, there was no collective doubting that he and his relatives were in some form present to assist at the sea-battle which took place within their geographical sphere of influence. In the context of his appearance at the Dionysia, not only was Ajax represented by an actor demonstrating skill in a competition but also, and *simultaneously*, Ajax manifested himself to the Athenians thanks to the inspiration of an actor. The modern western mind prefers the first half of this binary, wanting a comfortable awareness of dramatic illusion to remain unthreatened by the possibility that transcendental forces may have power over human life.

[88] Vernant (1990b: 25ff.). [89] Vernant (1990b: 65–6).

Sculpted images were the most important means by which Greeks apprehended the divine. Alongside the anonymous sculptor who made the tragic mask of Ajax, let us juxtapose Alcamenes, who created a new statue of Dionysos for the sanctuary in the later fifth century, a hollow structure with gold and ivory plating built up on a wooden armature, in all respects a mask save not housing an actor. Perhaps it too, like the great Spartan Apollo, or the columnar idol of Dionysos, was sometimes brought to life by being costumed. Other sculptors created what we would today term installations. Pausanias mentions that at the gates of Athens (where the procession entered at the start of the Dionysia), there was a building with clay images (*agalmata*), including Amphictyon king of Athens, feasting Dionysos and other gods. When Pausanias adds: 'Here also is Pegasus of Eleutherai who introduced the god to the Athenians',[90] in the normal Greek manner he slips from talking about an image of Pegasus to saying simply, here *is* Pegasus,[91] for the mythic figure was always in some sense present in his image. Regarding the 'ancient "failure" to distinguish between god and statue at the linguistic level', Richard Gordon comments that art was a 'problem' only to philosophers. Most people in the ancient world refused to develop a theory of the imagination and were happy to 'at once assert and deny that statues or painted figures are alive'. This 'gamble with the impermissible', or game of 'let's pretend' was necessary because without images there could be no cult of the gods. Statues which represent the gods are, in a paradoxical phrase, 'true illusions' because they are 'pictures of a world we cannot know'.[92]

To ask what Greek polytheists 'believed' about their sacred images is to pose a question which they had no vocabulary to answer. They had no equivalent to our word 'sculpture' which neatly separates object from function, and Pausanias' preferred term is *agalma*, literally an 'offering'. Plato's own views were heterodox, but he explains how normal Athenians 'set up *agalmata* as images, and when we worship [*agal-*] them, though they are without life (i.e. without *psychai*), we deem that living gods (i.e. with *psychai*) will thereby derive good-will and beneficence'.[93] The average Athenian knew on one level that the sculpted image was materially inert, but at the same time knew that if a human treated an *agalma* properly, because of its imagistic properties the represented god would be affected. It is salutary to ask an intelligent twenty-first-century Hindu how he or she understands the status of idols, and the practice of *darśan* when they behold images in an act of

---

[90] Pausanias i.2.5.  [91] Cf. Gordon (1979: 8); Jourdain-Annequin (1998: 242).
[92] Gordon (1979: 10, 16, 25).  [93] Plato *Laws* 11.931a.

worship. Answers received will be contradictory, complex and various. There has been a tension for many centuries between the idea that the image is a device for mediation, and the idea that it is an embodiment of the divine, an immediate form of the god.[94] The heart of Hindu worship lies not in forms of language but in practice. The eyes of the Hindu idol are critical to the practice of *darśan*, being carved last, and sealed with honey and ghee before being opened by a priest.[95] In Dionysian images and masks the eyes were no less crucial, because they opened a channel for interchange.

The sacredness of ancient statues related to their lifelike properties. If the statue is to respond to human prayers, then as Nigel Spivey explains, it 'must appear to have sensory powers'. Sculpture acquired what Benjamin terms an 'aura' because it was placed in sacred spaces, but also 'because the sculptor was conceived of as an essentially vicarious agent: through him came glimpses, or even revelations, of the divine'.[96] Both Sophocles and the actor who donned the mask of Ajax were vicarious agents in this sense. I should repeat once more that I am not in any way seeking to depoliticise tragedy when I argue that tragic, masked performance had a religious basis of this kind. When the Athenians abandoned their city to the Persians, they did not abandon the statue of Athena Polias, for the goddess was crucial to their 'political' and thus human identity. There is no evidence to suggest that Athenian society, which executed Socrates for impiety,[97] was set on a historical path leading to secularisation analogous to the trajectory of the modern west. Theatre historians must read against the grain of the philosophers if they are to reach that majority for whom reason was not the primary means of attaining truth. There was theory, and there was *theōria*.

[94] Eck (1985: 45–6); cf. Rutherford (2000: 144–6).   [95] Eck (1985: 7, 53).
[96] Spivey (1996: 50, 52).   [97] Parker (1996: 199–207).

# 11 | Mask and self

'I am an empty shell: an animal has eaten my inside without my noticing. Now I look into myself and I see that I am more dead than Agamemnon.'[1] Sartre's Aegisthus describes, from some ill-defined position of external agency, an interior space that should be the locus of feeling, where his authentic living self is supposed to reside. Sartre's vision of self as an interiority belongs to a modern and ever more globalised mode of understanding who we are, yet this 'inner self' is missing from the common-sense vocabulary of the ancient Greeks. The mask serves us conveniently today as a metaphor for Aegisthus' state of alienation, expressing the idea of a social façade with no substance behind or inside it, but for Greeks with a different concept of selfhood, the mask had different meanings. In Chapter 4 I examined the paradox that Sartre's Aegisthus had to be played without a mask. Only by displaying a naked face could the actor demonstrate that, beneath whatever psycho-social mask the character assumes in society, a unique individual lies concealed. Fascist collectivism made it imperative for Sartre to reassert the primacy of the individual moral agent, and *Les Mouches* was symptomatic of a retreat from a Nietzschean aesthetic.

In a celebrated lecture given in London in 1938, and thus likewise under the shadow of fascism, the French anthropologist and nephew of Durkheim, Marcel Mauss, laid the foundations for modern anthropological enquiry into the self. For him, the notion of the person (*personne*), which is to say the category of the self (*le moi*), was a recent, post-Kantian creation, and a precious acquisition that had to be cherished. 'Far from being the innate, primordial idea, clearly inscribed since Adam in the depths of our being, we see it carry on, almost to the present, slowly growing, clarifying, defining itself, becoming identified with self-knowledge, with psychological consciousness.'[2] Mauss traced an evolutionary line through human culture from the idea of the *personnage* – a theatrical term which translates as 'role' or 'character' – to the category of the person.

He offered his London audience a four-part historical schema, and the idea of the mask was central to this analysis. First came society of the clan,

---

[1] *Les Mouches* II.iv: Sartre 2005.   [2] Mauss (1938: 26).

accessible through anthropological field studies. Here ceremonial masking is central to the creation of a *personnage*, and a man's role in sacred drama is indistinguishable from his role in family life. In societies like the Kwakiutl, men use masks to 'manufacture a superimposed personality', and in the extreme example of Alaskan shutter masks different totemic identities are superimposed on top of each other. Men who wear many masks have many names, according to how they exist in relationship to different groups and activities, and in most such societies they are conceived as the fruit of their ancestors, whose spirits are reincarnated by masks.[3] In a related lecture given in Copenhagen, Mauss portrayed the Kwakiutl as men who 'spend their life in perpetual initiations, with mandatory ecstasy and possession required in order to obtain titles, prerogatives, marriage, wealth, office, prestige'. To be possessed by one's *role*, he added, remains a feature of modern life.[4]

Mauss located a decisive turning point in Rome, with its notion of the *persona* – the Latin term for a 'mask'. Originating in an Etruscan mask-based culture, the word came to represent a new category, the moral 'person' with rights at law. Whilst aristocrats continued to wear *imagines*, wax masks that assimilated them with their ancestors, Stoic philosophies of free will gave the mask new connotations. Used to translate the Greek term *prosōpon*, the term *persona* becomes ambivalent, since it is applied 'to the individual in his unclad nature, with all masks stripped off, and, conversely, the sense of artifice remains'. The word 'persona' evokes both the *personnage* and the intimacy of the *personne*. In the later Stoics, such ambiguity vanishes, and Epictetus, who was formerly a slave, offered the maxim: 'sculpt thy mask!' to mean: create your own *personnage*, type or character.[5] Christianity provided Mauss with his third phase, the three-in-one doctrine of the Trinity encapsulating the idea that divine and human meet in a single being. And finally, philosophers like Kant, political declarations of Human Rights, and puritans with their notion of individual responsibility to God, introduced the category of the *moi*, the self, as the 'condition of consciousness, of science, of Pure Reason'.[6]

Mauss' account of the Roman *persona* is supported by Cicero, who considered everyone to have two basic *personae*: one that is shared and distinguishes rational humans from animals, and one that is allocated to each individual. The calculating nature of Odysseus, for example, contrasts with the hot temper of Ajax, and people must manage such innate temperaments, not seek to change them. Cicero supports his theory of the double *persona* by analogy

---

[3] Mauss (1938: 14–15).  [4] Mauss (2004: 4–5).
[5] Mauss (1938: 22–3).  [6] Mauss (1938: 27).

with tragic actors, who select not the best play but the play that suits their natural talents. Aesopus, for example, regularly avoids Ajax, while Rupilius favours the victim role of Antiope; Clytaemnestra requires physicality (*gestus*), while the Seven who attacked Thebes need powerful voices. Cicero complicates the picture further with two subsidiary *personae*, one imposed by chance, another by choice of career.[7] This is all very different from the classical Greek concept of personhood, and of the tragic mask. Cicero has in mind a Roman theatrical convention whereby the mask reflects 'motions of the soul', and the unchanging mask worn by Ajax would be a marker of his fixed and given temperament.[8]

I have already cited Cicero's account of how the actor's eyes blaze through the eye-holes of the tragic mask.[9] This vignette of Telamon's rage and grief upon learning of Ajax' death was meant to give the aspirant orator a lesson in performance: the orator needs to live his part and feel the appropriate emotions, just like the actor whose authentic emotions have been glimpsed through the mask. Eyes, Cicero explains, are critical to the orator's performance, for nature gave humans eyes to indicate their feelings, just as it gave to horses and lions their manes, tails and ears. Not even the greatest of actors, Roscius, could 'win praise from the older generation when wearing a mask in some great play, for each action proceeds from the soul, and the face is an *imago* of the soul, the eyes its *indices*'.[10] The word *imago* refers to the aristocratic ancestor mask modelled from the life. These Roman elders were evidently hostile to the imported Greek convention of the tragic mask, which threatened their conception of human order. The word *persona*, unlike *prosōpon*, is not a synonym for face.[11] Cicero's account of the Roman mask reflects his everyday, common-sense experience of a gap between how he really is and the roles he has to play in Roman society.

In his developmental account of modern personhood, Mauss makes no mention of Nietzsche, whose fragmented vision of the self, as I argued in Chapter 4, saw masking as an inevitable accompaniment of the human condition, concealing a vulnerable psychic interiority. Nietzsche levelled against Euripides the charge of introducing a split between intent and action, and his assault on the rationality of the conscious self encouraged modernist experimentation with masking the actor.[12] For Mauss in 1938, such thinking was retrograde, dismissive of the moral agent imbued with Kantian reason. In the post-war era, however, individualism has come to look more and more

---

[7] *De Officiis* i.107–15.   [8] On the Roman mask see Dupont (2000: 125–39).
[9] *On the Orator* ii.193, cf. [74/4–8] above.   [10] *On the Orator* ii.221–2
[11] Cf. Frontisi-Ducroux (1995: 17).   [12] Cf. Jenkins (1998: 223).

like the ideology of global capitalism, asserting personal autonomy only to negate it. Modern neurology has modified contemporary perceptions of the self, eliminating on biological grounds the idea of a single interior centre of consciousness. Antonio Damasio's separation of autonomous emotions from conscious feelings has begun to be of interest to performers,[13] and raises fresh questions about the agency of the actor beneath the mask. Mauss' narrative of human progress culminating in the modern 'person' seems today to need reshaping.

Clifford Geertz has attempted to avoid evolutionary bias in his working definition of modern individualism. He argues that: 'The Western conception of the person as a bounded, unique, more or less integrated motivational and cognitive universe, a dynamic center of awareness, emotion, judgement, and action organised into a distinctive whole and set contrastively both against other such wholes and against its social and natural background, is, however incorrigible it may seem to us, a rather peculiar idea within the context of the world's cultures.' Geertz contrasts this western conception of the person with the dramaturgical conception of the Balinese, whereby: 'It is dramatis personae, not actors, that endure; indeed it is dramatis personae, not actors, that in the proper sense really exist. Physically men come and go, mere incidents in a happenstance history, of no genuine importance even to themselves. But the masks they wear, the stage they occupy, the parts they play, and, most important, the spectacle they mount remain and comprise not the façade but the substance of things, not least the self.'[14] We need to look at the classical Greeks with similar anthropological eyes to see how their experience of self was vested in external roles, and not try to absorb them as versions of the modern bounded and unique individual. David Napier, in his study of masks in polytheistic societies, points out the deep incompatibility between masking and the modern category of the person. Masks are 'heresy to any sort of positivistic psychology' since they imply abrupt changes and multiple selves, and they also 'challenge our perceptions of what is ethical' since the focus of responsibility keeps shifting. He argues for a positive value in the modern world of a 'polythetic' view of personality.[15] Edward LiPuma refines Geertz's binarism, arguing that tension between individual and 'dividual' experience is part of universal human experience, and it is ideology which consistently foregrounds one or the other.[16] Where Geertz argues for a formal decoding of symbolic systems, LiPuma allows the

---

[13] Damasio 1999. Cf. Becker (2004: 134ff.). Katie Mitchell's production of *Iphigenia at Aulis* for the Royal National Theatre (2004) drew inspiration from him: *The Guardian*, 25 September 2004.
[14] Geertz (1984: 126–9). First published in 1974.   [15] Napier (1986: 27–8).   [16] LiPuma 1998.

anthropologist more space for imaginative empathy, and for the analysis of contradictions within a given society.

In an essay published in 1960, Jean-Pierre Vernant mapped out an emergence of the *psychē*, which he described as the frame that 'allowed an interior world to become objectivised and take shape, a starting point for the progressive construction of structures of self'.[17] His later work on the Gorgon mask helped him modify this evolutionary view. He related the fatal gaze of the Gorgon to an extromissive theory of vision, which implied that rays from the eyes can be reflected back on oneself, leading him to the broader proposition that 'awareness of self is not directed towards the interior, but towards the exterior'. There are Lacanian overtones when he continues: 'The individual seeks and finds himself in others, in those mirrors comprised by all who are in his eyes his alter ego: parents, children, friends'. Arguing now for a complete absence of introspection, Vernant cites the pithy formulation: 'Consciousness of self is, for the Greek, awareness of a *He*, not of an *I*'.[18] He returns to vision in his essay 'Greek man', describing sight as a kind of prosthesis whereby a luminous arm extends from the eyes, like a tentacle. This non-Cartesian seeing physically conjoined the classical Greek to a world which had not yet been reified and 'cut off from man by the unbridgeable divide which separates matter from spirit, the physical from the psychic'.[19] This was a timocratic society where the 'identity of an individual coincides with his social reputation', and his human value depends on how the world regards him. Greek man has an individual life in the sense of a private life, but 'this individual never appears as the embodiment of inalienable and universal rights, nor as a person in the modern sense of the word, with his unique interior life, the secret world of his subjectivity, the foundational origin of his *self*'.[20]

In his earlier work Vernant maintains that the *psychē* or soul has no connection to a Greek sense of the individual, but is on the contrary an impersonal or supra-personal *daimon*. Its function is not to preserve the uniqueness of a given human being, but to 'liberate us from it by integrating us with the cosmic and divine order'.[21] In his later essay 'Psyche: double of the body or reflection of the divine?', having retreated from his idea of a nascent interiority, Vernant adopted the term 'double' to describe the Greek *psychē*, offering it as a translation of *eidōlon* ('image', 'phantom'). In Homer

---

[17] 'Aspects de la personne dans la religion grecque': Vernant (1990b: 369).
[18] 'La mort dans les yeux': Vernant (1996: 90–1), citing B. Groethuysen.
[19] Vernant (1996: 217, 214).
[20] Vernant (1996: 222–3). Vernant (1989: 224–9) develops a similar line of argument.
[21] Vernant (1996: 221); cf. Vernant (1990b: 370).

the *psychē* is a form of *eidōlon*, a ghost comparable to a shadow, dream or puff of smoke, appearing after death, and assuming the appearance of the dead person, but without material reality. If death is an emptying out of substance, but the image remains, it follows that humans can best help the dead by perpetuating that image, either by keeping it in the memory through epic performance, or by carving indestructible replicas in stone. Plato, Vernant argues, took from the Pythagoreans and Orphics the new notion that this 'double' did not simply emerge at death but also accompanied living beings through their lives, so that eventually a neo-Platonist double was taken for the true reality, a reflection of the divine, while the transient material body was judged of lower worth.[22]

Vernant's argument is suggestive for an understanding of tragic performance because the mask shares the qualities of the *psychē*, an ephemeral linen shell that lacks material substance but provides an idealised visible form of the dead person. Tragic performances preserved the memory of long-dead heroes by animating masks which were neither free products of the creative imagination, nor an attempt to reincarnate the living flesh of the dead hero, but corresponded to the *psychē* that lingers for ever. Greek spectators did not expect to see Ajax brought back to life, for such could never happen, but they could conceptualise the figure before them as a kind of *psychē*, and know that the Dionysia contributed to the well-being of Ajax through conserving his double in the public memory. Vernant does not, unfortunately, apply his theory to the theatre, which he regards as the product of a new philosophical split between being and appearances. As I pointed out in Chapter 9, worshipping the columnar idol is for Vernant a genuine means of making contact with the god. The ritual mask 'has the maximum of possessive presence and that presence is ever at the same time elsewhere, or nowhere, or in you [*en soi*]',[23] whilst theatre is relegated to the realm of the fictive, a mere product of aesthetic illusion. Given divergence between the nature of the Homeric hero and his staged civic counterpart, the tragic figure becomes 'problematic' and an 'enigma' in need of deciphering by the spectator. The theatre mask is not disorientating like the ritual mask, for its 'function is very clear: to proclaim the identity of the *personnage*, without ambiguity'. Tragedy is said to operate on familiar figures in 'a true experiment, I might even say simulation, as in physics or in chemistry'.[24]

Rejecting Nietzsche's spiritualised notion of Dionysism, Vernant effectively casts himself as a version of Nietzsche's Socrates, who appropriated

---

[22] Vernant (1996: 525–35). Translated in Vernant (1991: 186–92) as 'Psuche: simulacrum of the body or image of the divine?'

[23] 'Un théâtre de la cité': Vernant (1996: 430–1).   [24] Vernant (1996: 436–7, 427).

Greek tragedy on behalf of the intellect. Consigning tragedy to the realm of the fictive, Vernant placed dramatic art in a category that he apparently had no further interest in analysing, aside always from the privileged instance of the *Bacchae*. If, however, we reject this modern opposition of sacred and profane, Vernant's theory of the cultic Dionysos mask proves richly suggestive as a means of understanding the disturbing power of the mask in tragic performance. As I argued in Chapter 10, the gaze of Ajax presented itself to the viewer in no way differently from the mask or face of a newly sculpted idol. Vernant's account of theatrical spectatorship contradicts his own anti-Cartesian theory of Greek vision. Greek spectators who projected beams of light from their eyes, defining personal identity through social interaction, most surely did not view tragic performances as scientific experiments.

## *Seven Against Thebes*

In the remainder of this chapter I shall examine three Greek tragedies as engagements between masks and a living audience, and as re-enactments of past events involving heroes reanimated by their masks. I shall begin with *Seven Against Thebes* because of the way it has been eviscerated by generations of logocentric critics. If we take the play as a theoric spectacle, a tragic masquerade, we can grasp its artistry, its impact, and most importantly its engagement with the problem of self. If, on the other hand, we take it as essentially an oratorio, we are likely to emerge baffled by impenetrable linguistic enigmas. I shall interpret the play as an epiphanic spectacle offered to the eyes, and passing through four phases: the prologue and worship of the statues, the choosing of the warriors, the arming of Eteocles, and the lament over the corpses.

'Citizens of Cadmus!' The opening words of the play, uttered by Eteocles, have prompted most editors and translators, applying the logic of Cartesian vision and naturalistic stagecraft, to supply an otherwise redundant crowd of Theban men as addressees.[25] If, however, we start by recognising the importance of the gaze in Greek theatre, we shall see that Aeschylus' strategy is to engage the spectators with the mask, interpellating them in the action, and refusing them a position of detached omniscience. In line 3 Eteocles declares that he does not close his eyes in sleep, a phrase which recalls Tony

---

[25] Taplin (1977: 129–37) rejects the postulate of 'audience participation', and is followed for example in the Everyman translation – Ewans (1996: 39), and in the Oxford edition – Hutchinson (1985: 41). The deictic reference to 'these citizens' at l. 317 is ignored.

Harrison's Greek mask with 'eyes that never close'.[26] Driven from their own city by the Persians only twelve years previously, Athenians would not have found it hard to enter emotionally into the plight of besieged Thebans in the city of Cadmus.

The chorus of Theban women arrive in disorderly panic, declaring that they will cling to the statues, and deck them in robes and garlands (95–102).[27] They establish choreographic order with three strophic pairs addressed to the gods, presenting themselves as suppliants (111). Eight gods are invoked, and then invoked again in reverse sequence, which suggests that the women moved to and fro along a line of gods, adorning the statues before taking up their formal suppliant position at their feet.[28] Eteocles responds by calling the women away from the statues, and making his own calmer vow to a generalised group of gods, that includes both the visible statues and others on the Theban plain, promising a different adornment for the gods in the form of captured clothes and weaponry (265–78a). The audience thus witnessed two levels of animation: Aeschylus animating Eteocles and a set of female masks by the use of human performers – and the chorus animating a set of statues by dressing, addressing and embracing them as gods. The reservations which Eteocles expresses about the over-emotional behaviour of the chorus anticipate those which Plato would later express about the over-emotional Athenian audience. For the duration of the play, the adorned statues remain a powerful presence, leaving fluid the boundaries between mask and statue, human and divine.

In the central section of the play a messenger describes the seven warriors outside the seven gates who have been chosen by lot to fight as champions, each bearing an emblem on his shield. Eteocles then names seven Thebans who will engage with them, ending with himself who will fight his brother at the seventh gate. Pierre Vidal-Naquet and Froma Zeitlin have examined the semiotics of the shields, pointing in general terms to a mounting sense of threat,[29] but the difficulty in their analysis lies in the fact that only one Theban shield is described, and on the level of text there is no apparent logic. If, however, we start from the premise that a play is a theoric spectacle, then it would be strange indeed if the scene were not animated by the departure of Theban warriors, equipped with spectacular shields.[30] The

---

[26] Cf. p. 139.    [27] Line references are to Denys Page's Oxford Classical Text edition (1972).
[28] Thalmann (1978: 88–9) sets out the choreographic logic; cf. Wiles 1993.
[29] See 'The shields of the heroes' in Vernant and Vidal-Naquet (1990: 273–300); Zeitlin 1982.
[30] Building on Bacon 1964, the translation by Hecht and Bacon (1973) makes an effort to reconstruct the logic of visible shields. See Wiles (1993: 189–90).

chorus is allocated lines suitable to cover each exit, making an appropriate reference to divine intervention, and during the first of these exits it states unambiguously in the present tense, 'the champion comes forward' (419). Played as oratorio, the scene makes poor drama, for there is no indication of how word is transmitted to the unseen Theban warriors, or when those men depart for battle. Hutchinson in the Oxford edition insists that the Theban champions cannot be visible because the 'absence of support from the text is a fatal objection', but he then cancels Aeschylean lines which do not make sense to him because he has no visual context for what is being said. Paradoxically, the aspiration to foreground text over image results in the destruction of the text.[31]

The Argive champions have been chosen by lot, with stones cast from an inverted bronze helmet (458–9), and this use of lots is reiterated to establish the ritualised pattern (376, 423, 451, 457). Eteocles underlines the importance of chance when he states that Ares adjudges the outcome in dice (414), and that Hermes, who is god of dice and chance in general, has brought together two of the champions (508). In Homer, Ajax is chosen as champion by just this procedure: nine men, having volunteered to fight Hector in single combat and placed their marks on lots, pray to the gods before Nestor shakes one lot from Agamemnon's helmet.[32] As William Thalmann has pointed out, it would be odd if Eteocles did not use the same time-honoured procedure.[33]

It is exceptionally difficult to read this scene as oratorio because the tenses used by Eteocles when he sends his warriors to the seven gates, tenses located at different points in each speech, are apparently so illogical:

1. I shall oppose (408) + Justice sends (415): lines 12/19 of speech
2. has been designated (448): line 12
3. I would send (472) + he is sent (473): lines 1/2
4. was chosen (505): line 5
5. There is (553): line 4
6. we shall oppose (621): line 25
7. I go and will conjoin (672) + I shall engage (675): lines 20/23

The syntactical logic of tenses, moods and persons becomes obvious once we recognise that Eteocles is shaking a named ballot from a helmet at the start of each of his speeches. Given choice, he *would* send in l 472 the champion

---

[31] Hutchinson (1985: 105, with notes on 472–3, 650–2). Hutchinson is influenced by Taplin (1977: 149–56). On Taplin's theoretical position see Wiles 1987, Wiles (1993: 188–9), Wiles (1997: 5–14).
[32] *Iliad* vii.161–90.   [33] Thalmann (1978: 125–35).

who *is* nominated by the ballot at l 473, and there is no need for Hutchinson to cancel the first of these lines. Eteocles both is and is not the agent of sending. I, he says, will set six men with myself as seventh at the seven gates (282–4). He is the active instigator of a process which results in mutual fratricide because he sets up a framework whereby the will of the gods can be expressed. He is agent in that he shakes the helmet, yet has no agency because a divine force acts through him.

Thalmann interpreted the lottery in relation to how inheritance is 'allotted' (690, 731), but the issues are wider than this.[34] Aeschylus' *Eumenides* is the final play of its trilogy just like *Seven Against Thebes*, and the casting of ballots by democratic jurors provides a precise dramaturgical parallel. The *Eumenides* establishes a principle of democratic voting that retains its aetiological force in modern democracies, a force exploited, for example, in Peter Stein's 1994 production which used a cast from newly democratised Russia. Unlike the vote, however, sortition plays very little part in modern democratic processes, being alien to values of individual moral choice and meritocracy which the western world cherishes. The idea that the gods should have a role in shaping political outcomes is not something we today accept, and ideology contributes to the modern reluctance of scholars to picture a drawing of lots. Sortition, however, was at the core of the Greek democratic system. When the *Seven* was performed, a power struggle was in place between the Areopagites, who owed their position to birth and wealth, and the democrats, who wanted power to pass to juries and to the Council of Five Hundred, both egalitarian bodies whose members were chosen by lot.[35] Lottery was inseparably linked to democracy, and the Dionysia provides a localised example of its workings. The judges were selected from a huge panel by the public drawing of lots from a water-jar. The archon, himself appointed by lot, read out the ballots, but only a random five, or however many were needed to achieve a verdict thereafter. The allocation of poets to *choregoi* and actors to poets also became subject to the ethico-religious principle of sortition during the fifth century.[36]

The ideal of sortition turns upon a different concept of self. If selfhood is a function of the political community, then sortition is an efficient way to establish the collective will, and if gods can act through humans, then sortition provides them with their opportunity. If, however, the self resides in psychological interiors, then sortition denies 'me' my human right of

---

[34] Thalmann (1978: 63–78); on the democratic principle, see Sinclair (1988: 17–18).
[35] Aristotle *Constitution of Athens* 25.2, 43.2; cf. *Politics* ii.12. cf. Sinclair (1988: 195).
[36] Pickard-Cambridge (1968: 93–7); Csapo and Slater (1995: 157–65); Jedrkiewicz 1996; Wilson (2000: 67–8).

self-expression. The problem of agency is very much at issue in Aeschylus' play. After the announcement that Polyneices stands at the seventh gate, when we know the final lot to fall from the helmet must inevitably be that of Eteocles, the Messenger concludes: 'You yourself determine who should be sent! So you may not blame this man [i.e. 'me'] for his announcements, you yourself determine how to steer the city!' (650–2). Though Hutchinson finds the verbal repetition 'insufferable',[37] the repeated 'you yourself determine' has great theatrical force because it urges that Eteocles should override the ritual, and personally decide who the final combatant will be. Eteocles responds that Dikē (Justice) allows him no other course of action, as ruler, brother and foe (673–5). This is not a world of free existential choice, for Eteocles has no sense of identity outside the political and familial relationships which define him. The mask belonged naturally to a theatre where selfhood was a function of exterior relationships, and there was no question of the audience peering to see what was really going on inside Eteocles' mind.

Having determined to fight, Eteocles calls for his greaves. The chorus tells him to avoid the pollution of fratricide, but he replies that fame is preferable to shame; while the chorus pleads for calm, Eteocles in his antiphonal response sings of the gods and the curse of Oedipus. As Schadewaldt has argued, theatrical logic requires that Eteocles should be formally armed during this sequence.[38] Again, Homer provides the paradigm. When an attempt is made to resolve the Trojan War by single combat, Paris and Menelaus agree to fight, and lots are shaken in a helmet to determine who will throw their spear first. While the lots are being shaken, the people pray to Zeus that whichever is the guilty party will be killed. As soon as the lot is cast, the pair arm themselves in the following sequence: greaves, cuirass, sword, shield, helmet, spear. In the combat which follows, the gods do indeed intervene, and the attempt to avert war comes to nothing.[39] In Aeschylus' play, when Eteocles exits to walk to his death, the visual impact at this climactic moment would be much reduced if he had yet to prepare for combat. Eteocles' call for greaves implies that the Homeric sequence will be followed before the eyes of the audience.

In Euripides' telling of the tale, the two sons of Oedipus 'hide their bodies in bronze weaponry [*hopla*]'.[40] Just as masks transformed the wearer by hiding him, so did the armour of a Greek hoplite. I have already pointed out how the hoplite's helmet served as both preparation and analogue for wearing a theatrical mask. The visual transformation of Eteocles is not redundant

---

[37] Hutchinson (1985: 147).   [38] Schadewaldt 1961; Bacon 1964.
[39] *Iliad* iii.314–81.   [40] *Phoenician Women* 1242.

spectacle but an image crucial to the play's meaning. As a warrior, he is bound to a code of honour and obedience whereby private aspects of selfhood are of no account. After a musical passage expressing high emotion, eight tense lines of stichomythia culminate in Eteocles' exit, dramaturgically equivalent to the exchanges between Clytaemnestra and Agamemnon, or Orestes and Clytaemnestra, in the *Oresteia*. With each of his four utterances, Eteocles defines the identity or selfhood that drives him to fight: as a man he cannot obey women; he is 'sharpened', i.e. identified with his weapons, so cannot be blunted by words; he has the code of honour of a 'hoplite'; and the gods have disposed. His physical transformation is summed up in these four lines. He is bound by duty to his community, just like Athenian hoplites for whom warfare was part of citizenship,[41] and he identifies himself with Ares, god of war and bloodlust. As Eteocles' body vanishes into armour, the ontological status of the masked actor begins to merge with that of Ares' decorated statue.[42] Helen Bacon argues that Eteocles' shield should display an Erinye to counterbalance Dike (Justice) on his brother's shield, and suggests that the image on a round shield has the same mesmerising function as an eye or mask. Eteocles has dismissed the other Argive shields as a mere game of appearances, but if Bacon is correct, and a demonic face with apotropaic eyes does occupy his shield, then he now becomes identified with this shield that is also his mask.[43]

In his magisterial study of the self and its history, Charles Taylor examined Plato's ethic of reason and reflection, which required a unitary space for the mind, and saw it as the reaction against a warrior-citizen morality which placed fame and glory as the highest goals. This older morality set great store by a kind of possession or mania taking the form of a sudden access of strength and courage, and a warrior was heroic not in spite of divine help but because he was the locus of divine action. Prior to Plato, there was no single location for self and mind, but aspects of mind were associated with different parts of the body: the liver and the heart, together with the *thumos* and *phrenes* that have some association with the lungs.[44] In his antiphonal exchange with the chorus, it becomes clear that Eteocles is the locus for such intersecting forces. He is swept on by an *atē* or infatuation that is *thumos*-filled and spear-maddened (686–7), propelled by a personified lust called *Eros* or *himeros* (688, 692), and an Erinye or *daimon* haunts him (696, 710). In this demonic universe, evoked while Eteocles arms, we see the dissolution

---

[41] For bibliography on hoplites see Raaflaub 1999.
[42] Hecht and Bacon suggest that his pose should echo Ares' statue (1973: s.d. after l. 713).
[43] Bacon 1964.
[44] Taylor (1989: 117–18); cf. Onians 1951, Padel 1992.

of the autonomous moral agent who declared at the start of the play that he steered the ship of state (2). Now, he sings, 'since god drives the thing onwards, let the whole race of Laius, hated by Apollo, ride the crest of the allotted wave of Hells's river' (689–91). The nautical metaphor captures the ambiguities of agency, for the helmsman can only steer where the storm blows him (cf. 758–62, 795–6).

The mask articulates an ambivalence of agency which lies at the core of this and all Greek tragedies.[45] Actors characteristically experience themselves having to obey the dictates of their mask, and in much the same way Eteocles obeys an external force. Believing that Greek tragedy normally allows the development of a 'personality-viewpoint', whereby the spectator has privileged access to the personality of the hero resulting in empathetic response, Christopher Gill finds Eteocles' account of his behaviour 'bizarre' and 'deeply puzzling', with a 'curious' interplay of agency and passivity.[46] Gill is right to distance from Greek antiquity a Cartesian and Kantian 'I' endowed with rational autonomy and conscious acts of will, and right also to reject Snell's developmental concept of a Greek mind that only slowly became capable of free choice, but his own conception of a dialogic self assumes a theatre audience preoccupied with interrogating motivation. The sympathetic involvement of an audience, Gill argues, results from its understanding a character's ethical stance.[47] The quest for motivation underpins most naturalist theatre, but is not necessarily a helpful means of interpreting masked theatre. Ruth Padel remarks that the biological and the daemonic are not separate discourses in Greek tragedy,[48] and the mask helps us to see Eteocles as a psychosomatic whole, responsive to an environment imbued with daemonic forces. He may momentarily become an Ares, or an Erinye. When Michael Ewans pronounces that the visible arming of Eteocles would be a 'disastrous production error', obscuring the 'climax of the play', he starts from the premise that Eteocles is 'choosing, rationally' as well as recognising the *daimōn*.[49] My own contention is that, when he arms himself, Eteocles effectively dons a mask that tells him what to do. In theatrical terms, this seems a much more exciting option, in preference to the standard naturalist fare which involves a character explaining his motivation so the audience can form a rational understanding. In human terms, this account offers much more space to irrational forces driving human behaviour.

---

[45] Cf. Vernant's seminal essay 'Intimations of the will in Greek tragedy' in Vernant and Vidal-Naquet (1990: 49–84).
[46] Gill (1990: 26–7); cf. Gill (1996: 118).    [47] Gill (1996: esp. 34–41, 105–6). Cf. Halliwell 1990.
[48] Padel (1992: 3).    [49] Ewans (1996: 199).

Plato likened the human head to a charioteer, steering the chariot constituted by the body and its impulses,[50] but in Aeschylus, a century earlier, the mask clothed the face so the body as a whole became a wonder to behold, and the head did not yet represent a centre of agency, controlling the horses of passion. Plato's new attitude to the face is exemplified in the *Charmides*, where men gaze at an adolescent boy in the wrestling-school as if he were a statue. Socrates' companion comments that they are admiring the boy's fine *prosōpon*, but if the boy removed his clothes he would seem faceless, so beautiful is his bodily form. Socrates counters these carnal thoughts with an offer to cure the boy's headache, but insists that to do so he must treat the soul, citing a Thracian sage who believed that all good and evil springs from the *psychē*, and flows thence through the head to emerge at the eyes.[51] The face shifts from being an index of the body beautiful to being an index of the moral agent within. The Platonist association between head and *psychē*, *psychē* and agency, would inform the characterisation of Hellenistic masks, but has no bearing on fifth-century masking practice, which unified head with body.

Socrates in the *Charmides* masters his sexual desire in the search for wisdom. Although success or failure in self-mastery became the great theme of Hellenistic comedy, Greek tragedies were concerned with the very possibility of self-mastery in a world where gods intervene. It was when self-knowledge as distinct from self-mastery finally became the issue that the mask had to be banished from western theatre. Sophocles' Oedipus does not acquire knowledge of 'self' in this sense but knowledge of his parentage, for the fifth century has no concept of selfhood that can be isolated from external relationships. Oedipus' moral qualities, as a man capable of killing a traveller on the road, are of no relevance, and no moral qualities were inscribed on fifth-century masks. The self-knowledge of Aeschylus' Eteocles is likewise the recognition of who he actually is, son of the cursed Oedipus.

I conclude with the final epiphany of the play,[52] when 'not in word' but 'self-displaying' (847–8), two corpses are borne in, symmetrical in the way they have been wounded. The bodies are addressed as if Eteocles and Polyneices can hear what is being said to them, and the masks perpetuate the vitality of their features, while the actors have now assumed the masks of Antigone and Ismene. The symmetry of language and choreography is reinforced by the ability of the mask to do what is in nature a prodigy, to create pairs of identical faces, and perhaps also there is no longer any

---

[50] *Timaeus* 44D-E; cf. *Phaedrus* 245ff.   [51] *Charmides* 154E, 156E.
[52] The text from 1011 onwards is universally agreed to be non-Aeschylean, and I have taken no account of it.

distinction between the female masks of chorus and actors. There was an initial conflict between chorus and protagonist when distraught women trespassed into the public male domain, and in the central *agōn* the women of the chorus oppose Eteocles in an effort to avoid collective pollution, but in the final lament the actors revert to the function of chorus-leader and women assume their archaic ritual task of mourning the dead.[53] Identity in the classical Greek world was a collective affair, and lamentation for the dead served the function of bonding survivors. The mask insists that individuals are not unique, and transcending individuation is the main function of the tragic mask, for the wearer loses those normal boundaries comprised by the skin, and is forced to develop an intuitive kinaesthetic awareness of others, while the spectator sees individual faces unified to create a choral persona. The normal visible distinctions of daily life which separate brother from brother, actor from chorus, brother from sister, living from dead, are obliterated by the mask. And ultimately, the audience finds itself unified by the grief engendered by masked performers.

## Sophocles' *Electra*

In Sophocles' plays, the power of the demonic is less immediate, and it seems a more obvious requirement to discuss drama in terms of 'character'. In 1961 John Jones set out an influential theory of mask and character, arguing that the mask was not extraneous but an essential component of Greek tragedy because, in accordance with the principles of Aristotle's *Poetics*, it diverted attention from character to action. He substitutes the term 'stage-figure' for the confusing English term 'character'. For Jones the Greek mask is essentially a negative phenomenon, offering in terms of age, rank and sex limited pointers to a 'status-defined individuality'. What is important about the mask is its lack of interiority, such that: 'Its being is exhausted in its features'. Aristotle made no distinction 'between the actor playing Oedipus and Oedipus himself', and there could be no question of the spectator peering behind the mask, for this would have destroyed the mask convention.[54] The outward-facing nature of the mask is related to the 'centrifugal' nature of the Greek self, alien to modern 'individualistic humanism'.[55] Jones hints also that his notion of the mask as pure surface can be extended to the acoustic properties of the mask.[56]

---

[53] Cf. Foley (2001b: 49–51).
[54] Jones (1962: 45, 59). Goldhill (1990a: 111–12) also argues for the term 'figure', which he borrows from Barthes.
[55] Jones (1962: 232–3). On selfhood, cf. 195–8.   [56] Jones (1962: 234, cf. 44, 149).

In its day Jones' book provided a valuable counter to psychological analyses of Greek drama, but he did not find it easy to apply his own theoretical insights. In his chapter on Sophocles' *Electra*, starting from the premise that the execution of Apollo's command is morally unproblematic, he develops an Ibsenite conception of the play as 'an enquiry into motives'. Agents, who are increasingly 'personal' and endowed with will, deploy ritual forms like lamentation instrumentally, so that by comparison with Aeschylus we find 'a narrower definition of the bounds of selfhood, setting the individual over against his gods and his ritual life'. This analysis forms part of an evolutionary account of Greek tragedy which culminates in the human-interest drama of Euripides, where Jones identifies a 'characteristic penetrative enquiry which, precisely because it forces attention behind the surface show, threatens to destroy the masking convention'.[57] In order to support the premise that divine commands in *Electra* are beyond question, Jones insists repeatedly on Clytaemnestra's 'lustful disposition', basing his interpretation upon what the audience hears from Electra and the chorus, and not upon what is seen.[58] His theory of the mask ultimately sustained rather than challenged a logocentric bias in criticism.

In the years since Jones' book appeared, critics have increasingly balked at the monotheistic and hierarchical implications of the premise that Apollo's word has absolute moral authority, recognising the paradox in Apollo's Delphic mandate that Orestes should 'by sleight of hand steal just murders' (*doloisi klepsai cheiros endikous sphagas*) (37). In a society where selfhood is determined by how one is seen in the eyes of the other, the notion that goodness can be achieved by *dolos*, deception in the form of a broken oath (47), is a contradictory one.[59] In the political context of late fifth-century Athens, where democrats lived in fear of an aristocratic coup, the idea that the end could justify the means in this way was a sensitive one, especially given the premium which Electra and the chorus place on noble birth.[60] In a polytheistic context, the slippage from Orestes' statement that he has been sent by Apollo's oracle to the assertion that he is a purifier sent by plural 'gods' (70) is a significant one, for the play contains plentiful reminders of other divine forces, such as Zeus who oversees all, the Erinyes, and the anonymous *daimōn* who accompanies each individual.[61]

---

[57] Jones (1962: 260). [58] Jones (1962: 141–59). [59] Cf. the chorus' ideal in 1081–2.
[60] Electra: 257, 287, 989, 1081; chorus: 129, 226.
[61] On the authority of Zeus: 176; on Zeus and gratitude to parents among birds: 1060–93, cf. 1094–5; on the formal opposition of Dikē and Erinye, 472–93; on the *daimōn*: 917, 999, 1157, 1269, 1306.

Despite the limitations of his evolutionary model, Jones' basic lesson that the mask supports the primacy of action remains a valuable reminder. In the most recent article that I have seen on the play, Matthew Wright adds his name to the growing list of critics advocating a 'dark' reading of the play. Wright focuses on the apparently pivotal moment when Clytaemnestra learns of Orestes' death, and acknowledges that reliance cannot be placed on Electra's verbal account of Clytaemnestra's reaction: 'mad with joy'. He assumes, however, that the 'original audience would have had a clearer idea of Clytaemnestra's state of mind from the way she delivered her lines on stage'. Electra claims that Clytaemnestra departed laughing, but, Wright wonders, 'was Clytaemnestra really cackling (*vel sim.*) as she left the stage? If we had seen the scene which preceded this description, we would know for sure.'[62] Performance awareness is here badly misplaced. The first section of Jones' book should have made it clear that masked theatre provided no such construction of character, or insight into personal emotion. The value of the mask lay precisely in throwing attention back to the surface, so Clytaemnestra's utterances about her son's death could retain their rich ambiguity. The mask foregrounded language, and language in turn helped the audience project expression onto the mask/face. To underpin their respective moral positions, Electra and Clytaemnestra create two variants of the myth which explains the killing of Iphigeneia. Words are shown to be of their nature untrustworthy and the audience is offered no basis for determining which version is more authentic. For the audience, truth had finally to be a function of what it saw, and what it saw was action, not facial signals.

Jones failed to identify and describe the epiphanic aspect of the mask, which is to say, its power to arrest the gaze and mediate between a sense of life and a sense of death. This power helps us see why Sophocles chose to end his play just before the killing of Aegisthus. Wright echoes other 'dark' readings when he comments that the final scene 'creates a strong sense of unfinished business' and 'powerfully suggests further horrors to come'.[63] The play necessarily seems 'unfinished' when one pictures the visual revelation of matricide as merely the uncovering of a naked face, but the mask provided a stronger visual climax. When Orestes tells Aegisthus to remove the covering from the *eyes* of the shrouded corpse (1468), we are reminded of the power of the mask's eyes, with its associations of extromissive and reciprocal vision. In the modern theatre, a dummy face or an actress closing her eyes and

---

[62] Wright (2005: 185–6 – original italics). Wright nn. 1–5 provides a bibliography on light/dark approaches to the play.
[63] Wright (2005: 173).

struggling to breathe lightly under artificial lighting cannot exert the same hold over an audience. The repeated declaration that the dead now live again (1419, 1478) is supported by the ability of a mask to seem at once inert and alive. The lamentation which occupies much of the play turns on the supposed vitality of the dead,[64] and if Agamemnon retains power after death, so may Clytaemnestra. The Sophoclean climax is akin to that of Alcestis in its unveiling of a *prosōpon*. Once we abandon the Shakespearean assumption that a tragedy by definition ends with corpses, and recognise how Greek tragedies were structured around visual revelations, we can see that the play was aesthetically complete as well as morally ambivalent.

A dilettante Roman scholar preserved for us a philosophical parable about mimesis, recording how the fourth-century actor Polus playing Electra carried the ashes of his own son into the theatre: the story, we are told, was an 'appearance', while the pain was 'actus', i.e. actual or enacted.[65] The basis of the plot in deception has created in revivals of the play a special interest in the authenticity of the performer's emotion. Erika Fischer-Lichte invokes as a symbolic moment in European theatre history Reinhardt's 1903 production, when Gertrud Eysoldt in the title role did visible violence to her own body and entered an ecstatic state which imparted itself to the audience. For Fischer-Lichte, the production moved away from mimesis towards a new kind of transformative ritual, as the actress replaced a semiotic body with her phenomenal or real body, and the audience ceased to view as autonomous subjects engaged in purely mental processes.[66] A similar sense of authenticity and theatrical presence transcending illusion was generated by Fiona Shaw, who described her metamorphosis into Electra as 'physically and mentally very dangerous. I was physically wrecked from it – lame, thin, ill. You're psychically playing with illness, starvation and burning up enormous intellectual energy. It didn't do me any good, that. It did my soul good, but I don't think it did my body any good.'[67] When Zoe Wanamaker performed Electra in Agamemnon's greatcoat, she made it clear that the underlying subject of the play was her own relationship to her famous theatrical father who had died a few years previously, and she described each performance as 'a kind of exorcism'.[68] In all these performances we see an unmasking or exposure of the performer behind the role, but we see also, as Fischer-Lichte explains, a re-ritualisation of the dramatic event, with transformation effected in the here-and-now before the eyes of the audience.

[64] See Foley (2001b: 156).   [65] Aulus Gellius *Attic Nights* vi.5.
[66] Fischer-Lichte (2005: 1–14).
[67] Covington 1996. Production directed by Deborah Warner, RSC 1989–91.
[68] Plett (1998: 1). Production directed by David Leveaux, 1997–9.

The fifth-century Dionysia was also a transformative ritual, but the subject of transformation was not the individual representative of an audience comprising multiple individuals. The tragic mask was premised on a selfhood that connected the individual to the collective *polis* and to the cosmos. Possessing an individual selfhood located somewhere in the lonely space where her wounded body met her tormented soul, Fiona Shaw was compelled to find authentic emotion within herself, while the chorus were relegated to mere bystanders. In a fifth-century context, as Helene Foley has shown, Electra progressively engages the chorus in her oppositional ritual, for lament always had a social framework.[69] The choreographic structure of strophe and antistrophe integrated the original Electra with her peers, breaking down individuation in the same way as the mask. The mask turns selfhood outwards, in accordance with the 'dramaturgical' principle that how one is seen is how one is. After Orestes has sung in the finale that all is well if Apollo prophesied *kalōs* (well, finely, nobly, beautifully), Aegisthus declares that he should not be killed in the darkness indoors if the deed is *kalon* (1425, 1493–4). In post-Kantian theatre of the naked face, nobility is defined as a condition of the interior intentional self, so the ethics of homicide has to be referred back to Orestes' private motivation or will, and the Sophoclean ending makes a frustratingly inconclusive coda. In classical masked theatre, however, when Orestes hides his act from public view, he determines how his act will be seen by the city, and thus what sort of person he is. Orestes ends the play advocating summary justice as a universal principle (1505–7), and the mask simply calls attention to what he says, not allowing us to postulate a private self which thinks and feels otherwise.

The cosmic dimension of the Orestes mask can be discerned when we juxtapose it with another beautiful *prosōpon*, that of the god whom Orestes serves. Clytaemnestra and Electra both pray to Lycaean Apollo (645, 1379), whose statue must be visible throughout the play. When Orestes and Pylades exit to kill Clytaemnestra, Orestes says that before going in they will do obeisance to 'these' patronal gods before the door (1374–5), implying that alongside Apollo there is some visual reminder of the polytheistic pantheon. After Electra has implored Apollo to demonstrate how the gods reward impiety (1383), the chorus refers to gods other than Apollo. 'See . . . bloody Ares!' it sings in the strophe; 'Inside is the avenger . . . with blood on his hands!' it resumes in the antistrophe, adding, in a phrase which echoes Apollo's prophecy, that the avenger is led by Hermes who 'hides *dolos* in darkness' (1395–6). The chorus thus covers the fateful exit of Orestes and

---

[69] Foley (2001b: 147–71); cf. Foley 1993.

Pylades by interpreting them as incarnating, possessed by or directed by Ares and Hermes. When Orestes returns with bloody hands, it says he has sacrificed to Ares (1423). The presence of Apollo's statue alongside the masks of these heroes helps the audience experience the fluid boundaries of what it is to be human. The mask accords with the mentality of an idolatrous culture, where self can be a point of intersection for competing divine forces.

## Euripides' *Helen*

*Helen* dates from the same period as *Electra*, and deals likewise with illusion and deception. Times have changed since Richmond Lattimore was able to declare in the introduction to his widely used Chicago translation that this was a play about 'real, exciting love between two middle-aged people who are married to each other', eulogising Helen for her loveliness 'featuring, we guess, a most accomplished actor in a ravishing mask and with a voice that fairly demanded an extra allowance of solo lyrics'.[70] Doubtless this is how Broadway in the 1950s would have played Euripides' text, with a thin layer of greasepaint substituting for the material mask in order to compose the required ravishing face. By the 1980s Charles Segal was reading the play in more philosophical terms as a study of dualism which explored the manifold antitheses of appearance and reality, and he discerned a metatheatrical dimension when 'we become aware that the play *qua* play is a term in those antitheses'.[71] Lattimore's conception of the *real* had become untenable, but Segal's confident *we* also seems vulnerable from the perspective of a post 'postmodern' era. The abyss faced by any theatre historian is the knowledge that every generation constructs the past in accordance with its own preconceptions, and one's own will be no exception.

The security of knowledge was also a problem for Euripides. I have suggested that in general terms the Greek world found seeing the surest mode of apprehending truth, but in *Helen*, the seen proves no more reliable than what is heard. If Menelaus can mistake a cloud image for his wife, then no visual image can be secure, and the physical embrace of Menelaus and Helen suggests that touch may provide a higher level of certainty. It does not necessarily follow, however, from this theme of epistemological uncertainty that in performance the actor beneath the mask was perceived as a reassuring material and 'real' presence. In her introduction to the Oxford translation, Edith Hall cites Helen's wish that her beauty could be washed over, like an

---

[70] Lattimore (1956: 263–4).  [71] Segal (1986: 264).

*agalma* regaining its former dishonourable appearance (262–3), and this evocation of a statue losing its paint leads her to a metatheatrical interpretation of the play since "Helen' herself is but a male actor wearing a sculpted mask painted with beautiful colours. By drawing attention to this false 'face', the actor draws attention to one of the illusory conventions of the theatrical performance in which he is participating. Hall goes on to argue that the play confronts issues of 'self' and 'who is the "true" Helen?'[72] I do not share the view that this quest for the true Helen behind the name necessarily leads us to the actor behind the mask. Helen's concern is not with her inner qualities but with her good name, and how she is regarded, in accordance with the outward orientation of the mask.

At the start of the twenty-first century it is easier to engage with Euripides' philosophy than with his theology. Helen expresses uncertainty in the prologue about the story that Zeus was her father, but the chorus always refers to her as the daughter of Zeus, as do the Egyptian slaves. The chorus is troubled by the story of Helen's birth from an egg, for no one can witness divinity and report back, but it declares nevertheless that the word of the gods is the only thing to be relied on (1137–50). This 'word' is heard in the finale when Helen's deified brothers appear in the sky, promising that she will be called a god, and implicitly endorsing her status as a figure in Spartan cult.[73] For modern rationalists it is easier to take the *dei ex machina* as an exercise in irony and gratuitous spectacle, than an attestation to divine forces at work in the universe behind the mysterious play of appearances.

The deceptive nature of appearances extends to the costuming of both Menelaus and Helen. The entry of Menelaus in the 'wild' and 'formless' debris of a shipwreck, unrecognisable to his wife, was parodied by Aristophanes as an entry in a costume of seaweed.[74] In a well-known Spartan ritual, kings whose bodies were lost when they died in battle had to be buried in effigy,[75] and Helen seeks a similar ritual for the lost Spartan king who was her husband. In place of a dummy, however, Menelaus does duty as the effigy or double of himself, wearing the heroic armour that is to be cast overboard in a symbolic funeral. In a theatre which relied upon doubling, such a complete change of costume by the selfsame stage figure is unusual.[76] Seeing in Euripides' play no longer offers direct access to truth.

---

[72] Morwood (1997: xxiv–xxv).
[73] See Foley (1992: 144–7). Foley (2001b: 303–30) is a revised version of this essay.
[74] *Thesmophoriazousai* 910; cf. *Helen* 544, 554 etc.    [75] Herodotus vi.58.
[76] As Marshall points out (1995: 76–7). One may compare, however, the Furies dressing in purple, or Admetus in black mourning.

Helen's trajectory runs opposite to that of Menelaus. She starts the play beautiful, and Aristophanes' parody suggests that a veil was used to conceal and reveal her striking blonde hair.[77] Though Menelaus looks on her *opsis* (gaze), it is in her body that he recognises his lost wife, for faces are not the key to personal identity (548, 557, 559). In order to assume the part of a mourner, Helen decides to shear her hair, change her white dress for black, and lacerate her cheeks (1087–9), so her prodigious beauty will be destroyed. The Egyptian king attests to the black clothes and shorn hair (1186–90), and there seems no reason to doubt that bloodied cheeks were also visible to the audience.[78] Earlier in the play Helen described Trojan women shearing their hair and Greek women lacerating themselves after the war, linking this disfigurement to two nymphs turned animals, before blaming her own beauty for the war (362–85). There seems no reason to doubt that Helen acts as promised and disfigures herself in a way that needed no further verbal exposition. In the Aristophanic parody, the man who 'imitates the new Helen' is ashamed of his/her 'wronged jaws', a joke which refers overtly to nicks from his razor, but must play also on the facial disfigurement of the Euripidean Helen.[79] This alteration of the mask would complete the process that separates the name of Helen from the beauty which defines her as a heroic figure. This separation may remind us of how Plato would later picture the falsity of facial appearance through his construction of Alcibiades and Socrates, the first venal but beautiful, the second noble in his soul yet with the *prosōpon* of a satyr.[80] In contrast to Plato, Euripides does not envisage the soul as an interiority, but rather as a ghost, *eidōlon* or 'double'.

The new self that Helen acquires when she cuts her hair and destroys her beauty is not a modern unique self but a choral self, for she makes herself visually akin to the chorus of Greek slaves, whose status required that they be shorn. While Helen disfigures herself, the chorus prepares for her reappearance as a mourner by picturing wives cutting their hair (1125). The next choral ode links Helen's transposition to a foundation myth for the Dionysia. When Zeus ordains that song and dance are needed to assuage Demeter's grief, Aphrodite takes the lead, playing the trumpet and drums

---

[77] *Thesmophoriazousai* 890; *Helen* 1224 on blonde colour.

[78] The king refers to tears on her cheek, not in her eyes, and on a mask tears running through blood would be more visible.

[79] *Thesmophoriazousai* 850, 903. Csapo (1986: 387) identifies razor stubble in the extant vase image of the Aristophanic performer. For the change of mask, cf. Foley (1993: 110–11); Hall in Morwood (1997: xxv).

[80] See Zanker (1995: 32–9).

and presenting the Bacchic *aulos* to Demeter, who is first seduced by the entertainment and laughs, but is then enraged by it. The chorus sings that it was impiety for Aphrodite to take up the thyrsus and fawnskin of Dionysos, shake her hair ecstatically, and play his tambourine. On one level, this story anticipates the fact that Helen, Aphrodite's human counterpart, needs to shed her erotic beauty if she is to join the chorus of Dionysos, but we may also read this myth to signify that the carnal and desirable body of the performer has no place in tragedy, creating inappropriate emotions in the spectator. In the final choral ode, as Helene Foley demonstrates, members of the chorus 'invoke a Helen who presided in Spartan cult as a heroine over the initiation of young women on the verge of matrimony'.[81] There is a strong democratic force in the idea that, by abandoning the heroic face which made her unique, Helen will acquire a new and happier identity as a solidary part of the *polis*. The tendency in theatre of the naked face is to marginalise the chorus, turning tragedy into a story about heroic individuals. When we restore the chorus to its place at the centre of the dramatic event, the importance of the mask becomes clear: the mask is not a tool for revealing or concealing self but a tool for transcending individuation.

Inflected by Hollywood, Lattimore's reading of *Helen* reflects an age, post-Hitler and pre-Vietnam, when war could still be heroic. The idea that the Trojan War could have been fought to rescue a phantom formed of cloud seemed the sheerest fantasy. Today I write in the wake of an apparently fruitless war fought against Iraq on the basis of false information, and it no longer seems possible for me to read the play as a light romance. I surmise that the Athenians may have felt about Syracuse something akin to what is widely felt in 2006 about Iraq. Modern feminism informs my attitude to Helen's beauty, while post-colonial awareness prevents me from dismissing as irrelevant Menelaus' slaughter of innocent Egyptians to make his escape, and I can read Herodotus to back up this view.[82] But this does not of course mean that Lattimore is wrong and I am right, for I know that I read the play from the perspective of my own age, and readers a generation hence will see the play differently again. The epistemological doubt voiced by so many of the figures in Euripides' play cannot but touch me.

To take a specific example: I turn up in my files an essay published in 1980, where Froma Zeitlin pictures Euripides' *Orestes* as a 'self-reflective work' in which the 'repertory of tragedy and epic provides, as it were, a closet of masks for the actors to raid at will, characters in search of an identity, of a part to play'. Euripides is said to be working at the end of his life in 'a tradition

---

[81] Foley (1992: 145, 149–50).    [82] Herodotus ii.119.

which has reached the end of its organic development'.[83] I no longer, as I once did, find this a compelling account of the late fifth century. Zeitlin's metaphor of masks pulled from a cupboard does, however, give me a vivid picture of identity politics at the end of the 1970s, when Hollywood with its universalised Helens and Menelauses no longer served as an effective social bonding agent, and individual Americans found different identities stacked up in the cupboard: Latino, student, gay, New Yorker, war veteran, daughter, and so forth. Choosing a mask in order to present self in everyday life was a cultural reality, and Zeitlin viewed Euripides afresh through the eyes of her generation. The era of 'postmodernism' is now receding into history, with its taste for self-reflective theatre about theatre, and its notion that all identity is culturally constructed, but the nature of the present is inevitably much harder to discern. To reinterpret Euripides' *Helen* today is necessarily to interpret the present, but paradoxically that task is best accomplished through the application of professional historiographic rigour in a tireless search for what *actually happened* at the Dionysia in 412 BC.

As a historian, I am, in the last analysis, engaged in the same mythopoeic activity as Euripides. Euripides wanted to make sense of what happened in the Trojan War, and found that the versions preserved in Stesichorus and Herodotus accorded better with his sense of reality than Homer's version. In order to bring shades or doubles of long-dead heroes back before the Athenians, he had to make those figures credible, finding connections between the heroic age and his own. I in my turn am in pursuit of a long-dead Euripides who belongs to the heroic age of the theatre, and I want to make sense of my cultural inheritance. Determined all the while to preserve Euripides' historical otherness, I nevertheless cannot bring him back to the present without a measure of historical empathy. Pure scholarly detachment is not an available option. In a recent adaptation of *Electra* by the Polish company Gardzienice, Euripides came on at the end of the play with masks sewn to his gown, and gradually all the masks were pulled away to reveal the lonely person of the playwright, authentic ancestor of the modern reworking.[84] My own account of the Greek mask pushes in a rather different direction. The quest for the face behind the mask is a vain one. Expression in the mask is something that the spectator must project onto it, and the mask feels alive when the viewer has a sense of existing in the mask's eyes. The task of the historian, like that of the Greek spectator, is to look at the evidence on the surface and engage actively with it. There can be no probing behind

---

[83] Zeitlin (1980: 51, 69).
[84] Directed by W. Staniewski. UK performance: Barbican Theatre, 2005.

the mask, in a hopeless quest for ontological security, because the historian has no position of spectatorial detachment.

I have sought to engage in a dialogue with the past in this book. My journey through twentieth-century experiments with the tragic mask has revealed the potential power of the mask to grip an audience and to transform the psyche of a performer, but has also underscored the cultural otherness of masking. I have addressed the question of why the mask in antiquity seemed a natural part of tragedy, while in the modern West it offends our sense of the natural, unless we reduce it to a mode of disguise. To answer this question, in terms that extend beyond simple issues of stage technology, we are forced to address the question of who we ourselves are: rationalists, monotheists, individualists, patrons of what we call the arts, members of a hegemonic western culture. To understand the classical other is to understand ourselves in a reciprocal play of gazes.

# Epilogue: to the performer

Greek tragedy is a living form with a long genealogy. This book is written not just for theatre historians, but also for theatre practitioners, makers of theatre who help the form to renew itself. My argument in the last three chapters has been, primarily, an intervention in arguments among classicists, seeking to establish how masked theatre worked in a performance context remote from our own. In order to discuss ancient practicalities, it has been necessary to frame my discussion within a wider theoretical argument about the relation of theatre to ritual. I need now to spell out some implications of my historical argument for modern performance practice.

Student groups excited by Greek drama sometimes ask me: 'here's the play, should we do it in masks?' The answer to a question so phrased must inevitably be no – passionate though I am about masks – for it has been the burden of this book that masks are not an add-on element of spectacle to be incorporated if time and budget allow. If someone said to me, 'I want to work with masks, should I try a Greek tragedy?', the question would deserve more serious debate. Masks are at the core of what Greek tragedy *meant*, and working with masks is a matter of meaning, not style. In the contemporary world, masks all too easily become a design accessory because political, religious and psychological questions are placed in separate baskets, but in fifth-century Greece the mask provided a site of convergence.

Western culture has been uneasy about the mask ever since early Christians grew obsessed with laying bare the human soul. The mask became an emblem of the devil, and Harlequin began as Hell's King, licensed to commit diabolic mischief. Carnivalesque masks of this kind conferred a real or symbolic anonymity that allowed the wearer to break normal social rules. It is no easy matter to reconcile this western tradition of the mask as grotesque disguise with Greek tragedy, which places fine and good people in intolerable situations. To wear masks in Greek tragedy today just because the ancients did so is not sufficient reason, for we are not classical Greeks, and the mask today is laden with different cultural meanings. Equally unsatisfactory is the idea that masks are a device which will serve to 'ritualise' the performance. The power of rituals for individuals and communities lies in their specificity, and a penumbra of religiosity does little in my experience to enhance the power of a Greek text. Peter Brook's attack on 'something really sordid, nauseating (and very common to Western art theatre) which is also called a mask' deserves to be taken seriously.

There remain plenty of good reasons for using masks when performing Greek tragedy, and I shall suggest four that seem relevant in the first decade of the twenty-first century.

1. Distancing or 'alienation'. Acting with the naked face tends to give priority to character and the creation of unique individuals, in accordance with the norms of television and cinema. Masks may therefore disrupt our learned ways of viewing. There is still much force in Aristotle's dictum that the basis of tragedy lies in 'action' not 'character', even though we may judge Aristotle's notion of 'action' too disembodied. Psychologically oriented theatre is the manifestation of an individualistic ideology associated with a dominant economic system, and there are good reasons why one might wish to use masks in order to counter this way of seeing the world. The Brechtian half-mask, as used for example by Karolos Koun, now seems a rather dated convention. Borrowing from a specific non-western masking tradition, undertaken with respect and not as an act of cultural appropriation, seems currently a more productive means of distancing the play from western psychologism in order to touch other issues and other areas of human experience. Mnouchkine's *Les Atrides* is a seminal example.
2. Physicalisation. It is an obvious and observable feature of masks that they compel performers deprived of facial expression to make a richer use of the body. Given the power of television to capture facial movement, the rationale for live theatre depends increasingly on animating the body. Lecoq neutral masks, *ko-omote* masks and paper bags are all effective rehearsal devices for this purpose. Having used the mask in rehearsal to rediscover the body, however, one must then ask: why actually perform in a mask? There is an obvious reply. A physically animated body can render the masked face more expressive than the naked face, albeit only if the mask is sculpted with an uncommon level of skill. There is a further difficulty, however, for physical theatre is often concerned with the human body at the expense of the body's environment, and masks belong to *places* as black leotards belong to anonymous black-box *spaces*. Masks that seem naturalised inhabitants of an open-air theatre may have the awkwardness of refugees when trapped behind a proscenium arch.
3. Performance art. One can trace back to nineteenth-century puppetry, and to the cubist figures of the Bauhaus, the idea that the human form

is something the performer should mould as a totality, rejecting the natural visible body in order to create an artistic shape abstracted from it. Bread And Puppet Theatre Company, have worked in this way, creating figures bold enough to command an open landscape in Vermont, and on a smaller scale the actors of Trestle Theatre Company manipulate exciting mask creations without any spiritual identification. There is no reason, as Craig understood, why such methods should not be applied to Greek tragedy, treating the play as an extension of the visual arts.

4. Rediscovering antiquity. It is entirely reasonable that the performer should seek to rediscover the Greek mask, in the same spirit that one rediscovers a text by Sophocles through performing it. The meanings of a Sophoclean text are not given and fixed, but can only be pieced together and interpreted in the light of how we see the world today. The same applies to the mask, which only survives in the form of historical traces. To translate the classical play, for modernists like Ezra Pound and Walter Benjamin, was a means of renewing the language of the present, and interpreting the classical mask should, by the same token, be a means of enhancing the possibilities of contemporary performance.

I have shown how the modernist sensibility of the early twentieth century responded to the mask in a way that the post-war era did not. The 'postmodern' mentality, obsessed with unpicking the intellectual riddles of mimesis, could not accommodate the organicism associated with most forms of mask-work. The pendulum in the twenty-first century may be swinging back. The issue is not one of emotion, for sculpted faces can express feelings more powerfully than natural faces, but one of selfhood. The unique selves of actor and of character have long seemed coupled by virtue of their union in the face. This coupling is no longer so secure in an age when faces can be rebuilt by surgery, or even transplanted. Naturalistic theatre emerged in the age of the photograph, when faces could be scrutinised for what they revealed, but we now live in the age of digitised images, when synthetic faces can be constructed with photographic realism.[1] Neurology, with its account of a bilateral brain subdivided again into different areas of specialism, leaves untenable the idea that there is any single centre of selfhood, and performance methodologies like 'alpha emoting' turn on recognition that feeling is not just a function of consciousness but of the body as a whole. A new environmental politics is forcing humans to think of themselves as part of a greater biological organism. For reasons such as these, the hypothesis of

---

[1] See the images assembled in Kemp 2004.

a true and unitary 'self' concealed by the wearing of a mask has become harder to sustain.

To work with a mask requires technique. We have no textbooks on acting from the ancient world because skills were imparted through oral tradition, often from father to son, and in the twentieth century oral tradition has proved equally important. The influence of Copeau and Lecoq stems not from their writings but from the way they have taught actors who have taught other actors. Books can be a useful *aide-mémoire*, but they are not the normal means by which mask technique is learned.[2] One can set down in writing certain simple guidelines that almost all teachers agree upon. The mask in performance must not be touched for it destroys illusion. The mirror must be used sparingly, for it breeds self-consciousness. The eye cannot move so seeing must be articulated by the neck. The mask must be moved slowly, so its gaze can sweep about, its shifting expressions register. The movements of the body need to be larger and bolder to create configurations with the emboldened head . . . But rules of this kind are best learned in the rehearsal room, where their logic is instantly clear, and they can be absorbed kinaesthetically to become instinctual. The golden rule is to work in masks at all stages of the creative process, and avoid the example of Alan Howard, who only agreed to wear 'this bloody thing!' in the dress rehearsal.[3]

Masks transform consciousness, particularly Greek-style masks which envelope the whole head and impose a high level of sensory deprivation. Science has only a limited ability to explain consciousness, witness for example the phenomenon of 'blindsight' when people see without being conscious of seeing.[4] When stripped of one's face, one can feel either alarmed or released by the need to abandon the acquired sense of self that is related to one's unique facial imprint. The abandonment of selfhood in order to attain a state of mental emptiness is a common enough goal in eastern traditions, but offends against instinct in the west. One can work with the mask on the level of pure technique, holding it apart conceptually if not physically like a puppet, and steer clear of this challenge to personhood, but sustained work with the Greek-style helmet mask is likely to involve an experiential immersion, particularly when chorus-work is involved and the boundary between 'I' and 'we' is dissolved.

There are good and bad masks, masks which work and masks which don't, and no doubt there were two sides to the Alan Howard story.

---

[2] For Copeau's method see now Evans (2006: 135–45).
[3] In Hall's *Oedipus Plays*. Cited in Taplin 2002. Cf. Reynolds (1996: 23–4).
[4] Dennett (1993: 322–33).

Mask-making, like masked acting, requires technique. The mask is a face that must transform itself when moved in different ways in relation to the body, and the qualities that it has when sitting on a rehearsal room table, or on the collector's wall, are of little account. Masks need to be asymmetrical so their expression may seem to be in transition, while the planes defined by bone structure need to be adjusted in order to catch the light, creating the illusion that the mask itself moves when the angle of vision changes. Perfect faces seem inert, and the mask always needs a provisional quality, that might be perceived as 'crude'. Sculptural technique must be conjoined to something the Japanese call spirit. It is a curious but observable phenomenon that masks tend to echo the features of the person making them, for mask-makers put something of themselves into the images they create.[5] In a student context, masks often prove most successful when the mask is made by the wearer, because the wearer's spirit is in the mask. In a professional context, unless there is a close working relationship with the mask-maker, the mask will all too easily turn into 'this bloody thing' dumped upon the actor.

Masks in a contemporary context tend to attract devotees of physical theatre, dance or performance art. The Greek mask, however, belonged to a form of theatre where the contribution of the poet was of the first importance. There is thus an incompatibility between the Greek mask and the structures of contemporary theatre, for text-based theatre in the line of Shakespeare, Ibsen and Beckett has long been theatre of the naked face. Perhaps the greatest importance of the Greek mask for today's theatre lies in the challenges it offers to the dichotomy of language and body. To perform successfully in a Greek-style helmet mask, the actor needs to find the point where language and body converge in the voice and the breath that produce sound. Once word-sounds become disconnected from the embodied being that produced them, the mask becomes a redundant object, separating the visible person from word-thoughts that express an inner psychic reality. But when the connection of word and body is made, a present and organic entity is created. If this seems a holistic ideal that our theatre could never attain, so be it. The Greek world has a long and respectable history of providing posterity with a utopia.

[5] Cf. Rebecca Teele cited in Coldiron (2004: 147), and Plate 7.2.

# Bibliography

Alexander, Doris (1992). *Eugene O'Neill's Creative Struggle: the decisive decade, 1924–1933.* University Park: Pennsylvania University Press.
Allen, W. S. (1987). *Vox Graeca.* Cambridge: Cambridge University Press.
Antonaccio, Carla M. (1994). 'Contesting the past: hero cult, tomb cult and epic in early Greece'. *American Journal of Archaeology* 98: 389–410.
Arden, John (1967). *Theatre at Work*, ed. C. Marowitz and S. Trussler. London: Methuen.
Aronson, Arnold (2000). *Avant-garde Theatre: a history.* London: Routledge.
Artaud, Antonin (1970). *The Theatre and its Double*, trans. V. Corti. London: Calder & Boyars.
Ashmole, Bernard and Yalouris, Nicholas (1967). *Olympia: the sculptures of the Temple of Zeus.* London: Phaidon.
Aslan, Odette and Bablet, Denis, eds. (1985). *Le Masque: du rite au théâtre.* Paris: CNRS.
Astley, Neil, ed. (1991). *Tony Harrison.* Newcastle-upon-Tyne: Bloodaxe.
Bacon, Helen (1964). 'The shield of Eteocles'. *Arion* 3.3: 27–38.
Bacon, Helen (1994/5). 'The chorus in Greek life and drama'. *Arion* 3: 6–24.
Ball, Hugo (1974). *Flight out of Time: a Dada diary*, trans. A. Raimes. New York: Viking Press.
Barba, Eugenio and Savarese, Nicola (1991). *A Dictionary of Theatre Anthropology: the secret art of the performer.* London: Routledge.
Barker, Elton (2004). 'The fall-out from dissent: hero and audience in Sophocles' *Ajax*'. *Greece & Rome* 51: 1–20.
Barrault, Jean-Louis (1957). Interview in *World Theatre* 6: 274–7.
Barrault, Jean-Louis (1961). *The Theatre of Jean-Louis Barrault*, trans. J. Chiari. London: Barrie & Rockliff.
Barrault, Jean-Louis (1962). 'Problèmes de *l'Orestie*'. *Cahiers Renaud-Barrault*, 11 bis: 93–126.
Barrault, Jean-Louis (1974). *Memories for Tomorrow*, trans. J. Griffin. London: Thames & Hudson.
Barrault, Jean-Louis (1975). *Comme je le pense.* Paris: Gallimard.
Barrault, Jean-Louis (n.d.). Manuscript notebooks in the Renaud–Barrault archive, Bibliothèque Nationale. Transcript by Patricia Legangneux.
Barron, John (1981). *An Introduction to Greek Sculpture.* London: Athlone Press.

Barthes, Roland (1972). 'Putting on the Greeks' in *Critical Essays*, trans. R. Howard. Evanston, Ill.: Northwestern University Press. 59–66.
Barthes, Roland (1975). *Roland Barthes par Roland Barthes*. Paris: Seuil.
Barthes, Roland (1982). *Barthes: selected writings*, ed. Susan Sontag. London: Fontana.
Barthes, Roland (1983). *Selected Writings*, ed. Susan Sontag. London: Fontana.
Barthes, Roland (2002). *Ecrits sur le théâtre*, ed. J.-L. Rivière. Paris: Seuil.
Battezzato, Luigi (1999/2000). 'Dorian dress in Greek tragedy'. *Illinois Classical Studies* 24/5: 343–62.
Battezzato, Luigi (2003). Review of L. B. Brea *Maschere e personaggi nel teatro greco*. *Journal of Hellenic Studies* 123: 247–50.
Beare, William (1955). *The Roman Stage*. London: Methuen.
Beauvoir, Simone de (1981). *La Cérémonie des adieux: suivi de Entretiens avec Jean-Paul Sartre, août–septembre 1974*. Paris: Gallimard.
Beazley, J. D. (1927). *Corpus Vasorum Antiquorum: Oxford, Ashmolean Museum – Vol. 1*. Oxford: Oxford University Press.
Beazley, J. D. (1963). *Attic Red-Figure Vase-Painters*. Oxford: Oxford University Press.
Becker, Judith (2004). *Deep Listeners: music, emotion and trancing*. Bloomington: Indiana University Press.
Bell, Michael (1999). 'The metaphysics of modernism' in *The Cambridge Companion to Modernism*, ed. Michael Levenson. Cambridge: Cambridge University Press. 9–33.
Benedetti, Jean (1999). 'Stanislavsky and the Moscow Art Theatre, 1898–1938' in *A History of Russian Theatre*, ed. Robert Leach and Victor Borovsky. Cambridge: Cambridge University Press. 254–77.
Bérard, Claude and Bron, Christiane (1989). 'Satyric revels' in *A City of Images: iconography and society in ancient Greece*, ed. C. Bérard *et al.*, trans. D. Lyons. Princeton: Princeton University Press. 131–50.
Bérard, Claude and Bron, Christiane (1990). 'Le *liknon*, le "masque" et le poteau: images du rituel dionysiaque' in *Mélanges Pierre Lévêque 4: religion*, ed. M.-M. Mactoux and E. Geny. Paris: Les Belles Lettres. 29–44.
Berliner Ensemble (1961). *Theaterarbeit: 6 Aufführungen des Berliner Ensemble*, ed. R. Berlau *et al.* Berlin: Suhrkamp.
Bernabò Brea, Luigi (1981). *Menandro e il teatro greco nelle terracotte liparesi*. Genoa: Sagep.
Bernabò Brea, Luigi (2001). *Maschere e personaggi nel teatro greco nelle terracotte liparesi*. Rome: 'L'Erma' di Bretschneider.
Berti, Fede and Gasparri, Fede (1989). *Dionysos: mito e mistero*. Bologna: Nuova Alfa.
Bethe, Monica (1984). 'Okina: an interview with Takabyashi Kōji' in *Nō/Kyōgen Masks and Performance*, ed. Rebecca Teele. Claremont: Mime Journal. 93–103.
Bezerra de Meneses, U. (1970). 'Le Revêtement mural' in *L'Ilot de la Maison des Comédiens (Exploration archéologique de Délos, 27)*, ed. Ecole Française d'Athènes. Paris: Boccard. 151–94.

Bharucha, Rustom (1993). 'Peter Brook's *Mahabarata*: a view from India' in *Theatre and the World: performance and the problem of culture*. London: Routledge. 68–90.
Bieber, Margarete (1961). *The History of the Greek and Roman Theater*. Princeton: Princeton University Press.
Boardman, John (1985). *Greek Sculpture: the Classical Period*. London: Thames & Hudson.
Boardman, John, ed. (1993). *The Oxford History of Classical Art*. Oxford: Oxford University Press.
Bogard, Travis (1988). *Contour in Time: the plays of Eugene O'Neill*. New York: Oxford University Press.
Bohlmann, Otto (1982). *Yeats and Nietzsche*. London: Macmillan.
Bollini, A. et al. (1988). *Antike Helme*. Mainz: Römisch-Germanischen Zentralmuseums.
Boyle, Nicholas (2000). *Goethe: the poet and the age. Vol. 2*. Oxford: Oxford University Press.
Bradshaw, David J. (1991). 'The Ajax myth and the polis' in *Myth and the Polis*, ed. Dora C. Pozzi and John M. Wickersham. Ithaca: Cornell University Press. 99–125.
Bratton, Jacky and Bush-Bailey, Gilli (2002). 'Still working it out: an account of the practical workshop re-discovery of company practices and Romantic performance styles via Jane Scott's plays'. *Nineteenth Century Theatre & Film* 29.2: 6–21.
Brecht, Bertolt and Neher, Caspar (1949). *Antigonemodell 1948*, ed. R. Berlau. Berlin: Gebrüder Weiss.
Brecht, Bertolt (1977). *The Measures Taken, and other Lehrstücke*, trans. C. Mueller et al. London: Methuen.
Brecht, Bertolt (1978). *Brecht on Theatre*, ed. John Willett. London: Methuen.
Brindejont-Offenbach (1922). 'Une heure parmi les masques'. *Le Gaulois*, 1 March 1922.
Brinkmann, Vinzenz and Wünsche, Raimund (2004). *Bunte Götter: die Farbigkeit antiker Skulptur*. Munich: Glyptothek München.
Brook, Peter (1968). *The Empty Space*. London: MacGibbon & Kee.
Brook, Peter (1988). *The Shifting Point: 40 years of theatrical exploration 1946–1987*. London: Methuen.
Brook, Peter (1998). *Threads of Time: a memoir*. London: Methuen.
Browning, Robert (1928). *Balaustion's Adventure*. London: Macmillan.
Brual, Gérard (2000). *Les Renaud-Barrault*. Paris: Seuil.
Bruce, Vicki and Young, Andy (1998). *In the Eye of the Beholder: the science of face perception*. Oxford: Oxford University Press.
Bryant-Bertail, Sarah (1994). 'Gender, empire and body politic as mise en scène: Mnouchkine's *Les Atrides*'. *Theatre Journal* 46: 1–30.
Bullough, Geoffrey (1975). *Narrative and Dramatic Sources of Shakespeare. Vol. VIII*. London: RKP.

Buraud, Georges (1948). *Les Masques*. Paris: Seuil.
Burkert, Walter (1983). *Homo Necans: the anthropology of ancient Greek sacrificial ritual and myth*, trans. P. Bing. Berkeley: University of California Press.
Burkert, Walter (1985). *Greek Religion*, trans. J. Raffan. Oxford: Blackwell.
Buschor, Ernst and Von Massow, Wilhelm (1927). *Von Amyklaion. Athenische Mitteilungen* 52.
Butler, Christopher (1994). *Early Modernism: literature, music and painting in Europe 1900–1916*. Oxford: Oxford University Press.
Calame, Claude (1986). 'Facing otherness: the tragic mask of ancient Greece'. *History of Religions* 26: 125–42.
Calame, Claude (1999). 'Performative aspects of the choral voice in Greek tragedy: civic identity in performance' in *Performance Culture and Athenian Democracy*, ed. Simon Goldhill and Robin Osborne. Cambridge: Cambridge University Press. 125–53.
Calame, Claude (2005). *Masks of Authority: fiction and pragmatics in ancient Greek poetics*, trans. P. M. Burk. Ithaca: Cornell University Press.
Callery, Dymphna (2001). *Through the Body: a guide to physical theatre*. London: Nick Hern.
Calvert, Louis-Jean (1994). *Roland Barthes: a biography*, trans. S. Wykes. Cambridge: Polity Press.
Carlisle, Carol Jones (2000). *Helen Faucit: fire and ice on the Victorian stage*. London: Society for Theatre Research.
Carlson, Marvin (1978). *Goethe and the Weimar Theatre*. Ithaca: Cornell University Press.
Carpenter, Sarah and Twycross, Meg (2002). *Masks and Masking in Medieval and Early Tudor England*. Aldershot: Ashgate.
Carpenter, Thomas H. (1997). *Dionysiac Imagery in Fifth-Century Athens*. Oxford: Oxford University Press.
Carter, Susan Burr (1987). 'The masks of Ortheia'. *American Journal of Archaeology* 91: 355–83.
Caruso, Christiane (1987). 'Travestissements dionysiaques' in *Images et société en Grèce ancienne: l'iconographie comme méthode d'analyse*. ed. C. Bérard, C. Bron and A. Pomari. Lausanne: Institut d'Archéologie et d'Histoire Ancienne. 103–10.
Caskey, L. D. and Beazley J. D. (1931). *Attic Vase Paintings in the Museum of Fine Arts, Boston*. Oxford: Oxford University Press.
Chase, Michael (2000). Edited transcript of an interview with David Wiles, transcribed by Jane Belcher.
Christout, Marie-Françoise (1996). 'Le Langage du corps'. *Revue d'histoire du théâtre* 48: 183–206.
Cicero, Marcus Tullius (2001). *On the Ideal Orator*, trans. James M. May and Jakob Wisse. New York: Oxford University Press.
Cixous, Hélène (1976). 'The Laugh of the Medusa', trans. K. and P. Cohen. *Signs* 1: 875–93.

Clark, Barrett H. (1933). *Eugene O'Neill: the man and his plays.* London: Jonathan Cape.
Cocteau, Jean (1956). *The Hand of a Stranger* trans. A. Brown. London: Elek.
Cocteau, Jean (2003). *Théâtre complet.* Paris: Gallimard.
Coldiron, Margaret (2004). *Trance and Transformation of the Actor in Japanese Noh and Balinese Masked Dance-drama.* Lewiston: Edwin Mellen.
Connor, W. R. (1987). 'Tribes, festivals and processions: civic ceremonial and political manipulation in archaic Greece'. *Journal of Hellenic Studies* 107: 40–50.
Connor, W. R. (1988). 'Sacred and secular: *hiera kai hosia* and the classical Athenian concept of the state'. *Ancient Society* 19: 161–88.
Connor, W. R. (1990). 'City Dionysia and Athenian Democracy' in W. R. Connor, M. H. Hansen, K. A. Raaflaub and B. S. Strauss, *Aspects of Athenian Democracy.* Copenhagen: Museum Tusculanum Press. 7–32.
Copeau, Jacques (1955). *Notes sur le métier de comédien.* Paris: Marcel Brient.
Copeau, Jacques (1990). *Texts on Theatre,* ed. J. Rudlin and N. H. Paul. London: Routledge.
Copeau, Jacques (1991). *Journal 1901–1948.* Paris: Seghers.
Copeau, Jacques (1993). *Registres V: Les Registres du Vieux Colombier III,* ed. S. M. Saint-Denis and M.-H. Dasté. Paris: Gallimard.
Copeau, Jacques (2000). *Registres VI: l'Ecole du Vieux Colombier III, 1919–1924,* ed. C. Sicard. Paris: Gallimard.
Covington, Richard (1996). 'Portrait of the actress as a non-man' www.salon.com/11/features/shaw.
Craig, Edward Gordon (1983). *Craig on Theatre,* ed. J. Michael Walton. London: Methuen.
Croall, Jonathan (2002). *Peter Hall's Bacchai: the National Theatre at work.* London: NT Publications.
Csapo, Eric and Slater, William J. (1995). *The Context of Ancient Drama.* Ann Arbor: Michigan University Press.
Csapo, Eric (1986). 'A note on the Würtzburg bell-crater H5697 ("Telephus Travestitus")'. *Phoenix* 40: 379–92.
Csapo, Eric (1997). 'Riding the phallus for Dionysus: iconology, ritual and gender-role de/construction'. *Phoenix* 51: 253–95.
Damasio, Antonio (1999). *The Feeling of What Happens: body, emotion and the making of consciousness.* London: Heinemann.
Damasio, Antonio (2004). *Looking for Spinoza: joy, sorrow and the feeling brain.* London: Vintage.
Dasté, Jean (1977). *Voyage d'un comédien.* Paris: Stock.
Dasté, Jean (1987). *Qui êtes vous?* Lyon: La Manufacture.
Dennett, Daniel C. (1993). *Consciousness Explained.* Harmondsworth: Penguin.
Dentzer, Jean-Marie (1982). *Le Motif du banquet dans le Proche-Orient et le monde grec du VIIe au IVe siècle av. J.-C.* Rome: Ecole française de Rome.
Derrida, Jacques (1978). 'La parole soufflée' in *Writing and Difference,* trans. A. Bass. London: Routledge. 212–45.

Des Bouvrie, Synnve (1993). 'Creative euphoria: Dionysos and the theatre'. *Kernos* 6: 79–112.

Detienne, Marcel (1986). 'Dionysos en ses parousies: un dieu épidémique' in *L'Association dionysiaque dans les sociétés anciennes: actes de la table ronde organisée par L'Ecole Française de Rome, 24–5 mai 1984*. Rome: Ecole Française de Rome. 53–83.

Diderot, Jean, ed. (1765). *Encyclopédie Vol. IX*. Neuchâtel.

Diderot, Jean, ed. (1765). *Encyclopédie* Vol. X. Neuchâtel.

Diggle, James (1998). *Tragicorum Graecorum Fragmenta Selecta*. Oxford: Oxford University Press.

Dodds, E. R. (1951). *The Greeks and the Irrational*. Berkeley: University of California Press.

Dodds, E. R. (1983). 'On misunderstanding the Oedipus Rex' in *Oxford Readings in Greek Tragedy*, ed. Erich Segal. Oxford: Oxford University Press. 177–88.

Dodds, E. R., ed. (1960). *Euripides: Bacchae*. Oxford: Oxford University Press.

Doisy, Marcel. (1954). *Jacques Copeau, ou l'absolu dans l'art*. Paris: Le Cercle du Livre.

Dorcy, Jean (1958). *A la rencontre de la mime et des mimes*. Neuilly-sur-Seine: Les Cahiers de Danse et Culture.

Dorhoy, Marie (1924). Review of '*Antigone*' in *Bonsoir*, 23 March 1924.

Drewal, Margaret Thompson (1992). *Yoruba Ritual: performers, play, agency*. Bloomington: Indiana University Press.

Dullin, Charles (1946). *Souvenirs et notes de travail d'un acteur*. Paris: O. Lieutier.

Duncan, Anne (2006). *Performance and Identity in the Classical World*. Cambridge: Cambridge University Press.

Dupont, Florence (2000). *L'Orateur sans visage: essai sur l'acteur romain et son masque*. Paris: Presses Universitaires de France.

Dupont, Florence (2001). 'L'inscription de l'écriture tragique dans le temps rituel à Grèce et à Rome'. *Etudes de Lettres* 2: 75–95.

Easterling, P. E. (1988). 'Tragedy and ritual: <Cry "Woe, woe", but may the good prevail!>'. *Métis* 3.2: 88–109.

Easterling, Pat (2002). 'Actor as icon' in *Greek and Roman Actors: aspects of an ancient profession*, ed. Pat Easterling and Edith Hall. Cambridge: Cambridge University Press. 327–41.

Easterling, P. E. (2006). 'Sophocles – the first thousand years' in *Greek Drama III: essays in honour of Kevin Lee*, ed. John Davidson, Francis Muecke and Peter Wilson. London: Institute of Classical Studies. 1–15.

Easterling, P. E., ed. (1997). *The Cambridge Companion to Greek Tragedy*. Cambridge: Cambridge University Press.

Eck, Diana L. (1985). *Darśan: seeing the divine image in India*. Chambersburg: Anima.

Edinborough, Campbell (2003). '*Who wants to be neutral?*' *Jacques Lecoq's neutral mask as pedagogical tool*. MA dissertation. Royal Holloway University of London.

Edmunds, Lowell (1996). *Theatrical Space and Historical Space in Sophocles' Oedipus at Colonus.* Lanham: Rowman & Littlefield.

Eiseman, Fred B., Jr. (1990). *Bali: sekala and niskala.* Singapore: Periplus.

Ekman, Paul and Friesen, Wallace V. (1975). *Unmasking the Face: a guide to recognizing emotions from facial clues.* Englewood Cliffs: Prentice-Hall.

Eldredge, Sears (1996). *Mask Improvisation for Actor Training and Performance: the compelling image.* Evanston, Ill.: Northwestern University Press.

Eliade, Mircea (1986). *Symbolism, the Sacred, and the Arts*, ed. Diane Apostolos-Cappadona. New York: Crossroad Publishing Company.

Ellmann, Richard (1979). *Yeats: the man and the masks.* Oxford: Oxford University Press.

Elsner, Jas and Rutherford, Ian, eds. (2006). *Pilgrimage in Graeco-Roman and Early Christian Antiquity: seeing the gods.* Oxford: Oxford University Press.

Elsner, Jas (2000). 'Between mimesis and divine power: visuality in the Graeco-Roman world' in *Visuality Before and Beyond the Renaissance*, ed. Robert S. Nelson. Cambridge: Cambridge University Press. 45–69.

Emigh, John (1996). *Masked Performance: the play of self and other in ritual and theatre.* Philadelphia: University of Pennsylvania Press.

*Eos* (1998). *Anghelos Sikelianos, Eva Palmer Sikelianou: Delphikes Heortes.* Athens: Papadema.

Evans, Mark (2006). *Jacques Copeau.* London: Routledge.

Ewans, Michael (1996). *Aischylos: Suppliants and other dramas.* London: Dent.

Fay, Stephen (1995). *Power Play: the life and times of Peter Hall.* London: Hodder & Staughton.

Ferrari, Gloria (1986). 'Eye-cup'. *Revue archéologique.* 5–20.

Feugère, Michel (1994). *Casques antiques: les visages de la guerre de Mycènes à la fin de l'empire romain.* Paris: Errance.

Ffloyd, Virginia (1981). *Eugene O'Neill at Work.* New York: Frederick Ungar.

Fiedler, Jeannine and Feierabend, Peter, eds. (2000). *Bauhaus.* Cologne: Könemann.

Fischer-Lichte, Erika (2005). *Theatre, Sacrifice, Ritual: exploring forms of political theatre.* London: Routledge.

Flagge, Ingeborg (1975). *Untersuchungen zur Bedeutung des Greifen.* Sankt Augustin: Hans Richarz.

Flashar, Hellmut (1991). *Inszenierung der Antike: das griechische Drama auf der Bühne der Neuzeit.* Munich: Beck.

Flower, Harriet I. (1999). *Ancestor Masks and Aristocratic Power in Roman Culture.* Oxford: Oxford University Press.

Fo, Dario (1989). 'Hands off the mask' *New Theatre Quarterly* 55: 207–9.

Fo, Dario (1991). *The Tricks of the Trade*, trans. J. Farrell. London: Methuen.

Foley Helene (1985). *Ritual Irony: poetry and sacrifice in Euripides.* Ithaca: Cornell University Press.

Foley, Helene (1980). 'The Masque of Dionysus'. *Transactions of the American Philological Association* 110: 107–33.

Foley, Helene P. (1992). '*Anodos* dramas: Euripides' *Alcestis* and *Helen*' in *Innovations in Antiquity*, ed. Ralph Hexter and Daniel Selden. New York: Routledge. 133–60.

Foley, Helene (1993). 'The politics of tragic lamentation' in *Tragedy, Comedy and the Polis*, ed. A. H. Sommerstein, Stephen Halliwell, Jeffrey Henderson and Bernhard Zimmermann. Bari: Levante. 101–43.

Foley, Helene P. (2001a). '*Tantalus*'. *American Journal of Philology* 122: 415–28.

Foley, Helene P. (2001b). *Female Acts in Greek Tragedy*. Princeton: Princeton University Press.

Foley, Helene (2003). 'Choral identity in Greek tragedy'. *Classical Philology* 98: 1–30.

Fotopoulos, Dionysis (1980). *Maskes Theatro/Masks Theatre*. Athens: Kastaniotis.

Foucault, Michel (2001). 'Nietzsche, genealogy, history' in *Nietzsche*, ed. J. Richardson and B. Leiter. Oxford: Oxford University Press. 341–59.

Friedrich, Rainer (1996). 'Everything to do with Dionysos? Ritualism, the Dionysiac, and the tragic' in *Tragedy and the Tragic: Greek theatre and beyond*, ed. Michael Silk. Oxford: Oxford University Press. 257–83.

Froning, Heide (2002). 'Masken und Kostüme' in *Die Geburt des Theaters in der griechischen Antike*, ed. Susanne Moraw and Eckehart Nölle. Mainz: Philipp von Zabern. 70–95.

Frontisi-Ducroux (1986). 'Images du ménadisme féminin: les vases des "Lénéennes"' in *L'association dionysiaque dans les sociétés anciennes: actes de la table ronde organisée par L'Ecole Française de Rome, 24–5 mai 1984*. Rome: Ecole Française de Rome. 165–76.

Frontisi-Ducroux, Françoise (1989). 'In the mirror of the mask', in *A City of Images: iconography and society in ancient Greece*, trans. D. Lyons. Princeton: Princeton University Press. 151–65.

Frontisi-Ducroux, Françoise (1991). *Le Dieu-masque: une figure du Dionysos d'Athènes*. Paris: La Découverte and Rome: Ecole Française de Rome.

Frontisi-Ducroux, Françoise (1995). *Du masque au visage: aspects de l'identité en Grèce ancienne*. Paris: Flammarion.

Furness, Horace Howard (1898). *A New Variorum Edition of Shakespeare. Vol. XI. The Winter's Tale*. Philadelphia: Lippincott.

Galster, Ingrid (1986). *Le Théâtre de Jean-Paul Sartre devant ses premiers critiques*. Tübingen: Gunter Narr.

Gardiner, Cynthia P. (1987). *The Sophoclean Chorus*. Iowa: University of Iowa Press.

Garvie, A. F. (1998). *Sophocles: Ajax*. Warminster: Aris & Phillips.

Geertz, Clifford (1984). '"From the native's point of view": on the nature of anthropological understanding' in *Culture Theory: essays on mind, self and emotion*, ed. Richard A. Shweder and Robert A. LeVine. Cambridge: Cambridge University Press. 123–36.

Gell, Alfred (1998). *Art and Agency: an anthropological theory*. Oxford: Oxford University Press.

Ghiron-Bistagne, Paulette (1976). *Recherches sur les acteurs dans la Grèce antique*. Paris: Les Belles Lettres.

Ghiron-Bistagne, Paulette (1988). 'Acteurs de la transe dans l'antiquité'. *Cahiers du GITA* 4: 63–78.

Ghiron-Bistagne, Paulette (1989). 'Le masque, le personnage, l'acteur et la personne dans le théâtre des anciens grecs' in *II International Meeting of Ancient Greek Drama, Delphi 15–20 June 1986*. Athens: European Cultural Centre of Delphi. 83–8.

Gill, Christopher (1990). 'The character-personality distinction' in *Characterization and Individuality in Greek Literature*, ed. Christopher Pelling. Oxford: Oxford University Press. 1–31.

Gill, Christopher (1996). *Personality in Greek Epic, Tragedy, and Philosophy: the self in dialogue*. Oxford: Oxford University Press.

Gillibert, Jean (1955). 'Les Étudiants ont fait la relève'. *Cahiers Renaud-Barrault*, 11: 88–93.

Goethe, J. W. (1962). *Italian Journey*, trans. W. H. Auden and E. Mayer. London: Collins.

Goffman, Erving (1956). *The Presentation of Self in Everyday Life*. New York: Doubleday.

Golden, Mark (1998). *Sport and Society in Ancient Greece*. Cambridge: Cambridge University Press.

Goldhill, Simon (1989). 'Reading performance criticism'. *Greece & Rome* 36: 172–82.

Goldhill, Simon (1990a). 'Character and action, representation and reading: Greek tragedy and its critics' in *Characterization and Individuality in Greek Literature*, ed. Christopher Pelling. Oxford: Oxford University Press. 100–27.

Goldhill, Simon (1990b). 'The Great Dionysia and civic ideology' in *Nothing to do with Dionysos?* ed. John J. Winkler and Froma Zeitlin. Princeton: Princeton University Press. 97–129.

Goldhill, Simon (1996). 'Collectivity and otherness – the authority of the tragic chorus: response to John Gould', in *Tragedy and the Tragic: Greek theatre and beyond*, ed. M. S. Silk. Oxford: Oxford University Press. 244–56.

Goldhill, Simon (1997). 'Modern critical approaches to Greek tragedy' in *The Cambridge Companion to Greek Tragedy*, ed. P. E. Easterling. Cambridge: Cambridge University Press. 324–47.

Goldhill, Simon and Osborne, Robin, eds. (1999). *Performance Culture and Athenian Democracy*. Cambridge: Cambridge University Press.

Gombrich, Ernst (1960). *Art and Illusion: a study in the psychology of pictorial representation*. London: Phaidon.

Gombrich, E. H. (1977). *Art and Illusion: a study in the psychology of pictorial representation*. London: Phaidon.

Gordon, Richard (1979). 'The real and the imaginary: production and religion in the Graeco-Roman world'. *Art History* 2.1: 5–34.

Gould, John (1996). 'Tragedy and collective experience', in *Tragedy and the Tragic: Greek theatre and beyond*, ed. M. S. Silk. Oxford: Oxford University Press. 217–43.

Green, J. R. (1982). 'Dedications of masks'. *Revue archéologique*, 2: 237–48.
Green, J. R. (1991). 'On seeing and depicting the theatre in classical Athens'. *Greek, Roman and Byzantine Studies* 32: 15–50.
Green, J. R. (1994a). *Theatre in Ancient Greek Society*. London: Routledge.
Green, J. R. (1994b). 'The Theatre' in *The Cambridge Ancient History: plates to volumes V and VI*, ed. John Boardman. Cambridge: Cambridge University Press. 150–66.
Green, J. R. (1995). 'Oral tragedies? A question from St Petersburg' *Quaderni Urbinati di Cultura Classica*, N. S. 51: 66–77.
Green, J. R. (2002). 'Towards a reconstruction of performance style' in *Greek and Roman Actors: aspects of an ancient profession*, ed. Pat Easterling and Edith Hall. Cambridge: Cambridge University Press. 93–126.
Gregory, Richard L. (1998). *Eye and Brain: the psychology of seeing*. Oxford: Oxford University Press.
Griffiths, J. Gwyn (1980). *The Origins of Osiris and his Cult*. Leiden: Brill.
Grimes, Ronald L. (1992). 'The life history of a mask'. *The Drama Review* 36.3: 61–77.
Grotowski, Jerzy (1969). *Towards a Poor Theatre*. London: Methuen.
Habermas, Jürgen (2005). 'Religion in the public sphere'. Lecture of 4 March 2005. http://www.sandiego.edu/pdf/pdf_library/habermaslecture.
Hall, Edith and Macintosh, Fiona (2005). *Greek Tragedy and the British Theatre 1660–1914*. Oxford: Oxford University Press.
Hall, Edith (2006). *The Theatrical Cast of Athens: interactions between ancient Greek drama and society*. Oxford: Oxford University Press.
Hall, Peter (1993). *Making an Exhibition of Myself*. London: Sinclair-Stevenson.
Hall, Peter (1996). 'Peter Hall talks to Peter Stothard'. Platform Discussion, National Theatre, 21 September 1996. http://website-archive.nt-online.org/platforms/oedipus_1996.html.
Hall, Peter (2000). *Exposed by the Mask: form and language in drama*. London: Oberon.
Hallett, C. H. (1986). 'The origins of the classical style in sculpture'. *Journal of Hellenic Studies* 106: 71–84.
Halliwell, Stephen (1990). 'Traditional Greek conceptions of character' in *Characterization and Individuality in Greek Literature*, ed. Christopher Pelling. Oxford: Oxford University Press. 32–59.
Halliwell, Stephen (1993). 'The function and aesthetics of the Greek tragic mask'. *Drama* 2: 195–211 (= *Intertextualität in der griechisch-römischen Komödie*, ed. Niall W. Slater and Bernhardt Zimmermann. Stuttgart: Metzlerschen & Poeschel).
Hamilton, Richard (2003). 'Lenaia vases in context' in *Poetry, Theory, Praxis: the social life of myth, word and image in ancient Greece*, ed. Eric Csapo and Margaret M. Miller. Oxford: Oxbow. 48–68.

Harrison, Tony (1982a). *Aeschylus: the Oresteia*. London: Rex Collings.

Harrison, Tony (1982b). 'The *Oresteia* in the Making'. *Omnibus* 4.

Harrison, Tony (1992). *The Gaze of the Gorgon*. Newcastle-upon-Tyne: Bloodaxe.

Harrison, Tony (2002). *Plays Four*. London: Faber.

Haynes, Sybille (2000). *Etruscan Civilization: a cultural history*. London: British Museum Press.

Hecht, Anthony and Bacon, Helen H., trans. (1973). *Seven Against Thebes*. New York: Oxford University Press.

Hedreen, G. M. (1992). *Silens in Attic Black-figure Vase Painting*. Ann Arbor: Michigan University Press.

Heilpern, John (1989). *Conference of the Birds: the story of Peter Brook in Africa*. London: Methuen.

Henrichs, Albert (1978). 'Greek maenadism from Olympus to Messalina'. *Harvard Studies in Classical Philology* 82: 121–60.

Henrichs, Albert (1993a). '"He has a god in him": human and divine in modern perceptions of Dionysus' in *Masks of Dionysus*, ed. Thomas H. Carpenter and Christopher A. Faraone. Ithaca: Cornell University Press. 13–43.

Henrichs, Albert (1993b). 'The tomb of Aias and the prospect of hero cult in Sophokles'. *Classical Antiquity* 12: 165–80.

Henrichs, Albert (1994/5). '"Why Should I Dance?" choral self-referentiality in Greek tragedy'. *Arion* 3: 56–111.

Herbert, Jocelyn (1991). 'Filling the space: working with Tony Harrison on *The Oresteia* and *The Trackers of Oxyrhynchus*' in *Tony Harrison*, ed. Neil Astley. Bloodaxe Books: Newcastle-upon-Tyne. 281–6.

Herbert, Jocelyn (1993). *A Theatre Workbook*, ed. C. Courtney. London: Art Books International.

Herington, John (1985). *Poetry into Drama: early tragedy and the Greek poetic tradition*. Berkeley: University of California Press.

Hicks, Greg (2002a). Address given at Royal Holloway University of London at a Conference on the Greek mask, 21 April 2002. Transcript by Chris Vervain.

Hicks, Greg (2002b). Interview given to David Wiles on 16 December 2002.

Holsbehe, Mireille, ed. (1997). *The Object as Mediator: on the transcendental meaning of art in traditional cultures*. Antwerp: Etnografisch Museum.

Hölscher, Fernande (1981). *Corpus Vasorum Antiquorum: Würzburg, Martin von Wagner Museum – Band 2*. Munich: C. H. Beck.

Hooykas, C. (1973). *Religion in Bali*. Leiden: Brill.

Hornung Erik (1992). *Idea into Image: essays in ancient Egyptian thought*, trans. E. Bredeck. New York: Timken.

Hughes, Ted (1994). *Winter Pollen*, ed. W. Scammell. London: Faber.

Hutchinson, G. O., ed. (1985). *Aeschylus: Septem Contra Thebas*. Oxford: Oxford University Press.

Ibsen, Henrik (1961). 'The task of the poet' trans. A. Kildal and E. Sprinchorn, in *Playwrights on Playwriting*, ed. Toby Cole. New York: Hill & Wang. 3–4.
Jacquot Jean (1970). *Le Living Theatre: Les Voies de la création théâtrale*, vol. 1, Paris: CNRS.
James, Wendy (2003). *The Ceremonial Animal: a new portrait of anthropology*. Oxford: Oxford University Press.
Jannarone, Kimberly (2001). 'Puppetry and pataphysics: populism and the Ubu cycle'. *New Theatre Quarterly*, 67: 239–53.
Jedrkiewicz, Stefano (1996). 'Giustizio "giusto" ed alea nei concorsi drammatici del V secolo ad Atene'. *Quaderni Urbinati di Cultura Classica* 54: 85–101.
Jeffares, A. Norman and Knowland, A. S. (1975). *A Commentary on the Collected Plays of W. B. Yeats*. London: Macmillan.
Jenkins, Fiona (1998). 'Performative identity: Nietzsche on the force of art and language' in *Nietzsche, Philosophy and the Arts*, ed. Salim Kemal, Ivan Gaskell and Daniel M. Conway. Cambridge: Cambridge University Press. 212–38.
Johnstone, Keith (1981). *Impro: improvisation and the theatre*. London: Methuen.
Johnson, Martha (1992). 'Reflections of inner life: masks and masked acting in ancient Greek tragedy and Japanese Noh drama'. *Modern Drama* 35: 20–34.
Jones, John (1962). *On Aristotle and Greek Tragedy*. London: Chatto & Windus.
Jourdain-Annequin, Colette (1998). 'Représenter les dieux: Pausanias et le panthéon des cités' in *Les Panthéons des cités: des origines à la Périégèse de Pausanias*, ed. V. Pirenne-Delforge. Liège: Centre International d'Etude de la Religion Grecque. 241–61.
Kachler, Karl Gotthilf (1986). *Maskenspieler aus Basler Tradition 1936–1974*. Basel: Christian Merian.
Kachler, Karl Gotthilf (1991). *Zur Entstehung und Entwicklung der griechischen Theatermaske*. Basel: Verfasser.
Kanze, Hisao (1984). 'Life with the Nō mask,' trans. Don Kenny in *Nō/Kyōgen Masks and Performance*, ed. Rebecca Teele. Claremont: Mime Journal. 65–73.
Kearns, Emily (1989). *The Heroes of Attica*. London: Institute of Classical Studies.
Kemp, Sandra (2004). *Future Face: image, identity, innovation*. London: Profile Books.
Kleist, Heinrich von (1972). 'On the marionette theatre', trans. G. Neumiller. *The Drama Review* 16.3: 22–6.
Knoepfler, Denis (1993). *Les Imagiers de l'Orestie*. Neuchâtel: Akanthus.
Knox, Bernard M. W. (1964). *The Heroic Temper: studies in Sophoclean tragedy*. Berkeley: University of California Press.
Köhler, Joachim (2002). *Zarathustra's Secret*, trans. R. Taylor. New Haven: Yale University Press.
Komparu, Kunio (1983). *The Noh Theatre: principles and perspectives*. New York: Weatherhill/Tankosha.
Kongō Iwao (1984). 'Recollections and thoughts on Nō' in *Nō/Kyōgen Masks and Performance*, ed. Rebecca Teele. Claremont: Mime Journal. 74–92.

Korshak, Yvonne (1987). *Frontal Faces in Attic Vase Painting of the Archaic Period.* Chicago: Ares.

Kowalzig, Barbara (2004). 'Changing choral worlds: song-dance and society in Athens and beyond', in *Music and the Muses: the culture of Mousike in the classical Athenian city*, ed. Penelope Murray and Peter Wilson. Oxford: Oxford University Press, 39–65.

Kowalzig, Barbara (2006a). 'Mapping out *Communitas*: performances of *theôria* in their sacred and political context' in *Pilgrimage in Graeco-Roman and Early Christian Antiquity: seeing the gods*, ed. Jas Elsner and Ian Rutherford. Oxford: Oxford University Press. 41–72.

Kowalzig, Barbara (2006b). 'The aetiology of empire? Hero-cult and Athenian tragedy' in *Greek Drama III: essays in honour of Kevin Lee*, ed. John Davidson, Francis Muecke and Peter Wilson. London: Institute of Classical Studies. 79–98.

Kowalzig, Barbara (2007). '"And now all the world shall dance!" (Eur. *Bacch*. 114): Dionysus' *choroi* between drama and ritual' in *From Ritual to Drama*, ed. E. Csapo and M. Miller. Cambridge: Cambridge University Press. 221–54.

Kraiker, Wilhelm (1978). *Die rotfiguren attischen Vasen.* Mainz: Philipp von Zabern.

Krumeich, Ralf (2000). 'Die Weihgeschenke der Satyrn in Aischylos' *Theoroi* oder *Isthmiastaí*'. *Philologus* 144: 176–92.

Krumeich, Ralf (2002). '"Euaion ist schön"' in *Die Geburt des Theaters in der griechischen Antike*, ed. Susanne Moraw and Eckehart Nölle. Mainz: Philipp von Zabern. 141–5.

Kustow, Michael (2005). *Peter Brook: a biography.* London: Bloomsbury.

Lada-Richards, Ismene (1997). '"Estrangement" or "reincarnation"? Performers and performance on the classical Athenian stage'. *Arion* 5: 66–107.

Lada-Richards, Ismene (1999). *Initiating Dionysus: ritual and theatre in Aristophanes' Frogs.* Oxford: Oxford University Press.

Lada-Richards, Ismene (2002). 'The subjectivity of Greek performance' in *Greek and Roman Actors: aspects of an ancient profession*, ed. Pat Easterling and Edith Hall. Cambridge: Cambridge University Press. 395–418.

Lallias, Jean-Claude and Arnault, Jean-Jacques (1992). *Les Atrides au Théâtre du Soleil: Théâtre Aujourd'hui N° 1.* Paris: CNDP.

Lattimore, Richmond (1956). 'Introduction to *Helen*' in *The Complete Greek Tragedies: Euripides III.* Chicago: Chicago University Press. 261–4.

Layton, Robert (1991). *The Anthropology of Art.* Cambridge: Cambridge University Press.

Le groupe de théâtre antique de la Sorbonne (1962). *Le Théâtre antique à la Sorbonne.* Paris: L'Arche.

Leabhart, Thomas (1995). 'The mask as shamanic tool in the theatre training of Jacques Copeau'. *Mime Journal*, 82–113.

Lecoq, Jacques (2000). *The Moving Body,* trans. D. Bradby. London: Methuen.

Lehmann, Hans-Thies (2006). *Postdramatic Theatre*, trans. K. Jürs-Munby. London: Routledge.
Leigh, Barbara Kusler (1979). *Jacques Copeau's School for Actors* (= *Mime Journal* 9/10). Allendale: Performing Arts Center.
Levasseur-Legangneux, Patricia (2004). *Les Tragédies grecques sur la scène moderne: une utopie théâtrale*. Villeneuve d'Ascq: Presses Universitaires du Septentrion.
Lévi-Strauss, Claude (1961). 'Les Nombreux visages de l'homme'. *World Theatre* 10: 11–20.
*LIMC* = *Lexicon Iconographicum Mythologiae Classicae* (1981–99). Zurich: Artemis.
LiPuma, Edward (1998). 'Modernity and forms of personhood in Melanesia' in *Bodies and Persons: comparative perspectives from Africa and Melanesia*, ed. Michael Lambek and Andrew Strathern. Cambridge: Cambridge University Press. 53–79.
Lissarrague, François (1990). 'Why satyrs are good to represent' in *Nothing to do with Dionysos?* ed. John J. Winkler and Froma Zeitlin. Princeton: Princeton University Press. 228–36.
Lissarrague, François (1999). 'Publicity and performance: *kalos* inscriptions in Attic vase-painting' in *Performance Culture and Athenian Democracy*, ed. Simon Goldhill and Robin Osborne. Cambridge: Cambridge University Press. 359–73.
Lloyd-Jones, Hugh (1957). 'A new text of Fr.50' in *Aeschylus II*, trans. H. W. Smyth with appendix edited by H. Lloyd-Jones. London: Heinemann. 541–56.
Loraux, Nicole (1986). *The Invention of Athens: the funeral oration in the classical city*, trans. A. Sheridan. Cambridge, Mass.: Harvard University Press.
Louette, Jean-François (1996). *Sartre contra Nietzsche*. Grenoble: Presses Universitaires de Grenoble.
Lyons, Michael J., Campbell, Ruth, Plante André, Coleman, Mike, Kamachi, Miyuki and Akamatsu, Shigeru (2000). 'The Noh mask effect: vertical viewpoint dependence of facial expression perception'. *Proceedings of the Royal Society*, 267: 2239–45.
MacGowan, Kenneth and Rosse, Herman (1924). *Masks and Demons*. London: Martin Hopkinson.
Malik S. C., ed. (2001). *Mind, Man and Mask*, Delhi: Indira Gandhi Centre for the Arts.
Marshall, C. W. (1995). 'Idol speculation: the Protean stage of Euripides' *Helen*'. *Text & Presentation* 16: 74–9.
Marshall, C. W. (1999). 'Some fifth-century masking conventions', *Greece and Rome*, 46: 188–202.
Marshall, C. W. (2003). 'Casting the *Oresteia*'. *Classical Journal*, 98: 257–74.
Marshall, C. W. (2004). '*Alcestis* and the ancient rehearsal process (*P.Oxy*.4546)'. *Arion* 11.3: 27–45.
Martin, Jacqueline (1991). *Voice in Modern Theatre*. London: Routledge.

Martin, R. (1976). 'Bathyclès de Magnésie et le "trône" d'Apollon a Amyklae'. *Revue archéologique*. 205–18.

Martzel, Gérard (1982). *Le Dieu masqué: fêtes et théâtre au Japon*. Paris: Publications Orientalistes de France.

Massaro, Dominic W. (1998). *Perceiving Talking Faces*. Cambridge, Mass.: MIT Press.

Mauss, Marcel (1938). 'Une catégorie de l'esprit humain: la notion de personne celle de "moi"'. *Journal of the Royal Anthropological Institute* 68: 5–28.

Mauss, Marcel (1985). 'A category of the human mind: the notion of person, the notion of self' in *The Category of the Person*, ed. M. Carrithers, S. Collins and S. Lukes. Cambridge, Cambridge University Press. 1–25.

Mauss, Marcel (2004). 'Fait social et formation du caractère' *Sociologie et sociétés* 36: 135–40.

May, James M. and Wisse, Jakob, trans. (2001). *Cicero: on the ideal orator*. New York: Oxford University Press.

McCart, Greg (2007). 'Masks in Greek and Roman theatre' in *The Cambridge Companion to Greek and Roman Theatre*, ed. Marianne McDonald and J. Michael Walton. Cambridge: Cambridge University Press. 247–67.

Melchinger, Siegfried (1974). *Das Theater der Tragödie*. Munich: C. H. Beck

Mignon, Paul-Louis (1993). *Jacques Copeau*. Paris: Juillard.

Mignon, Paul-Louis (1999). *Jean-Louis Barrault: le théâtre total*. Monaco: Rocher.

Morris, Sarah (1992). *Daidalos and the Origins of Greek Art*. Princeton: Princeton University Press.

Morwood, James, ed. and trans. (1997). *Euripides: Medea, Hippolytus, Electra, Helen*. Oxford: Oxford University Press.

Murray, Penelope (1996). *Plato on Poetry*. Cambridge: Cambridge University Press.

Nagy, Gregory (1990). *Pindar's Homer: the lyric possession of an epic past*. Baltimore: Johns Hopkins University Press.

Nagy, Gregory (1994/5). 'Transformations of choral lyric traditions in the context of Athenian state theater'. *Arion* 3: 41–55.

Nagy, Gregory (1996). *Poetry as Performance: Homer and beyond*. Cambridge: Cambridge University Press.

Napier, A. David (1986). *Masks, Transformation and Paradox*. Berkeley: University of California Press.

Nearman, Mark J. (1984). 'Behind the Nō mask' in *Nō/Kyōgen Masks and Performance*, ed. Rebecca Teele. Claremont: Mime Journal. 20–64.

Nietzsche, Friedrich (1993). *The Birth of Tragedy*, trans. M. Tanner. Harmondsworth: Penguin.

Nietzsche, Friedrich (2001). *The Gay Science*, trans. J. Nauckhoff. Cambridge: Cambridge University Press.

Nietzsche, Friedrich (2002). *Beyond Good and Evil: prelude to a philosophy of the future*, trans. J. Norman. Cambridge: Cambridge University Press.

Nightingale, Andrea Wilson (2004). *Spectacles of Truth in Classical Greek Philosophy: theoria in its cultural context*. Cambridge: Cambridge University Press.

Nilsson, Martin P. (1925). *A History of Greek Religion*, trans. F. J. Fielden. Oxford: Oxford University Press.

Noirot, Claude (1838). 'L'Origine des masques' (1609). in *Collection de pièces relative à l'histoire de France* Vol. IX. ed. C. Leber. Paris.

Oakley, John H. (1990). *The Phiale Painter*. Mainz: Philipp von Zabern.

Okri, Ben (1997). *African Elegy*. London: Vintage.

O'Neill, Eugene (1961). 'Memoranda on masks' in *Playwrights on Playwriting*, ed. Toby Cole. New York: Hill & Wang. 65–71.

O'Neill, Eugene (1968). 'Author's foreword' in *Yale University Gazette*, vol. 43 (July): 29.

O'Neill, Eugene (1995). *Desire Under the Elms & The Great God Brown*. London Royal National Theatre & Nick Hern.

Onians, R. B. (1951). *The Origins of European Thought about the Body, the Mind, the Soul, the World, Time, and Fate*. Cambridge: Cambridge University Press.

Oranje, Hans (1984). *Euripides' Bacchae: the play and its audience*. Leiden: Brill.

Orgel, Stephen, ed. (1996). *William Shakespeare: The Winter's Tale*. Oxford: Oxford University Press.

Osborne, Robin (1997). 'The ecstasy and the tragedy: varieties of religious experience in art, drama and society' in *Greek Tragedy and the Historian*, ed. Christopher Pelling. Oxford: Oxford University Press. 187–210.

Osborne, Robin (1998). *Archaic and Classical Greek Art*. Oxford: Oxford University Press.

Otto, Walter F. (1965). *Dionysus: myth and cult*, trans. R. B. Palmer. Bloomington: Indiana University Press.

Padel, Ruth (1992). *In and Out of Mind: Greek images of the tragic self*. Princeton: Princeton University Press.

Palmer-Sikelianos, Eva (1993). *Upward Panic*. Amsterdam: Harwood Academic Publishers.

Parker, Robert (1996). *Athenian Religion: a history*. Oxford: Oxford University Press.

Parker, Robert (2005). *Polytheism and Society at Athens*. Oxford: Oxford University Press.

Peirce, Sarah (1998). 'Visual language and concepts of cult in the "Lenaian Vases"'. *Classical Antiquity* 17: 59–95.

Pemberton III, John and Aflayan, Funso S. (1996). *Yoruba Sacred Kingship: 'A power like that of gods'*. Washington: Smithsonian Institution.

Perrett, David *et al.* (1995). 'When is a face not a face?' in *The Artful Eye*, ed. R. Gregory, J. Harris, P. Heard and D. Rose. Oxford: Oxford University Press. 95–124.

Petterson, Michael (1992). *Cults of Apollo at Sparta: the Hyakinthia, the Gymnopaidiai, and the Karneia*. Stockholm: Svenska Institutet i Athen.

Piccirilli, Luigi (1967). 'Ricerche sul culto di Hyakinthos'. *Studi Classici ed Orientali* 16: 99–116.

Pickard-Cambridge, Arthur (1962). *Dithyramb, Tragedy and Comedy*, rev. T. B. L. Webster. Oxford: Oxford University Press.

Pickard-Cambridge, Arthur (1968). *The Dramatic Festivals of Athens*, rev. John Gould and D. M. Lewis. Oxford: Oxford University Press.

Picton, John (1990). 'What's in a mask?' *African Languages and Cultures* 3.2: 181–202.

Pizzato, Mark (2003). 'Soyinka's *Bacchae*, African gods, and postmodern mirrors'. *The Journal of Religion and Theatre* 2.1: 35–104.

Plett, Nicole (1998). 'Zoe Wanamaker and the Electra complex'. www.princetoninfo.com/199809/80916p01.html

Pollitt, J. J. (1985). 'Early classical art in a Platonic universe' in *Greek Art: archaic into classical*, ed. C. Boulter. Leiden: Brill. 96–111.

Pollitt, J. J. (1990). *The Art of Ancient Greece: sources and documents*. Cambridge: Cambridge University Press.

Pound, Ezra, trans. (1916). *Certain Noble Plays of Japan from the Manuscripts of Ernest Fenollosa*. Dundrum: Cuale Press.

Pound, Ezra (1956). *Women of Trachis*. London: Faber.

Prag, A. J. N. W. (1985). *The Oresteia: iconographic and narrative tradition*. Warminster: Aris & Phillips.

Prier, Raymond Adolph (1989). *Thauma idesthai*. Tallahassee: Florida State University Press.

Pucci, Pietro (1994). 'Gods' intervention and epiphany in Sophocles'. *American Journal of Philology* 115: 15–46.

Pulvers, Solrun Hoaas (1978). 'The Noh Mask and the Mask Making Tradition'. MA dissertation, Australian National University.

Raaflaub Kurt (1999). 'Archaic and classical Greece' in *War and Society in the Ancient and Medieval Worlds: Asia, the Mediterranean, Europe and Mesoamerica*, ed. K. Raaflaub and N. Rosenstein. Cambridge, Mass.: Harvard University Press. 129–61.

Radt, Stefan, ed. (1985). *Tragicorum Graecorum Fragmenta Vol. 3: Aeschylus*. Göttingen: Vandenhoek & Ruprecht.

Raz, Jacob (1993). *Audience and Actors: a study of their interaction in the Japanese traditional theatre*. Leiden: Brill.

*REB* (1989). = *The Revised English Bible*. Oxford and Cambridge: Oxford University Press and Cambridge University Press.

Rehm, Rush (1992). *Greek Tragic Theatre*. London: Routledge.

Reynolds, Peter (1996). *Unmasking Oedipus*. London: National Theatre.

Rhodes, P. J. (2003). 'Nothing to do with democracy: Athenian drama and the *polis*'. *Journal of Hellenic Studies* 125: 104–19.

Riccioni, Giuliana (1959). 'Cratere attico a figure rosse con scena di teatro'. *Arte antica e moderna* 2: 37–42.

Richter, Gisela M. (1984). *The Portraits of the Greeks*, rev. R. Smith. Ithaca: Cornell University Press.

Rodenburg, Patsy (2002). *The Actor Speaks: voice and the performer.* London: Palgrave.

Rolfe, Bari (1977). *Behind the Mask.* New York: Personabooks.

Rose, Peter W. (1995). 'Historicizing Sophocles' Ajax' in *History, Tragedy, Theory: dialogues on Athenian drama,* ed. Barbara Goff. Austin: University of Texas Press. 59–90.

Rosenmeyer, Thomas G. (1963). *The Masks of Tragedy: essays on six Greek dramas.* Austin: University of Texas Press.

Russell, D. A. and Winterbottom, M., ed. and trans. (1972). *Ancient Literary Criticism: the principal texts in new translations.* Oxford: Oxford University Press.

Rutherford, Ian (2000). '*Theoria* and *Darśan*: pilgrimage and vision in Greece and India'. *Classical Quarterly* 50: 133–46.

Rutherford, Ian (2004). '*Choros heis ek tēsde tēs poleōs . . .* (Xen. *Mem.* 3.3.12): song-dance and state-pilgrimage in Athens' in *Music and the Muses: the culture of 'Mousikē' in the classical Athenian city,* ed. Penelope Murray and Peter Wilson. Oxford: Oxford University Press. 67–90.

Saint-Denis, Michel (1960). *Theatre: the rediscovery of style.* London: Heinemann.

Salter, Denis (1993). 'Théâtre du Soleil: *Les Atrides.* An interview with Simon Akbarian, Nirupama Nityanandan, Juliana Carneiro da Cunha, Brontis Jodorowsky and Catherine Schaub'. *Theater* 24: 66–74.

Sampatakakis, Georgios (2004). 'Bakkhai-Model: the re-usage of Euripides' *Bakkhai* in text and performance'. Ph.D. dissertation. University of London.

Saraswati, Baidyanath (2001). 'Mind the elephant: a sacred science view of reality' in *Mind, Man and Mask,* ed. S. C. Malik. Delhi: Indira Gandhi Centre for the Arts. 81–92.

Sartori, Donato (2003). *Le maschere nell'antichità.* Pontedera: Villa Pacchiani.

Sartori, Donato and Lanata, Bruno (1984). *Maschera e maschere: storia, morfologia, tecnica.* Florence: Casa Usher.

Sartori, Donato and Piizzi, Paola (1996). *Maschere e mascheramenti: i Sartori tra arte e teatro.* Padua: Poligrafo.

Sartre, Jean-Paul (1992). *Un théâtre de situations,* ed. M. Contat and M. Rybalka. Paris: Gallimard.

Sartre, Jean-Paul (2005). *Théâtre complet,* ed. M. Contat. Paris: Gallimard.

Schadewaldt, W. (1961). 'Die Wappnung des Eteokles' in *Eranion: Festschrift für H. Hommel.* Tübingen: Niemeyer. 105–16.

Schechner, Richard (1988). *Performance Theory.* London: Routledge.

Schlegel, A. W. (1846). *A Course of Lectures on Dramatic Art and Literature,* trans. J. Black and A. T. W. Morrison. London: Bohn.

Schlesier, Renate (1993). 'Mixtures of masks: maenads as tragic models' in *Masks of Dionysus,* ed. Thomas H. Carpenter and Christopher A. Faraone. Ithaca: Cornell University Press. 89–114.

Scodel, Ruth (2003). 'The politics of Sophocles' *Ajax*'. *Scripta Classica Israelica* 22: 31–42.

Scullion, Scott (2002). '"Nothing to do with Dionysus": tragedy misconceived as ritual'. *Classical Quarterly* 52: 102–37.
Seaford, Richard, ed. (1996). *Euripides: Bacchae*. Warminster: Aris & Phillips.
Seaford, Richard (1998). 'In the mirror of Dionysos' in *The Sacred and the Feminine in Ancient Greece*, ed. Sue Blundell and Margaret Williamson. London: Routledge. 128–46.
Seaford, Richard (1994). *Reciprocity and Ritual: Homer and tragedy in the developing city-state*. Oxford: Oxford University Press.
Seaford, Richard, ed. (1984). *Euripides: Cyclops*. Oxford: Oxford University Press.
Seaford, Richard, ed. (2001). *Euripides: Bacchae*. Warminster: Aris & Phillips.
Segal, Charles (1986). *Interpreting Greek Tragedy: myth, poetry, text*. Ithaca: Cornell University Press.
Segal, C. P. (1993). *Euripides and the Poetics of Sorrow: art, gender, and commemoration in Alcestis, Hippolytus, and Hecuba*. Durham, NC: Duke University Press.
Segal, Charles (1995). *Sophocles' Tragic World: divinity, nature, society*. Cambridge, Mass.: Harvard University Press.
Segal, Charles (1997). *Dionysiac Poetics and Euripides' Bacchae*. Princeton: Princeton University Press.
Serban, Andrei (1976). 'The life in a sound' trans. E. Blumenthal. *The Drama Review* T72: 25–6.
Shapiro, H. A. (1989). *Art and Cult under the Tyrants in Athens*. Mainz: Philipp von Zabern.
Shaw, Fiona (1996). 'Electra Speechless' *Drama* 4: 131–8. (= *Sophocles' 'Electra' in Perfomance*, ed. Francis M. Dunn. Stuttgart: Metzlerschen & Poeschel).
Sherrard, Philip (1956). 'Anghelos Sikelianos' in *The Marble Threshing Floor*. London: Valentine, Mitchell & Co. 125–83.
Sherrard, Philip (1978). 'Anghelos Sikelianos and his vision of Greece' in *The Wound of Greece*. London: Rex Collings. 72–93.
Sifakis, G. M. (1995). 'The one-actor rule in Greek tragedy' in *Stage Directions: essays in honour of E. W. Handley*, ed. A. Griffiths. London: Institute of Classical Studies. 13–24.
Sikelianos, Anghelos (1998). 'Ta prosopeia sten tragodia *Prometheus*' in *Anghelos Sikelianos, Eva Palmer-Sikelianou: Delfikes Eortes*. Athens: Papadema. 81–7.
Simon, Erika (1982). *The Ancient Theatre*, trans. C. E. Vafopoulou-Richardson. London: Methuen.
Sinclair, R. K. (1988). *Democracy and Participation in Athens*. Cambridge: Cambridge University Press.
Slater, Niall W. (1985). 'Vanished players: two classical reliefs and theatre history'. *Greek, Roman and Byzantine Studies* 26: 333–44.
Slehoferova, Vera (1988). *Corpus Vasorum Antiquorum. Basel – Faszikel 3*. Bern: Peter Lang.
Smethurst, Mae (2000). 'The Japanese presence in Ninagawa's *Medea*' in *Medea in Performance 1500–2000*, ed. Edith Hall, Fiona Macintosh and Oliver Taplin. Oxford: Legenda. 191–216.

Smith, A. C. H. (1972). *Orghast at Persepolis.* London: Methuen.
Smith, Susan Harris (1984). *Masks in Modern Drama.* Berkeley: University of California Press.
Snodgrass, A. M. (1967). *Arms and Armour of the Greeks.* London: Thames & Hudson.
Sommerstein, Alan H., ed. (1989). *Aeschylus: Eumenides.* Cambridge: Cambridge University Press.
Sorell, Walter (1973). *The Other Face: the mask in the arts.* London: Thames & Hudson.
Sourvinou-Inwood, Christiane (2003). *Tragedy and Athenian Religion.* Lanham: Lexington Books.
Soyinka, Wole (1973). *Collected Plays: 1.* Oxford: Oxford University Press.
Soyinka, Wole (1976). *Myth, Literature and the African World.* Cambridge: Cambridge University Press.
Soyinka, Wole (1997). 'Wole Soyinka on Yoruba Religion: a conversation with Ulli Beier'. *Isokan Yoruba Magazine* 3.3. http://www.yoruba.org/Magazine/Summer97/File3.html
Spivey, Nigel (1996). *Understanding Greek Sculpture: ancient meanings, modern readings.* London: Thames & Hudson.
Stanford, W. B. (1983). *Greek Tragedy and the Emotions: an introductory study.* London: Routledge & Kegan Paul.
Stanislavski, Constantin (1950). *Building a Character*, trans. E. R. Hapgood. London: Methuen.
Stanislavski, Constantin (1967). *An Actor Prepares*, trans. E. R. Hapgood. Harmondsworth: Penguin.
Steegmuller, Frances (1970). *Cocteau: a biography.* London: Macmillan.
Steiner, Rudolf (1960). *Speech and Drama*, trans. M. Adams. London: Anthroposophical Publishing Co.
Stieber, Mary (1994). 'Aeschylus' *Theoroi* and realism in Greek art'. *Transactions of the American Philological Association* 124: 85–119.
Strong, Laura (2000). 'Egungun: the masked ancestors of the Yoruba'. http://www.mythicarts.com/writing/Egungun.html
Surel-Tupin, Monique (1974). 'La Recherche théâtrale de Charles Dullin étudiée à partir de ses écrits'. Doctoral thesis: Paris III.
Surel-Tupin, Monique (1984). *Charles Dullin.* Bordeaux: Presses Universitaires de Bordeaux.
Sutton, D. F. (1984). *The Greek Satyr Play.* Meisenheim: Hain.
Suzuki, Daisetz T. (1988). *Zen and Japanese Culture.* Tokyo: Tuttle.
Svenbro, Jesper (1993). *Phrasikleia: an anthropology of reading in ancient Greece.* Ithaca: Cornell University Press.
Talcott, Lucy (1939). 'Kourimos parthenos'. *Hesperia* 8: 267–73.
Taplin, Oliver (1977). *The Stagecraft of Aeschylus: the dramatic use of exits and entrances in Greek tragedy.* Oxford: Oxford University Press.
Taplin, Oliver (1978). *Greek Tragedy in Action.* London: Methuen.

Taplin, Oliver (1993). *Comic Angels: and other approaches to Greek drama through vase-paintings.* Oxford: Oxford University Press.

Taplin, Oliver (2002). 'Masks in Greek tragedy and in *Tantalus*'. *Didaskalia* 5.2.

Taplin, Oliver (2006). 'The Harrison version: "*So long ago that it's become a song?*"' in *Agamemnon in Performance 458 BC-AD 2004*, ed. Fiona Macintosh, Pantelis Michelakis, Edith Hall and Oliver Taplin. Oxford: Oxford University Press. 235–51.

Taxidou, Olga (1998). *The Mask: a periodical performance by Edward Gordon Craig.* Amsterdam: Harwood.

Taylor, Charles (1989). *Sources of the Self: the making of the modern identity.* Cambridge: Cambridge University Press.

Taylor, John H. (1994). 'Masks in ancient Egypt: the image of divinity' in *Masks: the art of expression*, ed. J. Mack. London: British Museum Press. 168–89.

Teele, Rebecca, ed. (1984). *Nō/Kyōgen Masks and Performance.* Claremont: Mime Journal.

Tenschert, Joachim (1961). 'The mask at the Berliner Ensemble'. *World Theatre* 10: 49–57.

Thalmann, William G. (1978). *Dramatic Art in Aeschylus's Seven against Thebes.* New Haven: Yale University Press.

Théâtre du Soleil (1992). *Les Atrides.* Paris: Théâtre du Soleil.

Theodossiev, Nikola (1998). 'The dead with golden faces: Dasaretian, Pelagonian, Mygdonian and Boeotian funeral masks'. *Oxford Journal of Archaeology* 17: 345–67.

Thornhill, Arthur H., III (1993). *Six Circles, One Dewdrop: the religio-aesthetic world of Komparu Zenchiko.* Princeton: Princeton University Press.

Todd, Andrew and Lecat, Jean-Guy (2003). *The Open Circle: Peter Brook's Theatre Environments.* London: Faber.

Trendall, A. D. and Cambitoglou, Alexander (1978). *Red-figured Vases of Apulia.* Vol. 1. Oxford: Oxford University Press.

Trevarthen, Colwyn (1995). 'Mother and Baby – seeing artfully eye to eye' in *The Artful Eye*, ed. R. Gregory, J. Harris, P. Heard and D. Rose. Oxford: Oxford University Press. 157–200.

Trevelyan, Humphrey (1941). *Goethe and the Greeks.* Cambridge: Cambridge University Press.

Trubotchkin, Dmitry (2005). '*Agamemnon* in Russia' in *Agamemnon in Performance 458 BC-AD 2004*, ed. Fiona Macintosh, Pantelis Michelakis, Edith Hall and Oliver Taplin. Oxford: Oxford University Press. 255–72.

Tseëlon, Efrat (2001). 'Reflections on mask and carnival' in *Masquerade and Identities: essays in gender, sexuality and marginality*, ed. E. Tseëlon. London: Routledge. 18–37.

Tsirivakos, Elias (1974). 'Eniochos technes tragikos'. *Deltion* 29: 88–94.

Tzachou-Alexandri, Olga (1997). 'Apeikoniseis ton Anthesterion kai o chous tis Hodou Peiraos to zographou tis Eretrias' in *Athenian Potters and Painters: the conference proceedings*, ed. John H. Oakley, William D. E. Coulson and Olga Palagia. Oxford: Oxbow. 473–90.

Underwood, Simeon (1998). 'Harrison's Aeschylus and Logue's Homer'. *Dialogos* 5: 76–100.

Vafopoulou-Richardson, C. E. (1981). *Greek Terracottas*. Oxford: Ashmolean Museum.

Van Wees, Hans (1998). 'A brief history of tears' in *When Men Were Men: masculinity, power and identity in classical antiquity*, ed. Lin Foxhall and John Salmon. London: Routledge. 10–53.

Vandiver, Elizabeth (1991). *Heroes in Herodotus: the interaction of myth and history*. Frankfurt: Peter Lang.

Vasseur-Legangneux, Patricia (2004). *Les Tragédies grecques sur la scène moderne: une utopie théâtrale*. Villeneuve d'Asq: Presses Universitaires du Septentrion.

Vernant, Jean-Pierre (1989). *L'individu, la mort, l'amour*. Paris: Gallimard.

Vernant, Jean-Pierre (1990a). *Mythe et pensée chez les grecs*. Paris: Editions la Découverte.

Vernant, Jean-Pierre (1990b). *Figures, idoles, masques*. Paris: Juillard.

Vernant, Jean-Pierre (1991). *Mortals and Immortals: collected essays*, ed. Froma Zeitlin. Princeton: Princeton University Press.

Vernant, Jean-Pierre (1996). *Entre mythe et politique*. Paris: Editions du Seuil.

Vernant, Jean-Pierre and Vidal-Naquet, Pierre (1990). *Myth and Tragedy in Ancient Greece*, trans. J. Lloyd. New York: Zone Books.

Vervain, Chris and Wiles, David (2001). 'The masks of Greek tragedy as point of departure for modern performance'. *New Theatre Quarterly* 67: 254–72.

Veyne, Paul (1988). *Did the Greeks Believe in their Myths? An essay in the constitutive imagination*, trans. P. Wissing. Chicago: Chicago University Press.

Vives, Juan Luis (1948). 'A Fable about Man', trans. N. Lenkeith, in *The Renaissance Philosophy of Man* ed. E. Cassirer, P. O. Kristeller and J. H. Randall. Chicago: University of Chicago Press. 387–93.

Von Reden, Sitta and Goldhill, Simon (1999). 'Plato and the performance of dialogue' in *Performance Culture and Athenian Democracy*, ed. Simon Goldhill and Robin Osborne. Cambridge: Cambridge University Press. 257–89.

Vovolis, Thanos and Zamboulakis, Giorgos (2004). 'The acoustical mask of Greek tragedy' in *The Face and Mask of the Actor: Methodica 2003*, ed. Martha Vestin and Grete Sneltved. Stockholm: Dramatiska Institutet. 107–31.

Wainscott, Ronald H. (1988). *Staging O'Neill: the experimental years 1920–1934*. New Haven: Yale University Press.

Walker, Susan and Bierbrier, Morris (1997). *Ancient Faces: mummy portraits from Roman Egypt*. London: British Museum Press.

Walton, J. Michael (1984). *The Greek Sense of Theatre: tragedy reviewed*. London: Methuen.

Walton, J. Michael (1991). *Greek Theatre Practice*. London: Methuen.

Walton, J. Michael (2002). '*Tantalus*'. *Didaskalia* 5.2.

Watt, H. F. (1992). 'Faces and Vision' in *Processing Images of Faces*, ed. V. Bruce and M. Burton. Norwood, NJ: Ablex. 88–125.

Webster, T. B. L. (1967). *Monuments Illustrating Tragedy and Satyr Play.* London: Institute of Classical Studies.

Webster, T. B. L. (1970). *The Greek Chorus.* London: Methuen.

Webster, T. B. L. (1978). *Monuments Illustrating Old and Middle Comedy*, rev. J. R. Green. London: Institute of Classical Studies.

Webster, T. B. L. (1995). *Monuments Illustrating New Comedy*, rev. J. R. Green. London: Institute of Classical Studies.

Wickersham, John M. (1991). 'Myth and identity in the archaic polis' in *Myth and the Polis*, ed. Dora C. Pozzi and John M. Wickersham. Ithaca: Cornell University Press. 16–31.

Wiles, David (1987). 'Reading Greek performance'. *Greece & Rome* 34: 136–51.

Wiles, David (1991). *The Masks of Menander: sign and meaning in Greek and Roman performance.* Cambridge: Cambridge University Press.

Wiles, David (1993). 'The seven gates of Aeschylus'. *Drama* 2: 180–94 (= *Intertextualität in der griechisch-römischen Komödie*, ed. Niall W. Slater and Bernhardt Zimmermann. Stuttgart: Metzlerschen & Poeschel) with printer's corrections in *Drama* 3 (1995). 190.

Wiles, David (1997). *Tragedy in Athens: performance space and theatrical meaning.* Cambridge: Cambridge University Press.

Wiles, David (2000). *Greek Theatre Performance: an introduction.* Cambridge: Cambridge University Press.

Wiles, David (2003). *A Short History of Western Performance Space.* Cambridge: Cambridge University Press.

Wiles, David (2004a). 'The mask in Greek tragedy'. *Dioniso* 3: 206–13.

Wiles, David (2004b). 'The use of masks in modern performances of Greek drama' in *Dionysus Since 69: Greek tragedy at the dawn of the new millenium*, ed. Edith Hall, Fiona Macintosh and Amanda Wrigley. Oxford: Oxford University Press. 245–63.

Wiles, David (2007). 'Aristotle's *Poetics* and ancient dramatic theory' in *The Cambridge Companion to Greek and Roman Theatre*, ed. Marianne McDonald and J. Michael Walton. Cambridge: Cambridge University Press. 92–107

Williams, David, ed. (1999). *Collaborative Theatre: the Théâtre du Soleil sourcebook.* London: Routledge.

Williams, Richard (2004). 'New Comedy in performance: Menander and the mask'. *Dioniso* 3: 148–53.

Wilson, Peter (2000). *The Athenian institution of the* Khoregia: *the chorus, the city and the stage.* Cambridge: Cambridge University Press.

Winkler, J. J. (1990). 'The ephebes' song: *tragôidia* and the *polis*', in *Nothing to do with Dionysos?* ed. John J. Winkler and Froma I. Zeitlin. Princeton: Princeton University Press. 20–62.

Winnington-Ingram, R. (1948). *Euripides and Dionysus: an interpretation of The Bacchae*. Cambridge: Cambridge University Press.

Woodford, Susan (2003). *Images of Myths in Classical Antiquity*. Cambridge: Cambridge University Press.

Wright, Matthew (2005). 'The joy of Sophocles' *Electra*'. *Greece & Rome* 52: 172–94.

Zanker, Paul (1995). *The Mask of Socrates: the image of the intellectual in antiquity*. Berkeley: University of California Press.

Zeami, Motokiyo (1984). *On the Art of the Nō Drama*, trans. J. Thomas Rimer and Yamazaki Masakazu. Princeton: Princeton University Press.

Zeitlin, Froma I. (1980). 'The closet of masks: role-playing and myth-making in the *Orestes* of Euripides'. *Ramus* 9: 51–77.

Zeitlin, Froma I. (1982). *Under the Sign of the Shield: semiotics and Aeschylus' Seven Against Thebes*. Rome: Ateneo.

Zeitlin, Froma I. (1990a). 'Playing the other: theatre, theatricality, and the feminine in Greek drama', in *Nothing to do with Dionysos?* ed. John J. Winkler and Froma I. Zeitlin. Princeton: Princeton University Press. 63–96.

Zeitlin, Froma I. (1990b). 'Thebes: theatre of self and society in Athenian drama' in *Nothing to do with Dionysos?* ed. John J. Winkler and Froma I. Zeitlin. Princeton: Princeton University Press. 130–67.

Zeitlin, Froma I. (1993). 'Staging Dionysus between Thebes and Athens' in *Masks of Dionysus*, ed. Thomas H. Carpenter and Christopher A. Faraone. Ithaca: Cornell University Press. 147–82.

Zeitlin, Froma I. (2004). 'Dionysus in 69' in *Dionysus Since 69: Greek tragedy at the dawn of the new millenium*, ed. Edith Hall, Fiona Macintosh and Amanda Wrigley. Oxford: Oxford University Press. 49–75.

# Index

actors (of the fifth century)  24, 29, 44, 48, 62, 172–4, 195
    prize for  201, 205–12, 257
    see also: *hypokrisis*
Aeschylus  15, 38, 62, 72, 90
    *Agamemnon*  149–51
    *Eumenides*  65, 66, 270
    *Isthmiastai*  201, 205–12, 219, 237
    *Lycurgeia*  210, 226
    *Oresteia*  86, 87, 98, 110–17, 125, 132–9, 154–5, 173, 203, 272
    *Persians*  18, 106, 111, 121, 126, 127, 169, 173
    *Prometheus*  80, 88–93
    *Seven Against Thebes*  267–75
    *Suppliants*  111
African masks  79, 116, 182–8
*agalma*  259, 281
agency  270–4
Alcamenes  220, 259
Alcmaeon  239
Althusser, Louis  249
ancestors  185–6, 190–1, 246–7, 262
angle of vision  50, 52–5, 56, 138, 165, 167, 199–200
animal masks  16–18, 228
Anthesteria  107, 186, 210, 213, 215, 216–19
Antigone, comic vase depicting  208
Apollonius  130, 131–2
Archive of Performances of Greek and Roman Drama  6
Arden, John  140
Aristophanes  2, 52, 210, 247
    *Knights*  16
    *Peace*  242
    *Thesmophoriazousai*  225, 226, 281, 282
Aristotle
    *Poetics*  10, 11, 15, 64, 65–6, 77, 98, 174, 194, 238, 275, 287
    *Protrepticus*  238–9
Artaud, Antonin  78, 81, 111, 112, 113, 125, 127–8, 160, 177
Artemis, mask cults of  223, 224

Ashmolean Museum  56–7
Athens Agora jug fragment  20–2
athletics  160, 207, 239
audience, constituents of  241
*aulos*  148

Bacon, Helen  176, 272
Balinese theatre  160, 165, 167, 188–96, 264
Ball, Hugo  78–9
Barrault, Jean-Louis  94, 102, 110–18, 122–3, 124, 125–6, 140, 157
Barrymore, John  86
Barthes, Roland  102, 116–24, 171
Barton, John  128
Basel krater  18–20, 26
Bauhaus  88, 287
Bell, Marie  117, 125
Benjamin, Walter  288
Bérard, C. and Bron, C.  42, 215, 216, 219
Berlin amphora  16–18
Bernabò Brea, Luigi  52–5
Bieber, Margarete  16
Billington, Michael  139
Birtwistle, Harrison  141
Boardman, John  62
Boston krater  25–6
Bramley, Peter  162, 163, 164
Bread and Puppet  288
Brecht, Bertolt  10, 77, 119–21, 139, 152, 287
Brindisi krater  195
Brinkmann, Vinzenz  51
British Museum, Orestes vases  59–60
Brook, Peter  126, 151, 184, 187, 188–90, 192–3, 200, 203, 251, 287
Browning, Robert  129–30
Bunraku  121
Burkert, Walter  213

Cagliari relief  46
Calame, Claude  42, 175–6, 227
carnival  73, 74, 286
Carpenter, Thomas  213
catharsis  77, 112, 158, 225, 245

character 144–5, 154, 165, 171, 193–4, 225, 275
Chase, Michael 156–64, 165, 167, 170, 171, 178
chorality 76, 108, 135
Christianity and masking 72, 151, 181, 234, 286
Cicero 3, 42, 61, 262–3
classical body 61, 70, 160
classical style 60–1, 65, 66–8
Claudel, Paul 117
Cleisthenes of Sicyon 244
Cocteau, Jean 81–4
Coldiron, Margaret 190, 192, 200
*commedia dell'arte* 75, 106, 112, 116, 153, 286
Copeau, Jacques 102–11, 122–4, 133, 146, 165, 167, 289
costume of ancient tragedy 20, 25, 28, 33, 38, 40, 45, 50, 52, 141, 185
Craig, Edward Gordon 86, 87, 102–4, 107, 109, 121, 135, 288
Cratylus 212
cross-dressing 37–8, 75, 174
Csapo, Eric 210, 214

Dada 78, 80
Daedalus 206, 211–12
Damasio, Antonio 264
*darsán* 259–60
Dasté, Jean 102, 106, 107, 109, 111, 119, 122
Dasté, Marie-Hélène ('Maïène') 105–8, 111–12, 122
death-masks 247–9, 255
dedication of masks 35, 201–2, 210
Delos wall-painting 50–2
Delphi Charioteer 45, 68, 71–2
Demosthenes 173
Derrida, Jacques 127–8, 132
Des Bouvrie, Synnøve 240–1
Detienne, Marcel 219
Devine, George 123, 135, 140
Diderot, Denis 73, 109
Diodorus 257, 258
Dionysos
 and afterlife 16, 231
 androgyny 43, 45, 226, 228, 231
 and Apollo 22, 76, 89
 as pillar god or mask-idol 175, 213–19, 224, 242, 266
 as Zarathustra 112
 Egyptian 103, 247–9
 epiphany of 219, 227, 232
 festival of 3, 224, 237, 238–57
 images of 220, 259
 statue in theatre 64, 191, 210, 213, 220, 235, 238, 240, 243
 temple of 210, 220
Dodds, E. R. 175, 221
Doisy, Marcel 108
Dorcy, Jean 107, 108
doubling 29, 88, 100, 172–4, 188
drag 37–8
dramatic illusion 208, 254, 258
Drewal, Margaret 185, 187–8, 229
Dullin, Charles 81, 93–8, 110, 111
Dupont, Florence 251–2

Easterling, Patricia 8, 10, 195
Egungun masquerade 185–7
Egyptian masks 247–8, 255
*eidōlon* 212, 253, 258, 266, 282
*ekkyklēma* 254
Ekman, Paul 3
Eleusinian Mysteries 90, 105, 112, 178, 186, 237
Eliade, Mircea 185, 186, 198
Elsner, Jas 237, 247, 255
Emigh, John 190, 192, 193–5
emotion 60, 64–5, 68, 73, 82, 118, 158, 177, 233, 241, 242–3, 288
Empedocles 239
Epidaurus 136, 138, 144, 163, 164, 169, 203
Erinyes 65, 66–7, 107, 116, 119, 272, 276
Etruscan masks 248, 262
Euaion 15, 172–3
Euripides 134, 186, 211
 *Alcestis* 129, 232–6
 *Bacchae* 24–6, 46, 108, 172, 185, 221–5, 227–8
 *Electra* 284
 *Helen* 280–4
 *Heracles* 173
 *Hippolytus* 8, 173
 *Ion* 75
 *Iphigeneia in Aulis* 100
 *Medea* 174, 199
 *Orestes* 283
 *Phoenician Women* 271
 *Suppliants* 247
Ewans, Michael 273
eye-contact 129, 255
Eysoldt, Gertrud 278

face recognition 131
Faucit, Helen 232–6, 254
Ferrara krater (end fifth century) 230–1

Ferrara krater (mid-fifth century) 22–5
Fischer-Lichte, Erika 278
Fo, Dario 153–4
Fokas, Antonis 93
Foley, Helene 128, 173, 221–2, 223, 224, 227, 279, 283
Frickenhaus, August 213
Friedrich, Rainer 10
Frontisi-Ducroux, Françoise 7, 213, 214–15, 223, 224, 227, 247, 256–7

Garbo, Greta 116, 123
Gardzienice 284
Garrick 109
gaze
    of the mask 31, 42, 70, 112, 130, 131–2, 138, 158, 231, 253, 267
    male gaze 234
Geertz, Clifford 264
Gell, Alfred 5, 16, 212
gender and masking 185–6, 197, 210, 215, 216, 230
gender-coding of masks 30, 41, 48, 50, 54, 59
Ghiron-Bistagne, Paulette 176–7, 178, 195, 247
Gill, Christopher 273
Gillibert, Jean 110, 111
Glasgow research project 52, 55
Glasshouse 156, 159
gods 59
    *daimones* 234, 265, 272, 276
    monotheism 180–2, 193, 221, 237
    polytheism 67, 180–204, 235–6, 257, 258, 259–60, 276
Goethe, Wolfgang 74–5, 160
Goffmann, Erving 85
Goldhill, Simon 227, 249, 251
Gombrich, Ernst 130, 132
Gorgon mask 139–40, 223, 224, 231, 235, 258, 265
Gould, John and Lewis, D. M. 24
Green, Richard 7, 18, 35, 54, 201, 205, 207
Grotowski, Jerzy 99, 189, 203
Groupe de Théâtre Antique 118
Gurdjieff, G. I. 189
Guthrie, Tyrone 79
gymnasium 61

Habermas, Jürgen 12
half-masks 86, 87, 113, 116, 123
Hall, Edith 172–3, 247, 280–1
Hall, Peter 102, 128, 129, 132–44, 155, 158, 163, 164, 169, 172, 200, 222, 228

Hallett, C. H. 67
Halliwell, Stephen 10–11, 16, 60
Hanley, Julian 161
Harrison, Tony 133, 135, 137, 139, 152, 154, 268
Heidelberg krater 36–8
helmets 57–8, 207–10, 248, 271
Henrichs, Albert 175, 226–8, 231
Herbert, Jocelyn 135–41, 177
Herington, John 237
hero cult 244–5, 250, 254, 255
Herodotus 103, 178, 182, 203, 244, 250, 283, 284
Hicks, Greg 128, 133, 137–8, 153, 172, 203
Hisao, Kanze 197
historiographic method 283–5
Homer 225, 239, 251, 254, 265, 269, 271, 284
hoplites 57–9, 271–2
    hoplite racing 207
Horace 15
Hottier, Philippe 124
Howard, Alan 289
Hughes, Ted 126, 151, 203
Hutchinson, G. O. 269, 270, 271
Hyacinthia 242–4
*hypokrisis* (acting) 72, 179, 247, 256

Ibsen, Henrik 251–2, 276
idealism 73–5, 107, 160
*imago* 61, 249, 262
improvisation 108, 125, 135, 139–40
Indian theatre 189
individualism 264
Isocrates 241, 246–7

James, Wendy 4
Johnstone, Keith 123, 124
Jones, John 10, 177, 221, 275–7
Jones, Robert Edmond 84, 86, 88
Jouvet, Louis 106

Kachler, Karl 227
Kant, Immanuel 73, 261, 262–3, 273, 279
Kathakali 100, 189
*kenosis* 165–6
Kiev krater 28
Kleist, Heinrich 75, 103
Knight, Malcolm 170–1
Knox, Bernard 249
Koun, Karolos 165, 287
Kowalzig, Barbara 245–6, 250
Krumeich, Ralf 206
Kwakiutl masks 262

Labisse, Félix 111
Lada-Richards, Ismene 2
language
   and embodiment 146–51, 290
   foregrounded by mask 77, 128
   sound and meaning 125–7
Lateran relief 49
Lattimore, Richard 280, 283
Layton, Robert 5
Lecoq, Jacques 67–70, 102, 123–4, 130, 132, 150, 289
Lehmann, Hans-Thies 12
'Lenaian' vases 213–20
Lévi-Strauss, Claude 3, 223
lighting 55–6, 128–9, 135–6, 139, 158, 235
Lipari terracotta miniatures 52–5, 65, 66, 129
LiPuma, Edward 264
Living Theatre 99
Lucian 57
Lyme Park relief 49
Lysippus 64, 65

MacGowan, Kenneth 84, 86
maenads 20, 22, 38–9, 44, 47, 48, 186, 214–15, 230
make-up masks 79, 82, 86, 87, 95, 100–1
Makron 214
Mamet, David 144
Marque, Albert 107
Marshall, C. W. 54
Martin, Jacqueline 127
Marx, Karl 120
mask elements
   asymmetry 24, 54, 55, 57, 167
   beard 214
   colour 15, 28, 30, 36, 41, 50, 105, 135, 139, 230
   cords or strap 21, 48
   ears 22, 24, 28, 41
   eyes 21–2, 24, 31, 37, 41, 42, 49, 57, 62, 70, 97, 135, 139–40, 188
   hair 20, 22, 36, 41, 48, 52, 53, 54, 64, 65
   headgear 29, 54
   materials 15, 156
   mouth 21, 41, 50, 72
   proportions 64, 65–6, 74, 197
mask technique 289
mask usage
   concealed in basket 214, 216–19
   putting on ('shoeing') 87, 106, 109, 113
   taking off 172
   tempo 157, 192
   unveiling of 219, 233, 236, 254, 255, 278, 282
'masked text' 140–1
mask-makers 290
   classical 57–8, 59, 62, 63
   Japanese 201, 202, 205–12
masks in antiquity
   acoustical properties 141–2, 153–79, 275
   casting process 61
   cloaks as masks 18–20, 26
   contemplation of 192
   etymology 1
   inhabited by a spirit 192–3, 201, 290
   'megaphone' theory of 73, 83, 90, 119, 126, 153–4, 177
   'melting' 15, 29, 37, 40, 46–7
   origin of 76, 105, 154
   viewed in profile 138, 219
masque 72
Mauriac, François 82
Mauss, Marcel 261–4
McCart, Greg 8
Melchinger, Siegfried 8, 65, 66, 227
Menander 49
metatheatricality 39, 175, 187, 222, 254, 280, 281
metre 145–8
Meyerhold, Vsevolod 157, 160
mimesis 20, 64, 65, 176, 188, 224, 226, 235, 238, 244, 252, 256, 258, 278
mirrors 135, 158, 200, 289
Mnouchkine, Ariane 9, 100–1, 102, 124, 287
modernism 70, 75–6, 88, 107
*mormolykeion* 210
Moscow Art Theatre 80
motivation 273, 276
music 33, 87, 106, 176
Mycenaean masks 248

Nagy, Gregory 243
Napier, David 7, 180, 264
Neher, Caspar 120
neurology 130–2, 288
neutral mask 42, 60, 67–70, 105, 107, 119, 137, 198
New Comedy masks 4, 38, 170, 177
New York terracotta figurines 50
Nietzsche, Friedrich 75–8, 79, 84, 88–9, 93, 98, 100, 101, 103, 104, 105, 112, 140, 185, 223, 226, 232, 235, 240, 261, 263, 266
Nigerian drama 184–8
Nilsson, Martin 213, 241

Noh masks  57, 79, 86, 88, 90, 99, 101, 108, 165, 167, 196–202
Noirot, Claude  72–3
Novelli, Ermete  103, 109

O'Neill, Eugene  84–8
occult  113
Okina ceremony  197, 219
Okri, Ben  182–4, 192, 212
Old Comedy  39–40, 49–50, 64, 65
    see also: Aristophanes
Olympia pediments  62–4
*onkos*  50, 52, 54, 64, 65
orators  3, 73, 263
orientalism  192, 196
Orthia, cult of  214, 216–19
Oskarson, Peter  163, 164
Otto, Walter  227, 255
outdoor performance  163–4, 235

Padel, Ruth  273
painting  50–1, 206
Palmer-Sikelianos, Eva  88–90, 97, 140, 164
pantomime  45, 71–2
Parker, Robert  10, 213, 244
Parthenon frieze  5, 49, 61, 64, 65
Pausanias  67, 259
Peiraeus plaque  44–7
Pentheus  18, 24, 29, 46, 59, 173, 220, 221, 222
person, category of  261–4
*persona*  262–3
Pheidias  61, 65, 66
physical theatre  106, 125, 157, 194, 287
physiognomics  55, 154–5
Picasso, Pablo  79, 81, 83, 84
Pickard-Cambridge, Arthur  7, 9, 227
Pindar  175
Piscator, Erwin  120
Plato  11, 150, 157, 177, 225, 237, 238–9, 241, 245, 256, 257, 258, 259, 266, 268, 272, 273
    *Alcibiades*  282
    *Charmides*  274
    *Ion*  225, 258
    *Theaetatus*  239
    *Timaeus*  169, 239
Pliny  13–14
Plutarch  134, 250, 256
Pollitt, J. J.  62, 64, 65
Pollux  54
Polus  278
Polycleitus  56, 64, 65
Polynesian masks  116
possession  110, 123–4, 187, 210, 223, 225, 226

postmodernism  101, 128, 280
Pound, Ezra  81, 99, 288
*proairesis*  98
Prometheus  65, 66
    represented on a chous  215, 216–19
Pronomos vase  28–33, 42, 44, 131, 173, 228
*prosōpeion*  1
*prosōpon*  1, 15, 237, 263
*psychē*  265–6, 274
puppetry  75, 77, 103–4, 121, 153, 287

Quintilian  73

reception in antiquity  257
Rehm, Rush  8
Reinhardt, Max  160, 278
ritual and theatre  3, 9, 155, 187, 190–1, 220, 229, 246, 266, 286
Roberts, Erica  162
Rodenburg, Patsy  168–9
Roman masks  1, 42, 129, 249, 252, 262–3
Roscius  57, 263
Rose, Peter  249

Saint-Denis, Michel  102, 123, 133, 135
Salamis tombstone  47–9, 195
Samothrace krater  35–6
Sartori, Amleto  69–70, 112, 139, 153
Sartori, Donato  154–6, 170, 177
Sartre, Jean-Paul  5, 93–9, 112, 203, 223, 261
satyr plays  11, 28–33, 201, 205–12, 234
satyriasis  210
satyrs  16–20, 215, 216–19, 231
Schadewaldt, W.  271
Schechner, Richard  5, 99, 222
Schlegel, August  74–5, 233
Schlesier, Renate  230
Scodel, Ruth  249
Scullion, Scott  9
Seaford, Richard  244
Segal, Charles  222–3, 224, 227, 254, 280
selfhood  96–7, 122, 124, 147, 193, 196, 261–83, 288–9
Seneca (the Elder)  65, 66
Seneca (the tragedian)  126, 140, 158
sensory deprivation  58, 121, 157, 167, 200, 289
Serban, Andrei  126–7
Shakespeare, William  143–51
    *Troilus and Cressida*  145–51
    *Winter's Tale*  232–5
Shaw, Fiona  278, 279
shield as mask  272

shutter masks 262
Sifakis, Gregory 174
sight 237–9, 242
　reliability of 280
Sikelianos, Anghelos 88–90, 164
Simon, Erika 18
*skeuopoios* 57, 64, 65
Skopas 64, 65
Smith, Susan Harris 84, 85
Snell, Bruno 273
Sommerstein, Alan 65, 66
Sophocles 53, 179, 240, 250, 260
　*Ajax* 173, 249–56, 258
　*Antigone* 81–4, 106, 120, 157, 158, 173, 174
　*Electra* 127, 275–80
　*Oedipus at Colonus* 50, 179
　*Oedipus Rex* 79, 84, 88, 120, 125, 143, 175–6, 184, 274
　*Philoctetes* 145–8, 240
　*Trackers* 208
　*Women of Trachis* 99, 173
*sōphrosynē* 198
sortition 270
Sourvinou-Inwood, Christiane 10, 175, 251
Soyinka, Wole 184–5
Spartan cult 214, 242, 281, 283
Spivey, Nigel 61, 62, 260
St Petersburg hydria 18, 46
Stanislavski, Konstantin 79–80, 106, 225, 226, 245
statues
　and idolatry 181, 234–5
　in performance 268, 279–80
　lifelike 61, 211, 242, 260
　see also: Dionysos
statuesque acting 74, 82, 232–3
Stein, Peter 270, 271
Steiner, Marie 159
Steiner, Rudolph 159–60, 163
Stoicism 262
Stravinski, Igor 84
Svenbro, Jesper 251

Taplin, Oliver 8, 128, 143
Taylor, Charles 272
Terence 75
Tertullian 72
Thalmann, William 269
Theatre of Dionysos 50–1, 55, 76

theatre space 50–1, 55–6, 143, 144, 184
*theōria* 205, 237–9, 242, 255
Thespis 16, 256
tombstones 48, 61
Topeng 188–96
trance 111, 165, 167, 186, 215, 216–19
Trestle Theatre Company 288

Varakis, Angeliki 162
vase painting as basis for modern performance 82, 90, 112
Vasseur-Legangneux, Patricia 8–9
Vatican krater 26–7
Vernant, Jean-Pierre 9, 174, 177, 223–5, 227, 231, 258, 265–7
Vidal-Naquet, Pierre 268
vision, theories of 130–2, 173, 239, 252, 265
visual basis of Greek tragedy 251
Vitruvius 169
Vives, Jean Luis 67, 71–2
voice
　as mask 82, 119
　choral 175, 176
　divine 178–9
Vovolis, Thanos 164–72, 174, 175, 176, 177

wall-painting 50–1
Walton, J. Michael 8, 135
Wanamaker, Zoe 278
Webster, T. B. L. 7, 20, 54
Weigel, Helene 119–20
Williams, Richard 52, 53, 177
wine 229, 240
Winkler, John 58
Woodford, Susan 66
Wright, Matthew 277
Würzburg gnathia fragment 194–5
Würzburg krater 33

Yeats, W. B. 79
Yemendzakis, Mirka 169
Yoruba drama 184–8

Zamboulakis, Giorgos 164–72
Zeami Motokiyo 196–202
Zeitlin, Froma 39, 227, 268, 283–4
Zempo, Komparu 199
Zenchiku, Komparu 201
Zurich krater 47

Made in the USA
Coppell, TX
29 November 2019